Most contemporary Christians are massively ignorant as to how the church got to where it is today and of how much current church practice is due simply to accumulated tradition, with little or no roots in Scripture. This book provides a useful service in peeling back the layers of tradition, showing the origins of much that we today call "church." Christians who want to be biblically faithful, regardless of their particular tradition or church form, can learn and benefit from the book.

DR. HOWARD SNYDER
Professor of history and theology of mission, Asbury Theological Seminary;
author of fourteen books including *The Community of the King*

Pagan Christianity? contains a wide variety of interesting and helpful historical information of which most Christians—or non-Christians—will be completely unaware. The book identifies—in part or in whole—the pagan roots of many of our current church practices, as well as indicates some borrowed from earlier Jewish or, occasionally, more recent customs.

DR. ROBERT BANKS
New Testament scholar and theologian;
author of *Paul's Idea of Community* and *Reenvisioning Theological Education*

Why do we "do church" the way we do? Most folks seem to assume that our Christian religious trappings can be traced all the way back to the first century. But they can't. The things we hold dear—sacred buildings to meet in, pulpits, sacramental tables, clergy, liturgies, etc.—were unknown among Paul's assemblies. *Pagan Christianity?* looks at our major church traditions and documents when and how they appeared in the ages long after the apostles. Haven't you ever wondered why people dress up in their best clothes for the Sunday morning service? *Pagan Christianity?* unfolds the answer to this and numerous other questions looming in the back of many folks' minds. Reading *Pagan Christianity?* will open your eyes to the fact that the ecclesiastical emperor really has no clothes on.

DR. JON ZENS
Editor of *Searching Together*

This is an important book that demonstrates that many of the practical aspects of contemporary church life, ministry, and structure have little or no biblical basis and are, in fact, inspired by a wide variety of non-Christian patterns and ideas, most of which are inimical to Christian life and growth. Many readers will find this book challenging in the extreme, but all who are concerned with the future of the church should read it.

DAVE NORRINGTON
Lecturer of religious studies at Blackpool and the Fylde College;
author of *To Preach or Not to Preach?*

Pagan Christianity? documents specific areas where contemporary church life violates biblical principles. Whether you agree with all the conclusions the authors draw or not, you will have no argument with their documentation. It is a scholarly work with an explosive conclusion. Particularly for those of us in the modern cell-church movement, this is a valuable tool to force rethinking the meaning of the word *ecclesia*.

DR. RALPH W. NEIGHBOUR
Author of *Where Do We Go from Here?*

Anyone interested in the worship of the New Testament church and how that was altered through the centuries will find *Pagan Christianity?* very useful. The authors' position is clear and quite well documented.

DR. GRAYDON F. SNYDER
Professor of New Testament (retired), Chicago Theological Seminary;
author of *Ante Pacem: Archaeological Evidence of Church Life before Constantine*

FRANK VIOLA
GEORGE BARNA

Pagan

CHRISTIANITY?

EXPLORING THE
ROOTS OF OUR
CHURCH PRACTICES

BARNA

AN IMPRINT OF TYNDALE HOUSE
PUBLISHERS, INC.

Visit Tyndale's exciting Web site at www.tyndale.com

TYNDALE is a registered trademark of Tyndale House Publishers, Inc.

Barna and the Barna logo are trademarks of George Barna.

BarnaBooks is an imprint of Tyndale House Publishers, Inc.

Pagan Christianity?: Exploring the Roots of Our Church Practices

Copyright © 2002, 2008 by Frank Viola and George Barna. All rights reserved. First printing by Present Testimony Ministry in 2002.

Cover photo of tree roots copyright © Tanja Mehl/iStockphoto. All rights reserved.

Designed by Stephen Vosloo

Library of Congress Cataloging-in-Publication Data

Viola, Frank.

    Pagan Christianity? : exploring the roots of our church practices / Frank Viola and George Barna.

      p. cm.

    Includes bibliographical references (p.   ).

    ISBN-13: 978-1-4143-1485-3 (hc)

    ISBN-10: 1-4143-1485-X (hc)

    1. Church renewal. 2. Church—Biblical teaching. 3. Bible. N.T.—Criticism, interpretation, etc. 4. Theology, Practical—History. I. Barna, George. II. Title.

BV600.3.V56 2007

262.001′7—dc22   2007025967

Printed in the United States of America

14   13   12   11   10   09   08

 9   8   7   6

To our forgotten brothers and sisters throughout the ages who coura-
geously stepped outside the safe bounds of institutional Christianity
at the risk of life and limb. You faithfully carried the torch, endured
persecution, forfeited reputation, lost family, suffered torture, and
spilled your blood to preserve the primitive testimony that Jesus
Christ is Head of His church. And that every believer is a priest . . .
a minister . . . and a functioning member of God's house. This book
is dedicated to you.

Dear Reader,

Perhaps you wonder why a publisher of Christian books would release a book that questions so many common church practices. Please be aware, however, that the authors are not questioning the validity or importance of the church. Instead, they are asking us to thoughtfully consider the source of our churches' traditions and then ask how these practices square with Scripture and the practices of the first-century church. Many in the church hold to tradition, even if it is not grounded in Scripture, and these same people wonder why the church seems to be losing its relevance and impact in the contemporary world.

Tyndale does not necessarily agree with all of the authors' positions and realizes that some readers may not either. At the same time, we stand united with Frank and George in our desire to see the church operate according to biblical principles and be a full expression of God's grace and truth. Furthermore, the authors raise important questions based on their careful research, study, and experiences, and we believe these questions should not be ignored. Our aim is for you to consider their conclusions and then pray seriously about your response.

The Publisher

Contents

"Experience supplies painful proof that traditions once called into being are first called useful, then they become necessary. At last they are too often made idols, and all must bow down to them or be punished."

—J. C. RYLE, NINETEENTH-CENTURY ENGLISH WRITER AND MINISTER

"All truth passes through three stages. First, it is ridiculed. Second, it is violently opposed. Third, it is accepted as self-evident."

—ARTHUR SCHOPENHAUER, NINETEENTH-CENTURY GERMAN PHILOSOPHER

NOT LONG AFTER I LEFT the institutional church to begin gathering with Christians in an organic way, I sought to understand how the Christian church ended up in its present state. For years I tried to get my hands on a documented book that traced the origin of every nonbiblical practice we Christians observe every week.[1]

I searched scores of bibliographies and card catalogs. I also contacted a raft of historians and scholars, asking if they knew of such a work. My quest yielded one consistent answer: No such book had ever been penned. So in a moment of insanity, I decided to put my hand to the plow.

I will admit that I wish someone else had taken on this overwhelming project—someone like a childless professor without a day job! It would have saved me an incalculable number of painstaking hours and a great deal of frustration. Nevertheless, now that the work is complete, I am glad I had the privilege of breaking new ground in this all-too-neglected area.

Some may wonder why I spent so much time and energy documenting the origin of our contemporary church practices. It's rather simple. Understanding the genesis of our church traditions can very well change the course of church history. As philosopher Søren Kierkegaard once put it, "Life is lived forwards but understood backwards." Without understanding the mistakes of the past, we are doomed to a flawed future. It is for this reason that I set out to make the first stab at this Himalayan project.

My hope in publishing this work is as simple as it is somber: that the Lord would use it as a tool to bring His church back to her biblical roots.

On that note, I would like to acknowledge the following people: my coauthor, George Barna, for making this a

---

[1] The only work that I could find that traces some of the origins of our modern church practices is Gene Edwards's little volume *Beyond Radical* (Jacksonville: Seedsowers, 1999), but it contains no documentation.

stronger book; Frank Valdez for your keen insight and your unwavering friendship; Mike Biggerstaff, Dan Merillat, Phil Warmanen, Eric Rapp, and Scott Manning for proofing the original manuscript; Howard Snyder for the matchless feedback that only scholars can give; Neil Carter for your willing tenacity to help me research everything under the sun; Chris Lee and Adam Parke for making repeated trips to the library and lugging countless stacks of dusty books into my study; Dave Norrington for periodically mailing me valuable leads from across the Atlantic; Gene Edwards for your pioneering efforts and your personal encouragement; those seminary professors whose names are too numerous to list for kindly responding to my endless and persistent inquiries; the Tyndale staff for your invaluable suggestions and superb editing; and Thom Black—without you this new edition would have never happened.

—*Frank Viola*

"Those who cannot remember the past are condemned to repeat it."
—GEORGE SANTAYANA, TWENTIETH-CENTURY SPANISH PHILOSOPHER AND POET

"Why do you yourselves transgress the commandment of God for the sake of your tradition?"
—JESUS CHRIST IN MATTHEW 15:3, NASB

WHEN THE LORD JESUS WALKED THIS EARTH, His chief opposition came from the two leading religious parties of the day: the Pharisees and the Sadducees.

The Pharisees added to the sacred Scriptures. They obeyed the law of God as it was interpreted and applied by the scribes, the experts in the Law who lived pious and disciplined lives. As the official interpreters of God's Word, the Pharisees were endowed with the power of creating tradition. They tacked on to the Word of God reams of human laws that were passed on to subsequent generations. This body of time-honored customs, often called "the tradition of the elders," came to be viewed as being on equal par with Holy Writ.[1]

The error of the Sadducees moved in the opposite direction. They subtracted whole segments of Scripture—deeming only the law of Moses worthy to be observed.[2] (The Sadducees denied the existence of spirits, angels, the soul, the afterlife, and the resurrection.[3])

No wonder that when the Lord Jesus entered the drama of human history, His authority was arduously challenged (see Mark 11:28). He did not fit into the religious mold of either camp. As a result, Jesus was viewed with suspicion by both the Pharisee and Sadducee parties. It did not take long for this suspicion to turn to hostility. And both the Pharisees and Sadducees took steps to put the Son of God to death.

History is repeating itself today. Contemporary Christianity has fallen into the errors of both the Pharisees and the Sadducees.

First, contemporary Christianity is guilty of the error of the Pharisees. That is, it has added a raft of humanly devised

---

[1] Herbert Lockyer Sr., ed., *Nelson's Illustrated Bible Dictionary* (Nashville: Thomas Nelson Publishers, 1986), 830–831, 957–958. See also Matthew 23:23-24.
[2] The law of Moses refers to the first five books of the Old Testament, i.e., Genesis to Deuteronomy. It is also called the Torah (the Law) and the Pentateuch, which is a Greek term meaning "five-volumed."
[3] I. Howard Marshall, *New Bible Dictionary*, 2nd ed. (Wheaton, IL: InterVarsity Fellowship, 1982), 1055.

traditions that have suppressed the living, breathing, functional headship of Jesus Christ in His church.

Second, in the tradition of the Sadducees, the great bulk of New Testament practices have been removed from the Christian landscape. Thankfully, such practices are presently being restored on a small scale by those daring souls who have taken the terrifying step of leaving the safe camp of institutional Christianity.

Even so, the Pharisees and the Sadducees both teach us this often-ignored lesson: It is harmful to dilute the authority of God's Word either by addition or by subtraction. We break the Scripture just as much by burying it under a mountain of human tradition as by ignoring its principles.

God has not been silent when it comes to the principles that govern the practice of His church. Let me explain by posing a question: Where do we find our practices for the Christian life? Where is our model for understanding what a Christian is in the first place? Is it not found in the life of Jesus Christ as portrayed in the New Testament? Or do we borrow it from somewhere else? Perhaps a pagan philosopher?

Few Christians would dispute that Jesus Christ, as He is presented in the New Testament, is the model for the Christian life. Jesus Christ *is* the Christian life. In the same way, when Christ rose from the dead and ascended, He gave birth to His church. That church was Himself in a different form. This is the meaning of the phrase "the body of Christ."[4]

Consequently, in the New Testament we have the genesis of the church. I believe the first-century church was the church in its purest form, before it was tainted or corrupted. That's not to say the early church didn't have problems—Paul's epistles make clear that it did. However, the conflicts Paul addresses are inevitable when a fallen people seek to be part of a close-knit community.[5]

---

[4] In 1 Corinthians 12:12, Paul refers to the church as the body of Christ. According to Pauline teaching, the church is the corporate Christ. The head is in heaven, while the body is on earth (Acts 9:4-5; Ephesians 5:23; Colossians 1:18, 2:19). Properly conceived, the church is a spiritual organism, not an institutional organization.

[5] Interestingly, an organic church will have problems identical to those in the first-century church. On the other hand, the institutional church faces a completely different set of problems, which have no biblical antidote since its structure is so distinct from the New Testament church. For instance, in an institutional church the laity may not like their preacher so they fire him. This never would have happened in the first century because there was no such thing as a hired pastor.

The church in the first century was an organic entity. It was a living, breathing organism that expressed itself far differently from the institutional church today. And that expression revealed Jesus Christ on this planet through His every-member functioning body. In this book, we intend to show how that organism was devoid of so many things that we embrace today.

The normative practices of the first-century church were the natural and spontaneous expression of the divine life that indwelt the early Christians. And those practices were solidly grounded in the timeless principles and teachings of the New Testament. By contrast, a great number of the practices in many contemporary churches are in conflict with those biblical principles and teachings. When we dig deeper, we are compelled to ask: Where did the practices of the contemporary church come from? The answer is disturbing: Most of them were borrowed from pagan culture. Such a statement short-circuits the minds of many Christians when they hear it. But it is unmovable, historical fact, as this book will demonstrate.

So we would argue that on theological grounds, historical grounds, and pragmatic grounds, the New Testament vision of church best represents the dream of God . . . the beloved community that He intends to create and re-create in every chapter of the human story. The New Testament church teaches us how the life of God is expressed when a group of people begin to live by it together.

Further, my own experience in working with organic churches confirms this finding. (An organic church is simply a church that is born out of spiritual life instead of constructed by human institutions and held together by religious programs. Organic churches are characterized by Spirit-led, open-participatory meetings and nonhierarchical leadership. This is in stark contrast to a clergy-led, institution-driven church.) My experience in the United States and overseas is that when a group of Christians begin to follow the life of the Lord who indwells them together, the same outstanding features that marked the New Testament church begin to emerge naturally.

This is because the church really is an organism. As such, it has DNA that will always produce these features if it is allowed to grow naturally. Granted, organic churches will have differences depending on the cultures in which they operate. But if the church is following the life of God who indwells it, it will never produce those nonscriptural practices this book addresses.[6] Such practices are foreign elements that God's people picked up from their pagan neighbors as far back as the fourth century. They were embraced, baptized, and called "Christian." And that is why the church is in the state it is in today, hampered by endless divisions, power struggles, passivity, and lack of transformation among God's people.

In short, this book is dedicated to exposing the traditions that have been tacked onto God's will for His church. Our reason for writing it is simple: We are seeking to remove a great deal of debris in order to make room for the Lord Jesus Christ to be the fully functioning head of His church.

We are also making an outrageous proposal: that the church in its contemporary, institutional form has neither a biblical nor a historical right to function as it does. This proposal, of course, is our conviction based upon the historical evidence that we shall present in this book. You must decide if that proposal is valid or not.

This is not a work for scholars, so it is by no means exhaustive. A thorough treatment of the origins of our contemporary church practices would fill volumes. But it would be read by few people. Although this is a single volume, it includes a great deal of history. Yet this book does not chase every historical sidelight. Rather, it focuses on tracing the central practices that define mainstream Christianity today.[7]

Because the roots of our contemporary church practices are so important to grasp, we wish that every literate Christian would read this work.[8] Consequently, we have chosen not to employ technical language, but to write in plain English.

---

[6] For a more in-depth discussion on this principle, see my articles "The Kingdom, the Church, and Culture" (http://www.ptmin.org/culture.htm) and "What Is an Organic Church?" (http://www.ptmin.org/organic.htm).

[7] This book focuses on *Protestant* Christian practices. And its main scope is "low church" Protestantism rather than "high church" denominations such as Anglican, Episcopal, and some stripes of Lutheran. By *high church*, I mean churches that emphasize the sacerdotal, sacramental, and liturgical Catholic elements of orthodox Christianity. The book touches on high-church practices only in passing.

[8] As the English philosopher Francis Bacon once said, "It is not St. Augustine's nor St. Ambrose's works that will make so wise a divine as ecclesiastical history thoroughly read and observed."

At the same time, footnotes containing added details and sources appear throughout each chapter.[9] Reflective Christians who wish to verify our statements and obtain a more in-depth understanding of the subjects covered should read the footnotes. Those who care little for such details may ignore them. The footnotes also occasionally qualify or clarify easily misunderstood statements.

Finally, I am delighted to have worked with George Barna on this revised edition. George's uncommon flair for readable research has made this a stronger work.

In short, this book demonstrates beyond dispute that those who have left the fold of institutional Christianity to become part of an organic church have a historical right to exist—since history demonstrates that many practices of the institutional church are not rooted in Scripture.

GAINESVILLE, FLORIDA
JUNE 2007

---

[9] Note that when I quote the church fathers, I have elected to cite their original works whenever possible. In those cases when I do not cite their original works, I have cited *Early Christians Speak*, 3rd ed., by Everett Ferguson (Abilene, TX: ACU Press, 1999), which is a compilation and translation of their original writings.

"But the Emperor has nothing at all on!" said a little child. "Listen to the voice of innocence!" exclaimed the father; and what the child had said was whispered from one to another. "But he has nothing on!" at last cried all the people. The Emperor was vexed, for he knew that the people were right; but he thought, "The procession must go on now!" And the lords of the bedchamber took greater pains than ever to appear holding up a train, although, in reality, there was no train to hold.

—HANS CHRISTIAN ANDERSEN

➤ WHAT HAPPENED TO THE CHURCH?

"There is perhaps nothing worse than reaching the top of the ladder and discovering that you're on the wrong wall."
—JOSEPH CAMPBELL, TWENTIETH-CENTURY AMERICAN WRITER

WE ARE LIVING IN THE MIDST of a silent revolution of faith. Millions of Christians throughout the world are leaving the old, accepted ways of "doing church" for even older approaches. Those older approaches are rooted in the Holy Scriptures and the eternal principles of the living God. Consequently, the motivation for this transition from the old to the older is not simply to get us in touch with our history or to reclaim our roots. It is borne out of a desire to return to our Lord with authenticity and fullness. It is a thrust to bond with Him through the Word of God, the Kingdom of God, and the Spirit of God.

The heart of the Revolutionaries is not in question. There is ample research to show that they are seeking more of God. They have a passion to be faithful to His Word and to be more in tune with His leading. They ardently want their relationship with the Lord to be their top priority in life. They are tired of the institutions, denominations, and routines getting in the way of a resonant connection with Him. They are worn out on the endless programs that fail to facilitate transformation. They are weary of being sent off to complete assignments, memorize facts and passages, and engage in simplistic practices that do not draw them into God's presence.

These are people who have experienced the initial realities of a genuine connection with God. They can no longer endure the spiritual teasing offered by churches and other well-intentioned ministries. God is waiting for them. They want Him. No more excuses.

But this revolution of faith is challenged. Those involved know what they are shifting from—lifeless, institutional forms of faith to breakthrough. But what are they shifting to? House churches, market-place ministries, cyberchurches, independent communitywide worship gatherings, intentional communities. These forms of church are all intriguing, but do they really represent a meaningful step toward God's highest purpose? Or are they just the same stuff presented in a different setting? Are they developing the same roles, but attaching new titles adopted by different role players? Are we living in a culture that is so infatuated with change that we have forgotten that the church is about transformation, not mere change?

As we grapple with such issues, there is much to be learned from the history of God's people. Followers of Christ appreciate the stories God has given us in His Word. We discover much about God, life, culture, and even ourselves by following the journey of God's people in both the Old and New Testaments. Consider how much we learn from Moses and the Israelites' pursuit of the Promised Land. Or the hard-won insights of David's rise from lowly shepherd boy to king of Israel. Or the plight of Jesus' disciples as they left their craft to follow the Lord before meeting with martyrdom. In the same way, much can be gleaned from the efforts of the earliest Christians—our physical and spiritual ancestors—as they sought to be the genuine church that Christ purchased with His blood.

But what do modern and postmodern Christians know about the

history of the church that would help to shape present-day attempts at honoring God and *being* the church? Precious little, it turns out. And therein lies a significant problem. Historians have long held that if we do not remember the past, we are doomed to repeat it. There is ample evidence to support that warning. Yet we often persist in our well-intentioned but ignorant efforts to refine life.

The recent story of the Christian church in America is a great example of this. The major changes in spiritual practice over the past half century have been largely window dressings. Pick a trend—megachurches, seeker churches, satellite campuses, vacation Bible school, children's church, affinity group ministries (e.g., ministries for singles, women, men, young marrieds), contemporary worship music, bigscreen projection systems, EFT giving, cell groups, downloadable sermons, sermon outlines in bulletins, Alpha groups. All of the above have simply been attempts to rely on marketing strategies to perform the same activities in different ways or places, or with particular segments of the aggregate population. Whatever difficulties were present in the larger institutional setting that spawned these efforts are invariably present in the smaller or divergent efforts as well.

This book will challenge you to consider making more significant changes in the way you practice your faith. Altering the ways in which we worship is no simple task. When people suggest significant changes in some of the hallowed practices, cries of "heretic" can be heard coming from all directions. Such protest is common largely because people have little knowledge of the true foundations of their faith.

That's where this book comes in. Rather than foster continued resistance to methodological innovations, it's time that the body of Christ get in touch with both the Word of God and the history of the church to arrive at a better understanding of what we can and should do—as well as what we cannot and should not do.

From personal experience, the authors of this book can tell you that such a journey of discovery is enlightening, to say the least. If you spend time searching God's Word for most of the common practices in conventional churches, you will rarely find them. If you go further and spend time tracing the history of those practices, you will soon discover that most of our religious habits are man-made choices. In fact, you're likely to discern a pattern about the way that we "do church" these days: If we do it, it's probably not in the Bible as one of the practices of the early church!

Does it surprise you that most of what we do in religious circles has no precedent in Scripture? This includes many of the activities within church services, the education and ordination of clergy, the routines commonly used in youth ministry, the methods of raising funds for ministry, the ways in which music is used in churches, even the presence and nature of church buildings. There were three historical periods when a bevy of changes were made in common Christian practices: the era of Constantine, the decades surrounding the Protestant Reformation, and the Revivalist period of the eighteenth and nineteenth centuries. But as you are about to find out, those changes were the result of passionate, though often ill-informed, followers of Christ. The believers during those periods simply went along for the ride, which resulted in new perspectives and practices that churches have held on to for many years. So many years, in fact, that you probably think of those routines as biblical in origin.

Not surprisingly, having changed the biblical model of the church, we have become adept at building support for our approaches through proof-texting. Proof-texting is the practice of taking disparate, unrelated verses of Scripture, often out of context, to "prove" that our position squares with the Bible. As you read this book, you may be stunned to discover how many of our esteemed practices are way off the mark biblically.

Does it really matter how we practice our faith, as long as the activities enable people to love God and obey Him? The preponderance of evidence shows that these perspectives, rules, traditions, expectations, assumptions, and practices often hinder the development of our faith. In other instances, they serve as barriers that keep us from encountering the living God. The way in which we practice our faith can, indeed, affect the faith itself.

Does that mean we must go back to the Bible and do everything exactly as the disciples did between AD 30 and 60? No. Social and cultural shifts over the last two thousand years have made it impossible to imitate some of the lifestyle and religious efforts of the early church. For example, we use cell phones, drive in automobiles, and utilize central heat and air. The first-century Christians had none of these forms of human convenience. Therefore, adhering to the *principles* of the New Testament does not mean reenacting the *events* of the first-century church. If so, we would have to dress like all first-century believers did, in sandals and togas!

Also, just because a practice is picked up from culture does not make it wrong in and of itself, though we must be discerning. As author Frank Senn notes, "We cannot avoid bringing our culture to church with us; it is a part of our very being. But in the light of tradition we need to sort out those cultural influences that contribute to the integrity of Christian worship from those that detract from it."[1]

It is in our best interest to scour the words of God to determine the core principles and ethos of the early church and to restore those elements to our lives. God has granted us great leeway in the methods we use to honor and connect with Him. But that does not mean we have free rein. Caution is advisable as we strive to be humble and obedient people who seek His central will. Our goal is to be true to His plan so that we may become the people He desires us to be and that the church may be all she is called to be.

So be prepared for a rude awakening as you find out how off track our current religious practices are. You probably know that today's jets use very sophisticated computer systems to constantly reorient a plane as it travels on its path. During the course of a trip from Los Angeles to New York, literally thousands of course corrections are made to ensure that the plane sets down on the appropriate landing strip.

---

[1] Frank C. Senn, *Christian Worship and Its Cultural Setting* (Philadelphia: Fortress Press, 1983), 51.

Without those course corrections, even a tiny one percent deviation from the original flight plan would land that airplane in a different county! The contemporary church is like a jet airplane that has no capacity for in-flight course corrections. A little change here, a minor deviation there, a slight alteration of this, a barely perceptible tweaking of that—and before you know it, the whole enterprise has been redefined!

Is this hard for you to believe? Then we encourage you to invest yourself in the process and do some of your own research. My coauthor, Frank Viola, spent many years laboriously tracking down the historical data that identified how the church got onto this crooked path. The references from his journey are supplied for you in each chapter. If you are skeptical—and we encourage healthy skepticism that leads to fact-finding and truth—then commit yourself to identifying exactly what did happen over the course of time. This matters! Your life is a gift from God and is to be lived for God. Furthermore, the church is one of God's deepest passions. He cares about her well-being, as well as how she expresses herself on the earth. So understanding how we got from the early church to the contemporary church, and figuring out what you will do about it, is very important.

Every good author writes in order to bring about positive, meaningful change. This book is no different. We want you to be informed by the Word of God and by church history. We want you to think carefully and biblically about how you practice your faith with other Christians. And we want you to influence others to understand what God leads you to discover. Part of the challenge of living in concert with a biblical view of the world is correlating your spiritual life with God's intentions, as outlined for us in the Bible. We pray that this book will help you to do your part in straightening out the crooked path of the contemporary church.

>delving DEEPER

Some Definitions

As you read this book, we feel it is important that you understand how we are using the terms below.

PAGAN

We are using this word to indicate those practices and principles that are not Christian or biblical in origin. In some cases, we use it to refer to those ancients who followed the gods of the Roman Empire. We are not using the word as a synonym for *bad*, *evil*, *sinful*, or *wrong*. A "pagan practice or mind-set" refers to a practice or mode of thinking that has been adopted from the church's surrounding culture. We believe that some pagan practices are neutral and can be redeemed for God's glory. We feel that others stand in direct conflict with the teachings of Jesus and the apostles and thus cannot be redeemed.

ORGANIC CHURCH

The term *organic church* does not refer to a particular model of church. (We believe that no perfect model exists.) Instead, we believe that the New Testament vision of church is organic. An organic church is a living, breathing, dynamic, mutually participatory, every-member-functioning, Christ-centered, communal expression of the body of Christ. Note that our goal in this book is not to develop a full description of the organic church but only to touch on it when necessary.

INSTITUTIONAL CHURCH

This term refers to a religious system (not a particular group of people). An institutional church is one that operates primarily as an organization that exists above, beyond, and independent of the members who populate it. It is constructed more on programs and rituals than on relationships. It is led by set-apart professionals ("ministers" or "clergy") who are aided by volunteers ("laity"). We also use the terms *contemporary church*, *traditional church*, *present-day church*, and *modern church* to refer to the institutional church of our day.

NEW TESTAMENT CHURCH, OR FIRST-CENTURY CHURCH

These terms do not refer to a particular form of church. We are instead speaking of the church of century one that we read about in our New Testament. (In this book, *first-century church* is used as a synonym for *New Testament church*.) We do not advocate a primitivistic return to a particular model of the early church. Instead, we believe that a return to the spiritual principles, the organic practices, and the spirit and ethos of the first-century church, along with the teachings of Jesus and the apostles, should guide our practice of the church in our day and time.

BIBLICAL, OR SCRIPTURAL

These words are used first and foremost as source statements and secondarily as value judgments. *Biblical* or *scriptural* refers to whether a practice has its origins in the New Testament Scriptures. References to *unbiblical* or *unscriptural* practices do not automatically imply error. These words can refer to the fact that a certain practice does not appear in the New Testament (in which case it should not be treated as sacred). But they can also refer to a practice that violates the principles or teachings of the New Testament. The context will determine how these words are used. We certainly do not agree with the doctrines of "the silence of Scripture" and "the regulative principle," which teach that if a practice is not mentioned in the New Testament then we should not follow it.

One day, through the primeval wood,
A calf walked home, as good calves should;
But made a trail all bent askew,
A crooked trail as all calves do.

Since then three hundred years have fled,
And, I infer, the calf is dead.
But still he left behind his trail,
And thereby hangs my moral tale.

The trail was taken up next day
By a lone dog that passed that way;
And then a wise bell-wether sheep
Pursued the trail o'er vale and steep,
And drew the flock behind him, too,
As good bell-wethers always do.
And from that day, o'er hill and glade,
Through those old woods a path was made.

And many men wound in and out,
And dodged, and turned, and bent about
And uttered words of righteous wrath
Because 'twas such a crooked path.[1]
But still they followed—do not laugh—
The first migrations of that calf,
And through this winding wood-way stalked,
Because he wobbled when he walked.

This forest path became a lane,
That bent, and turned, and turned again;
This crooked lane became a road,
Where many a poor horse with his load
Toiled on beneath the burning sun,
And traveled some three miles in one.
And thus a century and a half
They trod the footsteps of that calf.

---

[1] In this book, we sometimes refer to "the crooked path" that led the institutional church to its current form. This poem, written more than a century ago, served as the inspiration for that metaphor.

The years passed on in swiftness fleet,
The road became a village street;
And this, before men were aware,
A city's crowded thoroughfare;
And soon the central street was this
Of a renowned metropolis;
And men two centuries and a half
Trod in the footsteps of that calf.

Each day a hundred thousand rout
Followed the zigzag calf about;
And o'er his crooked journey went
The traffic of a continent.
A hundred thousand men were led
By one calf near three centuries dead.
They followed still his crooked way,
And lost one hundred years a day;
For thus such reverence is lent
To well-established precedent.

A moral lesson this might teach,
Were I ordained and called to preach;
For men are prone to go it blind
Along the calf-paths of the mind,

And work away from sun to sun
To do what other men have done.
They follow in the beaten track,
And out and in, and forth and back,

And still their devious course pursue,
To keep the path that others do.
They keep the path a sacred groove,
Along which all their lives they move.
But how the wise old wood-gods laugh,
Who saw the first primeval calf!
Ah! Many things this tale might teach—
But I am not ordained to preach.

—SAM WALTER FOSS

chapter one

➤ HAVE WE REALLY BEEN DOING IT BY THE BOOK?

"The unexamined life is not worth living."
—SOCRATES

"WE DO EVERYTHING by the Word of God! The New Testament is our guide for faith and practice! We live . . . and we die . . . by this Book!"

These were the words that thundered forth from the mouth of Pastor Farley as he delivered his Sunday morning sermon. Winchester Spudchecker, a member of Pastor Farley's church, had heard them dozens of times before. But this time it was different. Dressed in his blue suit, frozen in the back pew with his wife, Trudy, Winchester stared at the ceiling as Pastor Farley continued talking about "doing everything by the sacred Book."

One hour before Pastor Farley began his sermon, Winchester had had a fuming fight with Trudy. This was a common occurrence as Winchester, Trudy, and their three daughters, Felicia, Gertrude, and Zanobia, got ready for church on Sunday morning.

His mind began replaying the event. . . .

"Truuudyy! Why aren't the kids ready? We're always late! Why can't you ever get them prepared on time?" Winchester yelled as he anxiously glanced at the clock.

Trudy's response was typical. "If you ever thought to help me this wouldn't happen all the time! Why don't you start giving me a hand in this house?" The argument went back and forth until Winchester turned on the children: "Zanobia Spudchecker! . . . Why can't you respect us enough to get ready on time? . . . Felicia, how many times do I have to tell you to turn off your PlayStation before 9 a.m.?" Hearing the commotion, Gertrude burst into tears.

Wearing their Sunday best, the Spudchecker family finally drove to church at breakneck speed. (Winchester hated to be late and had received three speeding tickets this past year—all given to him on Sunday mornings!)

As they raced to the church building, the silence in the car was deafening. Winchester was steaming. Trudy was sulking. With heads down, the three Spudchecker daughters were trying to prepare their minds for something they hated . . . another long hour of Sunday school!

As they pulled in to the church parking lot, Winchester and Trudy gracefully exited the car, sporting large smiles. They held each other arm in arm and greeted their fellow church members, chuckling and putting on the pretense that all was well. Felicia, Gertrude, and Zanobia followed their parents with chins pointed upward.

These were the fresh yet painful memories that coursed through Winchester's mind that Sunday morning as Pastor Farley continued his sermon. Brooding in self-condemnation, Winchester began to ask himself some searching questions: *Why am I dressed up prim and proper looking like a good Christian when I acted like a heathen just an hour ago? . . . I wonder how many other families had this same pitiful experience this morning? Yet we're all smelling nice and looking pretty for God.*

Winchester was a bit shocked by these thoughts. Such questions had never before entered his consciousness.

As he peeked over to see Pastor Farley's wife and children sitting prim and proper on the front pew, Winchester mused to himself: *I wonder if Pastor Farley screamed at his wife and kids this morning? Hmmm . . .*

Winchester's mind continued to race in this direction as he watched Pastor Farley pound the pulpit for emphasis and raise his Bible with his right hand. "We at First Bible New Testament Community Church do everything by this Book! *Everything!* This is the Word of God, and we cannot stray from it . . . not even one millimeter!"

Suddenly Winchester had another new thought: *I don't remember reading anywhere in the Bible that Christians are supposed to dress up to go to church. Is that by the Book?*

This single thought unleashed a torrent of other barbed questions. As scores of frozen pew sitters filled his horizon, Winchester continued to ponder similar new questions. Questions that no Christian is supposed to ask. Questions like:

Is sitting in this uncushioned pew, staring at the back of twelve rows of heads for forty-five minutes, doing things by the Book? Why do we spend so much money to maintain this building when we're here only twice a week for a few hours? Why is half the congregation barely awake when Pastor Farley preaches? Why do my kids hate Sunday school? Why do we go through this same predictable, yawn-inspiring ritual every Sunday morning? Why am I going to church when it bores me to tears and does nothing for me spiritually? Why do I wear this uncomfortable necktie every Sunday morning when all it seems to do is cut off blood circulation to my brain?

Winchester felt unclean and sacrilegious to ask such things. Yet something was happening inside of him that compelled him to doubt his entire church experience. These thoughts had been lying dormant in Winchester's subconscious for years. Today, they surfaced.

Interestingly, the questions Winchester had that day are questions that never enter the conscious thinking of most Christians. Yet the sober reality is that Winchester's eyes had been opened.

As startling as it may sound, almost everything that is done in our contemporary churches has no basis in the Bible. As pastors preach from their pulpits about being "biblical" and following the "pure Word of God," their words betray them. The truth is that precious little that is observed today in contemporary Christianity maps to anything found in the New Testament church.

QUESTIONS WE NEVER THINK TO ASK

Socrates (470–399 BC)[1] is considered by some historians to be the father of philosophy. Born and raised in Athens, his custom was to go about the town relentlessly raising questions and analyzing the popular views of his day. Socrates believed that truth is found by dialoguing extensively about an issue and relentlessly questioning it. This method is known as *dialectic* or "the Socratic method." He thought freely on matters that his fellow Athenians felt were closed for discussion.

Socrates' habit of pelting people with searching questions and roping them into critical dialogues about their accepted customs eventually got him killed. His incessant questioning of tightly held traditions provoked the leaders of Athens to charge him with "corrupting the youth." As a result, they put Socrates to death. A clear message was sent to his fellow Athenians: All who question the established customs will meet the same fate![2]

Socrates was not the only provocateur to reap severe reprisal for his nonconformity: Isaiah was sawn in half, John the Baptist was beheaded, and Jesus was crucified. Not to mention the thousands of Christians who have been tortured and martyred through the centuries by the institutional church because they dared to challenge its teachings.[3]

As Christians, we are taught by our leaders to believe certain

---

[1] Note that on the first mention of historical figures (especially those who had a great impact on the development of the church), we generally include the dates of their births and deaths. You can also consult the appendix "Key Figures in Church History" on page 277 for these dates and a brief summary of these individuals' influence.

[2] For a concise treatment of Socrates' life and teaching, see Samuel Enoch Stumpf's *Socrates to Sartre* (New York: McGraw-Hill, 1993), 29–45.

[3] Ken Connolly, *The Indestructible Book* (Grand Rapids: Baker Books, 1996); *Foxe's Book of Martyrs* (Old Tappan, NJ: Spire Books, 1968).

ideas and behave in certain ways. We are also encouraged to read our Bibles. But we are conditioned to read the Bible with the lens handed to us by the Christian tradition to which we belong. We are taught to obey our denomination (or movement) and never to challenge what it teaches.

(At this moment, all the rebellious hearts are applauding and are plotting to wield the above paragraphs to wreak havoc in their churches. If that is you, dear rebellious heart, you have missed our point by a considerable distance. We do not stand with you. Our advice: Either leave your church quietly, refusing to cause division, or be at peace with it. There is a vast gulf between rebellion and taking a stand for what is true.)

If the truth be told, we Christians never seem to ask why we do what we do. Instead, we blithely carry out our religious traditions without asking where they came from. Most Christians who claim to uphold the integrity of God's Word have never sought to see if what they do every Sunday has any scriptural backing. How do we know this? Because if they did, it would lead them to some very disturbing conclusions that would compel them by conscience to forever abandon what they are doing.

Strikingly, contemporary church thought and practice have been influenced far more by postbiblical historical events than by New Testament imperatives and examples. Yet most Christians are not conscious of this influence. Nor are they aware that it has created a slew of cherished, calcified, humanly devised traditions[4]—all of which are routinely passed off to us as "Christian."[5]

A TERRIFYING INVITATION

We now invite you to walk with us on an untrodden path. It is a terrifying journey where you will be forced to ask questions that probably

---

[4] Edwin Hatch, *The Influence of Greek Ideas and Usages upon the Christian Church* (Peabody, MA: Hendrickson, 1895), 18. Hatch traces the detrimental effects of the church that is influenced by its culture rather than one that influences its culture.

[5] The Christian philosopher Søren Kierkegaard (1813–1855) said that modern Christianity is essentially a counterfeit. See Søren Kierkegaard, "Attack on Christendom," in *A Kierkegaard Anthology*, ed. Robert Bretall (Princeton, NJ: Princeton University Press, 1946), 59ff., 117, 150ff., 209ff.

have never entered your conscious thoughts. Tough questions. Nagging questions. Even frightening questions. And you will be faced squarely with the disturbing answers. Yet those answers will lead you face-to-face with some of the richest truths a Christian can discover.

As you read through the following pages, you may be surprised to discover that a great deal of what we Christians do for Sunday morning church did not come from Jesus Christ, the apostles, or the Scriptures. Nor did it come from Judaism. After the Romans destroyed Jerusalem in AD 70, Judaic Christianity waned in numbers and power. Gentile Christianity dominated, and the new faith began to absorb Greco-Roman philosophy and ritual. Judaic Christianity survived for five centuries in the little group of Syriac Christians called *Ebionim*, but their influence was not very widespread. According to Shirley J. Case, "Not only was the social environment of the Christian movement largely Gentile well before the end of the first century, but it had severed almost any earlier bonds of social contact with the Jewish Christians of Palestine. . . . By the year 100, Christianity is mainly a Gentile religious movement . . . living together in a common Gentile social environment."[6]

Strikingly, much of what we do for "church" was lifted directly out of pagan culture in the postapostolic period. (Legend tells us the last surviving apostle, John, died around AD 100.) According to Paul F. Bradshaw, fourth-century Christianity "absorbed and Christianized pagan religious ideas and practices, seeing itself as the fulfillment to which earlier religions had dimly pointed."[7] While today we often use the word *pagan* to describe those who claim no religion whatsoever, to the early Christians, pagans were those polytheists who followed the gods of the Roman Empire. Paganism dominated the Roman Empire until the fourth century, and many of its elements were absorbed by Christians in the first half of the first millennium, particularly during

---

[6] Will Durant, *Caesar and Christ* (New York: Simon & Schuster, 1950), 577. See also Shirley J. Case, *The Social Origins of Christianity* (New York: Cooper Square Publishers, 1975), 27–28. E. Glenn Hinson adds, "From the late first century on through, Gentiles came to outnumber Jews in the Christian assembly. They imported in subtle ways some of the ideas, attitudes, and customs of Greek and Roman culture" ("Worshiping Like Pagans?" *Christian History* 12, no. 1 [1993]: 17).

[7] Paul F. Bradshaw, *The Search for the Origins of Christian Worship* (New York: Oxford University Press, 1992), 65; Durant, *Caesar and Christ*, 575, 599–600, 610–619, 650–651, 671–672.

the Constantinian and early post-Constantinian eras (324 to 600).[8] Two other significant periods from which many of our current church practices originate were the Reformation era (sixteenth century) and the Revivalist era (eighteenth and nineteenth centuries).

Chapters 2 through 10 each trace an accepted traditional church practice. Each chapter tells the story of where this practice came from. But more importantly, it explains how this practice stifles the practical headship of Jesus Christ and hampers the functioning of His body.

Warning: If you are unwilling to have your Christianity seriously examined, do not read beyond this page. Give this book to Goodwill immediately! Spare yourself the trouble of having your Christian life turned upside down.

However, if you choose to "take the red pill" and be shown "how deep the rabbit hole goes"[9] . . . if you want to learn the true story of where your Christian practices came from . . . if you are willing to have the curtain pulled back on the contemporary church and its traditional presuppositions fiercely challenged . . . then you will find this work to be disturbing, enlightening, and possibly life changing.

Put another way, if you are a Christian in the institutional church who takes the New Testament seriously, what you are about to read may lead to a crisis of conscience. For you will be confronted by unmovable historical fact.

On the other hand, if you happen to be one of those people who gathers with other Christians outside the pale of institutional Christianity, you will discover afresh that not only is Scripture on your side—but history stands with you as well.

---

[8] The term *pagan* was used by the early Christian apologists to group non-Christians into a convenient package. At its root, a "pagan" is a country dweller, an inhabitant of the *pagus* or rural district. Because Christianity primarily spread in the cities, the country bumpkins, or pagans, were regarded as those who believed in the old gods. See Joan E. Taylor, *Christians and the Holy Places: The Myth of Jewish-Christian Origins* (Oxford: Clarendon Press, 1993), 301.

[9] The idea of the red pill comes from the thought-provoking hit movie *The Matrix*. In the film, Morpheus gives Neo the choice between living in a deceptive dreamworld or understanding reality. His words are applicable to the subject at hand: "After this, there's no turning back. You take the blue pill, the story ends, you wake up in your bed and believe whatever you want to believe. You take the red pill . . . and I show you how deep the rabbit hole goes." We hope that all of God's people would dare to take the red pill!

>delving DEEPER

1. I don't see how the Spudcheckers' family squabbles before church had anything to do with church itself—other than frustrating Winchester and making him cynical about everything that went on at his church. Why did you lead off the book with this story?

You're right—Winchester's Sunday morning troubles were what put him in the frame of mind to question church practices he normally sat through without giving any thought to at all. The story was simply a humorous way to illustrate how scores of Christians go through the motions on Sunday morning without considering why they do what they do.

2. While you say that contemporary church practice has been influenced far more by postbiblical historical events than New Testament principles, isn't it true that there aren't many specifics in the Gospels, Acts, or Paul's letters about church practice? What Scriptures would you point to as outlining what Christians should do when gathering for worship?

The New Testament actually includes many details about how the early Christians gathered. For example, we know that the early church met in homes for their regular church meetings (Acts 20:20; Romans 16:3, 5; 1 Corinthians 16:19). They took the Lord's Supper as a full meal (1 Corinthians 11:21-34). Their church gatherings were open and participatory (1 Corinthians 14:26; Hebrews 10:24-25). Spiritual gifts were employed by each member (1 Corinthians 12–14). They genuinely saw themselves as family and acted accordingly (Galatians 6:10; 1 Timothy 5:1-2; Romans 12:5; Ephesians 4:15; Romans 12:13; 1 Corinthians 12:25-26; 2 Corinthians 8:12-15). They had a plurality of elders to oversee the community (Acts 20:17, 28-29; 1 Timothy 1:5-7). They were established and aided by itinerant apostolic workers (Acts 13-21; all the apostolic letters). They were fully united and did not denominate themselves into separate organizations in the same city (Acts 8:1, 13:1, 18:22; Romans 16:1; 1 Thessalonians 1:1). They did not use honorific titles (Matthew 23:8-12). They did not organize themselves hierarchically (Matthew 20:25-28; Luke 22:25-26).

Offering a complete biblical basis for these practices and explaining why they should be emulated today is beyond the scope of this book. One book that does so is *Paul's Idea of Community* by Robert Banks (Peabody, MA: Hendrickson, 1994). I (Frank) also treat this subject comprehensively in the book *Reimagining Church* (Colorado Springs: David C. Cook), which will be released in summer 2008.

chapter two

›THE CHURCH BUILDING: INHERITING THE EDIFICE COMPLEX

"In the process of replacing the old religions, Christianity became a religion."
—ALEXANDER SCHMEMANN, TWENTIETH-CENTURY EASTERN ORTHODOX PRIEST, TEACHER, AND WRITER

"That the Christians in the apostolic age erected special houses of worship is out of the question. . . . As the Saviour of the world was born in a stable, and ascended to heaven from a mountain, so his apostles and their successors down to the third century, preached in the streets, the markets, on mountains, in ships, sepulchres, eaves, and deserts, and in the homes of their converts. But how many thousands of costly churches and chapels have since been built and are constantly being built in all parts of the world to the honor of the crucified Redeemer, who in the days of his humiliation had no place of his own to rest his head!"
—PHILIP SCHAFF, NINETEENTH-CENTURY AMERICAN CHURCH HISTORIAN AND THEOLOGIAN

MANY CONTEMPORARY CHRISTIANS have a love affair with brick and mortar. The edifice complex is so ingrained in our thinking that if a group of believers begins to meet together, their first thoughts are toward securing a building. For how can a group of Christians rightfully claim to be a church without a building? (So the thinking goes.)

The "church" building is so connected with the idea of church that we unconsciously equate the two. Just listen to the vocabulary of the average Christian today:

"Wow, honey, did you see that beautiful church we just passed?"

"My goodness! That is the largest church I have ever seen! I wonder what the electric costs to keep it going?"

"Our church is too small. I'm developing claustrophobia. We need to extend the balcony."

"The church is chilly today; I am freezing my buns off in here!"

"We have gone to church every Sunday this past year except for the Sunday when Aunt Mildred dropped the microwave oven on her toe."

Or how about the vocabulary of the average pastor:

"Isn't it wonderful to be in the house of God today?"

"We must show reverence when we come into the sanctuary of the Lord."

Or how about the mother who tells her happy child (in subdued tones), "Wipe that smile off your face; you're in church now! We behave ourselves in the house of God!"

To put it bluntly, none of these thoughts have anything to do with New Testament Christianity. Rather they reflect the thinking of other religions—primarily Judaism and paganism.

TEMPLES, PRIESTS, AND SACRIFICES

Ancient Judaism was centered on three elements: the Temple, the priesthood, and the sacrifice. When Jesus came, He ended all three, fulfilling them in Himself. He is the temple who embodies a new and living house made of living stones—"without hands." He is the priest who has established a new priesthood. And He is the perfect and finished sacrifice.[1] Consequently, the Temple, the professional priesthood, and the sacrifice of Judaism all passed away with the coming of Jesus Christ.[2] Christ is the fulfillment and the reality of it all.[3]

In Greco-Roman paganism, these three elements were also present: Pagans had their temples, their priests, and their sacrifices.[4] It was only the Christians who did away with all of these elements.[5] It can be rightly said that Christianity was the first non-temple-based religion ever to emerge. In the minds of the early Christians, the people—not the architecture—constituted a sacred space. The early Christians understood that they themselves—corporately—were the temple of God and the house of God.[6]

Strikingly, nowhere in the New Testament do we find the terms *church (ekklesia)*, *temple*, or *house of God* used to refer to a building. To the ears of a first-century Christian, calling an *ekklesia* (church) a building would have been like calling your wife a condominium or your mother a skyscraper![7]

The first recorded use of the word *ekklesia* to refer to a Christian

---

[1] For references to Christ as Temple, see John 1:14, where the Greek word used for *dwelt* literally means "tabernacled," and John 2:19-21. For additional references to Christ as a new house made of living stones, see Mark 14:58; Acts 7:48; 2 Corinthians 5:1, 6:16; Ephesians 2:21-22; Hebrews 3:6-9, 9:11, 24; 1 Timothy 3:15. For references to Christ as priest, see Hebrews 4:14; 5:5-6, 10; and 8:1. The new priesthood is mentioned in 1 Peter 2:9 and Revelation 1:6. Scriptures that point to Christ as the final sacrifice include Hebrews 7:27; 9:14, 25–28; 10:12; 1 Peter 3:18. Hebrews continually stresses that Jesus offered Himself "once for all time," emphasizing the fact that He need not be sacrificed again.

[2] Stephen's message in Acts 7 indicates that "the temple was merely a man-made house originating with Solomon; it had no connection with the tent of meeting that Moses had been commanded to set up on a Divinely revealed pattern and that had continued until David's time." See Harold W. Turner, *From Temple to Meeting House: The Phenomenology and Theology of Places of Worship* (The Hague: Mouton Publishers, 1979), 116–117. See also Mark 14:58, where Jesus says that the Temple of Solomon (and Herod) was made "with hands," while the Temple that He would raise up would be made "without hands." Stephen uses the same wording in Acts 7:48. In other words, God does not dwell in temples "made with hands." Our heavenly Father is not a temple dweller!

[3] See Colossians 2:16-17. That Christ came to fulfill the shadows of the Jewish law is the central theme of the book of Hebrews. The New Testament writers all affirm that God does not require any holy sacrifices nor a mediating priesthood. All things are fulfilled in Jesus—the sacrifice and the mediating priest.

[4] Ernest H. Short dedicates an entire chapter to the architecture of Greek temples in his book *History of Religious Architecture* (London: Philip Allan & Co., 1936), ch. 2. David Norrington states, "Religious buildings were, nonetheless, an integral part of Graeco-Roman religion" in his book *To Preach or Not to Preach? The Church's Urgent Question* (Carlisle, UK: Paternoster Press, 1996), 27. Pagans also had "holy" shrines. Michael Grant, *The Founders of the Western World: A History of Greece and Rome* (New York: Charles Scribner's Sons, 1991), 232–234. For more on pagan rituals, see Robin Lane Fox, *Pagans and Christians* (New York: Alfred Knopf, 1987), 39, 41–43, 71–76, 206.

[5] John O. Gooch, "Did You Know? Little-Known or Remarkable Facts about Worship in the Early Church," *Christian History* 12, no. 1 (1993): 3.

[6] See 1 Corinthians 3:16; Galatians 6:10; Ephesians 2:20-22; Hebrews 3:5-6; 1 Timothy 3:15; 1 Peter 2:5, 4:17. All of these passages refer to God's people, not to a building. Arthur Wallis writes, "In the Old Testament, God had a sanctuary for His people; in the New, God has His people as a sanctuary" *The Radical Christian* (Columbia, MO: Cityhill Publishing, 1987), 83.

[7] According to the New Testament, the church is the bride of Christ, the most beautiful woman in the world: John 3:29; 2 Corinthians 11:2; Ephesians 5:25-32; Revelation 21:9.

meeting place was penned around AD 190 by Clement of Alexandria (150–215).[8] Clement was also the first person to use the phrase "go to church"—which would have been a foreign thought to the first-century believers.[9] (You cannot go to something you are!) Throughout the New Testament, *ekklesia* always refers to an assembly of people, not a place. *Ekklesia*, in every one of its 114 appearances in the New Testament, refers to an assembly of people. (The English word *church* is derived from the Greek word *kuriakon*, which means "belonging to the Lord." In time, it took on the meaning of "God's house" and referred to a building.)[10]

Even so, Clement's reference to "going to church" is not a reference to attending a special building for worship. It rather refers to a private home that the second-century Christians used for their meetings.[11] Christians did not erect special buildings for worship until the Constantinian era in the fourth century. New Testament scholar Graydon F. Snyder states, "There is no literary evidence nor archaeological indication that any such home was converted into an extant church building. Nor is there any extant church that certainly was built prior to Constantine." In another work he writes, "The first churches consistently met in homes. Until the year 300 we know of no buildings first built as churches."[12]

Neither did they have a special priestly caste that was set apart to serve God. Instead, every believer recognized that he or she was a priest unto God. The early Christians also did away with sacrifices. For they understood that the true and final sacrifice (Christ) had come. The only sacrifices that they offered were the spiritual

---

[8] Clement of Alexandria, *The Instructor*, Book 3, ch. 11.

[9] The nineteenth-century church historian Adolf von Harnack said of the first- and second-century Christians, "One thing is clear—the idea of a special place for worship had not yet arisen. The Christian idea of God and of Divine service not only failed to promote this, but excluded it, while the practical circumstances of the situation retarded its development." *The Mission and Expansion of Christianity in the First Three Centuries*, vol. 2 (New York: G. P. Putnam's Sons, 1908), 86.

[10] Robert L. Saucy, *The Church in God's Program* (Chicago: Moody Publishers, 1972), 11, 12, 16; A. T. Robertson, *A Grammar of the Greek New Testament in the Light of Historical Research* (Nashville: Broadman & Holman, 1934), 174. As William Tyndale translated the New Testament, he refused to translate *ekklesia* as *church*. He translated it more correctly as *congregation*. Unfortunately, the translators of the King James Version did use *church* as the translation of *ekklesia*. They rejected the correct translation of *ekklesia* as *congregation* because it was the terminology of the Puritans. See "The Translators to the Reader" from the preface to the 1611 translation in Gerald Bray, *Documents of the English Reformation* (Cambridge: James Clarke, 1994), 435.

[11] Clement, *The Instructor*, Book 3, ch. 11. Clement writes, "Woman and man are to go to church decently attired."

[12] Graydon F. Snyder, *Ante Pacem: Archaeological Evidence of Church Life Before Constantine* (Macon, GA: Mercer University Press, 1985), 67; Graydon F. Snyder, *First Corinthians: A Faith Community Commentary* (Macon, GA: Mercer University Press, 1991), 3.

sacrifices of praise and thanksgiving (see Hebrews 13:15 and 1 Peter 2:5).

When Roman Catholicism evolved in the fourth to the sixth centuries, it absorbed many of the religious practices of both paganism and Judaism. It set up a professional priesthood. It erected sacred buildings.[13] And it turned the Lord's Supper into a mysterious sacrifice.

Following the path of the pagans, early Catholicism adopted the practice of burning incense and having vestal (sacred) virgins.[14] The Protestants dropped the sacrificial use of the Lord's Supper, the burning of incense, and the vestal virgins. But they retained the priestly caste (the clergy) as well as the sacred building.

FROM HOUSE CHURCHES TO HOLY CATHEDRALS

The early Christians believed that Jesus is the very presence of God. They believed that the body of Christ, the church, constitutes a temple.

When the Lord Jesus was on earth, He made some radically negative statements about the Jewish Temple.[15] The one that angered many Jews most was His announcement that if the Temple was destroyed, He would build a new one in three days! (See John 2:19-21.) Though Jesus was referring to the Temple that existed in the architectural sense, He was really speaking of His body. Jesus said that after this temple was destroyed, He would raise it up in three days. He was referring to the real temple—the church—which He raised up in Himself on the third day (Ephesians 2:6).

Since Christ has risen, we Christians have become the temple of God. At His resurrection, Christ became a "life-giving spirit" (1 Corinthians 15:45, NIV). Therefore, He could take up residence

---

[13] "According to Canon Law, a church is a sacred building dedicated to Divine worship for the use of all the faithful and the public exercise of religion." Peter F. Anson, *Churches: Their Plan and Furnishing* (Milwaukee: Bruce Publishing Co., 1948), 3.

[14] Fox, *Pagans and Christians*, 71, 207, 27, 347, 355. Fox states that "in modern Christianity, there are more than 1.6 million adults vowed to virginity" (p. 355). They are called nuns and priests.

[15] Stephen also spoke negatively about the Temple. Interestingly, both Jesus and Stephen were charged with the same exact crime— speaking against the Temple (see Mark 14:58; Acts 6:13-14).

in the believers, thus making them His Temple, His house. It is for this reason that the New Testament always reserves the word *church* (*ekklesia*) for the people of God. It never uses this word to refer to a building of any sort.

Jesus' act of clearing the Temple not only showed His anger at the money changers' disrespect for the Temple, which was a picture of God's true house, but it also signified that the "Temple worship" of Judaism would be replaced with Himself.[16] With Jesus' coming, God the Father would no longer be worshipped in a mountain or a temple. He would instead be worshipped in spirit and in reality.[17]

When Christianity was born, it was the only religion on the planet that had no sacred objects, no sacred persons, and no sacred spaces.[18] Although surrounded by Jewish synagogues and pagan temples, the early Christians were the only religious people on earth who did not erect sacred buildings for their worship.[19] The Christian faith was born in homes, out in courtyards, and along roadsides.[20]

For the first three centuries, the Christians did not have any special buildings.[21] As one scholar put it, "The Christianity that conquered the Roman Empire was essentially a home-centered movement."[22] Some have argued that this was because the Christians were

---

[16] John 2:12-22; Mark 2:22. See Oscar Cullmann, *Early Christian Worship* (London: SCM Press, 1969), 72–73, 117.

[17] John 4:23. The Bible teaches that the church, the community of the believers, is the real Temple (2 Corinthians 3:16; Ephesians 2:21). It is the living habitation of God on Earth. Worship, therefore, is not spatially located nor extracted from the totality of life. Biblically speaking, the Christians' "holy place" is as omnipresent as their ascended Lord. Worship is not something that happens in a certain place at a certain time. It is a lifestyle. Worship happens in spirit and reality inside of God's people, for that is where God lives today. See J. G. Davies, *The Secular Use of Church Buildings* (New York: The Seabury Press, 1968), 3–4.

[18] James D. G. Dunn, "The Responsible Congregation, 1 Corinthians 14:26-40," in *Charisma und Agape* (Rome: Abbey of St. Paul before the Wall, 1983), 235–236.

[19] The third-century Christian apologist Minucius Felix wrote, "We have no temples and no altars." *The Octavius of Minucius Felix*, ch. 32. See also Robert Banks, *Paul's Idea of Community* (Peabody, MA: Hendrickson Publishers, 1994), 8–14, 26–46.

[20] See Acts 2:46, 8:3, 20:20; Romans 16:3, 5; 1 Corinthians 16:19; Colossians 4:15; Philemon 1:1-2; 2 John 1:10. It should be noted that on occasion, the Christians used *already existing* buildings for special and temporary purposes. Solomon's porch and the school of Tyrannus are examples (Acts 5:12, 19:9). Their normal church meetings, however, were always set in a private home.

[21] Snyder, *Ante Pacem*, 166. John A. T. Robinson writes, "In the first three centuries the church had no buildings." See *The New Reformation* (Philadelphia: Westminster Press, 1965), 89.

[22] Robert Banks and Julia Banks, *The Church Comes Home* (Peabody, MA: Hendrickson Publishers, 1998), 49–50. The house at Dura-Europos was destroyed in AD 256. According to Frank Senn, "Christians of the first several centuries lacked the publicity of the pagan cults. They had no shrines, temples, statues, or sacrifices. They staged no public festivals, dances, musical performances, or pilgrimages. Their central ritual involved a meal that had a domestic origin and setting inherited from Judaism. Indeed, Christians of the first three centuries usually met in private residences that had been converted into suitable gathering spaces for the Christian community. . . . This indicates that the ritual bareness of early Christian worship should not be taken as a sign of primitiveness, but rather as a way of emphasizing the spiritual character of early Christian worship." *Christian Liturgy: Catholic and Evangelical* (Minneapolis: Fortress Press, 1997), 53.

not permitted to erect church buildings. But that is not true.[23] Meeting in homes was a conscious choice of the early Christians.

As Christian congregations grew in size, they began to remodel their homes to accommodate their growing numbers.[24] One of the most outstanding finds of archaeology is the house of Dura-Europos in modern Syria. This is the earliest identifiable Christian meeting place. It was simply a private home remodeled as a Christian gathering place around AD 232.[25]

The house at Dura-Europos was essentially a house with a wall torn out between two bedrooms to create a large living room.[26] With this modification, the house could accommodate about seventy people.[27] Remodeled houses like Dura-Europos cannot rightfully be called "church buildings." They were simply homes that had been refurbished to accommodate larger assemblies.[28] Further, these homes were never called temples, the term that both pagans and Jews used for their sacred spaces. Christians did not begin calling their buildings temples until the fifteenth century.[29]

THE CREATION OF SACRED SPACES AND OBJECTS

In the late second and third centuries a shift occurred. The Christians began to adopt the pagan view of reverencing the dead.[30] Their focus

---

[23] Some have argued that the pre-Constantine Christians were poor and could not own property. But this is false. Under the persecution of Emperor Valerian (253–260), for example, all property owned by Christians was seized. See Philip Schaff, *History of the Christian Church* (Grand Rapids: Eerdmans, 1910), 2:62. L. Michael White points out that the early Christians had access to higher socioeconomic strata. Also, the Greco-Roman environment of the second and third century was quite open to many groups adapting private buildings for communal and religious use. *Building God's House in the Roman World* (Baltimore: Johns Hopkins University Press, 1990), 142–143. See also Steve Atkerson, *Toward a House Church Theology* (Atlanta: New Testament Restoration Foundation, 1998), 29–42.

[24] Snyder, *Ante Pacem*, 67. These restructured homes are called *domus ecclesiae*.

[25] Everett Ferguson, *Early Christians Speak: Faith and Life in the First Three Centuries*, 3rd ed. (Abilene, TX: A.C.U. Press, 1999), 46, 74. White, *Building God's House*, 16–25.

[26] John F. White, *Protestant Worship and Church Architecture* (New York: Oxford University Press, 1964), 54–55.

[27] "Converting a House into a Church," *Christian History* 12, no. 1 (1993): 33.

[28] Norrington, *To Preach or Not*, 25. In addition to remodeling private homes, Alan Kreider states that "by the mid-third century, congregations were growing in numbers and wealth. So Christians who met in *insulae* (islands), multi-storied blocks containing shops and housing, unobtrusively began to convert private spaces into domestic complexes tailored to fit congregational needs. They knocked out walls to unite spaces, thereby creating the varied spaces, large and small, that were required by the lives of their growing communities." *Worship and Evangelism in Pre-Christendom* (Oxford: Alain/GROW Liturgical Study, 1995), 5.

[29] Turner, *From Temple to Meeting House*, 195. The Renaissance theorists Alberti and Palladio studied the temples of ancient Rome and began using the term *temple* to refer to the Christian church building. Later, Calvin referred to Christian buildings as temples, adding it to the Reformation vocabulary (p. 207). See also Davies, *Secular Use of Church Buildings*, 220–222, for the thinking that led Christians to begin using the term *temple* to refer to a church building.

[30] Snyder, *Ante Pacem*, 83, 143–144, 167.

was on honoring the memory of the martyrs. So prayers for the saints (which later devolved into prayers *to* them) began.[31]

The Christians picked up from the pagans the practice of having meals in honor of the dead.[32] Both the Christian funeral and the funeral dirge came straight out of paganism in the third century.[33]

Third-century Christians had two places for their meetings: their homes and the cemetery.[34] They met in the cemetery because they wished to be close to their dead brethren.[35] It was their belief that to share a meal at a cemetery of a martyr was to commemorate him and to worship in his company.[36]

Since the bodies of the "holy" martyrs resided there, Christian burial places came to be viewed as "holy spaces." The Christians then began to build small monuments over these spaces—especially over the graves of famous saints.[37] Building a shrine over a burial place and calling it holy was also a pagan practice.[38]

In Rome, the Christians began to decorate the catacombs (underground burial places) with Christian symbols.[39] So art became associated with sacred spaces. Clement of Alexandria was one of the first Christians advocating the visual arts in worship. (Interestingly, the cross as an artistic reference for Christ's death cannot be found prior to the time of Constantine.[40] The crucifix, an artistic representation of

---

[31] "Praying to the 'Dead,'" *Christian History* 12, no. 1 (1993): 2, 31.

[32] Snyder, *Ante Pacem*, 65; Johannes Quasten, *Music and Worship in Pagan and Christian Antiquity* (Washington DC: National Association of Pastoral Musicians, 1983), 153–154, 168–169.

[33] Quasten, *Music and Worship*, 162–168. Tertullian demonstrates the relentless efforts of the Christians to do away with the pagan custom of the funeral procession. Yet eventually the Christians succumbed to it. Christian funeral rites, which drew heavily from pagan forms, begin to appear in the third century. See David W. Bercot, ed., *A Dictionary of Early Christian Beliefs* (Peabody, MA: Hendrickson, 1998), 80; Everett Ferguson, ed., *Encyclopedia of Early Christianity* (New York: Garland Publishing, 1990), 163. The practice of Christians praying for the dead seems to have begun around the second century. Tertullian tells us that it was common in his day. See Tertullian, *de cor.* 4.1, and F. L. Cross and E. A. Livingstone, eds., *The Oxford Dictionary of the Christian Church*, 3rd ed. (New York: Oxford University Press, 1997), 456.

[34] Snyder, *Ante Pacem*, 83.

[35] Haas, "Where Did Christians Worship?" *Christian History* 12, no. 1 (1993): 35; Turner, *From Temple to Meeting House*, 168–172.

[36] Haas, "Where Did Christians Worship?" 35; Josef A. Jungmann, *The Early Liturgy: To the Time of Gregory the Great* (Notre Dame: Notre Dame Press, 1959), 141.

[37] White, *Protestant Worship and Church Architecture*, 60. These monuments would later be transformed into magnificent church buildings.

[38] Jungmann, *Early Liturgy*, 178; Turner, *From Temple to Meeting House*, 164–167.

[39] Schaff, *History of the Christian Church*, 2:292. "The use of catacombs lasted about three centuries, from the end of the second to the end of the fifth" (Snyder, *Ante Pacem*, 84). Contrary to popular belief, there is not a shred of historical evidence that Roman Christians hid in the catacombs to escape persecution. They met there to be close to the dead saints. See "Where Did Christians Worship?" 35; "Early Glimpses," *Christian History* 12, no.1 (1993): 30.

[40] Snyder, *Ante Pacem*, 27. "Jesus does not suffer or die in pre-Constantinian art. There is no cross symbol, nor any equivalent" (p. 56). Philip Schaff says that following Constantine's victory over Maxentius in AD 312, crosses were seen on helmets, bucklers, crowns, etc. (Schaff, *History of the Christian Church*, 2:270).

the Savior attached to the cross, made its first appearance in the fifth century.[41] The custom of making the "sign of the cross" with one's hands dates back to the second century.)[42]

At about the second century, Christians began to venerate the bones of the saints, regarding them as holy and sacred. This eventually gave birth to relic collecting.[43] Reverence for the dead was the most powerful community-forming force in the Roman Empire. Now the Christians were absorbing it into their own faith.[44]

In the late second century there was also a shift in how the Lord's Supper was viewed. The Supper had devolved from a full meal to a stylized ceremony called Holy Communion. (For more on how this transition occurred, see chapter 9.) By the fourth century, the cup and the bread were seen as producing a sense of awe, dread, and mystery. As a result, the churches in the East placed a canopy over the altar table where the bread and cup sat. (In the sixteenth century, rails were placed upon the altar table.[45] The rails signified that the altar table was a holy object only to be handled by holy persons—i.e., the clergy.[46])

So by the third century, the Christians not only had sacred spaces, they also had sacred objects. (They would soon develop a sacred priesthood.) In all of this, the second- and third-century Christians began to assimilate the magical mind-set that characterized pagan thinking.[47] All of these factors made the Christian terrain ready for the man who would be responsible for creating church buildings.

---

[41] Snyder, *Ante Pacem*, 165.

[42] Schaff, *History of the Christian Church*, 2:269–70.

[43] A relic is the material remains of a saint after his death as well as any sacred object that has been in contact with his body. The word *relic* comes from the Latin word *reliquere*, meaning "to leave behind." The first evidence of the veneration of relics appears around AD 156 in the *Martyrium Polycarpi*. In this document, the relics of Polycarp are considered more valuable than precious stones and gold. See Cross and Livingstone, *Oxford Dictionary of the Christian Church*, 1379; Michael Collins and Matthew A. Price, *The Story of Christianity* (New York: DK Publishing, 1999), 91; Jungmann, *Early Liturgy*, 184–187.

[44] Snyder, *Ante Pacem*, 91; Turner, *From Temple to Meeting House*, 168–172.

[45] This is the table where the Holy Communion was placed. The altar table signifies what is offered to God (the altar) and what is given to man (the table). White, *Protestant Worship and Church Architecture*, 40, 42, 63. Side altars did not come into use until Gregory the Great. Schaff, *History of the Christian Church*, 3:550.

[46] In the fourth century, the laity was forbidden to go to the altar. Edwin Hatch, *The Growth of Church Institutions* (London: Hodder and Stoughton, 1895), 214–215.

[47] Norman Towar Boggs, *The Christian Saga* (New York: The Macmillan Company, 1931), 209.

CONSTANTINE—FATHER OF THE CHURCH BUILDING

While the emperor Constantine (ca. 285–337) is often lauded for granting Christians freedom of worship and expanding their privileges, his story fills a dark page in the history of Christianity. Church buildings began with him.[48] The story is astonishing.

By the time Constantine emerged on the scene, the atmosphere was ripe for Christians to escape their despised, minority status. The temptation to be accepted was just too great to resist, and Constantine's influence began in earnest.

In AD 312, Constantine became caesar of the Western Empire.[49] By 324, he became emperor of the entire Roman Empire. Shortly afterward, he began ordering the construction of church buildings. He did so to promote the popularity and acceptance of Christianity. If the Christians had their own sacred buildings—as did the Jews and the pagans—their faith would be regarded as legitimate.

It is important to understand Constantine's mind-set—for it explains why he was so enthusiastic about the establishment of church buildings. Constantine's thinking was dominated by superstition and pagan magic. Even after he became emperor, he allowed the old pagan institutions to remain as they were.[50]

Following his conversion to Christianity, Constantine never abandoned sun worship. He kept the sun on his coins. And he set up a statue of the sun god that bore his own image in the Forum of Constantinople (his new capital). Constantine also built a statue of the mother-goddess Cybele (though he presented her in a posture

[48] Ilion T. Jones, *A Historical Approach to Evangelical Worship* (New York: Abingdon Press, 1954), 103; Schaff, *History of the Christian Church*, 3:542. Schaff's opening words are telling: "After Christianity was acknowledged by the state and empowered to hold property, it raised houses of worship in all parts of the Roman Empire. There was probably more building of this kind in the fourth century than there has been in any period, excepting perhaps the nineteenth century in the United States." Norrington points out that as the bishops of the fourth and fifth centuries grew in wealth, they funneled it into elaborate church building programs (*To Preach or Not*, 29). Ferguson writes, "Not until the Constantinian age do we find specially constructed buildings, at first simple halls and then the Constantinian basilicas." Before Constantine, all structures used for church gatherings were "houses or commercial buildings modified for church use" (*Early Christians Speak*, 74).
[49] That year Constantine defeated the western emperor Maxentius at the battle of Milvian Bridge. Constantine claimed that on the eve of the battle, he saw a sign of the cross in the heavens and was converted to Christ (Connolly, *Indestructible Book*, 39–40).
[50] This included the temples, priestly offices, college of pontiffs, vestal virgins, and the title (reserved for himself) *Pontifex Maximus*. See Louis Duchesne, *Early History of the Christian Church* (London: John Murray, 1912), 49–50; M. A. Smith, *From Christ to Constantine* (Downers Grove, IL: InterVarsity, 1973), 172.

of Christian prayer).[51] Historians continue to debate whether or not Constantine was a genuine Christian. The fact that he is reported to have had his eldest son, his nephew, and his brother-in-law executed does not strengthen the case for his conversion.[52] But we will not probe that nerve too deeply here.

In AD 321, Constantine decreed that Sunday would be a day of rest—a legal holiday.[53] It appears that Constantine's intention in doing this was to honor the god Mithras, the Unconquered Sun.[54] (He described Sunday as "the day of the sun.") Further demonstrating Constantine's affinity with sun worship, excavations of St. Peter's in Rome uncovered a mosaic of Christ as the Unconquered Sun.[55]

Almost to his dying day, Constantine "still functioned as the high priest of paganism."[56] In fact, he retained the pagan title *Pontifex Maximus*, which means chief of the pagan priests![57] (In the fifteenth century, this same title became the honorific title for the Roman Catholic pope.)[58]

When Constantine dedicated Constantinople as his new capital on May 11, 330, he adorned it with treasures taken from heathen temples.[59] And he used pagan magic formulas to protect crops and heal diseases.[60]

Further, all historical evidence indicates that Constantine was an egomaniac. When he built the Church of the Apostles in Constantinople, he included monuments to the twelve apostles. The twelve monuments surrounded a single tomb, which lay at the center. That tomb was reserved for Constantine himself—thus making himself the thirteenth and chief apostle. Thus Constantine not only continued

[51] Paul Johnson, *A History of Christianity* (New York: Simon & Schuster, 1976), 68.
[52] He is also charged with the death of his second wife, though some historians believe this is a false rumor. Taylor, *Christians and Holy Places*, 297; Schaff, *History of the Christian Church*, 3:16–17; Ramsay MacMullen, *Christianizing the Roman Empire: AD 100–400* (London: Yale University Press, 1984), 44–58.
[53] Kim Tan, *Lost Heritage: The Heroic Story of Radical Christianity* (Godalming, UK: Highland Books, 1996), 84.
[54] Constantine seems to have thought that the Unconquered Sun (a pagan god) and Christ were somehow compatible. Justo L. Gonzalez, *The Story of Christianity* (Peabody, MA: Prince Press, 1999), 1:122–123.
[55] Hinson, "Worshiping Like Pagans?" 20; Jungmann, *Early Liturgy*, 136.
[56] Gonzalez, *Story of Christianity*, 123.
[57] Fox, *Pagans and Christians*, 666; Durant, *Caesar and Christ*, 63, 656.
[58] Cross and Livingstone, *Oxford Dictionary of the Christian Church*, 1307.
[59] Robert M. Grant, *Early Christianity and Society* (San Francisco: Harper & Row Publishers, 1977), 155.
[60] Durant, *Caesar and Christ*, 656.

the pagan practice of honoring the dead, he also sought to be included as one of the significant dead.[61]

Constantine also borrowed from the pagans (not the Jews) the notion of the sacredness of objects and places.[62] Largely due to his influence, relic mongering became common in the church.[63] By the fourth century, obsession with relics got so bad that some Christian leaders spoke out against it, calling it "a heathen observance introduced in the churches under the cloak of religion . . . the work of idolaters."[64]

Constantine is also noted for bringing to the Christian faith the idea of the holy site, which was based on the model of the pagan shrine. Because of the aura of "sacredness" that the fourth-century Christians attached to Palestine, it had become known as "the Holy Land" by the sixth century.[65]

After Constantine's death, he was declared to be "divine." (This was the custom for all pagan emperors who died before him.)[66] It was the senate who declared him to be a pagan god at his death.[67] And no one stopped them from doing so.

At this point, a word should be said about Constantine's mother, Helena. This woman was most noted for her obsession with relics. In AD 326, Helena made a pilgrimage to Palestine.[68] In AD 327 in Jerusalem, she reportedly found the cross and nails that were used to crucify Jesus.[69] It is reported that Constantine promoted the idea that the bits of wood that came from Christ's cross possessed spiritual powers.[70] Truly,

---

[61] Johnson, *History of Christianity*, 69; Duchesne, *Early History of the Christian Church*, 69. In the Eastern Church, Constantine is actually named the thirteenth apostle and is venerated as a saint (Cross and Livingstone, *Oxford Dictionary of the Christian Church*, 405; Taylor, *Christians Holy Places*, 303, 316; Snyder, *Ante Pacem*, 93).

[62] Taylor, *Christians and the Holy Places*, 308; Davies, *Secular Use of Church Buildings*, 222–237.

[63] The notion that relics had magical power cannot be credited to the Jews, for they believed that any contact with a dead body was a pollution. This idea was completely pagan (Boggs, *Christian Saga*, 210).

[64] Johnson, *History of Christianity*, 106. This is a quote from Vigilantius.

[65] Taylor, *Christians and Holy Places*, 317, 339–341.

[66] Boggs, *Christian Saga*, 202.

[67] Gonzalez, *Story of Christianity*, 123.

[68] Cross and Livingstone, *Oxford Dictionary of the Christian Church*, 1379. Helena made her pilgrimage to the Holy Land immediately following the execution of Constantine's son and the "suicide" of his wife (Fox, *Pagans and Christians*, 670–671, 674).

[69] Oscar Hardman, *A History of Christian Worship* (Nashville: Parthenon Press, 1937). Helena gave Constantine two of these nails: one for his diadem and the other for his horse's bit (Johnson, *History of Christianity*, 106; Duchesne, *Early History of the Christian Church*, 64–65). "The cross was said to have miraculous powers, and pieces of wood claiming to come from it were found all over the Empire" (Gonzalez, *Story of Christianity*, 126). The legend of Helena's discovery of the cross originated in Jerusalem in the second half of the fourth century and rapidly spread over the entire Empire.

[70] Taylor, *Christians and Holy Places*, 308; Boggs, *Christian Saga*, 206–207.

a pagan magical mind was at work in Emperor Constantine—the father of the church building.

CONSTANTINE'S BUILDING PROGRAM

Following Helena's trip to Jerusalem in AD 327, Constantine began erecting the first church buildings throughout the Roman Empire, some at public expense.[71] In so doing, he followed the path of the pagans in constructing temples to honor God.[72]

Interestingly, he named his church buildings after saints—just as the pagans named their temples after gods. Constantine built his first church buildings upon the cemeteries where the Christians held meals for the dead saints.[73] That is, he built them over the bodies of dead saints.[74] Why? Because for at least a century beforehand, the burial places of the saints were considered "holy spaces."[75]

Many of the largest buildings were built over the tombs of the martyrs.[76] This practice was based on the idea that the martyrs had the same powers that they had once ascribed to the gods of paganism.[77] The Christians adopted this view completely.

The most famous Christian "holy spaces" were St. Peter's on the Vatican Hill (built over the supposed tomb of Peter), St. Paul's Outside the Walls (built over the supposed tomb of Paul), the dazzling and astonishing Church of the Holy Sepulcher in Jerusalem (built over the supposed tomb of Christ), and the Church of the Nativity in Bethlehem (built over the supposed cave of Jesus' birth). Constantine built nine churches in Rome and many others in Jerusalem, Bethlehem, and Constantinople.[78]

---

[71] Fox, *Pagans and Christians*, 667–668.

[72] Taylor, *Christians and Holy Places*, 309.

[73] Snyder, *Ante Pacem*, 65. These places are referred to as *martyria*.

[74] Ibid., 92; Haas, "Where Did Christians Worship?" *Christian History*, 35.

[75] Taylor, *Christians and Holy Places*, 340–341. As Davies says, "As the first Christians had no holy shrines, the need for consecration did not arise. It was only in the fourth century, with the peace of the church, that the practice of dedicating buildings began" (Davies, *Secular Use of Church Buildings*, 9, 250).

[76] Short, *History of Religious Architecture*, 62.

[77] Johnson, *History of Christianity*, 209.

[78] Snyder, *Ante Pacem*, 109. St. Peter's was 835 feet long, according to Haas, "Where Did Christians Worship?" 35. Details on St. Paul's found in Cross and Livingstone, *Oxford Dictionary of the Christian Church*, 1442; on Holy Sepulcher in Edward Norman, *The House of God: Church Architecture, Style, and History* (London: Thames and Hudson, 1990), 38–39; on the Church of the Nativity, Ibid., 31; on the nine other churches in John White, *Protestant Worship and Church Architecture*, 56; White, *Building God's House*, 150; Grant, *Early Christianity and Society*, 152–155.

EXPLORING THE FIRST CHURCH BUILDINGS

Because the church building was regarded as sacred, congregants had to undergo a purification ritual before entering. So in the fourth century, fountains were erected in the courtyard so the Christians could wash before they entered the building.[79]

Constantine's church buildings were spacious and magnificent edifices that were said to be "worthy of an Emperor." They were so splendid that his pagan contemporaries observed that these "huge buildings imitated" the structure of pagan temples.[80] Constantine even decorated the new church buildings with pagan art.[81]

The church edifices built under Constantine were patterned exactly after the model of the basilica.[82] These were the common government buildings,[83] designed after Greek pagan temples.[84]

Basilicas served the same function as high school auditoriums do today. They were wonderful for seating passive and docile crowds to watch a performance. This was one of the reasons why Constantine chose the basilica model.[85]

He also favored it because of his fascination with sun worship. Basilicas were designed so that the sun fell upon the speaker as he faced the congregation.[86] Like the temples of the Greeks and Romans, the Christian basilicas were built with a facade (front) facing east.[87]

[79] Turner, *From Temple to Meeting House*, 185.

[80] This quote comes from the anti-Christian writer Porphyry (Davies, *Secular Use of Church Buildings*, 8). Porphyry said that the Christians were inconsistent because they criticized pagan worship yet erected buildings that imitated pagan temples! (White, *Building God's House*, 129).

[81] Gonzalez, *Story of Christianity*, 122. According to Professor Harvey Yoder, Constantine built the original church of Hagia Sophia (the Church of Holy Wisdom) on the site of a pagan temple and imported 427 pagan statues from across the Empire to decorate it. "From House Churches to Holy Cathedrals" (lecture given in Harrisburg, VA, October 1993).

[82] Grant, *Founders of the Western World*, 209. The first basilica was the Church of St. John Lateran built from an imperial palace donated in AD 314 (White, *Building God's House*, 18). "Constantine, when deciding what the pioneer church of St. John Lateran was to be like, chose the basilica as a model, thereby establishing it as standard for Rome's Christian places of worship." Lionel Casson, *Everyday Life in Ancient Rome* (Baltimore: Johns Hopkins University Press, 1998), 133.

[83] Hinson, "Worshiping Like Pagans?" 19; Norman, *House of God*, 24; Jungmann, *Early Liturgy*, 123. The word *basilica* comes from the Greek word *basileus*, which means "king." "The Christian architects adapted the pagan plan, installing an altar near the large, rounded recess, or apse, at one end of the edifice, where the king or judge sat; the bishop was now to take the place of the pagan dignitary." Collins and Price, *Story of Christianity*, 64.

[84] White, *Protestant Worship and Church Architecture*, 56. One Catholic scholar states, "Long before the Christian epoch, various pagan sects and associations had adapted the basilica type of building to worship" (Jungmann, *Early Liturgy*, 123); see also Turner, *From Temple to Meeting House*, 162–163. Furthermore, Constantine's churches in Jerusalem and Bethlehem, built between AD 320 and 330, were modeled on Syrian pagan sanctuaries. Gregory Dix, *The Shape of the Liturgy* (London: Continuum International Publishing Group, 2000), 26.

[85] Michael Gough, *The Early Christians* (London: Thames and Hudson, 1961), 134.

[86] Ibid.

[87] Jungmann, *Early Liturgy*, 137.

Let's explore the inside of the Christian basilica. It was an exact duplicate of the Roman basilica that was used for Roman magistrates and officers. Christian basilicas possessed an elevated platform where the clergy ministered. The platform was usually elevated by several steps. There was also a rail or screen that separated the clergy from the laity.[88]

In the center of the building was the altar. It was either a table (the altar table) or a chest covered with a lid.[89] The altar was considered the most holy place in the building for two reasons. First, it often contained the relics of the martyrs.[90] (After the fifth century, the presence of a relic in the church altar was essential to make the church legitimate.)[91] Second, upon the altar sat the Eucharist (the bread and the cup).

The Eucharist, now viewed as a sacred sacrifice, was offered upon the altar. No one but the clergy, who were regarded as "holy men," were allowed to receive the Eucharist within the altar rails.[92]

In front of the altar stood the bishop's chair, which was called the cathedra.[93] The term *ex cathedra* is derived from this chair. *Ex cathedra* means "from the throne."[94] The bishop's chair, or "throne" as it was called, was the biggest and most elaborate seat in the building. It replaced the seat of the judge in the Roman basilica.[95] And it was surrounded by two rows of chairs reserved for the elders.[96]

The sermon was preached from the bishop's chair.[97] The power and authority rested in the chair, which was covered with a white linen cloth. The elders and deacons sat on either side of it in a semicircle.[98]

---

[88] White, *Protestant Worship and Church Architecture*, 57, 73–74. "The church building in this view was no longer the house of the people of God for their common worship, but the House of God which they were allowed to enter with due reverence. They must remain in the nave (where the congregants sit or stand) and refrain from entering the chancel (the clergy platform) which was for the choir or the sanctuary reserved for the priesthood." Turner, *From Temple to Meeting House*, 244; Hatch, *Growth of Church Institutions*, 219–220.

[89] Altars were first made of wood. Then, beginning in the sixth century, they were made of marble, stone, silver, or gold. Johnson, *History of Christianity*, 3: 550.

[90] Snyder, *Ante Pacem*, 93; White, *Protestant Worship and Church Architecture*, 58; William D. Maxwell, *An Outline of Christian Worship: Its Developments and Forms* (New York: Oxford University Press, 1936), 59.

[91] Kenneth Scott Latourette, *A History of Christianity* (New York: Harper and Brothers, 1953), 204.

[92] Johnson, *History of Christianity*, 3: 549–550, 551. In the Protestant church building, the pulpit is in the foreground and the altar table is in the background.

[93] Short, *History of Religious Architecture*, 64.

[94] Cross and Livingstone, *Oxford Dictionary of the Christian Church*, 302.

[95] White, *Protestant Worship and Church Architecture*, 57.

[96] Davies, *Secular Use of Church Buildings*, 11; Dix, *Shape of the Liturgy*, 28.

[97] White, *Protestant Worship and Church Architecture*, 59.

[98] Dix, *Shape of the Liturgy*, 28.

The hierarchical distinction embedded in the basilican architecture was unmistakable.

Interestingly, most present-day church buildings have special chairs for the pastor and his staff situated on the platform behind the pulpit. (Like the bishop's throne, the pastor's chair is usually the largest of them all.) All of this is a clear carryover from the pagan basilica.

In addition to all of this, Constantine did not destroy pagan temples on a large scale. Neither did he close them.[99] In some places, existing pagan temples were emptied of their idols and converted into Christian edifices.[100] The Christians used materials stripped from pagan temples and built new church buildings on pagan temple sites.[101]

MAJOR INFLUENCES ON WORSHIP

The advent of the church building brought significant changes to Christian worship. Because the emperor was the number one "layperson" in the church, a simple ceremony was not sufficient. In order to honor him, the pomp and ritual of the imperial court was incorporated into the Christian liturgy.[102]

It was the custom of the Roman emperors to have lights carried before them whenever they appeared in public. The lights were accompanied by a basin of fire filled with aromatic spices.[103] Taking his cue from this custom, Constantine introduced candles and the burning of incense as part of the church service. And they were brought in when the clergy entered the room.[104]

Under Constantine's reign, the clergy, who had first worn every-

[99] Grant, *Early Christianity and Society*, 155.

[100] Norman, *House of God*, 23–24.

[101] Hinson, "Worshiping Like Pagans?" 19. Gregory the Great (540–604) was the first to prescribe the use of holy water and Christian relics to purify pagan temples for Christian use. Bede, *A History of the Christian Church and People*, trans. Leo Sherley-Price (New York: Dorset Press, 1985), 86–87 (bk. 1, chapter 30). These pages contain instructions from Gregory the Great on how pagan temples were to be sanctified for Christian use. See also John Mark Terry, *Evangelism: A Concise History* (Nashville: Broadman and Holman, 1994), 48–50; Davies, *Secular Use of Church Buildings*, 251.

[102] Hinson, "Worshiping Like Pagans?" 20; White, *Protestant Worship and Church Architecture*, 56.

[103] Jungmann, *Early Liturgy*, 132.

[104] Richard Krautheimer, *Early Christian and Byzantine Architecture* (London: Penguin Books, 1986), 40–41. Krautheimer gives a vivid description of the parallels between the Roman imperial service and the Christian liturgy under Constantine.

day clothes, began dressing in special garments. What were those special clothes? They were the garments of Roman officials. Further, various gestures of respect toward the clergy, comparable to those used to honor Roman officials, were introduced in the church.[105]

The Roman custom of beginning a service with processional music was adopted as well. For this purpose, choirs were developed and brought into the Christian church. (See chapter 7 for more on the origin of the choir.) Worship became more professional, dramatic, and ceremonial.

All of these features were borrowed from the Greco-Roman culture and carried straight into the Christian church.[106] Fourth-century Christianity was being profoundly shaped by Greek paganism and Roman imperialism.[107] The upshot of it all was that there was a loss of intimacy and open participation. The professional clergy performed the acts of worship while the laity looked on as spectators.[108]

As one Catholic scholar wrote, with the coming of Constantine "various customs of ancient Roman culture flowed into the Christian liturgy . . . even the ceremonies involved in the ancient worship of the emperor as a deity found their way into the church's worship, only in their secularized form."[109]

Constantine brought peace for all Christians.[110] Under his reign, the Christian faith had become legitimate. In fact, it had risen to a status greater than Judaism and paganism.[111]

For these reasons, the Christians saw Constantine's rise to emperor as an act of God. Here was God's instrument who had come

---

[105] Jungmann, *Early Liturgy*, 129–133.

[106] Gonzalez, *Story of Christianity*, 125.

[107] Kenneth Scott Latourette traces the strong influence of Greco-Roman paganism into the Christian faith in his book *A History of Christianity*, 201–218.

[108] White, *Protestant Worship and Church Architecture*, 56.

[109] Jungmann, *Early Liturgy*, 130, 133.

[110] Historians call the period of Constantine's reign "the Peace." The Peace actually came with the Edict of Galerian (also called the Edict of Toleration) in AD 311. It was then popularized by the Edict of Milan in AD 313. These edicts stopped Diocletian's vicious persecution of the Christians that was launched in AD 303. Just eleven years after the Edict of Milan, Constantine, the first Christian emperor, became sole ruler of the Roman Empire. Gonzalez, *Story of Christianity*, 106–107; Durant, *Caesar and Christ*, 655.

[111] Adolf von Harnack estimates that there were three to four million Christians in the Empire at the beginning of Constantine's reign. *Mission and Expansion of Christianity*, 325. Others estimate it was only 4 or 5 percent of the Empire's population. Taylor, *Christians and Holy Places*, 298.

to their rescue. Christianity and Roman culture were now melded together.[112]

The Christian building demonstrates that the church, whether she wanted it or not, had entered into a close alliance with pagan culture.[113] As Will Durant, author of *The Story of Civilization* (a sweeping, eleven-volume work on world history that earned him a Pulitzer Prize), put it, "Pagan isles remained in the spreading Christian sea."[114] This was a tragic shift from the primitive simplicity that the church of Jesus Christ first knew.

The first-century Christians were opposed to the world's systems and avoided any contact with paganism. This all changed during the fourth century when the church emerged as a public institution in the world and began to "absorb and Christianize pagan religious ideas and practices."[115] As one historian put it, "Church buildings took the place of temples; church endowments replaced temple lands and funds."[116] Under Constantine, tax exempt status was granted for all church property.[117]

Consequently, the story of the church building is the sad saga of Christianity borrowing from heathen culture and radically transforming the face of our faith.[118] To put it bluntly, the church buildings of the Constantinian and post-Constantinian era essentially became holy shrines.[119] The Christians embraced the concept of the physical temple. They imbibed the pagan idea that there exists a special place where God dwells in a special way. And that place is made "with hands."[120]

As with other pagan customs that were absorbed into the Christian faith (such as the liturgy, the sermon, clerical vestments, and hierarchical leadership structure), third- and fourth-century Christians

---

[112] Johnson, *History of Christianity*, 126; Hinson, "Worshiping Like Pagans?" 19.
[113] Jungmann, *Early Liturgy*, 123.
[114] Will Durant, *The Age of Faith* (New York: Simon and Schuster, 1950), 8.
[115] Bradshaw, *Search for the Origins of Christian Worship*, 65.
[116] Grant, *Early Christianity and Society*, 163.
[117] Durant, *Caesar and Christ*, 656.
[118] "Inside Pagan Worship" *Christian History* 12, no. 1 (1993): 20.
[119] Turner, *From Temple to Meeting House*, 167, 180. Constantine built Christian shrines at the sites of biblical-historical locations (Fox, *Pagans and Christians*, 674).
[120] Contrast this with Mark 14:58; Acts 7:48; 2 Corinthians 5:1; Hebrews 9:11; and Hebrews 9:24.

incorrectly attributed the origin of the church building to the Old Testament.[121] But this was misguided thinking.

The church building was borrowed from pagan culture. "Dignified and sacramental ritual had entered the church services by way of the mysteries [the pagan cults], and was justified, like so many other things, by reference to the Old Testament."[122]

To use the Old Testament as a justification for the church building is not only inaccurate, but it is self-defeating. The old Mosaic economy of sacred priests, sacred buildings, sacred rituals, and sacred objects has been forever destroyed by the cross of Jesus Christ. In addition, it has been replaced by a nonhierarchical, nonritualistic, nonliturgical organism called the ekklesia (church).[123]

THE EVOLUTION OF CHURCH ARCHITECTURE

Following the Constantinian era, church buildings passed through various stages. (They are too complex for us to detail here.) To quote one scholar, "Changes in church architecture are the result of mutation rather than a steady line of evolution." These mutations did little to change the dominant architectural features that fostered a monopolizing clergy and an inert congregation.[124]

Let's quickly survey the evolution of church architecture:

> After Constantine, Christian architecture passed from the basilica phase to the Byzantine phase.[125] Byzantine churches had wide central domes and decorative icons and mosaics.[126]

[121] Norrington, *To Preach or Not*, 29. J. D. Davies writes, "When Christians began to build their great basilicas, they turned for guidance to their Bible and were soon applying all that was said about the Jerusalem Temple to their new edifices, seemingly ignorant of the fact that in so doing they were behaving contrary to the New Testament outlook." Davies goes on to say that the cult of the saints (revering dead saints) and its steady penetration of church buildings finally set its seal upon the outlook of the church as a holy place, "towards which Christians should adopt the same attitude as Jews to the Jerusalem Temple and pagans to their shrines" (*Secular Use of Church Buildings*, 16–17). Oscar Hardman writes, "The Roman system of administration and the architecture of its larger houses and public halls lent suggestive guidance to the church in the grading of its hierarchy and the subsequent defining of spheres of jurisdiction, and in the building of its places of worship" (*History of Christian Worship*, 13–14).
[122] Boggs, *Christian Saga*, 209.
[123] Mark 14:58; Acts 7:48, 17:24; Galatians 4:9; Colossians 2:14-19; Hebrews 3–11; 1 Peter 2:4-9.
[124] White, *Protestant Worship and Church Architecture*, 51, 57.
[125] Krautheimer, *Early Christian and Byzantine Architecture*.
[126] Norman, *House of God*, 51–71. The Hagia Sophia (the Church of Holy Wisdom), which opened in AD 360 and was rebuilt in AD 415, is touted by the Eastern church to be the perfect embodiment of a church building.

➤ Byzantine architecture was followed by Romanesque architecture.[127] Romanesque buildings were characterized by a three-story elevation, massive pillars supporting round arches, and colorful interiors.[128] This form of building arose shortly after Charlemagne became emperor of the Holy Roman Empire on Christmas day AD 800.

➤ Following the Romanesque period was the Gothic era of the twelfth century. Gothic architecture gave rise to the spell-binding Gothic cathedrals with their cross-ribbed vaults, pointed arches, and flying buttresses.[129] The term *cathedral* is derived from *cathedra*. It is the building that houses the cathedra, the bishop's chair.[130]

Colored glass was first introduced to church buildings in the sixth century by Gregory of Tours (538–594).[131] The glass was set into the narrow windows of some Romanesque churches. Suger (1081–1151), abbot of St. Denis, took colored glass to another level. He adorned the glass with sacred paintings. He thus became the first to use stained-glass windows in church buildings, placing them in his Gothic cathedrals.[132]

Great panels of tinted glass came to fill the walls of Gothic churches to emit brilliant, bright colored light.[133] Rich and dark colors were also employed to create the effect of the new Jerusalem. The stained-glass windows of the twelfth and thirteenth centuries have rarely been equaled in their beauty and quality. With their dazzling colors, stained-glass windows effectively created a soulish sense of majesty and splendor. They induced feelings associated with the worship of a mighty, fear-inspiring God.[134]

---

[127] Short, *History of Religious Architecture*, ch. 10.

[128] Norman, *House of God*, 104–135.

[129] For details see Short, *History of Religious Architecture*, ch. 11–14, and Otto von Simson's classic volume *The Gothic Cathedral: Origins of Gothic Architecture and the Medieval Concept of Order* (Princeton: Princeton University Press, 1988).

[130] Krautheimer, *Early Christian and Byzantine Architecture*, 43.

[131] Durant, *Age of Faith*, 856.

[132] von Simson, *Gothic Cathedral*, 122. Frank Senn writes, "More space between the pillars could be filled in with larger windows, which gave a lightness and a brightness to the new buildings that the old Romanesque buildings lacked. The windows could be filled with stained-glass, which could tell the biblical stories or employ the theological symbols that were previously painted on the walls" (*Christian Liturgy*, 214).

[133] Durant, *Age of Faith*, 856.

[134] Norman, *House of God*, 153–154; Paul Clowney and Teresa Clowney, *Exploring Churches* (Grand Rapids: Eerdmans, 1982), 66–67.

As with the Constantinian basilicas, the root of the Gothic cathedral is completely pagan. Gothic architects relied heavily on the teachings of the pagan Greek philosopher Plato. Plato taught that sound, color, and light have lofty mystical meanings. They can induce moods and help bring one closer to the "Eternal Good."[135] The Gothic designers took Plato's teachings and set them to brick and stone. They created awe-inspiring lighting to elicit a sense of overwhelming splendor and worship.[136]

Color is one of the most powerful emotive factors available. Thus the Gothic stained-glass windows were employed skillfully to create a sense of mystery and transcendence. Drawing inspiration from the grandiose statues and towers of ancient Egypt, Gothic architecture sought to recapture the sense of the sublime through its exaggerated heights.[137]

It was said of the Gothic structure that "the whole building seems chained to earth in fixed flight. . . . It rises like an exhalation from the soil. . . . No architecture so spiritualizes, refines and casts heaven-ward the substance which it handles."[138] It was the ultimate symbol of heaven joining the earth.[139]

So with its use of light, color, and excessive height, the Gothic cathedral fostered a sense of mystery, transcendence, and awe.[140] All of these features were borrowed from Plato and passed off as Christian.[141]

Basilica, Romanesque, and Gothic church buildings are a human

---

[135] von Simson, *Gothic Cathedral*, 22–42, 50–55, 58, 188–191, 234–235. Von Simson shows how the metaphysics of Plato shaped Gothic architecture. Light and luminosity reach their perfection in Gothic stained-glass windows. Numbers of perfect proportions harmonize all elements of the building. Light and harmony are images of heaven; they are the ordering principles of creation. Plato taught that light is the most notable of natural phenomena—the closest to pure form. The Neoplatonists conceived light as a transcendental reality that illuminates our intellect to grasp truth. The Gothic design was essentially a blending together of the visions of Plato, Augustine, and Denis the pseudo-Areopagite (a noted Neoplatonist).

[136] White, *Protestant Worship and Church Architecture*, 6.

[137] Neil Carter, "The Story of the Steeple" (unpublished manuscript, 2001). The full text, which is documented, can be accessed at http://www.christinyall.com/steeple.html.

[138] Turner, *From Temple to Meeting House*, 190.

[139] The baroque architecture of the seventeenth and eighteenth centuries followed the path of the Gothic in inducing the senses with its harmonious richness and decoration (Clowney and Clowney, *Exploring Churches*, 75–77). J. G. Davies states that in the West during the Middle Ages, cathedrals were regarded as models of the cosmos (Davies, *Secular Use of Church Buildings*, 220).

[140] White, *Protestant Worship and Church Architecture*, 131.

[141] For a detailed discussion of the historical specificities of Gothic architecture, see Durant, *Age of Faith*, ch. 32. Although antiquated, Gothic architecture made a reappearance among Protestants with the Gothic revival in the mid-nineteenth century. But Gothic construction ceased after World War II (White, *Protestant Worship and Church Architecture*, 130–142; Norman, *House of God*, 252–278).

attempt to duplicate that which is heavenly and spiritual.[142] In a very real way, the church building throughout history reflects man's quest to sense the divine with his physical senses. While being surrounded by beauty can certainly turn a person's heart toward God, He desires so much more for His church than an aesthetic experience. By the fourth century, the Christian community had lost touch with those heavenly realities and spiritual intangibles that cannot be perceived by the senses, but which can only be registered by the human spirit (see 1 Corinthians 2:9-16).

The main message of Gothic architecture is: "God is transcendent and unreachable—so be awed at His majesty." But such a message defies the message of the gospel, which says that God is very accessible—so much so that He has taken up residence inside of His people.

THE PROTESTANT CHURCH BUILDING

In the sixteenth century, the Reformers inherited the aforementioned building tradition. In a short period of time, thousands of medieval cathedrals became their property as the local rulers who controlled those structures joined the Reformation.[143]

Most of the Reformers were former priests. Hence, they had been unwittingly conditioned by the thought patterns of medieval Catholicism.[144] So even though the Reformers did some remodeling to their newly acquired church buildings, they made little functional change in the architecture.[145]

Even if the Reformers wanted to bring radical changes to the practice of the church, the masses were not ready for it.[146] Martin Luther was quite clear that the church was not a building or an insti-

---

[142] Senn, *Christian Liturgy*, 604.

[143] White, *Protestant Worship and Church Architecture*, 64. The first Protestant church building was the castle at Torgua, built in 1544 for Lutheran worship. There was no chancel, and the altar had become a simple table (Turner, *From Temple to Meeting House*, 206).

[144] White, *Protestant Worship and Church Architecture*, 78.

[145] Jones, *Historical Approach to Evangelical Worship*, 142–143, 225. Interestingly, the nineteenth and twentieth centuries have seen a major revival of medieval architecture among all Protestant bodies (White, *Protestant Worship and Church Architecture*, 64).

[146] White, *Protestant Worship and Church Architecture*, 79.

tution.[147] Yet it would have been impossible for him to overturn more than a millennium of confusion on the subject.[148]

The central architectural change that the Reformers made reflected their theology. They made the pulpit the dominant center of the building rather than the altar table.[149] The Reformation was built on the idea that people could not know God nor grow spiritually unless they heard preaching. Thus when the Reformers inherited existing church buildings, they adapted them toward that end.[150]

THE STEEPLE

Ever since the inhabitants of Babel erected a tower to "reach to the heavens," civilizations have followed suit by building structures with pointed tops.[151] The Babylonians and Egyptians built obelisks and pyramids that reflected their belief that they were progressing toward immortality. When Greek philosophy and culture came along, the direction of architecture changed from upward and vertical to downward and horizontal. All of this suggested the Greek belief in democracy, human equality, and earthbound gods.[152]

However, with the rise of the Roman Catholic Church, the practice of crowning buildings with pointed tops reemerged. Toward the end of the Byzantine period, Catholic popes drew inspiration from the obelisks of ancient Egypt.[153] As religious architecture entered the Romanesque period, points began to appear on the surfaces and

---

[147] "Of all the great teachers of Christianity, Martin Luther perceived most clearly the difference between the *Ecclesia* of the New Testament and the institutional church, and reacted most sharply against the *quid pro quo* which would identify them. Therefore he refused to tolerate the mere word 'church': he called it an obscure ambiguous term. In his translation of the Bible, he rendered *ecclesia* by 'congregation.' . . . He realized that the New Testament *ecclesia* is just not an 'it,' 'a thing,' an 'institution,' but rather a unity of persons, a people, a communion. . . . Strong as was Luther's aversion to the word 'church,' the facts of history prove stronger. The linguistic usage of both the Reformation and the post-Reformation era had to come to terms with the so powerfully developed idea of the church, and consequently all the confusion dependent upon the use of this 'obscure ambiguous' word penetrated Reformation theology. It was impossible to put the clock back one millennium and a half. The conception 'church' remained irrevocably moulded by this historical process of 1500 years." Emil Brunner, *The Misunderstanding of the Church* (London: Lutterworth Press, 1952), 15–16.

[148] Martin Luther, *Luther's Works* (Philadelphia: Fortress Press, 1965), 53–54.

[149] White, *Protestant Worship and Church Architecture*, 82.

[150] Clowney and Clowney, *Exploring Churches*, 72–73. The altar table was moved from the lofty position of "altar" and moved down the chancel (clergy platform) steps, giving it a position of less prominence. The pulpit was moved closer to the nave where the people sat, so as to make the sermon a fixed part of the service.

[151] See Genesis 11:3-9. Carter, "The Story of the Steeple."

[152] Zahi Havass, *The Pyramids of Ancient Egypt* (Pittsburgh: Carnegie Museum of Natural History, 1990), 1; Short, *History of Religious Architecture*, 13, 167.

[153] Norman, *House of God*, 160.

corners of every cathedral built in the Roman Empire. This trend reached its pinnacle during the era of Gothic architecture with Abbot Suger's construction of the cathedral at St. Denis.

Unlike Greek architecture, the characteristic line of Gothic architecture was vertical to suggest striving upward. By this time, all throughout Italy, towers began to appear near the entrances of church buildings. The towers housed bells to call the people to worship.[154] These towers represented contact between heaven and earth.[155]

As the years passed, Gothic architects (with their emphasis on verticality) sought to add a tall spire to every tower.[156] Spires (also called steeples; *spires* is the British/Anglican term) were a symbol of man's aspiration to be united with His Creator.[157] In the centuries that followed, the towers grew taller and thinner. They eventually became a visual focal point for the architecture. They also reduced in number, from the double-towered "westwork" to the singular spire that so characterized the churches of Normandy and Britain.

In the year 1666, something happened that changed the course of tower architecture. A fire swept across the city of London and damaged most of its eighty-seven church edifices.[158] Sir Christopher Wren (1632–1723) was then commissioned to redesign all the churches of London. Using his own stylistic innovations in modifying the Gothic spires of France and Germany, Wren created the modern steeple.[159] From that point on, the steeple became a dominant feature of Anglo-British architecture.

Later the Puritans made their church buildings far simpler than their Catholic and Anglican predecessors. But they kept the steeple and brought it into the new world of the Americas.[160]

---

[154] Charles Wickes, *Illustrations of Spires and Towers of the Medieval Churches of England* (New York: Hessling & Spielmeyer, 1900), 18.

[155] Clowney and Clowney, *Exploring Churches*, 13.

[156] Durant, *Age of Faith*, 865.

[157] Clowney and Clowney, *Exploring Churches*, 13.

[158] Gerald Cobb, *London City Churches* (London: Batsford, 1977), 15ff.

[159] Viktor Furst, *The Architecture of Sir Christopher Wren* (London: Lund Humphries, 1956), 16. Because the churches of London were so tightly sandwiched between other buildings, little room was left for emphasis on anything other than the spire itself. Consequently, Wren established the trend of building churches with relatively plain sides featuring a disproportionately tall and ornate spire on one end. Paul Jeffery, *The City Churches of Sir Christopher Wren* (London: The Hambledon Press, 1996), 88.

[160] Peter Williams, *Houses of God* (Chicago: University of Illinois Press, 1997), 7–9; Colin Cunningham, *Stones of Witness* (Gloucestershire, UK: Sutton Publishing, 1999), 60.

The message of the steeple is one that contradicts the message of the New Testament. Christians do not have to reach into the heavens to find God. He is here! With the coming of Immanuel, God is with us (see Matthew 1:23). And with His resurrection, we have an indwelling Lord. The steeple defies these realities.

THE PULPIT

The earliest sermons were delivered from the bishop's chair, or cathedra, which was positioned behind the altar.[161] Later the ambo, a raised desk on the side of the chancel from which Bible lessons were read, became the place where sermons were delivered.[162] The ambo was taken from the Jewish synagogue.[163] However, it has earlier roots in the reading desks and platforms of Greco-Roman antiquity. John Chrysostom (347–407) was noted for making the ambo a place for preaching.[164]

As early as AD 250, the ambo was replaced by the pulpit. Cyprian of Carthage (200–258) speaks of placing the leader of the church into public office upon the pulpitum.[165] Our word *pulpit* is derived from the Latin word *pulpitum* which means "a stage."[166] The pulpitum, or pulpit, was propped up in the highest elevated place in the congregation.[167]

In time, the phrase "to ascend the platform" (*ad pulpitum venire*) became part of the religious vocabulary of the clergy. By AD 252, Cyprian alludes to the raised platform that segregated the clergy from the laity as "the sacred and venerated congestum of the clergy."[168]

---

[161] Arthur Pierce Middleton, *New Wine in Old Wineskins* (Wilton, Connecticut: Morehouse-Barlow Publishing, 1988), 76.

[162] *Ambo* is the Latin term for pulpit. It is derived from *ambon* which means "crest of a hill." Most *ambos* were elevated and reached by steps (Ferguson, *Encyclopedia of Early Christianity*, 29; Peter F. Anson, *Churches: Their Plan and Furnishing*, 154; Middleton, *New Wine in Old Wineskins*, 76).

[163] Gough, *Early Christians*, 172; Ferguson, *Encyclopedia of Early Christianity*, 29. The predecessor of the ambo is the migdal of the synagogue. *Migdal* means "tower" in Hebrew.

[164] Ferguson, *Encyclopedia of Early Christianity*, 29.

[165] Latin for "pulpit." White, *Building God's House*, 124.

[166] Christian Smith, *Going to the Root* (Scottdale, PA: Herald Press, 1992), 83.

[167] White, *Building God's House*, 124.

[168] Ibid.

By the end of the Middle Ages the pulpit became common in parish churches.[169] With the Reformation, it became the central piece of furniture in the church building.[170] The pulpit symbolized the replacement of the centrality of ritualistic action (the Mass) with clerical verbal instruction (the sermon).[171]

In Lutheran churches, the pulpit was moved to the front of the altar.[172] In Reformed churches the pulpit dominated until the altar finally disappeared and was replaced by the "Communion table."[173]

The pulpit has always been the centerpiece of the Protestant church. So much so that a well-known pastor who spoke during a conference sponsored by the Billy Graham Evangelistic Association claimed: "If the church is alive, it's because the pulpit is alive—if the church is dead, it's because the pulpit is dead."[174]

The pulpit elevates the clergy to a position of prominence. True to its meaning, it puts the preacher at center "stage"—separating and placing him high above God's people.

THE PEW AND BALCONY

The pew is perhaps the greatest inhibitor of face-to-face fellowship. It is a symbol of lethargy and passivity in the contemporary church and has made corporate worship a spectator sport.[175]

The word *pew* is derived from the Latin *podium*. It means a seat raised up above floor level or a "balcony."[176] Pews were unknown to the church building for the first thousand years of Christian history. In the early basilicas, the congregation stood throughout the entire service.[177] (This is still the practice among many Eastern Orthodox.)[178]

---

[169] Middleton, *New Wine in Old Wineskins*, 76.

[170] Clowney and Clowney, *Exploring Churches*, 26.

[171] Frank C. Senn, *Christian Worship and Its Cultural Setting* (Philadelphia: Fortress Press, 1983), 45.

[172] Owen Chadwick, *The Reformation* (London: Penguin Books, 1964), 422. In the sixteenth century, the pulpit was combined with the reading desk (or lectern) to make a single structure—the "two decker." The reading desk was the lower-level part of the pulpit (Middleton, *New Wine in Old Wineskins*, 77).

[173] Senn, *Christian Worship and Its Cultural Setting*, 45.

[174] Scott Gabrielson, "All Eyes to the Front: A Look at Pulpits Past and Present," *Your Church*, January/February 2002, 44.

[175] James F. White, *The Worldliness of Worship* (New York: Oxford University Press, 1967), 43.

[176] Cross and Livingstone, *Oxford Dictionary of the Christian Church*, 1271; Smith, *Going to the Root*, 81.

[177] Davies, *Secular Use of Church Buildings*, 138. Occasionally a few wooden or stone benches were provided for the aged and sick.

[178] Middleton, *New Wine in Old Wineskins*, 73.

By the thirteenth century, backless benches were gradually introduced into English parish buildings.[179] These benches were made of stone and placed against the walls. They were then moved into the body of the building (the area called the nave).[180] At first, the benches were arranged in a semicircle around the pulpit. Later they were fixed to the floor.[181]

The modern pew was introduced in the fourteenth century, though it was not commonly found in churches until the fifteenth century.[182] At that time, wooden benches supplanted the stone seats.[183] By the eighteenth century, box pews became popular.[184]

Box pews have a comical history. They were furnished with cushioned seats, carpets, and other accessories. They were sold to families and considered private property.[185] Box-pew owners set out to make them as comfortable as possible.

Some decorated them with curtains, cushions, padded armchairs, fireplaces—even special compartments for pet dogs. It was not uncommon for owners to keep their pews sealed with lock and key. After much criticism from the clergy, these embellished pews were replaced with open seats.[186]

Because box pews often had high sides, the pulpits had to be elevated so as to be seen by the people. Thus the "wineglass" pulpit was born during colonial times.[187] Eighteenth-century family box pews were replaced with slip pews so that all the people faced the newly erected high platform where the pastor conducted the service.[188]

So what is the pew? The meaning of the word tells it all. It is a lowered "balcony"—detached seating from which to watch performances on a stage (the pulpit). It immobilizes the congregation of

---

[179] Ibid., 74. By the end of the Middle Ages, these pews were elaborately decorated with pictures of saints and fanciful animals. Norrington, *To Preach or Not*, 31; J. G. Davies, *The Westminster Dictionary of Worship* (Philadelphia: Westminster Press, 1972), 312.

[180] Doug Adams, *Meeting House to Camp Meeting* (Austin: The Sharing Company, 1981), 14.

[181] Clowney and Clowney, *Exploring Churches*, 28.

[182] Senn, *Christian Liturgy*, 215; Clowney and Clowney, *Exploring Churches*, 28.

[183] Davies, *Secular Use of Church Buildings*, 138.

[184] White, *Protestant Worship and Church Architecture*, 101.

[185] Clowney and Clowney, *Exploring Churches*, 28.

[186] Ibid.; Davies, *Secular Use of Church Buildings*, 139. Some clergymen attacked the abuse of pew decorum. One preacher is noted for giving a sermon lamenting the pew, saying that the congregation "wants nothing but beds to hear the Word of God on."

[187] Middleton, *New Wine in Old Wineskins*, 74.

[188] Adams, *Meeting House to Camp Meeting*, 14.

the saints and renders them mute spectators. It hinders face-to-face fellowship and interaction.

Galleries (or church balconies) were invented by the Germans in the sixteenth century. They were popularized by the Puritans in the eighteenth century. Since then balconies have become the trademark of the Protestant church building. Their purpose is to bring the congregation closer to the pulpit. Again, ensuring that congregants will be able to clearly hear the preacher has always been the main consideration in Protestant church design.[189]

CONTEMPORARY CHURCH ARCHITECTURE

Over the last two hundred years, the two dominating architectural patterns employed by Protestant churches are the divided chancel form (used in liturgical churches) and the concert stage form (used in evangelical churches).[190] The chancel is the area where the clergy (and sometimes the choir) conduct the service.[191] In the chancel-style church, a rail or screen that separates the clergy from the laity still exists.

The concert-style church building was profoundly influenced by nineteenth-century revivalism.[192] It is essentially an auditorium. The building is structured to emphasize the dramatic performance of the preacher and the choir.[193] Its structure implicitly suggests that the choir (or worship team) performs for the congregation to stimulate their worship or entertain them.[194] It also calls excessive attention to the preacher whether he is standing or sitting.

In the concert-style building, a small Communion table may appear on the floor below the pulpit. The Communion table is typically decorated with brass candlesticks, a cross, and flowers. Two candles on the Communion table have become the sign of orthodoxy in most Protestant churches today. As with so many parts of the church

---

[189] White, *Protestant Worship and Church Architecture*, 85, 107. Clowney and Clowney, *Exploring Churches*, 74.
[190] White, *Protestant Worship and Church Architecture*, 118.
[191] Clowney and Clowney, *Exploring Churches*, 17.
[192] White, *Protestant Worship and Church Architecture*, 121ff.
[193] Turner, *From Temple to Meeting House*, 237, 241.
[194] White, *Protestant Worship and Church Architecture*, 140.

service, the presence of candles was borrowed from the ceremonial court of the Roman Empire.[195]

Yet despite these variations, all Protestant architecture produces the same sterile effects that were present in the Constantinian basilicas. They continue to maintain the unbiblical division between clergy and laity. And they encourage the congregation to assume a spectator role. The arrangement and mood of the building conditions the congregation toward passivity. The pulpit platform acts like a stage, and the congregation occupies the theater.[196] In short, Christian architecture has stalemated the functioning of God's people since it was born in the fourth century.

EXEGETING THE BUILDING

At this point, you may be thinking to yourself, *So what's the big deal? Who cares if the first-century Christians did not have buildings? Or if church buildings were patterned after pagan beliefs and practices? Or if medieval Catholics based their architecture on pagan philosophy? What has that got to do with us today?*

Consider this next sentence: The social location of the church meeting expresses and influences the character of the church.[197] If you assume that where the church gathers is simply a matter of convenience, you are tragically mistaken. You are overlooking a basic reality of humanity. Every building we encounter elicits a response from us. By its interior and exterior, it explicitly shows us what the church is and how it functions.

To put it in the words of Henri Lefebvre, "Space is never empty; it always embodies a meaning."[198] This principle is also expressed in

---

[195] Ibid., 129, 133, 134. Some churches have built-in baptistries behind the pulpit and choir. In the Catholic tradition, candles were not commonly placed on the altar table until the eleventh century (Jungmann, *Early Liturgy*, 133).

[196] White, *Protestant Worship and Church Architecture*, 120, 125, 129, 141.

[197] As J. G. Davies says, "The question of church building is inseparable from the question of the church and of its function in the modern world" (*Secular Use of Church Buildings*, 208).

[198] Leonard Sweet, "Church Architecture for the 21st Century," *Your Church*, March/April 1999, 10. In this article, Sweet tries to envision postmodern church buildings that break out of the old mold of architecture, which promotes passivity. Ironically, Sweet writes from the old paradigm of viewing church buildings as sacred spaces. He writes, "Of course, you are not just putting up a building when you build a church; you are constructing sacred space." This sort of thinking runs quite deep.

the architectural motto "form follows function." The form of the building reflects its particular function.[199]

The social setting of a church's meeting place is a good index of that church's understanding of God's purpose for His body. A church's location teaches us how to meet. It teaches us what is important and what is not. And it teaches us what is acceptable to say to each other and what is not.

We learn these lessons from the setting in which we gather—whether it be a church edifice or a private home. These lessons are by no means neutral. Go into any given church building and exegete the architecture. Ask yourself what objects are higher and which are lower. Ask yourself what is at the front and what is at the back. Ask yourself in what ways it might be possible to "adjust" the direction of the meeting on the spur of the moment. Ask yourself how easy or hard it would be for a church member to speak where he is seated so that all may see and hear him.

If you look at the church building setting and ask yourself these questions (and others like them), you will understand why the contemporary church has the character it does. If you ask the same set of questions about a living room, you will get a very different set of answers. You will understand why being a church in a house setting (as were the early Christians) has the character it does.

The church's social location is a crucial factor in church life. It cannot be assumed as simply "an accidental truth of history."[200] Social locations can teach good and godly people very bad lessons and choke their lives together. Calling attention to the importance of the social location of the church (house or church edifice) helps us to understand the tremendous power of our social environment.

To put a finer point on it, the church building is based on the benighted idea that worship is removed from everyday life. People vary, of course, on how profoundly they emphasize this disjunction.

---

[199] Senn, *Christian Liturgy*, 212, 604. The auditorium-styled church building turns the congregation into a passive audience while the Gothic-style scatters it through a long, narrow nave or into nooks and crannies.
[200] A quote from Gotthold Lessing (*Lessing's Theological Writings*).

Some groups have gone out of their way to emphasize it by insisting that worship could occur only in specific kinds of spaces designed to make you feel differently than you feel in everyday life.

The disjunction between worship and everyday life characterizes Western Christianity. Worship is seen as something detached from the whole fabric of life and packaged for group consumption. Centuries of Gothic architecture have taught us badly about what worship really is. Few people can walk into a powerful cathedral without experiencing the power of the space.

The lighting is indirect and subdued. The ceilings are high. The colors are earthy and rich. Sound travels in a specific way. All these things work together to give us a sense of awe and wonder. They are designed to manipulate the senses and create a "worshipful atmosphere."[201]

Some traditions add smells to the mix. But the effect is always the same: Our senses interact with our space to bring us to a particular state of the soul—a state of awe, mystery, and transcendence that equals an escape from normal life.[202]

We Protestants have replaced some of the grander architectural embellishments with a specific use of music intended to achieve the same end. Consequently, in Protestant circles "good" worship leaders are those who can use music to evoke what other traditions use space to evoke; specifically, a soulish sense of worshipfulness.[203] But this is disjointed from everyday life and is inauthentic. Jonathan Edwards rightfully pointed out that emotions are transient and cannot be used to measure one's relationship with God.[204]

This disjunction between secular and spiritual is highlighted by the fact that the typical church building requires you to "process" in by walking up stairs or moving through a narthex. This adds to the sense that you are moving from everyday life to another life. Thus a transition

---

[201] White, *Protestant Worship and Church Architecture*, 5.
[202] White, *Worldliness of Worship*, 79–83.
[203] Plato was fearful of exposing the youth to certain types of music because it might excite the wrong emotions (*The Republic*, 3:398).
[204] White, *Protestant Worship and Church Architecture*, 19.

is required. All of this flunks the Monday test. No matter how good Sunday was, Monday morning still comes to test our worship.[205]

Watch a choir don their robes before the church service. They smile, laugh, and even joke. But once the service starts, they become different people. You will not often catch them smiling or laughing. This false separation of secular and sacred—this "stained-glass mystique" of Sunday morning church—flies in the face of truth and reality.

In addition, the church building is far less warm, personal, and friendly than someone's home—the organic meeting place of the early Christians.[206] The church building is not designed for intimacy nor fellowship. In most church buildings, the seating consists of wooden pews bolted to the floor. The pews (or chairs) are arranged in rows, all facing toward the pulpit. The pulpit sits on an elevated platform, which is often where the clergy also sits (remnants of the Roman basilica).

This arrangement makes it nearly impossible for one worshipper to look into the face of another. Instead, it creates a sit-and-soak form of worship that turns functioning Christians into "pew potatoes." To state it differently, the architecture emphasizes fellowship between God and His people via the pastor! Yet despite these facts, we Christians still treat the building as if it is sacred.

Granted, you may object to the idea that the church building is hallowed. But (for most of us) our actions and words betray our belief. Listen to Christians speak of the church building. Listen to yourself as you speak of it. Do you ever hear it referred to as "church"? Do you ever hear it spoken of as "God's house"? The general consensus among Christians of all denominations is that "a church is essentially a place set apart for worship."[207] This has been true for the last 1,700 years. Constantine is still living and breathing in our minds.

---

[205] These insights owe much to Frank's friend Hal Miller.

[206] Robert Sommer speaks of a "sociofugal space" as a place where people tend to avoid personal contact with one another. The modern church building fits Sommer's description rather nicely. "Sociofugal Space," *American Journal of Sociology* 72 (1967): 655.

[207] Davies, *Secular Use of Church Buildings*, 206.

THE INCREDIBLY HIGH COST OF OVERHEAD

Most contemporary Christians mistakenly view the church building as a necessary part of worship. Therefore, they never question the need to financially support a building and its maintenance.

The church edifice demands a vast infusion of money. In the United States alone, real estate owned by institutional churches today is worth over $230 billion. Church building debt, service, and maintenance consumes about 18 percent of the $50 to $60 billion tithed to churches annually.[208] Point: Contemporary Christians are spending an astronomical amount of money on their buildings.

All the traditional reasons put forth for "needing" a church building collapse under careful scrutiny.[209] We so easily forget that the early Christians turned the world upside down without them (see Acts 17:6). They grew rapidly for three hundred years without the help (or hindrance) of church buildings.

In the business world, overhead kills. Overhead is what gets added on to the "real" work a business does for its clients. Overhead pays for the building, the pencils, and the accounting staff. Furthermore, church buildings (as well as salaried pastors and staff) require very large ongoing expenses rather than onetime outlays. These budget busters take their cut out of a church's monetary giving not just today, but next month, next year, and so on.

Contrast the overhead of a traditional church, which includes salaried staff and church buildings, with the overhead of a house church. Rather than such overhead siphoning off 50 to 85 percent of the house church's monetary giving, its operating costs amount to a small percentage of the budget, freeing more than 95 percent of its shared money for delivering real services like ministry, mission, and outreach to the world.[210]

---

[208] Smith, *Going to the Root*, 95. George Barna's research indicates that Christians give $50 to $60 billion annually to churches.

[209] Howard Snyder demolishes most common arguments for "needing" church buildings in his book *Radical Renewal: The Problem of Wineskins Today* (Houston: Touch Publications, 1996), 62–74.

[210] For a discussion on why the early Christians met in homes and how large congregations can move into house churches, see Frank Viola, *Reimagining Church* (Colorado Springs: David C. Cook, 2008).

CAN WE DEFY THIS TRADITION?

Most of us are completely unaware of what we lost as Christians when we began erecting places devoted exclusively for worship. The Christian faith was born in believers' homes, yet every Sunday morning, scores of Christians sit in a building with pagan origins that is based upon pagan philosophy.

There does not exist a shred of biblical support for the church building.[211] Yet scores of Christians pay good money each year to sanctify their brick and stone. By doing so, they have supported an artificial setting where they are lulled into passivity and prevented from being natural or intimate with other believers.[212]

We have become victims of our past. We have been fathered by Constantine who gave us the prestigious status of owning a building. We have been blinded by the Romans and Greeks who forced upon us their hierarchically structured basilicas. We have been taken by the Goths who imposed upon us their Platonic architecture. We have been hijacked by the Egyptians and Babylonians who gave us our sacred steeples. And we have been swindled by the Athenians who imposed on us their Doric columns.[213]

Somehow we have been taught to feel holier when we are in "the house of God" and have inherited a pathological dependency upon an edifice to carry out our worship to God. At bottom, the church building has taught us badly about what church is and what it does. The building is an architectural denial of the priesthood of all believers. It is a contradiction of the very nature of the ekklesia—which is a countercultural community. The church building impedes our understanding and experience that the church is

---

[211] The Temple in Jerusalem was a type and a shadow of the church of Jesus Christ, along with the sacrificial system that went with it. Thus the Temple cannot be used as a justification for owning church buildings any more than slaying lambs can be used to justify that practice today. The church in Jerusalem met under a roof in the Temple courts and Solomon's Porch on special occasions when it suited their needs (Acts 2:46, 5:12). Paul temporarily rented a school as his apostolic base while he was in Ephesus (Acts 19:1-10). Consequently, buildings are by no means inherently wrong or bad. They *can* be used for God's glory. However, the "church building" that is depicted in this chapter is at odds with biblical principles for the reasons stated herein.

[212] One English Catholic writer puts it this way: "If there is one simple method of saving the church's mission it is probably the decision to abandon church buildings for they are basically unnatural places . . . and they do not correspond to anything which is normal in everyday life" (Turner, *From Temple to Meeting House*, 323).

[213] Richard Bushman, *The Refinement of America* (New York: Knopf, 1992), 338. Between 1820 and 1840, American churches began to appear with Doric columns reminiscent of Greek classicalism and archways reminiscent of ancient Rome (Williams, *Houses of God*, 12).

Christ's functioning body that lives and breathes under His direct headship.

It is high time we Christians wake up to the fact that we are being neither biblical nor spiritual by supporting church buildings. And we are doing great damage to the message of the New Testament by calling man-made buildings "churches." If every Christian on the planet would never call a building a church again, this alone would create a revolution in our faith.

John Newton rightly said, "Let not him who worships under a steeple condemn him who worships under a chimney." With that in mind, what biblical, spiritual, or historical authority does any Christian have to gather under a steeple in the first place?

>delving DEEPER

1. Church buildings enable a large number of people to gather together for worship. How did the early church manage to worship in homes with so many people and still see themselves as a single body of believers? Practically, how do organic churches today maintain every-member functioning as they grow in size?

Today Christians often assume that the early churches were large like many contemporary institutional churches. This, however, was not the case. The early Christians met in homes for their church gatherings (Acts 2:46; 20:20; Romans 16:3, 5; 1 Corinthians 16:19; Colossians 4:15; Philemon 2). Given the size of first-century houses, the early Christian churches were rather small compared to today's standards. In his book *Paul's Idea of Community*, New Testament scholar Robert Banks says the average-sized church included thirty to thirty-five people.[214]

Some first-century churches, such as the one in Jerusalem, were much larger. Luke tells us that the church in Jerusalem met in homes all throughout the city (Acts 2:46). Yet each home gathering didn't see itself as a separate church or denomination but as part of the one church in the city. For this reason, Luke always refers to this church as "the church at Jerusalem," never as the "churches at Jerusalem" (Acts 8:1, 11:22, 15:4). When the entire church needed to come together for a specific

---

[214] Robert Banks, *Paul's Idea of Community* (Peabody, MA: Hendrickson, 1994), 35.

purpose (i.e., Acts 15), it met in an already existing facility that was large enough to accommodate everyone. The porch of Solomon outside the Temple was used for such occasions (Acts 5:12).

Today, when an organic church grows too large to gather in a single home, it will typically multiply into separate home meetings throughout the city. Yet it will often still see itself as one church meeting in different locations. If the home groups need to congregate together for special occasions, they often rent or borrow a large space to accommodate everyone.

2. I'm not sure I understand the problem with church buildings. Are you saying that they are bad because the first ones were modeled on large public buildings or promoted by an emperor with suspect theological grounding? Is there anything in Scripture that prohibits the body of Christ from meeting in them?

The answer to the first question is no, that is not what we are saying. By detailing their origin, however, we are showing that they developed apart from any scriptural mandate, contrary to what some Christians believe. Furthermore, we believe they detract from a proper understanding of the church as the body of believers.

Although Scripture never discusses the topic specifically, church buildings teach us a number of bad lessons that run contrary to New Testament principles. They limit the involvement of and fellowship between members. Often their grandeur distances people from God rather than reminding them that Christ indwells each believer. As Winston Churchill said: "First we shape our buildings. Thereafter, they shape us." This has definitely been the case with the church building.

The idea that the church building is "the house of God" and is constantly referred to as "church" is not only unbiblical, it violates the New Testament understanding of what the ekklesia really is. We believe that this is why the early Christians did not erect such buildings until the era of Constantine.

Church historian Rodney Stark says, "For far too long, historians have accepted the claim that the conversion of the Emperor Constantine (ca. 285–337) caused the triumph of Christianity. To the contrary, he destroyed its most attractive and dynamic aspects, turning a high-intensity, grassroots movement into an arrogant institution controlled by an elite who often managed to be both brutal and lax. . . . Constantine's 'favor' was his decision to divert to the Christians the massive state funding on which the pagan temples had always depended. Overnight, Christianity became 'the most-favoured recipient of the near limitless resources of imperial favors.' A faith that had been meeting in humble structures was suddenly housed in magnificent public buildings—the new church of Saint Peter in Rome was modeled on the basilican form used for imperial throne rooms."[215]

3. Just because Plato, a pagan philosopher, was the first to articulate how sound, light, and color influence mood and elicit splendor, awe, and worship, why is it wrong for churches to consider how to maximize these factors when designing their buildings? Isn't it appropriate to employ these to the fullest in Christian worship? After all, Scripture makes clear that we are to remember God's holiness and righteousness.

Our point in that brief discussion on Plato was simply to show that pagan philosophy had a hand in engineering sacred buildings to create a psychological experience in those who occupy them. To our minds, psychological experience ought never to be confused with spiritual experience.

4. Since believers are in a church building only two to three hours a week, how can you say that these structures stymie the functioning of God's people?

Most Christians equate church services in a church building with "church." Church leaders often quote Hebrews 10:25 ("not forsaking the assembling of ourselves together") when telling members they should "go to church" on Sunday mornings. This reinforces the misconception that when the New Testament writers talk about church, what they had in mind is passively sitting through a service in a special building once a week.

But the fact is, the New Testament vision of the church meeting is one in which every member functions and participates in the gathering. And as we have established, the church building defeats this purpose by its architecture.

Case in point: I (Frank) have met a number of pastors who came to the conviction that the New Testament teaches that church meetings are to be open and participatory. Shortly after making this discovery, these pastors "opened up" their church services to allow members to freely function. In every case, it did not work. The members were still passive. The reason: the architecture of the building. Pews and elevated floors, for example, are not conducive for open sharing. They obstruct it. By contrast, when these same congregations began meeting in homes, functioning and every-member participation flourished.

To put it another way: If we equate church with sitting in a pew and taking a mostly passive role, then church buildings are appropriate for the task (but we

[215] Rodney Stark, *For the Glory of God: How Monotheism Led to Reformations, Science, Witch-Hunts, and the End of Slavery* (Princeton, NJ: Princeton University Press, 2003), 33–34.

still cannot claim that they are biblical since the New Testament knows nothing of church buildings).

On the other hand, if we believe that God's idea of a church meeting is for every member to participate in ministering spiritually to one another, then church buildings as we know them today greatly hinder that process.

5. Wasn't the concept of "sacred space" a Jewish idea as well as a pagan idea?

Yes, the Jews believed in sacred spaces (the Temple), a sacred priesthood (the Levites), and sacred rituals (the Old Testament sacrifices). However, these things were done away with by Christ's death, and the New Testament Christians knew nothing of them. Later, the Christians picked up these concepts from the pagans, not the Jews. This chapter supplies evidence for that statement.

6. Do you think it's always wrong for a group of Christians to use a building for worship or ministry?

Not at all. Paul rented a building (the Hall of Tyrannus) when he was in Ephesus, and the church of Jerusalem used the outer courts of the Temple for special gatherings. What we are establishing in this chapter are five key points: (1) it is unbiblical to call a building a "church," "the house of God," "the temple of God," "the sanctuary of the Lord," and other similar terms; (2) the architecture of the typical church building hinders the church from having open-participatory meetings; (3) it is unscriptural to treat a building as though it were sacred; (4) a typical church building should not be the site of all church meetings because the average building is not designed for face-to-face community; and (5) it is a profound error to assume that all churches should own or rent buildings for their gatherings. It is our opinion that each church should seek the Lord's guidance on this question rather than assume the presence of a building to be the Christian norm. Tracing the history of the "church" building helps us to understand why and how we use them today.

chapter three

> THE ORDER OF WORSHIP: SUNDAY MORNINGS SET IN CONCRETE

"Custom without truth is error grown old."
    —TERTULLIAN, THIRD-CENTURY THEOLOGIAN

"Son of man, describe to the people of Israel the Temple I have shown you, so they will be ashamed."
    —EZEKIEL 43:10, NLT

IF YOU ARE A CHURCHGOING CHRISTIAN, it is likely that you observe the same perfunctory order of worship every time you go to church. It does not matter what stripe of Protestantism you belong to—be it Baptist, Methodist, Reformed, Presbyterian, Evangelical Free, Church of Christ, Disciples of Christ, CMA, Pentecostal, Charismatic, or nondenominational—your Sunday morning service is virtually identical to that of all other Protestant churches.[1] Even among the so-called cutting-edge denominations (like the Vineyard and Calvary Chapel), the variations are minor.

Granted, some churches use contemporary choruses while others use hymns. In some churches, congregants raise their hands. In others, their hands never get above their hips. Some churches observe the Lord's Supper weekly. Others observe it quarterly. In some churches, the liturgy (order of worship) is written out in a bulletin.[2] In others, the liturgy is unwritten, yet it is just as mechanical and predictable as if it were set to print. Despite these slight variations, the order of worship is essentially the same in virtually all Protestant churches.

THE SUNDAY MORNING ORDER OF WORSHIP

Peel away the superficial alterations that make each church service distinct and you will find the same prescribed liturgy. See how many of the following elements you recall from the last weekend service you attended:

The Greeting. As you enter the building, you are greeted by an usher or an appointed greeter—who should be smiling! You are then handed a bulletin or announcement page. (Note: If you are part of some newer denominations, you may drink coffee and eat doughnuts before you are seated.)

Prayer or Scripture Reading. Usually given by the pastor or song leader.

---

[1] There are three exceptions to this point. The Plymouth Brethren (both Open and Closed) have an encased liturgy where there is some open sharing among the congregants at the beginning of the service. Nevertheless, the order of service is the same every week. Old-school Quakers have an open meeting where the congregants are silent until someone is "enlightened," after which they share. The third exception are "high church" Protestant churches, which retain the "smells and bells" of an elaborate Catholic Mass—including a prescribed order of service.

[2] The word *liturgy* is derived from the Greek word *leitourgia*, which referred to the performance of a public task expected of citizens of ancient Athens; in other words, it was the fulfilling of civil obligations. Christians picked it up to refer to the public ministry to God. A liturgy, therefore, is simply a worship service or a prescribed order of worship. White, *Protestant Worship and Church Architecture,* 22; Ferguson, *Early Christians Speak,* 83. See also J. D. Davies, *The New Westminster Dictionary of Liturgy and Worship* (Philadelphia: Westminster Press, 1986), 314.

The Song Service. Led by a professional song leader, choir, or worship team. In charismatic-styled churches, this part of the service typically lasts thirty to forty-five consecutive minutes. In other churches, it is shorter and may be divided into several segments.

The Announcements. News about upcoming events. Usually given by the pastor or some other church leader.

The Offering. Sometimes called "the offertory," it is usually accompanied by special music by the choir, worship team, or a soloist.

The Sermon. Typically, the pastor delivers an oration lasting twenty to forty-five minutes.[3] The current average is thirty-two minutes.

Your service may also have included one or more of the following post-sermon activities:

An after-the-sermon pastoral prayer,
An altar call,
More singing led by the choir or worship team,
The Lord's Supper,
Prayer for the sick or afflicted.

The Benediction. This may be in the form of a blessing from the pastor or a song to end the service.

With some minor rearrangements, this is the unbroken liturgy that 345 million Protestants across the globe observe religiously week after week.[4] And for the last five hundred years, few people have questioned it.

Look again at the order of worship. Notice that it includes a

---

[3] See chapter 4 for a complete discussion on the roots of the sermon.
[4] There are an estimated 345,855,000 Protestants in the world: 70,164,000 are in North America, and 77,497,000 are in Europe. *The World Almanac and Book of Facts 2003* (New York: World Almanac Education Group, 2003), 638.

threefold structure: (1) singing, (2) the sermon, and (3) closing prayer or song. This order of worship is viewed as sacrosanct in the eyes of many present-day Christians. But why? Again, it is due simply to the titanic power of tradition. And that tradition has set the Sunday morning order of worship in concrete for five centuries . . . never to be moved.[5]

WHERE DID THE PROTESTANT ORDER OF WORSHIP COME FROM?

Pastors who routinely tell their congregations that "we do everything by the Book" and still perform this ironclad liturgy are simply not correct. (In their defense, the lack of truthfulness is due to ignorance rather than overt deception.)

You can scour your Bible from beginning to end, and you will never find anything that remotely resembles our order of worship. This is because the first-century Christians knew no such thing. In fact, the Protestant order of worship has about as much biblical support as does the Roman Catholic Mass.[6] Both have few points of contact with the New Testament.

The meetings of the early church were marked by every-member functioning, spontaneity, freedom, vibrancy, and open participation (see, for example, 1 Corinthians 14:1-33 and Hebrews 10:25).[7] The first-century church meeting was a fluid gathering, not a static ritual. And it was often unpredictable, unlike the contemporary church service.

Further, the first-century church meeting was not patterned after

---

[5] One scholar defines tradition as "inherited worship practices and beliefs that show continuity from generation to generation" (White, *Protestant Worship and Church Architecture*, 21).

[6] The medieval Mass is a blending of Roman, Gallic, and Frankish elements. For more details, see Edmund Bishop's essay "The Genius of the Roman Rite" in *Studies in Ceremonial: Essays Illustrative of English Ceremonial*, ed. Vernon Staley (Oxford: A. R. Mowbray, 1901) and Louis Duchesne's *Christian Worship: Its Origin and Evolution* (New York: Society for Promoting Christian Knowledge, 1912), 86–227. The ceremonial aspects of the Mass, such as the incense, candles, and arrangement of the church building were all borrowed from the ceremonial court of the Roman emperors (Jungmann, *Early Liturgy*, 132–133, 291–292; Smith, *From Christ to Constantine*, 173).

[7] The New Testament church meeting is being observed today on a growing scale. While such gatherings are often considered radical and revolutionary by mainline Christianity, they are no more radical or revolutionary than the New Testament church. For a scholarly discussion on the early church meeting, see Banks, *Paul's Idea of Community*, ch. 9–11; Banks and Banks, *Church Comes Home*, ch. 2; Eduard Schweizer, *Church Order in the New Testament* (Chatham, UK: W. & J. Mackay, 1961), 1–136.

the Jewish synagogue services as some recent authors have suggested.[8] Instead, it was totally unique to the culture.

So where did the Protestant order of worship come from? It has its basic roots in the medieval Catholic Mass.[9] Significantly, the Mass did not originate with the New Testament; it grew out of ancient Judaism and paganism.[10] According to Will Durant, the Catholic Mass was "based partly on the Judaic Temple service, partly on Greek mystery rituals of purification, vicarious sacrifice, and participation."[11]

Gregory the Great (540–604), the first monk to be made pope, is the man responsible for shaping the medieval Mass.[12] While Gregory is recognized as an extremely generous man and an able administrator and diplomat, Durant notes that Gregory was also an incredibly superstitious man whose thinking was influenced by magical paganistic concepts. He embodied the medieval mind, which was influenced by heathenism, magic, and Christianity. It is no accident that Durant calls Gregory "the first completely medieval man."[13]

The medieval Mass reflected the mind of its originator. It was a blending of pagan and Judaistic ritual sprinkled with Catholic theology and Christian vocabulary.[14] Durant points out that the Mass was

---

[8] See Banks, *Paul's Idea of Community*, 106–108, 112–117; Bradshaw, *Origins of Christian Worship*, 13–15, 27–29, 159–160, 186. Bradshaw argues against the idea that first-century Christianity inherited its liturgical practices from Judaism. He points out that this idea began around the seventeenth century. David Norrington states, "We have little evidence to suggest that the first Christians attempted to perpetuate the style of the synagogue" (*To Preach or Not*, 48). Moreover, the Jewish synagogue was a human invention. Some scholars believe it was created during the Babylonian captivity (sixth century BC), when worship at the Jerusalem Temple was impossible; others believe they emerged in the third or second century BC with the rise of the Pharisees. Even though the synagogue became the center of Jewish life after the Jerusalem Temple was destroyed in AD 70, there is no Old Testament (or divine) precedent for such an institution. Joel B. Green, ed., *Dictionary of Jesus and the Gospels* (Downers Grove, IL: InterVarsity, 1992), 781–782; Alfred Edersheim, *The Life and Times of Jesus the Messiah* (Mclean, VA: MacDonald Publishing Company, 1883), 431. Furthermore, the architectural inspiration for the synagogue was pagan (Norrington, *To Preach or Not*, 28).

[9] The word *mass*, which means "dismissal" of the congregation (*mission, dismissio*) became, at the end of the fourth century, the word for the worship service that celebrated the Eucharist (Schaff, *History of the Christian Church* 3:505).

[10] The story of the origin of the Mass is far beyond the scope of this book. Suffice it to say that the Mass was essentially a blending together of a resurgence of Gentile interest in synagogue worship and pagan influence that dates back to the fourth century (Senn, *Christian Liturgy*, 54; Jungmann, *Early Liturgy*, 123, 130–144).

[11] Durant, *Caesar and Christ*, 599.

[12] Gregory's major reforms shaped the Catholic Mass into what it was all throughout the medieval period up until the Reformation. Schaff, *History of the Christian Church*, 4:387–388.

[13] Durant, *Age of Faith*, 521–524.

[14] Philip Schaff outlines the various Catholic liturgies which climax in Gregory's liturgy. Gregory's liturgy dominated the Latin church for centuries and was sanctioned by the Council of Trent (Schaff, *History of the Christian Church*, 3:531–535). Gregory is also the person who developed and popularized the Catholic doctrine of "purgatory," although he extracted it from several speculative comments from Augustine (Gonzalez, *Story of Christianity*, 247). In effect, Gregory made Augustine's teachings the foundational theology of the Western church. "Augustine," says Paul Johnson, "was the dark genius of imperial Christianity, the ideologue of the Church-State alliance, and the fabricator of the medieval mentality. Next to Paul, who supplied the basic theology, he did more to shape Christianity than any other human being" (*History of Christianity*, 112). Durant says Augustine's theology dominated Catholic philosophy until the thirteenth century. Augustine also gave it a Neoplatonic tinge (Durant, *Age of Faith*, 74).

deeply steeped in pagan magical thinking as well as Greek drama.[15] He writes, "The Greek mind, dying, came to a transmigrated life in the theology and liturgy of the church; the Greek language, having reigned for centuries over philosophy, became the vehicle of Christian literature and ritual; the Greek mysteries passed down into the impressive mystery of the Mass."[16]

In effect, the Catholic Mass that emerged in the sixth century was fundamentally pagan. Christians incorporated the vestments of the pagan priests, the use of incense and holy water in purification rites, the burning of candles in worship, the architecture of the Roman basilica for their church buildings, the law of Rome as the basis of "canon law," the title *Pontifex Maximus* for the head bishop, and the pagan rituals for the Catholic Mass.[17]

Once established, the Mass changed little over a thousand years.[18] But the liturgical deadlock underwent its first revision when Martin Luther (1483–1546) entered the scene. As various other Protestant denominations were born, they also helped reshape the Catholic liturgy. While the transformation was a complex one that is too vast to chronicle in this book, we can survey the basic story.

LUTHER'S CONTRIBUTION

In 1520, Luther launched an impassioned campaign against the Roman Catholic Mass.[19] The high point of the Catholic Mass has always been the Eucharist,[20] also known as "Communion" or "the Lord's Supper."

---

[15] Durant, *Caesar and Christ*, 599–600, 618–619, 671–672; Durant, *Age of Faith*, 1027.
[16] Durant, *Caesar and Christ*, 595.
[17] Ibid., 618–619.
[18] The modern Mass has changed little since the 1500s (James F. White, *Protestant Worship: Traditions in Transition* (Louisville: Westminster/John Knox Press, 1989), 17). The form used today was issued in the Roman Missal, Sacramentary, and Lectionary of 1970 (Senn, *Christian Liturgy*, 639). Even so, the Mass of the sixth century strongly resembles the present-day Mass (Jungmann, *Early Liturgy*, 298).
[19] This campaign was articulated in Luther's radical treatise, *The Babylonian Captivity of the Church*. This book was a bombshell dropped on the Roman Catholic system challenging the core theology behind the Catholic Mass. In *The Babylonian Captivity*, Luther attacked the following three features of the Mass: (1) the withholding of the cup from the laity, (2) transubstantiation (the belief that the bread and the wine turn into the *actual* body and blood of Christ), and (3) the concept that the Mass is a human work offered up to God as a sacrifice of Christ. Although Luther rejected transubstantiation, he nevertheless believed that the "real presence" of Christ's body and blood is in, with, and under the elements of bread and wine. This belief is called "consubstantiation." In *Captivity*, Luther also denied the seven sacraments, accepting only three: baptism, penance, and the bread (Senn, *Christian Liturgy*, 268). Luther later dropped penance as a sacrament.
[20] The word *Eucharist* is derived from the Greek word *eucharisteo* which means "to give thanks." It appears in 1 Corinthians 11:23-24. There we are told that Jesus took bread, gave thanks, and broke it. Postapostolic Christians referred to the Lord's Supper as the "Eucharist."

Everything centers on and leads up to the moment when the priest breaks the bread and gives it to the people. To the medieval Catholic mind, the offering of the Eucharist was the resacrificing of Jesus Christ. As far back as Gregory the Great, the Catholic church taught that Jesus Christ is sacrificed anew through the Mass.[21]

Luther railed (often uncouthly) against the miters and staffs of the Roman Catholic leadership and its teaching on the Eucharist.[22] The cardinal error of the Mass, said Luther, was that it was a human "work" based on an inaccurate understanding of Christ's sacrifice.[23] So in 1523, Luther set forth his own revisions to the Catholic Mass.[24] These revisions are the foundation for worship in most Protestant churches.[25] The heart of them is this: Luther made preaching, rather than the Eucharist, the center of the gathering.[26]

Accordingly, in the contemporary Protestant worship service, the pulpit, rather than the altar table, is the central element.[27] (The altar table is where the Eucharist is placed in Catholic, Anglican, and Episcopal churches.) Luther gets the credit for making the sermon the climax of the Protestant service.[28] Read his words: "A Christian congregation should never gather together without the preaching of God's Word and prayer, no matter how briefly". . . "the preaching and teaching of God's Word is the most important part of Divine service."[29]

---

[21] Luther penned his liturgical revisions in a treatise called *Form of the Mass* (Gonzalez, *Story of Christianity*, 247). Note that for the past seventy years, most Catholic theologians have said that the Mass is a *representation* of the one sacrifice rather than a new sacrifice, as did the medieval Catholic church.

[22] The miters (caps) and staffs were the symbolic décor that the bishops wore, which represented their authority and separated them from the laity.

[23] The Eucharist was often referred to as an "oblation" or "sacrifice" in the third through fifth centuries. James Hastings Nichols, *Corporate Worship in the Reformed Tradition* (Philadelphia: Westminster Press, 1968), 25. See also Senn, *Christian Liturgy*, 270–275. Loraine Boettner critiques the medieval Catholic Mass in chapter 8 of his book *Roman Catholicism* (Phillipsburg, NJ: The Presbyterian and Reformed Publishing Company, 1962).

[24] The Latin name for it is *Formula Missae.*

[25] White, *Protestant Worship*, 36–37.

[26] Ibid., 41-42. While Luther had a very high view of the Eucharist, he stripped the Mass of all sacrificial language, only keeping the Eucharist itself. He was a strong believer in both Word and sacrament. So his German Mass assumed both Holy Communion and preaching.

[27] Some "liturgical" churches in the Protestant tradition still have the altar table somewhere near the pulpit.

[28] Before the medieval age, both the sermon and the Eucharist had a prominent place in the Christian liturgy. However, the sermon fell into serious decline during the medieval period. Many priests were too illiterate to preach, and other elements crowded out the preaching of Scripture. Maxwell, *An Outline of Christian Worship*, 72. Gregory the Great sought to restore the place of the sermon in the Mass. However, his efforts failed. It was not until the Reformation that the sermon was brought to a central place in the worship service (Schaff, *History of the Christian Church*, 4:227, 399–402).

[29] These Luther quotes are from "Concerning the Order of Public Worship," *Luther's Works*, LIII, 11 and "The German Mass," *Luther's Works*, LIII, 68. Luther arranged for three services on Sunday morning. They were all accompanied by a sermon (Schaff, *History of the Christian Church*, 7:488). Roland Bainton counted 2,300 extant sermons preached by Luther in his lifetime. *Here I Stand: A Life of Martin Luther* (Nashville: Abingdon Press, 1950), 348–349.

Luther's belief in the centrality of preaching as the mark of the worship service has stuck till this day. Yet making preaching the center of the church gathering has no biblical precedent.[30] As one historian put it, "The pulpit is the throne of the Protestant pastor."[31] For this reason ordained Protestant ministers are routinely called "preachers."[32]

But aside from this change, Luther's liturgy varied little from the Catholic Mass,[33] since Luther tried to preserve what he thought were the "Christian" elements in the old Catholic order.[34] Consequently, if you compare Luther's order of worship with Gregory's liturgy, it is virtually the same.[35] He kept the ceremony, believing it was proper.[36]

For instance, Luther retained the act that marked the high moment of the Catholic Mass: the elevation of the bread and cup to consecrate them, a practice that began in the thirteenth century and was based mostly on superstition.[37] Luther merely reinterpreted the meaning of this act, seeing it as an expression of the grace Christ has extended to God's people.[38] Yet it is still observed by many pastors today.

In like manner, Luther did drastic surgery to the Eucharistic prayer, retaining only the "words of institution"[39] from 1 Corinthians 11:23ff. (WEB)—"That the Lord Jesus on the night in which he was betrayed took bread . . . and said, 'Take, eat. This is my body.'" Even today, Protestant pastors religiously recite this text before administering Communion.

---

[30] Acts 2:42 (NLT) tells us that "the believers devoted themselves to the apostles' teaching." In this passage, Luke is describing the apostolic meetings, which took place over four years and were designed to lay the foundation for the Jerusalem church. Because the church was so large, these meetings were held in the Temple courts. However, the believers also met for regular open-participatory worship in homes (Acts 2:46).

[31] Schaff, *History of the Christian Church*, 7:490.

[32] White, *Protestant Worship*, 20.

[33] Luther still followed the historic Western Ordo. The main difference was that Luther eliminated the offertory prayers and the prayers of the Canon after the Sanctus that spoke of offerings. In sum, Luther struck from the Mass everything smacking of "sacrifice." He, along with other Reformers, removed many of the decadent late-medieval elements of the Mass. They did so by rendering the liturgy in the common vernacular, including congregational songs (chants and chorales for the Lutherans; metrical psalms for the Reformed), the centrality of the sermon, and allowing the congregants to participate in Holy Communion (Senn, *Christian Worship*, 84, 102).

[34] Schaff, *History of the Christian Church*, 7:486–487. The German Reformer Carlstadt (1480–1541) was more radical than Luther. During Luther's absence Carlstadt abolished the entire Mass, destroying the altars along with the pictures.

[35] Frank Senn includes the early Catholic liturgy in his book (*Christian Liturgy*, 139). Luther even retained the word *mass*, which came to mean the entire worship service (p. 486).

[36] Luther pointed to the ceremonial in the courts of kings and believed this should be applied to the worship of God (Senn, *Christian Worship*, 15). See chapter 2 of this book for how imperial protocol made its way into the Christian liturgy during the fourth century with the reign of Constantine.

[37] Senn, *Christian Worship*, 18–19.

[38] When the Catholic priest held up the sacrament, he was doing so to inaugurate the sacrifice.

[39] White, *Protestant Worship*, 41–42; Maxwell, *Outline of Christian Worship*, 75.

In the end, Luther's liturgy was nothing more than a truncated version of the Catholic Mass.[40] And the Lutheran order of service contributed to the same problems: The congregants were still passive spectators (though they could now sing), and the entire liturgy was still directed by an ordained clergyman (the pastor had replaced the priest). This was in stark contradiction to the glorious, free-flowing, open-participatory, every-member-functioning church meetings led by Jesus Christ that the New Testament envisions (see 1 Corinthians 14:26; Hebrews 10:24-25).

In Luther's own words, "It is not now nor ever has been our intention to abolish the liturgical service of God completely, but rather to purify the one that is now in use from the wretched accretions which corrupt it."[41] Tragically, Luther did not realize that new wine cannot be repackaged into old wineskins.[42] At no time did Luther (or any of the other mainstream Reformers) demonstrate a desire to return to the principles of the first-century church. These men set out merely to reform the theology of the Catholic church.

In sum, the major enduring changes that Luther made to the Catholic Mass were as follows: (1) he performed the Mass in the language of the people rather than in Latin, (2) he gave the sermon a central place in the gathering, (3) he introduced congregational singing,[43] (4) he abolished the idea that the Mass was a sacrifice of Christ, and (5) he allowed the congregation to partake of the bread and cup (rather than just the priest, as was the Catholic practice). Other than these differences, Luther kept the same order of worship as found in the Catholic Mass.

Worse, although Luther talked much about the "priesthood of all

---

[40] Luther retained the basic order of the medieval Mass along with the ceremonial aspects of lights, incense, and vestments (Maxwell, *Outline of Christian Worship*, 77).

[41] Luther, *Luther's Works*, LIII, 20.

[42] Ironically, Luther insisted that his German Mass should not be adopted legalistically, and if it became outdated it should be discarded (*Christian Worship and Its Cultural Setting*, 17). This never happened.

[43] A lover of music, Luther made music a key part of the service (White, *Protestant Worship*, 41; Hinson, "Worshiping Like Pagans?" *Christian History* 12, no. 1 (1993): 16–19. Luther was a musical genius. So powerful was his gifting in music that the Jesuits said that Luther's songs "destroyed more souls than his writings and speeches." It is not surprising that one of the greatest musical talents in church history happened to be a Lutheran. His name was Johann Sebastian Bach. For details on Luther's musical contribution to the Protestant liturgy see Senn, *Christian Liturgy*, 284–287; White, *Protestant Worship*, 41, 47–48; Will Durant, *Reformation* (New York: Simon and Schuster, 1957), 778–779.

believers," he never abandoned the practice of an ordained clergy.[44] In fact, so strong was his belief in an ordained clergy that he wrote, "The public ministry of the Word ought to be established by holy ordination as the highest and greatest of the functions of the church."[45] Under Luther's influence, the Protestant pastor simply replaced the Catholic priest. And for the most part, there was little practical difference in the way these two offices functioned.[46] This is still the case, as we will consider in chapter 5.

What follows is Luther's order of worship.[47] The general outline should look very familiar to you—for it is the taproot of the Sunday morning church service found in most Protestant denominations.[48]

Singing
Prayer
Sermon
Admonition to the people
Lord's Supper
Singing[49]
Post-Communion prayer
Benediction

ZWINGLI'S CONTRIBUTION

With the advent of Gutenberg's printing press (about 1450), the bulk production of liturgical books accelerated the liturgical changes that

---

[44] White, *Protestant Worship*, 41.

[45] "Concerning the Ministry," *Luther's Works*, XL, 11.

[46] The Catholic priest administered seven sacraments, while the Protestant pastor only administered two (baptism and the Eucharist). However, both priest and pastor were viewed as having the exclusive authority of proclaiming the Word of God. For Luther, the use of clerical robes, candles on the altar, and the attitude of the minister while praying were matters of indifference (Schaff, *History of the Christian Church*, 7:489). But though he was indifferent about them, he did advise that they be retained (Senn, *Christian Liturgy*, 282). Hence, they are still with us today.

[47] This liturgy was published in his *German Mass and Order of Service* in the year 1526.

[48] Senn, *Christian Liturgy*, 282–283.

[49] Notice the sermon was both preceded by and followed by singing and prayer. Luther believed that sandwiching the sermon with songs strengthened the sermon and provided a devotional response to it (Senn, *Christian Liturgy*, 306). Most of the songs sung in Luther's German Mass were versifications of Latin liturgical chants and creeds. (Versification is making verse out of prose.) To Luther's credit, he himself wrote about 36 hymns (*Luther's Works*, LIII). And he was a genius at taking contemporary songs and redeeming them with Christian lyrics. His feeling was, "Why let the devil have all the good tunes?" Marva J. Dawn, *Reaching Out without Dumbing Down: A Theology of Worship for the Turn-of-the-Century Culture* (Grand Rapids: Eerdmans, 1995), 189. (Note that others have been credited with this quote also, William Booth of the Salvation Army being one of them.)

the Reformers attempted to make.[50] Those changes were now set to movable type and printed in mass quantity.

The Swiss Reformer Ulrich Zwingli (1484–1531) made a few of his own reforms that helped shape today's order of worship. He replaced the altar table with something called "the Communion table" from which the bread and wine were administered.[51] He also had the bread and cup carried to the people in their pews using wooden trays and cups.[52]

Most Protestant churches still have such a table. Two candles typically sit upon it—a custom that came directly from the ceremonial court of Roman emperors.[53] And most carry the bread and cup to the people seated in their pews.

Zwingli also recommended that the Lord's Supper be taken quarterly (four times a year). This was in opposition to taking it weekly as other Reformers advocated.[54] Many Protestants follow the quarterly observation of the Lord's Supper today. Some observe it monthly.

Zwingli is also credited with championing the "memorial" view of the Supper. This view is embraced by mainstream American Protestantism.[55] It is the view that the bread and cup are mere symbols of Christ's body and blood.[56] Nevertheless, aside from these variations, Zwingli's liturgy was not much different from Luther's.[57] Like Luther, Zwingli emphasized the centrality of preaching, so much so that he and his coworkers preached fourteen times a week.[58]

---

[50] Senn, *Christian Liturgy*, 300.
[51] Hardman, *History of Christian Worship*, 161. On this point, Frank Senn writes, "In Reformed churches, the pulpit dominated the altar so totally that in time the altar disappeared and was replaced by a table used for Holy Communion only a few times a year. The preaching of the Word dominated the service. This has been taken as a consequence of the so-called rediscovery of the Bible. But the rediscovery of the Bible was the invention of the printing press, a cultural phenomenon" (*Christian Worship*, 45).
[52] Senn, *Christian Liturgy*, 362; White, *Protestant Worship*, 62.
[53] Jungmann, *Early Liturgy*, 132–133, 291–292; Smith, *From Christ to Constantine*, 173.
[54] Senn, *Christian Liturgy*, 363.
[55] White, *Protestant Worship*, 60.
[56] Zwingli's view was more complex than this. However, his idea of the Eucharist was not as "high" as that of Calvin or Luther (Maxwell, *Outline of Christian Worship*, 81). Zwingli is the father of the modern Protestant view of the Lord's Supper. Of course, his view would not be representative of the "liturgical" Protestant churches, which celebrate both Word and Sacrament weekly.
[57] Zwingli's order of service is listed in Senn, *Christian Liturgy*, 362–364.
[58] White, *Protestant Worship*, 61.

THE CONTRIBUTION OF CALVIN AND COMPANY

Reformers John Calvin (1509–1564), John Knox (1513–1572), and Martin Bucer (1491–1551) added to the liturgical molding. These men created their own orders of worship between 1537 and 1562. Even though their liturgies were observed in different parts of the world, they were virtually identical.[59] They merely made a few adjustments to Luther's liturgy. Most notable was the collection of money that followed the sermon.[60]

Like Luther, Calvin stressed the centrality of preaching during the worship service. He believed that each believer has access to God through the preached Word rather than through the Eucharist.[61] Given his theological genius, the preaching in Calvin's Geneva church was intensely theological and academic. It was also highly individualistic, a mark that never left Protestantism.[62]

Calvin's Geneva church was held up as the model for all Reformed churches. Thus its order of worship spread far and wide. This accounts for the cerebral character of most Protestant churches today, particularly the Reformed and Presbyterian brand.[63]

Because musical instruments were not explicitly mentioned in the New Testament, Calvin did away with pipe organs and choirs.[64] All singing was a cappella. (Some contemporary Protestants, like the Church of Christ, still follow Calvin's rigid noninstrumentalism.) This changed in the mid-nineteenth century when Reformed churches began using instrumental music and choirs.[65] However, the Puritans

---

[59] These liturgies were used in Strasbourg, Germany (1537), Geneva, Switzerland (1542), and Scotland (1562).

[60] The collection was alms for the poor (Senn, *Christian Liturgy*, 365–366). Calvin wrote, "No assembly of the church should be held without the Word being preached, prayers being offered, the Lord's Supper being administered, and alms given" (Nichols, *Corporate Worship*, 29). Although Calvin desired to have the Lord's Supper weekly, his Reformed churches followed Zwingli's practice of taking it quarterly (White, *Protestant Worship*, 65, 67).

[61] Stanley M. Burgess and Gary B. McGee, eds., *Dictionary of Pentecostal and Charismatic Movements* (Grand Rapids: Zondervan, 1988), 904. The "Word" in Reformed usage meant the Bible and the preached word as conveying the incarnated Word. Both the sermon and Scripture-reading were connected and were viewed as the "Word" (Nichols, *Corporate Worship*, 30). The idea that the preaching of the Bible is the very "Word of God" appears in the *Confessio Helvetica Posterior* of 1566.

[62] The rugged individualism of the Renaissance influenced the message of the Reformers. They were a product of their times. The gospel they preached was centered on individual needs and personal development. It was not communitarian as was the message of the first-century Christians. This individualistic emphasis was picked up by the Puritans, Pietists, and Revivalists, and it pervaded all areas of American life and thought (Senn, *Christian Worship*, 100, 104; Terry, *Evangelism*, 125).

[63] White, *Protestant Worship*, 65.

[64] Ibid., 66. Zwingli, a musician himself, shared Calvin's conviction that music and choirs ought not to be part of the church service (p. 62).

[65] Ibid., 76. For Calvin, all songs had to include the words of Old Testament Scripture, so hymns were excluded (page 66).

(English Calvinists) continued in the spirit of Calvin, condemning both instrumental music and choir singing.[66]

Probably the most damaging feature of Calvin's liturgy is that he led most of the service himself from his pulpit.[67] Christianity has not yet recovered from this. Today, the pastor is the MC and CEO of the Sunday morning church service—just as the priest is the MC and CEO of the Catholic Mass. This is in stark contrast to the church meeting envisioned in Scripture. According to the New Testament, the Lord Jesus Christ is the leader, director, and CEO of the church meeting. In 1 Corinthians 12, Paul tells us that Christ speaks through His entire body, not just one member. In such a meeting, His body freely functions under His headship (direct leadership) through the working of His Holy Spirit. First Corinthians 14 gives us a picture of such a gathering. This kind of meeting is vital for the spiritual growth of God's people and the full expression of His Son in the earth.[68]

Another feature that Calvin contributed to the order of worship is the somber attitude that many Christians are encouraged to adopt when they enter the building. That atmosphere is one of a profound sense of self-abasement before a sovereign and austere God.[69]

Martin Bucer is equally credited with fostering this attitude. At the beginning of every service, he had the Ten Commandments uttered to create a sense of veneration.[70] Out of this mentality grew some rather outrageous practices. Puritan New England was noted for fining children who smiled in church! Add to this the creation of the "Tithingman" who would wake up sleeping congregants by poking them with a heavily-knobbed staff.[71]

---

[66] Ibid., 126.

[67] Ibid., 67. This was also the practice of Calvin's contemporary, Martin Bucer. (White, *Protestant Worship and Church Architecture*, 83).

[68] Note that the New Testament presents to us different kinds of meetings. Some meetings are characterized by a central speaker like an apostle or evangelist preaching to an audience. But these kinds of meetings were sporadic and temporary in nature. They weren't the ordinary, normative meeting of first-century believers. The "church meeting," however, is the regular gathering of Christians that is marked by mutual functioning, open participation from every member, freedom and spontaneity under the headship of Jesus Christ.

[69] Horton Davies, *Christian Worship: Its History and Meaning* (New York: Abingdon Press, 1957), 56.

[70] White, *Protestant Worship*, 74.

[71] Alice Morse Earle, "Sketches of Life in Puritan New England," *Searching Together* 11, no. 4 (1982): 38–39.

Such thinking is a throwback to the late medieval view of piety.[72] Yet it was embraced and kept alive by Calvin and Bucer. While many contemporary Pentecostals and Charismatics broke with this tradition, it is mindlessly followed in many churches today. The message is: "Be quiet and solemn, for this is the house of God!"[73]

One further practice that the Reformers retained from the Mass was the practice of the clergy walking to their allotted seats at the beginning of the service while the people stood singing. This practice started in the fourth century when the bishops walked into their magnificent basilica churches. It was a practice copied straight from the pagan imperial court ceremony.[74] When the Roman magistrates entered into the courtroom, the people would stand singing. This practice is still observed today in many Protestant churches.

As Calvinism spread throughout Europe, Calvin's Geneva liturgy was adopted in most Protestant churches. It was transplanted and took root in multiple countries.[75] Here is what it looks like:[76]

Prayer
Confession
Singing (Psalm)
Prayer for enlightenment of the Spirit in the preaching
Sermon
Collection of alms
General prayer
Communion (at the appointed times) while Psalm is sung
Benediction

---

[72] The medievals equated somberness with holiness and moroseness with godliness. By contrast, the early Christians were marked by an attitude of gladness and joy. See Acts 2:46, 8:8, 13:52, 15:3, 1 Peter 1:8.

[73] By contrast, the Psalms beckon God's people to enter His gates with joy, praise, and thanksgiving (See Psalm 100).

[74] Senn, *Christian Worship*, 26–27. This so-called "entrance rite" included psalmody (Introit), the litany prayer (Kyrie), and a song of praise (Gloria). It was borrowed from the imperial court ceremony (Jungmann, *Early Liturgy*, 292, 296). As Constantine saw himself as God's vicar on earth, God came to be viewed as the emperor of heaven. Thus the Mass turned into a ceremony performed before God and before His representative, the bishop—just like the ceremony performed before the emperor and his magistrate. The bishop, clad in his garments of a high magistrate, entered the church building in solemn procession preceded by candles. He was then seated on his special throne—the *sella curulis* of a Roman official. The fourth-century church had borrowed both the ritual and flavor of Roman officialdom in its worship (Krautheimer, *Early Christian and Byzantine Architecture*, 184).

[75] The Geneva liturgy was "a fixed Reformed liturgy used without variation or exception not only for the celebration of the sacraments but for ordinary Sunday worship as well" (White, *Protestant Worship*, 69).

[76] James Mackinnon, *Calvin and the Reformation* (New York: Russell and Russell, 1962), 83–84. For a more detailed version of the Geneva liturgy, see Senn, *Christian Liturgy*, 365–366.

It should be noted that Calvin sought to model his order of worship after the writings of the early church fathers[77]—particularly those who lived in the third through sixth centuries.[78] This accounts for his lack of clarity on the character of the New Testament church meeting. The early fathers of the third through sixth centuries were intensely liturgical and ritualistic.[79] They did not have a New Testament Christian mind-set.[80] They were also theoreticians more than practitioners.

To put it another way, the church fathers of this period represent nascent (early) Catholicism. And that is what Calvin took as his main model for establishing a new order of worship.[81] It is no wonder that the so-called Reformation brought very little reform in the way of church practice.[82] As was the case with Luther's order of worship, the liturgy of the Reformed church "did not try to change the structures of the official [Catholic] liturgy but rather it tried to maintain the old liturgy while cultivating extra-liturgical devotions."[83]

THE PURITAN CONTRIBUTION

The Puritans were Calvinists from England.[84] They embraced a rigorous biblicism and sought to adhere tightly to the New Testament order of worship.[85] The Puritans felt that Calvin's order of worship

---

[77] Hughes Oliphant Old, *The Patristic Roots of Reformed Worship* (Zurich: Theologischer Verlag, 1970), 141–155. Calvin also took the postapostolic fathers as his model for church government. Hence, he embraced a single pastorate (Mackinnon, *Calvin and the Reformation*, 81).

[78] Nichols, *Corporate Worship*, 14.

[79] The church fathers were greatly influenced by their Greco-Roman culture. Many of them, in fact, were pagan philosophers and orators before they became Christians. As already stated, this is why their church services reflected a blending of pagan culture and Jewish synagogue forms. Further, recent scholarship has shown that the writings of the fathers on Christian worship were written later than assumed and have been reshaped by various layers of tradition (Bradshaw, *Origins of Christian Worship*, ch. 3).

[80] The church fathers were heavily influenced by paganism and Neoplatonism. Will Durant, *Caesar and Christ*, 610–619, 650–651. See also Durant's *Age of Faith*, 63, 74, 521–524.

[81] Since this study focuses on the unscriptural contributions of the Reformers, listing their positive contributions is beyond the scope of this book. Nevertheless, let it be known that the authors are well aware that Luther, Zwingli, Calvin, et al., contributed many positive practices and beliefs to the Christian faith. At the same time, they failed to bring us to a complete reformation.

[82] The Protestant Reformation was mainly an intellectual movement (White, *Protestant Worship*, 37). While the theology was radical compared to that of Roman Catholicism, it hardly touched ecclesiastical practice. Those who went further in their reforms, letting it touch their practice of the church, are referred to as the "Radical Reformation." For a discussion on the Radical Reformers, see *The Pilgrim Church* by E. H. Broadbent (Grand Rapids: Gospel Folio Press, 1999); *The Reformers and Their Stepchildren* by Leonard Verduin (Grand Rapids: Eerdmans, 1964); *The Radical Reformation* by George H. Williams (Philadelphia: Westminster Press, 1962); *The Torch of the Testimony* by John Kennedy (Bombay: Gospel Literature Service, 1965).

[83] Old, *Patristic Roots of Reformed Worship*, 12.

[84] Senn, *Christian Liturgy*, 510.

[85] White, *Protestant Worship*, 118.

was not biblical enough. Consequently, when pastors sermonize about "doing everything by the Word of God," they are echoing Puritan sentiments. But the Puritan effort to restore the New Testament church meeting did not succeed.

The forsaking of clerical vestments, icons, and ornaments, as well as clergymen writing their own sermons (as opposed to reading homilies), were positive contributions that the Puritans gave us. However, because of their emphasis on "spontaneous" prayer, the Puritans also bequeathed to us the long pastoral prayer that precedes the sermon.[86] This prayer in a Sunday morning Puritan service could easily last an hour or more![87]

The sermon reached its zenith with the American Puritans. They felt it was almost supernatural, since they saw it as God's primary means of speaking to His people. And they punished church members who missed the Sunday morning sermon.[88] New England residents who failed to attend Sunday worship were fined or put in stocks.[89] (Next time your pastor threatens you with God's unbridled wrath for missing "church," be sure to thank the Puritans.)

It is worth noting that in some Puritan churches the laity was allowed to speak at the end of the service. Immediately after the sermon, the pastor would sit down and answer the congregation's questions. Congregants would also be allowed to give testimonies. But with the advent of Frontier-Revivalism in the eighteenth century, this practice faded away, never again to be adopted by mainstream Christianity.[90]

All in all, the Puritan contribution in shaping the Protestant liturgy did little in releasing God's people to freely function under Christ's headship. Like the liturgical reforms that preceded them, the

---

[86] White, *Protestant Worship*, 119, 125; Senn, *Christian Liturgy*, 512. The Puritans also allowed the congregation to question the pastor's handling of the biblical text when he finished his sermon. White, *Protestant Worship*, 129.

[87] Cassandra Niemczyk, "Did You Know? Little-Known Facts about the American Puritans," *Christian History* 13, no. 1 (1994): 2.

[88] One Puritan leader wrote that "the preaching of the Word is the Scepter of Christ's Kingdom, the glory of a nation, and the chariot upon which life and salvation comes riding." A Puritan might hear 15,000 hours of preaching in his lifetime.

[89] Niemczyk, "Did You Know?" 2; Allen C. Guelzo, "When the Sermon Reigned," *Christian History* 13, no. 1 (1994): 23.

[90] White, *Protestant Worship*, 126, 130. Adams, *Meeting House to Camp Meeting*, 13, 14.

Puritan order of worship was highly predictable. It was written out in detail and followed uniformly in every church.[91]

What follows is the Puritan liturgy.[92] Compare it to the liturgies of Luther and Calvin and you will notice that the central features did not change.

> Call to worship
> Opening prayer
> Reading of Scripture
> Singing of the Psalms
> Pre-sermon prayer
> Sermon
> Post-sermon prayer
> (When Communion is observed, the minister exhorts the congregation, blesses the bread and cup, and passes them to the people.)

In time, the Puritans spawned their own offshoot denominations.[93] Some of them were part of the "Free Church" tradition.[94] The Free Churches created what is called the "hymn-sandwich,"[95] and this order of service is quite similar to that used by most evangelical churches today. Here is what it looks like:

> Three hymns
> Scripture reading
> Choir music
> Unison prayers
> Pastoral prayer
> Sermon

---

91 White, *Protestant Worship*, 120, 127.
92 Senn, *Christian Liturgy*, 514–515. The Puritan's basic liturgy is contained in a work called *A Directory of the Public Worship of God* written in 1644 (White, *Protestant Worship*, 127). This was a revision of the Anglican *Book of Common Prayer* which was first drafted in 1549. The *Directory* was used by English (not Scottish) Presbyterians and Congregationalists.
93 The descendants of Puritanism are the Baptists, Presbyterians, and Congregationalists (White, *Protestant Worship*, 129).
94 The so-called "Free Church" tradition includes Puritans, Separatists, Baptists, Quakers in the seventeenth and eighteenth centuries, Methodists in the late eighteenth century, and Disciples of Christ in the early nineteenth century (Adams, *Meeting House to Camp Meeting*, 10).
95 White, *Protestant Worship*, 133.

Offering

Benediction

Does this look familiar to you? Rest assured, you cannot find it in the New Testament.

METHODIST AND FRONTIER-REVIVAL CONTRIBUTIONS

Eighteenth-century Methodists brought to the Protestant order of worship an emotional dimension. People were invited to sing loudly with vigor and fervor. In this way, the Methodists were the forerunners of the Pentecostals.

Like the Puritans, the Methodists spiced up the pastor's Sunday morning pre-sermon prayer. The Methodist clerical prayer was long and universal in its scope. It swallowed up all other prayers, covering the waterfront of confession, intercession, and praise. But more importantly, it was always offered up in Elizabethan English (i.e., Thee, Thou, Thy, etc.).[96]

Even today, in the twenty-first century, the Elizabethan pastoral prayer lives and breathes.[97] Many contemporary pastors still pray in this outdated language—even though it has been a dead dialect for four hundred years! Why? Because of the power of tradition.

The Methodists also popularized the Sunday evening worship service. The discovery of incandescent gas as a means of lighting enabled John Wesley (1703–1791) to make this innovation popular.[98] Today, many Protestant churches have a Sunday evening service—even though it is typically poorly attended.

The eighteenth and nineteenth centuries brought a new challenge to American Protestantism. It was the pressure to conform to the ever-popular American Frontier-Revivalist services. These services greatly influenced the order of worship for scores of churches. Even today, the

---

[96] Ibid., 153, 164.

[97] Ibid., 183. The "pastoral prayer before the sermon" was prescribed in detail in the *Westminster Directory of Worship.*

[98] Horton Davies, *Worship and Theology in England: 1690–1850* (Princeton: Princeton University Press, 1961), 108. Evening prayer services were common in the Catholic church since the fourth century. And Sunday vespers (evening services) were a stable part of cathedral and parish liturgical life for many centuries. However, the Methodists are noted for bringing into the Protestant faith the Sunday evening worship service.

changes they injected into the bloodstream of American Protestantism are evident.[99]

First, the Frontier-Revivalists changed the goal of preaching. They preached exclusively with one aim: to convert lost souls. To the mind of a Frontier-Revivalist, nothing beyond salvation was involved in God's plan.[100] Salvation was God's supreme purpose for church and all of life. This emphasis finds its seeds in the innovative preaching of George Whitefield (1714–1770).[101]

Whitefield was the first modern-day evangelist to preach to outdoor crowds in the open air.[102] He is the man that shifted the emphasis in preaching from God's plans for the church to God's plans for the individual. The popular notion that "God loves you and has a wonderful plan for your life" became prominent after Whitefield.[103]

Second, Frontier-Revivalist music spoke to the soul and sought to elicit an emotional response to the salvation message.[104] All the great revivalists had a musician on their team for this purpose.[105] Worship began to be viewed as primarily individualistic, subjective, and emotional.[106] This shift in emphasis was picked up by the Methodists, and it began to penetrate many other Protestant subcultures. The main goal of the church shifted from experiencing and expressing the

---

[99] White, *Protestant Worship*, 91, 171; Iain H. Murray, *Revival and Revivalism: The Making and Marring of American Evangelicalism* (Carlisle, PA: Banner of Truth Trust, 1994).

[100] American revivalism gave birth to the "missionary society" at the end of the eighteenth century. This included the Baptist Missionary Society (1792), the London Missionary Society (1795), the General Methodist Missionary Society (1796), and the Church Missionary Society (1799). Tan, *Lost Heritage*, 195.

[101] Whitefield is called "the father of American revivalism." Whitefield's central message was "the new birth" of the individual Christian. With this he led the First Great Awakening in New England, which reached its peak in the early 1740s. In 45 days, Whitefield preached 175 sermons. A superb orator, his voice could be heard by 30,000 people in one meeting. As many as 50,000 would come to hear him speak. Remarkably, it is said that Whitefield's voice could be heard at a range of one mile without amplification. And his oratorical powers were so great that he could make an audience weep with his pronunciation. Positively, Whitefield is credited for recovering the lost practice of itinerant ministry. He also shared credit with the Puritans for restoring extemporaneous prayer and preaching (Yngve Brilioth, *A Brief History of Preaching* (Philadelphia: Fortress Press, 1965), 165. See also *Christian History* 12, no. 2 (1993), which is devoted to George Whitefield; "The Great Awakening," *Christian History* 9, no. 4 (1990): 46; J. D. Douglas, *Who's Who in Christian History* (Carol Stream, IL: Tyndale House, 1992), 716–717; Terry, *Evangelism*, 100, 110, 124–125.

[102] Davies, *Worship and Theology in England*, 146; "The Great Awakening," *Christian History* 9, no. 4 (1990): 46; "George Whitefield," *Christian History* 8, no. 3 (1989): 17.

[103] Mark A. Noll, "Father of Modern Evangelicals?" Interview in *Christian History* 12, no. 2 (1993): 44; "The Second Vatican Council," *Christian History* 9, no. 4 (1990): 47. The Great Awakening under Whitefield stamped American Protestantism with an individualistic-revivalistic character from which it has never recovered.

[104] Senn, *Christian Liturgy*, 562–565; White, *Protestant Worship and Church Architecture*, 8, 19.

[105] Finney used Thomas Hastings. Moody used Ira D. Sankey. Billy Graham continued the tradition by using Cliff Barrows and George Beverly Shea (Senn, *Christian Liturgy*, 600). Music was extremely instrumental in furthering the goals of revivalism. George Whitefield and John Wesley are credited with being the first to employ music to induce conviction and a readiness to hear the gospel (Terry, *Evangelism*, 110).

[106] White, *Protestant Worship and Church Architecture*, 11.

Lord Jesus Christ corporately to the making of individual converts. In doing so, the church by and large lost sight of the fact that while Christ's atonement is absolutely essential to getting humanity back on track and restoring our relationship with God, it is not His sole purpose. God has an eternal purpose that goes beyond salvation. That purpose has to do with enlarging the eternal fellowship He has with His Son and making it visible on planet Earth. The theology of revivalism did not discuss God's eternal purpose and put little to no emphasis on the church.[107]

Methodist choral music was designed to soften the hard hearts of sinners. Lyrics began to reflect the individual salvation experience as well as personal testimony.[108] Charles Wesley (1707–1788) is credited for being the first to write invitational hymns.[109]

Pastors who gear their Sunday morning sermons exclusively toward winning the lost still reflect the revivalist influence.[110] This influence has pervaded the majority of today's television and radio evangelism. Many Protestant churches (not just Pentecostal and charismatic) begin their services with rousing songs to prepare people for the emotionally targeted sermon. But few people know that this tradition began with the Frontier-Revivalists little more than a century ago.

Third, the Methodists and the Frontier-Revivalists gave birth to the "altar call." This practice began with the Methodists in the eighteenth century.[111] The practice of inviting people who want prayer to stand to their feet and walk to the front to receive prayer was given to us by a Methodist evangelist named Lorenzo Dow.[112]

Later, in 1807 in England, the Methodists created the "mourner's

[107] For a full discussion on God's eternal purpose, see Viola, *God's Ultimate Passion* (Gainesville, FL: Present Testimony Ministry, 2006).

[108] White, *Protestant Worship*, 164–165, 184–185.

[109] R. Alan Streett, *The Effective Invitation* (Old Tappan, NJ: Fleming H. Revell Co., 1984), 190. Charles Wesley wrote over 6,000 hymns. Charles was the first hymn writer to introduce a congregational style of singing that expressed the feelings and thoughts of the individual Christian.

[110] The Baptists are the most noted for making the winning of the lost the goal of the Sunday morning service. Revivalism's call to make "personal decisions" for Christ both reflected and appealed to the cultural ideology of American individualism just as the "new measures" under Charles Finney reflected and appealed to American pragmatism (Terry, *Evangelism*, 170–171).

[111] Murray, *Revival and Revivalism*, 185–190.

[112] Streett, *Effective Invitation*, 94–95. Reverend James Taylor was among the first to call inquirers to the front of his church in 1785 in Tennessee. The first recorded use of the altar in connection with a public invitation occurred in 1799 at a Methodist camp meeting in Kentucky. See also White, *Protestant Worship*, 174.

bench."[113] Anxious sinners now had a place to mourn for their sins when they were invited to walk down the sawdust trail. This method reached the United States a few years later and was given the name the "anxious bench" by Charles Finney (1792–1875).[114]

The "anxious bench" was located in the front where preachers stood on an erected platform.[115] It was there that both sinners and needy saints were called forward to receive the minister's prayers.[116] Finney's method was to ask those who wished to be saved to stand up and come forward. Finney made this method so popular that "after 1835, it was an indispensable fixture of modern revivals."[117]

Finney later abandoned the anxious seat and simply invited sinners to come forward into the aisles and kneel at the front of the platform to receive Christ.[118] Aside from popularizing the altar call, Finney is credited with inventing the practice of praying for persons by name, mobilizing groups of workers to visit homes, and displacing the routine services of the church with special services every night of the week.

In time, the "anxious bench" in the outdoor camp meeting was replaced by the "altar" in the church building. The "sawdust trail" was replaced by the church aisle. And so was born the famous "altar call."[119]

Perhaps the most lasting element that Finney unwittingly contributed to contemporary Christianity was pragmatism. Pragmatism is the philosophy that teaches that if something works, it should be embraced regardless of ethical considerations. Finney believed that

---

[113] Finney was an innovator in the business of winning souls and starting revivals. Employing his so-called "new measures," he argued that there existed no normative forms of worship in the New Testament. But whatever was successful in leading sinners to Christ was approved (Senn, *Christian Liturgy*, 564; White, *Protestant Worship*, 176–177).

[114] Streett, *Effective Invitation*, 95. Finney began using this method exclusively following his famous Rochester, New York, crusade of 1830. The first historically traceable use of the phrase "anxious seat" comes from Charles Wesley: "Oh, that blessed anxious seat." For a critique on the anxious bench, see J. W. Nevin's *The Anxious Bench* (Chambersburg, PA: German Reformed Church, 1843).

[115] White, *Protestant Worship*, 181; James E. Johnson, "Charles Grandison Finney: Father of American Revivalism," *Christian History* 7, no. 4 (1988): 7; "Glossary of Terms," *Christian History* 7, no. 4 (1988): 19.

[116] "The Return of the Spirit: The Second Great Awakening," *Christian History* 8, no. 3 (1989): 30; Johnson, "Charles Grandison Finney," 7; Senn, *Christian Liturgy*, 566.

[117] Murray, *Revival and Revivalism*, 226, 241–243, 277.

[118] Streett, *Effective Invitation*, 96.

[119] Burgess and McGee, *Dictionary of Pentecostals*, 904. For further study, see Gordon L. Hall's *The Sawdust Trail: The Story of American Evangelism* (Philadelphia: Macrae Smith Company, 1964). The "sawdust trail" later became equated with the dust-covered aisle of the evangelist's tent. This usage ("hit the sawdust trail") was popularized by the ministry of Billy Sunday (1862–1935). See Terry, *Evangelism*, 161.

the New Testament did not teach any prescribed forms of worship.[120] He taught that the sole purpose of preaching was to win converts. Any devices that helped accomplish that goal were acceptable.[121] Under Finney, eighteenth-century revivalism was turned into a science and brought into mainstream churches.[122]

Contemporary Christianity still reflects this ideology. Pragmatism is unspiritual, not just because it encourages ethical considerations to be secondary, but because it depends on techniques rather than on God to produce the desired effects. Genuine spirituality is marked by the realization that in spiritual things, we mortals are utterly and completely dependent on the Lord. Recall the Lord's word that "unless the Lord builds the house, those who build it labor in vain" (Psalm 127:1, ESV) and "without me ye can do nothing" (John 15:5). Unfortunately, pragmatism ("if it works let's do it"), not biblical principle or spirituality, governs the activities of many present-day churches. (Many "seeker sensitive" churches have excelled at following in Finney's footsteps.) Pragmatism is harmful because it teaches "the end justifies the means." If the end is considered "holy," just about any "means" are acceptable.

The philosophy of pragmatism opens the door for human manipulation and a complete reliance upon oneself rather than upon God. Note that there is a monumental difference between well-motivated humans working for God in their own strength, wisdom, and power versus God working through humans.[123]

Because of his far-reaching impact, Charles Finney has been called "the most influential liturgical Reformer in American history."[124] Finney believed that the revivalist methods that worked in his camp meetings could be imported into the Protestant churches

---

[120] White, *Protestant Worship*, 177.

[121] *Pastor's Notes: A Companion Publication to Glimpses* 4, no. 2 (Worcester, PA: Christian History Institute, 1992), 6.

[122] White, *Protestant Worship and Church Architecture*, 7.

[123] Two books that explain this difference well are Watchman Nee: *The Normal Christian Life* (Carol Stream, IL: Tyndale House, 1977) and *The Release of the Spirit* (Indianapolis: Sure Foundation, 1965). For a further discussion on the non-Christian nature of pragmatism, see Ronald Rolheiser's *The Shattered Lantern: Rediscovering God's Presence in Everyday Life* (London: Hodder & Stoughton, 1994), 31–35.

[124] White, *Protestant Worship*, 176; *Pastor's Notes* 4, no. 2: 6. Iain Murray points out that the camp meetings under the Methodists were a precursor to Finney's systematic evangelistic techniques (*Revival and Revivalism*, 184–185).

to bring revival there. This notion was popularized and put into the Protestant mind-set via his 1835 book *Lectures on Revival*. To the contemporary Protestant mind, doctrine must be vigorously checked with Scripture before it is accepted. But when it comes to church practice, just about anything is acceptable as long as it works to win converts.

In all of these ways, American Frontier-Revivalism turned church into a preaching station. It reduced the experience of the ekklesia into an evangelistic mission.[125] It normalized Finney's revivalist methods and created pulpit personalities as the dominating attraction for church. It also made the church an individualistic affair rather than a corporate one.

Put differently, the goal of the Frontier-Revivalists was to bring individual sinners to an individual decision for an individualistic faith.[126] As a result, the goal of the early church—mutual edification and every-member functioning to corporately manifest Jesus Christ before principalities and powers—was altogether lost.[127] Ironically, John Wesley, an early revivalist, understood the dangers of the revivalist movement. He wrote, "Christianity is essentially a social religion . . . to turn it into a solitary religion is indeed to destroy it."[128] With Albert Blake Dick's invention of stencil duplicating in 1884, the order of worship began to be printed and distributed.[129] Thus was born the famous "Sunday morning bulletin."[130]

THE STAGGERING INFLUENCE OF D. L. MOODY

The seeds of the "revivalist gospel" were spread throughout the Western world by the mammoth influence of D. L. Moody (1837–1899).

---

[125] Properly conceived, the goal of preaching is not the salvation of souls. It is the birth of the church. As one scholar put it, "Conversion can only be the means; the goal is the extension of the visible church." Karl Muller, ed., *Dictionary of Mission: Theology, History, Perspectives* (Maryknoll, NY: Orbis Books, 1997), 431. Scholar D. J. Tidball has echoed the same thought saying, "Paul's primary interest was not in the conversion of individuals but in the formation of Christian communities." *Dictionary of Paul and His Letters* (Downers Grove, IL: InterVarsity, 1993), 885. The Frontier-Revivalists had no concept of the ekklesia.

[126] White, *Protestant Worship and Church Architecture*, 121–124.

[127] See 1 Corinthians 12–14; Ephesians 1–3.

[128] John Wesley, "Sermon on the Mount IV," *Sermons on Several Occasions* (London: Epworth Press, 1956), 237.

[129] Ibid., 132. See http://www.officemuseum.com/copy_machines.htm for details on Dick's mimeograph stencil invention.

[130] Ferguson, *Early Christians Speak*, 84. *Written* liturgies first came into being in the fourth century. But they were not put into bulletin form until the nineteenth century.

He traveled more than one million miles and preached to more than 100 million people—in the century before airplanes, microphones, television, or the Internet. Moody's gospel, like Whitefield's, had but one center—salvation for the sinner. He preached the gospel with a focus on individuals, and his theology was encapsulated in the three Rs: ruined by sin, redeemed by Christ, and regenerated by the Spirit. While those are certainly critical elements of the faith, Moody apparently did not recognize that the eternal purpose of God goes far beyond redemption.[131]

Moody's preaching was dominated by this single interest—individual salvation. He instituted the solo hymn that followed the pastor's sermon. The invitational solo hymn was sung by a soloist until George Beverly Shea encouraged Billy Graham to employ a choir to sing songs like "Just As I Am" as people came forward to receive Christ.[132]

Moody gave us door-to-door witnessing and evangelistic advertising/campaigning.[133] He gave us the "gospel song" or "gospel hymn."[134] And he popularized the "decision card," an invention of Absalom B. Earle (1812–1895).[135]

In addition, Moody was the first to ask those who wanted to be saved to stand up from their seats and be led in a "sinner's prayer."[136] Some fifty years later, Billy Graham upgraded Moody's technique. He introduced the practice of asking the audience to bow their heads, close their eyes ("with no one looking around"), and raise their hands in response to the salvation message.[137] (All of these methods have met

---

[131] *Christian History* 9, no. 1 (1990); Douglas, *Who's Who in Christian History*, 483–485; Terry, *Evangelism*, 151–152; H. Richard Niebuhr and Daniel D. Williams, *The Ministry in Historical Perspectives* (San Francisco: Harper & Row Publishers, 1956), 256. While God certainly wants souls to be redeemed by Christ, that is just the first step in what He is ultimately after. We are not against evangelism, but when we make that our entire focus, evangelism becomes a duty rather than something that happens spontaneously when Christians are consumed with Christ. Believers in the early church were completely Christ-focused, which is why our evangelism methods and outlook are so different from theirs. For a thorough discussion of God's eternal purpose, see Viola, *God's Ultimate Passion*.

[132] Streett, *Effective Invitation*, 193–194, 197.

[133] Terry, *Evangelism*, 153–154, 185.

[134] David P. Appleby, *History of Church Music* (Chicago: Moody Press, 1965), 142.

[135] Streett, *Effective Invitation*, 97. "Each person who came forward signed a card to indicate his pledge to live a Christian life and to show a church preference. This portion of the card was retained by the personal worker, so some form of follow-up could be worked out. Another portion of the card was given to the new Christian as a guide for Christian living" (pages 97–98).

[136] Ibid., 98. For more information on the "sinner's prayer," see chapter 9.

[137] Ibid., 112–113. In his forty-fifth year of ministry, Graham had preached to 100 million people in 85 different countries (*Pastor's Notes* 4, no. 2: 7).

fierce opposition by those who argue that they are psychologically manipulative.)[138]

For Moody, "the church was a voluntary association of the saved."[139] So staggering was his influence that by 1874 the church was not seen as a grand corporate body but as a gathering of individuals.[140] This emphasis was picked up by every revivalist who followed him.[141] And it eventually entered into the marrow and bones of evangelical Christianity.

It is also worth noting that Moody was heavily influenced by the Plymouth Brethren teaching on the end times. This was the teaching that Christ may return at any second before the great Tribulation. (This teaching is also called "pretribulational dispensationalism.")[142]

Pretribulational dispensationalism gave rise to the idea that Christians must act quickly to save as many souls as possible before the world ends.[143] With the founding of the Student Volunteer Movement by John Mott in 1888, a related idea sprang forth: "The evangelization of the world in one generation."[144] The "in one generation" watchword still lives and breathes in the church today.[145] Yet it does not map well with the mind-set of the first-century Christians who did not appear to be pressured into trying to get the entire world saved in one generation.[146]

---

[138] Iain H. Murray, *The Invitation System* (Edinburgh: Banner of Truth Trust, 1967). Murray distinguishes between "revival" which is an authentic, spontaneous work of God's Spirit and "revivalism" which is the human methods of obtaining (at least in appearance) the signs of conviction, repentance, and rebirth. The use of psychological and social pressures to bring converts is part of "revivalism" (pp. xvii–xix). See also Jim Ehrhard, "The Dangers of the Invitation System" (Parkville, MO: Christian Communicators Worldwide, 1999), http://www.gracesermons.com/hisbygrace/invitation.html.

[139] Niebuhr and Williams, *Ministry in Historical Perspectives*, 256.

[140] Sandra Sizer, *Gospel Hymns and Social Religion* (Philadelphia: Temple University Press, 1978), 134.

[141] Moody along with Great Awakening preachers like George Whitefield strongly appealed to the emotions. They were influenced by the philosophy of Romanticism, the body of thought stressing the will and emotions. This was a reaction to the stress on reason that marked earlier Christian thinking that was shaped by the Enlightenment (David W. Bebbington, "How Moody Changed Revivalism," *Christian History* 9, no. 1 (1990): 23). The Awakening preachers' emphasis was the individual's heartfelt response to God. Conversion came to be viewed as the paramount goal of divine activities. As J. Stephen Lang and Mark A. Noll point out, "Because of the preaching of the Awakening, the sense of *religious self* intensified. The principle of individual choice became forever ingrained in American Protestantism and is still evident today among evangelicals and many others" (J. Stephen Lang and Mark A. Noll, "Colonial New England: An Old Order, A New Awakening," *Christian History* 4, no. 4 [1985]: 9–10).

[142] John Nelson Darby spawned this teaching. The origin of Darby's pretribulational doctrine is fascinating. See Dave MacPherson, *The Incredible Cover-Up* (Medford, OR: Omega Publications, 1975).

[143] Bebbington, "How Moody Changed Revivalism," 23–24.

[144] Daniel G. Reid, *Concise Dictionary of Christianity in America* (Downers Grove, IL: InterVarsity, 1995), 330.

[145] Example: The AD 2000 and Beyond movement, etc.

[146] The apostles stayed in Jerusalem for many years before they went "unto the uttermost parts of the earth" as Jesus predicted. They were in no hurry to evangelize the world. Equally, the church in Jerusalem did not evangelize anyone for the first four years of its life. They, too, were in no hurry to evangelize the world. Finally, there is not the faintest whisper in any of the New Testament epistles where an apostle tells a church to evangelize because "the hour is late and the days are few." In short, there is nothing wrong with Christians having a burden to save as many souls as they can within a specific time frame. But there is no biblical justification or divine precedent to put that particular burden on all of God's people.

THE PENTECOSTAL CONTRIBUTION

Beginning around 1906, the Pentecostal movement gave us a more emotional expression of congregational singing. This included the lifting of one's hands, dancing in pews, clapping, speaking in tongues, and the use of tambourines. The Pentecostal expression was in harmony with its emphasis on the ecstatic working of the Holy Spirit.

What few people realize is that if you removed the emotional features from a Pentecostal church service, it would look just like a Baptist liturgy. Thus no matter how loudly Pentecostals claim that they are following New Testament patterns, the typical Pentecostal or charismatic church follows the same order of worship as do most other Protestant bodies. There is simply more freedom for emotional expression in the pew.

Another interesting feature of Pentecostal worship occurs during the song service. Sometimes the singing will be punctuated by an occasional utterance in tongues, an interpretation of tongues, or word of "prophecy." But such utterances rarely last more than a minute or two. Such a pinched form of open participation cannot accurately be called "body ministry."[147] The Pentecostal tradition also gave us solo or choral music (often tagged as "special music") that accompanies the offering.[148]

As in all Protestant churches, the sermon is the climax of the Pentecostal meeting. However, in the garden-variety Pentecostal church, the pastor will sometimes "feel the Spirit moving." At such times he will suspend his sermon until the following week. The congregation will then sing and pray for the rest of the service. For many Pentecostals, this is the pinnacle of a great church service.

The way congregants describe these special services is fascinating. They typically say, "The Holy Spirit led our meeting this week. Pastor Cheswald did not get to preach." Whenever such a remark is made, it begs the question, *Isn't the Holy Spirit supposed to lead all of our church meetings?*

---

[147] By "pinched" we mean very restricted. Pentecostal and charismatic churches that have services that are completely open for the congregation to minister and share freely without any restrictions are not at all typical today.

[148] White, *Protestant Worship*, 204.

Even so, as a result of being born in the afterglow of Frontier-Revivalism, Pentecostal worship is highly subjective and individualistic.[149] In the mind of the Pentecostal, as in the minds of most other Protestants, worshipping God is not a corporate affair, but a solo experience.[150]

MANY ADJUSTMENTS, NO VITAL CHANGE

Our study of the liturgical history of the Lutherans (sixteenth century), Reformed (sixteenth century), Puritans (seventeenth century), Methodists (eighteenth century), Frontier-Revivalists (eighteenth to nineteenth centuries), and Pentecostals (twentieth century) uncovers one inescapable point: For the last five hundred years, the Protestant order of worship has undergone minimal change.[151]

In the end, all Protestant traditions share the same unbiblical features in their order of worship: They are officiated and directed by a clergyman, they make the sermon central, and the people are passive and not permitted to minister.[152]

The Reformers accomplished a great deal in changing the theology of Roman Catholicism. But in terms of actual practice, they made only minor adjustments that did little to bring worship back to the New Testament model. The result: God's people have never broken free from the liturgical constraints they inherited from Roman Catholicism.[153]

---

[149] White, *Protestant Worship and Church Architecture*, 129.

[150] The Great Awakening of the eighteenth century set the tone for an individualistic faith, something foreign to the first-century church. America was fast becoming a nation of rugged individualists, so this new emphasis sat well with the country (Terry, *Evangelism*, 122–123).

[151] Frank Senn's *Christian Liturgy* compares scores of various liturgies down through the ages. Anyone who compares them will readily spot their common features.

[152] Senn compares five modern written liturgies side by side: *Roman Catholic Missal, Lutheran Book of Worship, Book of Common Prayer*, the Methodist order of worship, and *Book of Common Worship*. The similarities are striking. (*Christian Liturgy*, 646–647).

[153] Some scholars have tried to tease out of the writings of the church fathers a unified, monolithic liturgy observed by all churches. But recent scholarship has shown that none of their writings can be universalized to represent what was happening in all the churches at a given time (Bradshaw, *Origins of Christian Worship*, 67–73, 158–183). Furthermore, archaeological findings have demonstrated that the writings of the church fathers, who were theologians, do not provide an accurate view of the beliefs or practices of the garden-variety Christians of those times. New Testament professor Graydon F. Snyder's *Ante Pacem* is a study of the archaeological evidence that contradicts the portrait that the church fathers give of church life before Constantine. According to one seminary writer, "Snyder raises the question, do the writings of the intellectuals in early Christianity give us adequate portrait of the church of their times? The question can only be asked for the obvious answer 'no' to be heard on our lips. Do the intellectuals of any age tell it like it is in the trenches? Do Barth, Tillich, or even the Niebuhrs describe in any way what popular twentieth-century American Christianity has been like? We all know they don't, and yet we have assumed that the New Testament and the so-called 'Patristic' theologians give us accurately a description of Christianity of the first three centuries. In part, of course, this has been assumed because we have thought they are the only sources we have, and to a large extent this is true, as far as *literary* documents are concerned" (Robin Scroggs, *Chicago Theological Seminary Register 75*, no. 3 [Fall 1985]: 26).

As one author put it, "The Reformers accepted in substance the ancient Catholic pattern of worship[154]. . . the basic structures of their services were almost universally taken from the late medieval orders of various sorts."[155]

In the end, then, the Reformers reformed the Catholic liturgy only slightly. Their main contribution was in changing the central focus. In the words of one scholar, "Catholicism increasingly followed the path of the [pagan] cults in making a rite the center of its activities, and Protestantism followed the path of the synagogue in placing the book at the center of its services."[156] Unfortunately, neither Catholics nor Protestants were successful in allowing Jesus Christ to be the center and head of their gatherings. Nor were they successful at liberating and unleashing the body of Christ to minister one to another in the gathering, as the New Testament envisions.

Because of the Reformation, the Bible replaced the Eucharist and the pastor replaced the priest. But there is still a person directing God's people, rendering them as silent spectators. The centrality of the Author of the Book was never restored. Hence, the Reformers dramatically failed to put their finger on the nerve of the original problem: a clergy-led worship service attended by a passive laity.[157] It is not surprising, then, that the Reformers viewed themselves as reformed Catholics.[158]

WHAT IS WRONG WITH THIS PICTURE?

It is clear that the Protestant order of worship did not originate with the Lord Jesus, the apostles, or the New Testament Scriptures.[159] This in itself does not make the order of worship misguided. It just means it has no biblical basis.

---

[154] Nichols, *Corporate Worship in the Reformed Tradition*, 13.

[155] Ibid., 13. "Much of traditional [i.e., Catholic] theological terminology and concepts are truly part of the Lutheran approach as well as they were part of the Roman Catholic approach." Kenan B. Osborne, *Priesthood: A History of the Ordained Ministry in the Roman Catholic Church* (New York: Paulist Press, 1988), 223.

[156] Banks, *Paul's Idea of Community*, 108; Hatch, *Influence of Greek Ideas and Usages*, 308–309.

[157] Chapter 2 discusses the influence of fourth-century church architecture on the active clergy and the passive congregation. In this vein, Horton Davies writes, "The passing of three or four centuries shows a great alteration in the character of Christian worship. . . . In the fourth century, worship is not celebrated in private houses, but in stately cathedrals and magnificent churches; not in free and simple forms of service, but in fixed and ordered worship" (*Christian Worship: History and Meaning*, 26).

[158] Nichols, *Corporate Worship*, 155.

[159] Some liturgical scholars, like Anglican Gregory Dix, have tried to argue that the New Testament contains a primitive model of the Mass. However, a careful examination of their arguments shows that they are merely reading their present tradition back into the biblical text (Bradshaw, *Origins of Christian Worship*, ch. 2).

The use of chairs and pile carpets in Christian gatherings has no biblical support either. And both were invented by pagans.[160] Nonetheless, who would claim that sitting in chairs or using carpets is "wrong" simply because they are postbiblical inventions authored by pagans?

The fact is that we do many things in our culture that have pagan roots. Consider our accepted calendar. The days of our week and the months of our year are named after pagan gods.[161] But using the accepted calendar does not make us pagans.[162]

So why is the Sunday morning order of worship a different matter than the type of chairs and carpeting we use in the place we worship? Not only is the traditional order of service unscriptural and heavily influenced by paganism (which runs contrary to what is often preached from the pulpit), it does not lead to the spiritual growth God intended.[163] Consider the following.

First, the Protestant order of worship represses mutual participation and the growth of Christian community. It puts a choke hold on the functioning of the body of Christ by silencing its members. There is absolutely no room for anyone to give a word of exhortation, share an insight, start or introduce a song, or spontaneously lead a prayer. You are forced to be a muted, staid pewholder! You are prevented from being enriched by the other members of the body as well as being able to enrich them yourself.

Like every other "lay person," you may open your mouth only during the congregational singing or prayer. (If you happen to be part

---

[160] The earliest known chairs were made in Egypt. For thousands of years, they were used only by royalty, nobility, priests, and the wealthy. Chairs did not come into common use among the general populace until the sixteenth century. *Encarta Encyclopedia*, 1999 ed., s.v. "Chairs." Pile carpets were developed in India in the eleventh century and spread throughout the rest of the Eastern world. *Encarta Encyclopedia*, 1998 ed., s.v. "Floor and Floor Coverings."

[161] The seven-day week originated in ancient Mesopotamia and became part of the Roman calendar in AD 321. January is named after the Roman god Janus; March is named after the Roman god Mars; April comes from *Aprilis*, the sacred month of Venus; May is named for the goddess Maia; and June is named for the goddess Juno. Sunday celebrates the sun god; Monday is the day of the moon goddess; Tuesday is named after the warrior god *Tiw*; Wednesday is named after the Teutonic god *Wotan*; Thursday is named after the Scandinavian god *Thor*; Friday is named after the Scandinavian goddess *Frigg*; and Saturday is named after Saturn, the Roman god of agriculture (see *Months of the Year* at www.ernie.cummings.net/calendar.htm).

[162] To those of you who are wondering why Christmas, Easter, and Christians gathering on Sunday are not addressed in this book, please see Frank's full comments at http://www.ptmin.org/answers.htm.

[163] David Norrington makes the point that although there is nothing intrinsically wrong with the church embracing ideas from the surrounding culture, because they are pagan they are often contrary to biblical faith. Thus syncretism and acculturation are frequently harmful to the church (*To Preach or Not*, 23).

of a typical Pentecostal/charismatic church, you may be permitted to give a one-minute ecstatic utterance. But then you must sit down and be quiet.)

Even though open sharing in a church meeting is completely scriptural,[164] you would be breaking the liturgy if you dared try something so outrageous! You would be considered "out of order" and asked to behave yourself or leave.

Second, the Protestant order of worship strangles the headship of Jesus Christ.[165] The entire service is directed by one person. You are limited to the knowledge, gifting, and experience of one member of the body—the pastor. Where is the freedom for our Lord Jesus to speak through His body at will? Where in the liturgy may God give a brother or a sister a word to share with the whole congregation? The order of worship allows for no such thing. Jesus Christ has no freedom to express Himself through His body at His discretion. He too is rendered a passive spectator.

Granted, Christ may be able to express Himself through one or two members of the church—usually the pastor and the music leader. But this is a very limited expression. The Lord is stifled from manifesting Himself through the other members of the body. Consequently, the Protestant liturgy cripples the body of Christ. It turns it into one huge tongue (the pastor) and many little ears (the congregation). This does violence to Paul's vision of the body of Christ, where every member functions in the church meeting for the common good (see 1 Corinthians 12).

Third, for many Christians, the Sunday morning service is shamefully boring. It is without variety or spontaneity. It is highly predictable, highly perfunctory, and highly mechanical. There is little in the way of freshness or innovation. It has remained frozen for five centuries. Put bluntly, the order of worship embodies the ambiguous

---

[164] 1 Corinthians 14:26. The New Testament teaches that all Christians are to use their gifts as functioning priests to edify one another when they gather together (Romans 12:3-8; 1 Corinthians 12:7; Ephesians 4:7; Hebrews 10:24-25, 13:15-16; 1 Peter 2:5, 9).

[165] In the words of Arthur Wallis, "Liturgies, whether ancient or modern, written or unwritten, are a human device to keep the religious wheels turning by doing what is customary, rather than exercising faith in the immediate presence and operation of the Spirit."

power of the rote. And the rote very quickly decays into the routine, which in turn becomes tired, meaningless, and ultimately invisible.

Seeker-sensitive churches have recognized the sterile nature of the contemporary church service. In response, they have incorporated a vast array of media and theatrical modernizations into the liturgy. This is done to market worship to the unchurched. Employing the latest electronic technology, seeker-sensitive churches have been successful at swelling their ranks. As a result, they have garnered a large portion of the American Protestant market share.[166]

But despite the added entertainment it affords, the market-driven seeker-sensitive service is still held captive by the pastor, the threefold "hymn sandwich" remains intact, and the congregants continue to be muted spectators (only they are more entertained in their spectating).[167]

Fourth, the Protestant liturgy that you quietly sit through every Sunday, year after year, actually hinders spiritual transformation. It does so because (1) it encourages passivity, (2) it limits functioning, and (3) it implies that putting in one hour per week is the key to the victorious Christian life.

Every Sunday you attend the service to be bandaged and recharged, like all other wounded soldiers. Far too often, however, the bandaging and the recharging never takes place. The reason is quite simple. The New Testament never links sitting through an ossified ritual that we mislabel "church" as having anything to do with spiritual transformation. We grow by functioning, not by passively watching and listening.

Let's face it. The Protestant order of worship is largely unscriptural, impractical, and unspiritual. It has no analog in the New Testament. Rather, it finds its roots in the culture of fallen man.[168] It rips at the heart of primitive Christianity, which was informal and free of ritual. Five centuries after the Reformation, the Protestant order of

---

[166] For details, see Gary Gilley, *This Little Church Went to Market: The Church in the Age of Entertainment* (Webster, NY: Evangelical Press, 2005).

[167] See my (Frank's) book *Reimagining Church* for more on this topic.

[168] The purpose of the first-century church meeting was not for evangelism, sermonizing, worship, or fellowship. It was rather for mutual edification through manifesting Christ corporately (Viola, *Rethinking the Wineskin*, ch. 1).

worship still varies little from the Catholic Mass—a religious ritual that is a fusion of pagan and Judaistic elements.

As one liturgical scholar put it, "The history of Christian worship is the story of the give and take between cult and culture. As the gospel was preached in different times and places, missionaries brought with them the forms and styles of worship with which they were familiar."[169]

I (Frank) am no armchair liturgist. What I have written about open meetings under the headship of Christ is not fanciful theory. I have participated in such meetings for the last nineteen years.

Such meetings are marked by incredible variety. They are not bound to a one-man, pulpit-dominated pattern of worship. There is a great deal of spontaneity, creativity, and freshness. The overarching hallmark of these meetings is the visible headship of Christ and the free yet orderly functioning of the body of Christ. I was in such a meeting not too long ago. Let me describe it to you.

About thirty of us gathered together in a home and greeted one another. Some of us stepped into the center of the living room and began singing a capella. Quickly, the entire church was singing in unison, arms around one another. Someone else began another song, and we all joined in. Between each song, prayers were uttered by different people. Some of the songs had been written by the members themselves. We sang several of the songs several times. Some people turned the words of the songs into prayers. On several occasions, a few of the members exhorted the church in relation to what we had just sung.

After we sang, rejoiced, spontaneously prayed, and exhorted one another, we sat down. Then, very quickly, a woman stood and began explaining what the Lord had showed her during the week. She spoke for about three minutes. After she sat down, a man stood up and shared a portion of Scripture and exalted the Lord Jesus through it. Next another gentleman stood up to add a few very edifying words

---

[169] Senn, *Christian Worship and Its Cultural Setting*, 38, 40.

to what he said. A woman then broke into a new song that went right along with what the two men had just shared. The whole church sang with her. Another woman stood and read a poem that the Lord had given her during the week . . . and it meshed perfectly with what the others had shared up to that point.

One by one, brothers and sisters in Christ stood up to tell us what they had experienced in their relationship with the Lord Jesus Christ that week. Exhortations, teaching, encouragements, poems, songs, and testimonies all followed one right after the other. And a common theme, one that revealed the glories of Jesus Christ, emerged. Some of those gathered wept.

None of this was rehearsed, prescribed, or planned. Yet the meeting was electric. It was so rich, so glorious, and so edifying that it became evident to everyone that someone was indeed leading the meeting. But He was not visible. It was the Lord Jesus Christ! His headship was being made manifest among His people. We were reminded again that He in fact is alive . . . alive enough to direct His church.

The New Testament is not silent with respect to how we Christians are to meet. Shall we, therefore, opt for man's tradition when it clearly runs contrary to God's thought for His church? Shall we continue to undermine the functioning headship of Christ for the sake of our sacrosanct liturgy? Is the church of Jesus Christ the pillar and ground of truth or the defender of man's tradition (1 Timothy 3:15)?

Perhaps the only sure way to thaw out God's frozen people is to make a dramatic break with the Sunday morning ritual. May we not be found guilty of our Lord's bone-rattling words: "Full well do you reject the commandment of God, that you may keep your tradition."[170]

---

[170] Mark 7:9, WEB. See also Matthew 15:2-6; Mark 7:9-13; Colossians 2:8.

>delving DEEPER

1. Isn't it true that the Bible's description of church gatherings seems to allow for a lot of latitude in how our worship is structured? My church's order of worship contains almost all the practices mentioned in 1 Corinthians 14. What, then, is so wrong with a standard order of worship?

Most gatherings in institutional churches do include singing and teaching; however, they're done in an atmosphere far different from the one prescribed in 1 Corinthians 14. This passage describes a gathering with open participation by every member to bring a teaching, a revelation, a song, an exhortation, etc. (verse 26); interjections by the members while others are speaking (verse 30); and spontaneous prophesying by everyone (verses 24, 31).

If your church gathering possesses all of these elements, that is wonderful. We just would not describe it as a "standard order of worship" since it is not the standard practice today.

2. In 1 Corinthians 14, Paul admonishes the believers to do things in an orderly way. How does an organic church keep their worship time from becoming a free-for-all—or dominated by one or two individuals? Doesn't an organic church's style lend itself to disorder?

This is an excellent question. The fact that Paul admonishes the believers to meet in an orderly fashion clearly demonstrates that an open meeting does not have to be a tumultuous free-for-all. To Paul's mind, there is a wonderful synergy between an open meeting and an orderly one. If God's people are properly equipped on how to function under Christ's headship, an open-participatory meeting can be a glorious event with harmony and order.

Let's ask ourselves: What happened when Paul faced the frenzied morass in Corinth? The apostle did not shut down the meetings and hand out a liturgy. Nor did he introduce human officiation. Instead, he supplied the church with a number of broad guidelines to facilitate order and edification in the gatherings (see 1 Corinthians 14).

What is more, Paul was confident the church would adhere to those guidelines. This sets forth an important principle. Every church in the first century had at its disposal an itinerant apostolic worker who helped it navigate through common problems. Sometimes the worker's help came in the form of letters. At other times, it came during personal visits from the worker himself. Such outside help can be highly beneficial in keeping an organic church centered on Christ and focused in its meetings.

3. You question the church's focus on bringing lost souls to Christ. Yet until people come to Christ, they cannot partake in God's great, eternal purpose, which Paul discusses in Ephesians 1. Therefore, isn't it critical that churches make the gospel's proclamation a priority?

Yes, it is. In fact, we believe that embodying the gospel in life and proclaiming it in word is a natural outgrowth of the life of a healthy organic church. If God's people are learning to love their Lord and one another with greater intensity, they will naturally want to share Him with others in both word and deed.

4. You imply that Finney and other Revivalists began using such things as the altar call strictly because they were pragmatists who invented certain practices to win converts. But how can we say for sure that these men weren't led by the Holy Spirit to employ new methods that would help people recognize their need for Christ?

Our point about Finney was simply that the Revivalists made salvation God's governing purpose. Salvation was turned into something that took on a life of its own, often isolated from a holistic Christian experience, and thus many innovations were created to facilitate a conversion experience but not a full Christian experience. God's eternal purpose was not in view at all.

As far as modern pragmatism goes, Christians should decide for themselves whether a particular practice is of the Holy Spirit or if it is mere human ingenuity at work. We leave such judgments to the individual reader.

5. You seem very critical that Moody was so concerned about bringing lost souls to Christ. Yet as an evangelist, wasn't it natural that that was his focus?

We certainly commend Moody for bringing souls to Christ. However, we believe that by viewing redemption as God's ultimate purpose, he failed to communicate the scope of God's complete plan.

No evangelist or apostle in the New Testament brought souls to Christ simply to save them from hell. Such a thought was unknown to the early Christians. The early Christians won people to the Lord to bring them into God's community, the church.

In the first century, people were saved with the idea of adding them to the ekklesia. Conversion and community were not separate; they were inextricably intertwined. In the words of Gilbert Bilezikian: "Christ did not die just to save us from sins, but to bring us together into community. After coming to Christ, our next step is to be involved in community. A church that does not experience community is a parody, a sham."[171]

---

[171] John McNeil, " 'Denatured' Church Facing Extinction," ASSIST News Service, February 19, 2006.

In this regard, mainstream evangelicalism has made the profound error of divorcing soteriology (salvation) from ecclesiology (church practice). The message conveyed is that soteriology is a required course, while ecclesiology is an elective. So church practice does not really matter. But this thinking does not reflect God's curriculum. The church is not a footnote in the gospel. It stands at the center of God's beating heart.

In fact, when the church functions as she should, she is the greatest evangelism known to humankind. When God's people are living in authentic community, their lives together are a sign to the world of God's coming reign.[172]

6. You say that "neither Catholics nor Protestants were successful in allowing Jesus Christ to be the center and head of their gatherings." I must disagree. In my church, the songs we sing, the Scripture we read, the message that is proclaimed all center on Jesus. Furthermore, we are given practical instruction on how to make Christ our Lord every day of the week.

The central issue we were addressing is not, "Is Jesus talked about and given honor in the service?" We agree that in many institutional churches, He is. The issue we were addressing is, "Is Jesus Christ the functional head of the gathering?" There is a significant difference between making Jesus the invisible guest of honor and allowing Him to be the practical leader of the gathering.

Let's suppose the authors of this book attend your church service. And let's suppose that the Lord Jesus Christ puts something on our hearts to share with the rest of His body. Would we have the freedom to do so spontaneously? Would everyone else have the freedom to do it? If not, then we would question whether your church service is under Christ's headship.

You see, a meeting that is under the headship of Christ means that He may speak through every member of the body in the gathering. This is the very argument of 1 Corinthians 12–14. Paul begins this section by saying that Jesus Christ is not speechless like the idols the Corinthians once worshipped. And through whom does Christ speak? He speaks through His body using the various gifts and ministries granted by the Spirit (1 Corinthians 12). In the next chapter, Paul says that believers' gifts and ministries are to be used in love, as love seeks to edify everyone else (rather than to take for itself). Paul then moves on to the specifics of the church meeting where "every one of you hath" something to bring and "ye may all prophesy one by one" (1 Corinthians 14).

In this connection, if you were to attend an organic church gathering that met

---

172 See also Stanley Grenz, *Created for Community* (Grand Rapids: Baker Books, 1998).

in New Testament fashion, you would have both the right and the privilege to share whatever the Lord laid on your heart in the manner in which the Spirit led you. Not only that, but you would be expected to. In other words, Jesus Christ would be the functional head of that gathering.

7. You often use the phrase headship of Christ to refer to Christ's leadership and authority in the church. I read somewhere that head in the New Testament means "source" rather than "authority." What do you think?

It actually means both. We are using *headship of Christ* to refer to the idea that Jesus Christ is both the authority over the church as well as the source of the church. There is good scholarly support for this usage.[173]

8. Didn't the early church hold their services in the synagogues? I remember reading that the apostles went to the synagogues to preach. And didn't Paul and Peter preach to a passive audience?

The apostles, as well as gifted people like Stephen, visited the synagogues for evangelistic purposes. But these meetings were not church meetings. They were not for believers. Rather, they were opportunities for the apostles to preach the gospel to the Jews. (In that day, a visitor could visit a synagogue and preach to the audience.) Yes, Paul and Peter preached in certain settings, but again, these were not at church meetings. They preached at apostolic meetings designed to evangelize the lost or to equip and encourage an existing church. Apostolic and evangelistic meetings were temporary and sporadic, while church meetings were normative and ongoing.

9. Are you saying that just because the first-century church had open-participatory meetings, we should too—even though we live in the twenty-first century?

No. We are suggesting that open-participatory meetings are rooted in New Testament theology, namely the doctrine of the priesthood of all believers and the every-member functioning of Christ's body. We are also suggesting that Christians have a spiritual instinct to share what God has shown them with others for their edification. And we are raising three key questions: (1) After exploring where the modern Protestant order of worship came from, is it really successful at transforming people and expressing Jesus Christ? (2) Is it possible that open-participatory church meetings are more in line with what God had in mind for His church than the Protestant order of worship? (3) Would it be worth our time to begin exploring new ways to gather and express Christ in our church life together?

---

173 F. F. Bruce, *The Epistles to the Colossians, to Philemon, and to the Ephesians* (Grand Rapids: Eerdmans, 1984), 68–69, 274–275; Francis Foulkes, *Ephesians* (Grand Rapids: Eerdmans, 1989), 73–74.

chapter four

> THE SERMON: PROTESTANTISM'S MOST SACRED COW

"Christianity did not destroy paganism; it adopted it."
—WILL DURANT, TWENTIETH-CENTURY AMERICAN HISTORIAN

"And my speech and my preaching was not with enticing words of man's wisdom, but in demonstration of the Spirit and of power: That your faith should not stand in the wisdom of men, but in the power of God."
—PAUL OF TARSUS IN 1 CORINTHIANS 2:4-5

WE NOW COME to one of the most sacrosanct church practices of all: the sermon. Remove the sermon and the Protestant order of worship becomes in large part a songfest. Remove the sermon and attendance at the Sunday morning service is doomed to drop.

The sermon is the bedrock of the Protestant liturgy. For five hundred years, it has functioned like clockwork. Every Sunday morning, the pastor steps up to his pulpit and delivers an inspirational oration to a passive, pew-warming audience.[1] So central is the sermon that it is the very reason many Christians go to church. In fact, the entire service is often judged by the quality of the sermon. Ask a person how church was last Sunday and you will most likely get a description of the message. In short, the contemporary Christian mind-set often equates the sermon with Sunday morning worship.[2] But it does not end there.

Remove the sermon and you have eliminated the most important source of spiritual nourishment for countless numbers of believers (so it is thought). Yet the stunning reality is that today's sermon has no root in Scripture. Rather, it was borrowed from pagan culture, nursed and adopted into the Christian faith. That's a startling statement, is it not? But there is more.

The sermon actually detracts from the very purpose for which God designed the church gathering. And it has very little to do with genuine spiritual growth. Don't faint dead away . . . we will prove these words in the following pages.

THE SERMON AND THE BIBLE

Doubtlessly, someone reading the previous few paragraphs will retort: "People preached all throughout the Bible. Of course the sermon is scriptural!"

Granted, the Scriptures do record men and women preaching. However, there is a world of difference between the Spirit-inspired preaching and teaching described in the Bible and the contemporary sermon. This difference is virtually always overlooked because we have been unwittingly conditioned to read our modern-day practices back into the Scripture. So we mistakenly embrace today's pulpiteerism as being biblical. Let's unfold that a bit. The present-day Christian sermon has the following features:

---

[1] "Nothing is more characteristic of Protestantism than the importance it attaches to preaching." Niebuhr and Williams, *Ministry in Historical Perspectives*, 110.

[2] In France, the Protestant church service is called *aller à sermon* ("go to a sermon") (White, *Protestant Worship*, 20).

> **It is a regular occurrence**—delivered faithfully from the pulpit at least once a week.
> **It is delivered by the same person**—most typically the pastor or an ordained guest speaker.
> **It is delivered to a passive audience**—essentially it is a monologue.
> **It is a cultivated form of speech**—possessing a specific structure. It typically contains an introduction, three to five points, and a conclusion.

Contrast this with the kind of preaching mentioned in the Bible. In the Old Testament, men of God preached and taught. But their speaking did not map to the contemporary sermon. Here are the features of Old Testament preaching and teaching:

> Active participation and interruptions by the audience were common.[3]
> Prophets and priests spoke extemporaneously and out of a present burden, rather than from a set script.
> There is no indication that Old Testament prophets or priests gave regular speeches to God's people.[4] Instead, the nature of Old Testament preaching was sporadic, fluid, and open for audience participation. Preaching in the ancient synagogue followed a similar pattern.[5]

Come now to the New Testament. The Lord Jesus did not preach a regular sermon to the same audience.[6] His preaching and teaching took many different forms. And He delivered His messages to many different audiences. (Of course, He concentrated most of His

---

[3] Norrington, *To Preach or Not*, 3.
[4] The prophets spoke in response to specific events (Deuteronomy 1:1, 5:1, 27:1, 9; Joshua 23:1–24:15; Isaiah; Jeremiah; Ezekiel; Daniel; Amos; Haggai; Zechariah; etc.). Norrington, *To Preach or Not*, 3.
[5] Norrington, *To Preach or Not*, 4. The only difference in synagogue preaching is that a message delivered on a biblical text was a *regular* occurrence. Even so, most synagogues allowed for any member to preach to the people who wished to do so. This, of course, is in direct contradiction to the modern sermon where only religious "specialists" are allowed to address the congregation.
[6] Augustine was the first to title Matthew 5–7 in his book *The Lord's Sermon on the Mount* (written between 392 and 396). But the passage was not generally referred to as the Sermon on the Mount until the sixteenth century (Green, *Dictionary of Jesus and the Gospels*, 736; Douglas, *Who's Who in Christian History*, 48). Despite its name, the Sermon on the Mount is quite different from the modern sermon in both style and rhetoric.

teaching on His disciples. Yet the messages He brought to them were consistently spontaneous and informal.)

Following the same pattern, the apostolic preaching recorded in Acts possessed the following features:

> It was sporadic.[7]
> It was delivered on special occasions in order to deal with specific problems.[8]
> It was extemporaneous and without rhetorical structure.[9]
> It was most often dialogical (meaning it included feedback and interruptions from the audience) rather than monological (a one-way discourse).[10]

In like manner, the New Testament letters show that the ministry of God's Word came from the entire church in their regular gatherings.[11] From Romans 12:6-8, 15:14, 1 Corinthians 14:26, and Colossians 3:16, we see that it included teaching, exhortation, prophecy, singing, and admonishment. This "every-member" functioning was also conversational (1 Corinthians 14:29) and marked by interruptions (1 Corinthians 14:30). Equally so, the exhortations of the local elders were normally impromptu.[12]

In short, the contemporary sermon delivered for Christian consumption is foreign to both Old and New Testaments. There is nothing in Scripture to indicate its existence in the early Christian gatherings.[13]

---

[7] Norrington, *To Preach or Not*, 7–12. Norrington analyzes the speeches in the New Testament and contrasts them with the modern-day sermon.

[8] Acts 2:14-35; 15:13-21, 32; 20:7-12, 17-35; 26:24-29. Norrington, *To Preach or Not*, 5–7.

[9] The spontaneous and nonrhetorical character of the apostolic messages delivered in Acts is evident upon close inspection. See for instance Acts 2:14-35, 7:1-53, 17:22-34.

[10] Jeremy Thomson, *Preaching As Dialogue: Is the Sermon a Sacred Cow?* (Cambridge: Grove Books, 1996), 3–8. The Greek word often used to describe first-century preaching and teaching is *dialegomai* (Acts 17:2, 17; 18:4, 19; 19:8-9; 20:7, 9; 24:25). This word means a two-way form of communication. Our English word *dialogue* is derived from it. In short, apostolic ministry was more dialogue than it was monological sermonics. William Barclay, *Communicating the Gospel* (Sterling: The Drummond Press, 1968), 34–35.

[11] 1 Corinthians 14:26, 31; Romans 12:4ff.; Ephesians 4:11ff.; Hebrews 10:25.

[12] Kreider, *Worship and Evangelism in Pre-Christendom*, 37.

[13] Norrington, *To Preach or Not*, 12.

WHERE DID THE CHRISTIAN SERMON COME FROM?

The earliest recorded Christian source for regular sermonizing is found during the late second century.[14] Clement of Alexandria lamented the fact that sermons did so little to change Christians.[15] Yet despite its recognized failure, the sermon became a standard practice among believers by the fourth century.[16]

This raises a thorny question. If the first-century Christians were not noted for their sermonizing, from whom did the postapostolic Christians pick it up? The answer is telling: The Christian sermon was borrowed from the pagan pool of Greek culture!

To find the headwaters of the sermon, we must go back to the fifth century BC and a group of wandering teachers called sophists. The sophists are credited for inventing rhetoric (the art of persuasive speaking). They recruited disciples and demanded payment for delivering their orations.[17]

The sophists were expert debaters. They were masters at using emotional appeals, physical appearance, and clever language to "sell" their arguments.[18] In time, the style, form, and oratorical skill of the sophists became more prized than their accuracy.[19] This spawned a class of men who became masters of fine phrases, "cultivating style for style's sake." The truths they preached were abstract rather than truths that were practiced in their own lives. They were experts at imitating form rather than substance.[20]

The sophists identified themselves by the special clothing they wore. Some of them had a fixed residence where they gave regular sermons to the same audience. Others traveled to deliver their polished orations. (They made a good deal of money when they did.)

---

[14] Ibid., 13. The first recorded Christian sermon is contained in the so-called *Second Letter of Clement* dated between AD 100 and AD 150. Brilioth, *Brief History of Preaching*, 19–20.

[15] Norrington, *To Preach or Not*, 13.

[16] Hatch, *Influence of Greek Ideas and Usages*, 109.

[17] Douglas J. Soccio, *Archetypes of Wisdom: An Introduction to Philosophy* (Belmont, CA: Wadsworth/ITP Publishing, 1998), 56–57.

[18] Ibid.

[19] We get our words *sophistry* and *sophistical* from the sophists. *Sophistry* refers to specious and fallacious (bogus) reasoning used to persuade (Soccio, *Archetypes of Wisdom*, 57). The Greeks celebrated the orator's style and form over the accuracy of the content of his sermon. Thus a good orator could use his sermon to sway his audience to believe what he knew to be false. To the Greek mind, winning an argument was a greater virtue than distilling truth. Unfortunately, an element of sophistry has never left the Christian fold (Norrington, *To Preach or Not*, 21–22; Hatch, *Influence of Greek Ideas and Usages*, 113).

[20] Hatch, *Influence of Greek Ideas and Usages*, 113.

Sometimes the Greek orator would enter his speaking forum "already robed in his pulpit-gown." He would then mount the steps to his professional chair to sit before he brought his sermon.

To make his points, he would quote Homer's verses. (Some orators studied Homer so well that they could repeat him by heart.) So spellbinding was the sophist that he would often incite his audience to clap their hands during his discourse. If his speaking was very well received, some would call his sermon "inspired."

The sophists were the most distinguished men of their time. Some even lived at public expense. Others had public statues erected in their honor.[21]

About a century later, the Greek philosopher Aristotle (384–322 BC) gave to rhetoric the three-point speech. "A whole," said Aristotle, "must have a beginning, a middle, and an end."[22] In time, Greek orators implemented Aristotle's three-point principle into their discourses.

The Greeks were intoxicated with rhetoric.[23] So the sophists fared well. When the Romans took over Greece, they too became obsessed with rhetoric.[24] Consequently, Greco-Roman culture developed an insatiable appetite for hearing someone give an eloquent oration. This was so fashionable that a "sermonette" from a professional philosopher after dinner was a regular form of entertainment.[25]

The ancient Greeks and Romans viewed rhetoric as one of the greatest forms of art.[26] Accordingly, the orators in the Roman Empire were lauded with the same glamorous status that Americans assign to movie stars and professional athletes. They were the shining stars of their day.

Orators could bring a crowd to a frenzy simply by their powerful speaking skills. Teachers of rhetoric, the leading science of the

---

[21] Ibid., 54, 56, 91–92, 96, 97–98, 112.
[22] Aristotle, *On Poetics*, ch. 7. Although Aristotle was speaking about writing "Plot" or "Fable," his principle was nonetheless applied to delivering speeches.
[23] The love of speech was second nature to the Greeks. "They were a nation of talkers" (Hatch, *Influence of Greek Ideas and Usages*, 27).
[24] Norrington, *To Preach or Not*, 21.
[25] Hatch, *Influence of Greek Ideas and Usages*, 40.
[26] Brilioth, *Brief History of Preaching*, 26.

era, were the pride of every major city.[27] The orators they produced were given celebrity status. In short, the Greeks and Romans were addicted to the pagan sermon—just as many contemporary Christians are addicted to the "Christian" sermon.

THE ARRIVAL OF A POLLUTED STREAM

How did the Greek sermon find its way into the Christian church? Around the third century a vacuum was created when mutual ministry faded from the body of Christ.[28] At this time the last of the traveling Christian workers who spoke out of a prophetic burden and spontaneous conviction left the pages of church history.[29] To fill their absence, the clergy began to emerge. Open meetings began to die out, and church gatherings became more and more liturgical.[30] The "church meeting" was devolving into a "service."

As a hierarchical structure began to take root, the idea of a "religious specialist" emerged.[31] In the face of these changes, the functioning Christians had trouble fitting into this evolving ecclesiastical structure.[32] There was no place for them to exercise their gifts. By the fourth century, the church had become fully institutionalized.

As this was happening, many pagan orators and philosophers were becoming Christians. As a result, pagan philosophical ideas unwittingly made their way into the Christian community.[33] Many of these men became the theologians and leaders of the early Christian church. They are known as the "church fathers," and some of their writings are still with us.[34]

Thus the pagan notion of a trained professional speaker who delivers orations for a fee moved straight into the Christian bloodstream.

---

[27] Robert A. Krupp, "Golden Tongue and Iron Will," *Christian History* 13, no. 4 (1994): 7.
[28] Norrington, *To Preach or Not*, 24.
[29] Hatch, *Influence of Greek Ideas and Usages*, 106–107, 109.
[30] Norrington, *To Preach or Not*, 24–25.
[31] Ibid.; see chapter 5 of this book.
[32] Ibid., 25.
[33] Ibid., 22; Smith, *From Christ to Constantine*, 115.
[34] Among them are Tertullian, Cyprian, Arnobius, Lactantius, and Augustine (Norrington, *To Preach or Not*, 22). See also Hatch, *Influence of Greek Ideas and Usages*, 7–9, 109; Richard Hanson, *Christian Priesthood Examined* (Guildford, UK: Lutterworth Press, 1979), 53.

Note that the concept of the "paid teaching specialist" came from Greece, not Judaism. It was the custom of Jewish rabbis to take up a trade so as to not charge a fee for their teaching.[35]

The upshot of the story is that these former pagan orators (now turned Christian) began to use their Greco-Roman oratorical skills for Christian purposes. They would sit in their official chair[36] and "expound the sacred text of Scripture, just as the sophist would supply an exegesis of the near-sacred text of Homer."[37] If you compare a third-century pagan sermon with a sermon given by one of the church fathers, you will find both the structure and the phraseology to be quite similar.[38]

So a new style of communication was being birthed in the Christian church—a style that emphasized polished rhetoric, sophisticated grammar, flowery eloquence, and monologue. It was a style that was designed to entertain and show off the speaker's oratorical skills. It was Greco-Roman rhetoric.[39] And only those who were trained in it were allowed to address the assembly![40] (Does any of this sound familiar?)

One scholar put it this way: "The original proclamation of the Christian message was a two-way conversation . . . but when the oratorical schools of the Western world laid hold of the Christian message, they made Christian preaching something vastly different. Oratory tended to take the place of conversation. The greatness of the orator took the place of the astounding event of Jesus Christ. And the dialogue between speaker and listener faded into a monologue."[41]

In a word, the Greco-Roman sermon replaced prophesying, open sharing, and Spirit-inspired teaching.[42] The sermon became the elit-

---

[35] F. F. Bruce, *Paul: Apostle of the Heart Set Free* (Grand Rapids: Eerdmans, 1977), 220. The noted Jewish rabbi Hillel said, "He who makes a worldly crown of the Torah shall waste away" (107–108).

[36] Hatch, *Influence of Greek Ideas and Usages*, 110.

[37] Norrington, *To Preach or Not*, 22. An exegesis is an interpretation and explanation of a biblical text.

[38] Hatch, *Influence of Greek Ideas and Usage*, 110.

[39] A student who studied rhetoric completed his studies when he could talk offhand on any subject that was presented to him. Logic, in the form of debate, was common in the study of rhetoric. Every student learned how to argue and argue well. Logic was natural to the Greek mind. But it was logic divorced from practice and built on theoretical arguments. This entire mind-set seeped into the Christian faith early on (Hatch, *Influence of Greek Ideas and Usages*, 32–33).

[40] Ibid., 108. Hatch writes, "with the growth of organization there grew up also, not only a fusion of teaching and exhortation, but also the gradual restriction of the liberty of addressing the community to the official class."

[41] Wayne E. Oates, *Protestant Pastoral Counseling* (Philadelphia: Westminster Press, 1962), 162.

[42] Ibid., 107.

ist privilege of church officials, particularly the bishops. Such people had to be educated in the schools of rhetoric to learn how to speak.[43] Without this education, a Christian was not permitted to address God's people.

As early as the third century, Christians called their sermons *homilies*, the same term Greek orators used for their discourses.[44] Today, one can take a seminary course called homiletics to learn how to preach. Homiletics is considered a "science, applying rules of rhetoric, which go back to Greece and Rome."[45]

Put another way, neither homilies (sermons) nor homiletics (the art of sermonizing) have a Christian origin. They were stolen from the pagans. A polluted stream made its entrance into the Christian faith and muddied its waters. And that stream flows just as strongly today as it did in the fourth century.

CHRYSOSTOM AND AUGUSTINE

John Chrysostom was one of the greatest Christian orators of his day.[46] (*Chrysostom* means "golden-mouthed.")[47] Never had Constantinople heard "sermons so powerful, brilliant, and frank" as those preached by Chrysostom.[48] Chrysostom's preaching was so compelling that people would sometimes shove their way toward the front to hear him better.[49]

Naturally endowed with the orator's gift of gab, Chrysostom learned how to speak under the leading sophist of the fourth century, Libanius.[50] Chrysostom's pulpit eloquence was unsurpassed. So

---

[43] Brilioth, *Brief History of Preaching*, 26, 27.

[44] Hatch, *Influence of Greek Ideas and Usages*, 109; Brilioth, *Brief History of Preaching*, 18.

[45] J. D. Douglas, *New Twentieth Century Encyclopedia of Religious Knowledge* (Grand Rapids: Baker Book House, 1991), 405.

[46] On his deathbed, Libanius (Chrysostom's pagan tutor) said that he would have been his worthiest successor "if the Christians had not stolen him" (Hatch, *Influence of Greek Ideas and Usages*, 109).

[47] Tony Castle, *Lives of Famous Christians* (Ann Arbor, MI: Servant Books, 1988), 69; Hatch, *Influence of Greek Ideas and Usages*, 6. John was nicknamed golden-mouth (*Chrysostomos*) because of his eloquent and uncompromising preaching (Krupp, "Golden Tongue and Iron Will," *Christian History*, 7).

[48] Durant, *Age of Faith*, 63.

[49] Kevin Dale Miller, "Did You Know? Little-Known Facts about John Chrysostom," *Christian History* 13, no. 4 (1994): 3. Of the sermons that Chrysostom preached, more than 600 survive.

[50] Krupp, "Golden Tongue and Iron Will," 7; Schaff, *History of the Christian Church*, 3:933–941; Durant, *Age of Faith*, 9. Chrysostom imbibed rhetoric from Libanius, but he was also a student of pagan philosophy and literature (Durant, *Age of Faith*, 63).

powerful were his orations that his sermons would often get interrupted by congregational applause. Chrysostom once gave a sermon condemning the applause as unfitting in God's house.[51] But the congregation loved the sermon so much that after he finished preaching, they applauded anyway.[52] This story illustrates the untamable power of Greek rhetoric.

We can credit both Chrysostom and Augustine (354–430), a former professor of rhetoric,[53] for making pulpit oratory part and parcel of the Christian faith.[54] In Chrysostom, the Greek sermon reached its zenith. The Greek sermon style indulged in rhetorical brilliance, the quoting of poems, and focused on impressing the audience. Chrysostom emphasized that "the preacher must toil long on his sermons in order to gain the power of eloquence."[55]

In Augustine, the Latin sermon reached its heights.[56] The Latin sermon style was more down to earth than the Greek style. It focused on the "common man" and was directed to a simpler moral point. Zwingli took John Chrysostom as his model in preaching, while Luther took Augustine as his model.[57] Both Latin and Greek styles included a verse-by-verse commentary form as well as a paraphrasing form.[58]

Even so, Chrysostom and Augustine stood in the lineage of the Greek sophists. They gave us polished Christian rhetoric. They gave us the "Christian" sermon: biblical in content, but Greek in style.[59]

THE REFORMERS, THE PURITANS, AND THE GREAT AWAKENING

During medieval times, the Eucharist dominated the Roman Catholic Mass, and preaching took a backseat. But with the coming of Mar-

---

[51] The enthusiastic applause from an audience to a sophist's homily was a Greek custom.
[52] Schaff, *History of the Christian Church*, 3:938.
[53] Durant, *Age of Faith*, 65.
[54] Norrington, *To Preach or Not*, 23.
[55] Niebuhr and Williams, *Ministry in Historical Perspectives*, 71.
[56] Brilioth, *Brief History of Preaching*, 31, 42.
[57] Senn, *Christian Liturgy*, 366. Both Lutheran and Reformed preaching tended to be a verse-by-verse exposition. This was characteristic of the patristic fathers like Chrysostom and Augustine.
[58] John McGuckin, professor of early church history at Union Theological Seminary, e-mail message to Frank Viola, September 29, 2002.
[59] Norrington, *To Preach or Not*, 23

tin Luther, the sermon was again given prominence in the worship service.[60] Luther viewed the church as the gathering of those who listen to the Word of God being spoken to them. For this reason, he once called the church building a *Mundhaus* (mouth-house or speech-house)![61]

Taking his cue from Luther, John Calvin argued that the preacher is the "mouth of God."[62] (Ironically, both men vehemently railed against the idea that the pope was the vicar of Christ.) It is not surprising that many of the Reformers had studied rhetoric and were deeply influenced by the Greco-Roman sermons of Augustine, Chrysostom, Origen, and Gregory the Great.[63]

Thus the flaws of the church fathers were duplicated by the Reformers and the Protestant subcultures that were created by them. This was especially true of the Puritans.[64] In fact, the contemporary evangelical preaching tradition finds its most recent roots in the Puritan movement of the seventeenth century and the Great Awakening of the eighteenth century.

The Puritans borrowed their preaching method from Calvin. What was that method? It was the systematic exposition of Scripture week after week. It was a method taken from the early church fathers that became popular during the Renaissance. Renaissance scholars would provide a sentence-by-sentence commentary on a writing from classical antiquity. Calvin was a master at this form. Before his conversion, he employed this style while writing a commentary on a work by the pagan author Seneca. When he was converted and turned to sermonizing, he applied the same analytical style to the Bible.

Following the path of John Calvin, the Puritans centered all

---

[60] White, *Protestant Worship*, 46–47.

[61] Niebuhr and Williams, *Ministry in Historical Perspectives*, 114.

[62] Thomson, *Preaching as Dialogue*, 9–10.

[63] Old, *Patristic Roots of Reformed Worship*, 79ff.

[64] Tracing the evolution of sermon *content* from the Reformation to today is beyond the scope of this book. Suffice it to say that sermons during the Enlightenment period degenerated into barren moral discourses for improving human society. The Puritans brought back the verse-by-verse expositional preaching that began with the church fathers. Social justice themes became prominent in nineteenth-century Methodism. And with the advent of Frontier-Revivalism, preaching in evangelical churches was dominated by a salvation call. The Puritans also made contributions to modern sermonic rhetoric. Their sermons were written out ahead of time in a four-part outline (Scripture reading, theological statement, proof and illustration of doctrine, and application) with a detailed organizational structure. White, *Protestant Worship*, 53, 121, 126, 166, 183; Allen C. Guelzo, "When the Sermon Reigned," *Christian History* 13, no.1 (1994): 24–25.

their church services around a systematic teaching of the Bible. As they sought to Protestantize England (purifying it from the flaws of Anglicanism), the Puritans centered all of their church services around highly structured, methodical, logical, verse-by-verse expositions of Scripture. They stressed that Protestantism was a religion of "the Book." (Ironically, "the Book" knows nothing of this type of sermon.)

The Puritans also invented a form of preaching called "plain-style." This style was rooted in the memorization of sermon notes. Their dividing, subdividing, and analyzing of a biblical text raised the sermon to a fine science.[65] This form is still used today by countless pastors. In addition, the Puritans gave us the one-hour sermon (though some Puritan sermons lasted ninety minutes), the practice of congregants taking notes on the sermon, the tidy four-part sermon outline, and the pastor's use of crib notes while delivering his oration.[66]

Another influence, the Great Awakening, is responsible for the kind of preaching that was common in early Methodist churches and is still used in contemporary Pentecostal churches. Strong outbursts of emotion, which include screaming and running up and down the platform, are all carryovers from this tradition.[67]

Summing up the origin of the contemporary sermon, we can say the following: Christianity had taken Greco-Roman rhetoric and adapted it for its own purposes, baptized it, and wrapped it in swaddling clothes. The Greek homily made its way into the Christian church around the second century. It reached its height in the pulpit orators of the fourth century—namely Chrysostom and Augustine.[68]

The Christian sermon lost its prominence from the fifth century until the Reformation, when it became encased and enshrined

---

[65] Meic Pearse and Chris Matthews, *We Must Stop Meeting Like This* (E. Sussex, UK: Kingsway Publications, 1999), 92–95.

[66] White, *Protestant Worship*, 53, 121, 126, 166, 183; Guelzo, "When the Sermon Reigned," 24–25. The ghosts of Puritan preaching are still with us today. Every time you hear a Protestant pastor sermonize, underneath you will find the Puritan sermon style which has its roots in pagan rhetoric.

[67] Pearse and Matthews, *We Must Stop Meeting Like This*, 95.

[68] Brilioth, *Brief History of Preaching*, 22.

as the central focus of the Protestant worship service. Yet for the last five centuries, most Christians have never questioned its origin or its effectiveness.[69]

HOW SERMONIZING HARMS THE CHURCH

Though revered for five centuries, the conventional sermon has negatively impacted the church in a number of ways.

First, the sermon makes the preacher the virtuoso performer of the regular church gathering. As a result, congregational participation is hampered at best and precluded at worst. The sermon turns the church into a preaching station. The congregation degenerates into a group of muted spectators who watch a performance. There is no room for interrupting or questioning the preacher while he is delivering his discourse. The sermon freezes and imprisons the functioning of the body of Christ. It fosters a docile priesthood by allowing pulpiteers to dominate the church gathering week after week.[70]

Second, the sermon often stalemates spiritual growth. Because it is a one-way affair, it encourages passivity. The sermon prevents the church from functioning as intended. It suffocates mutual ministry. It smothers open participation. This causes the spiritual growth of God's people to take a nosedive.[71]

As Christians, we must function if we are to mature (see Mark 4:24-25 and Hebrews 10:24-25). We do not grow by passive listening week after week. In fact, one of the goals of New Testament–styled preaching and teaching is to get each of us to function (Ephesians 4:11-16).[72] It is to encourage us to open our mouths in the church meeting (1 Corinthians 12–14).[73] The conventional sermon hinders this very process.

---

[69] The nineteenth-century historian Edwin Hatch was one of the first to challenge the sermon.
[70] The sermon sells itself as the major facilitator of Christian growth. But this idea is both misleading and misdirected.
[71] For more on this topic, see Viola, *Reimagining Church.*
[72] This passage also points out that functioning is necessary for spiritual maturity.
[73] The meeting that is described in this passage is clearly a church gathering.

Third, the sermon preserves the unbiblical clergy mentality. It creates an excessive and pathological dependence on the clergy. The sermon makes the preacher the religious specialist—the only one having anything worthy to say. Everyone else is treated as a second-class Christian—a silent pew warmer. (While this is not usually voiced, it is the unspoken reality.)[74]

How can the pastor learn from the other members of the body of Christ when they are muted? How can the church learn fully from the pastor when its members cannot ask him questions during his oration?[75] How can the brothers and sisters learn from one another if they are prevented from speaking in the meetings?

The sermon makes "church" both distant and impersonal.[76] It deprives the pastor of receiving spiritual sustenance from the church. And it deprives the church of receiving spiritual nourishment from one another. For these reasons, the sermon is one of the biggest roadblocks to a functioning priesthood![77]

Fourth, rather than equipping the saints, the sermon de-skills them. It matters not how loudly ministers drone on about "equipping the saints for the work of the ministry," the truth is that the contemporary sermon preached every week has little power to equip God's people for spiritual service and functioning.[78] Unfortunately, however, many of God's people are just as addicted to hearing sermons as many preachers are addicted to preaching them.[79] By contrast, New Testament–styled preaching and teaching equips the church so that it can function without the presence of a clergyman.[80]

For instance, I (Frank) recently attended a conference where a

---

74 Some pastors have been known to give voice to the mindless idea that "all that sheep do is say 'baa' and eat grass."

75 Reuel L. Howe, *Partners in Preaching: Clergy and Laity in Dialogue* (New York: Seabury Press, 1967), 36.

76 George W. Swank, *Dialogical Style in Preaching* (Valley Forge: Hudson Press, 1981), 24.

77 Kevin Craig, "Is the Sermon Concept Biblical?" *Searching Together* 15, no. 1-2 (1986), 22.

78 While many pastors talk about "equipping the saints" and "liberating the laity," promises to free the flaccid laity and equip the church for ministry virtually always prove to be empty. So long as the pastor is still dominating the church service by his sermonics, God's people are not free to function in the gathering. Therefore, "equipping the saints" is typically empty rhetoric.

79 For those of us who regard the sermon to be exotically boring, we understand the feeling of being "preached to death." The quote by the nineteenth-century English writer and clergyman Sydney Smith captures the sentiment: "He deserves to be preached to death by wild curates!"

80 Consider Paul's method of preaching to an infant church, then leaving it on its own for long periods of time. For details, see Frank Viola, *So You Want to Start a House Church? First-Century Styled Church Planting for Today* (Jacksonville, FL: Present Testimony Ministry, 2003).

contemporary church planter spent an entire weekend with a network of house churches. Each day, the church planter submerged the churches in a revelation of Jesus Christ. But he also gave them very practical instruction on *how* to experience what he preached. He then left them on their own, and he probably will not return for months. The churches, having been equipped that weekend, have been having their own meetings where every member has contributed something of Christ in the gathering through exhortations, encouragements, teachings, testimonies, writing new songs, poems, etc. This is essentially New Testament apostolic ministry.

Fifth, today's sermon is often impractical. Countless preachers speak as experts on that which they have never experienced. Whether it be abstract/theoretical, devotional/inspirational, demanding/compelling, or entertaining/amusing, the sermon fails to put the hearers into a direct, practical experience of what has been preached. Thus the typical sermon is a swimming lesson on dry land! It lacks any practical value. Much is preached, but little ever lands. Most of it is aimed at the frontal lobe. Contemporary pulpiteerism generally fails to get beyond disseminating information and on to equipping believers to experience and use that which they have heard.

In this regard, the sermon mirrors its true father—Greco-Roman rhetoric. Greco-Roman rhetoric was bathed in abstraction.[81] It "involved forms designed to entertain and display genius rather than instruct or develop talents in others."[82] The contemporary polished sermon can warm the heart, inspire the will, and stimulate the mind. But it rarely if ever shows the team how to leave the huddle. In all of these ways, the contemporary sermon fails to meet its billing at promoting the kind of spiritual growth it promises. In the end, it actually intensifies the impoverishment of the church.[83] The sermon acts like a momentary stimulant. Its effects are often short-lived.

Let's be honest. There are scores of Christians who have been

[81] Craig, "Is the Sermon Concept Biblical?" 25.
[82] Norrington, *To Preach or Not*, 23.
[83] Clyde H. Reid, *The Empty Pulpit* (New York: Harper & Row Publishers, 1967), 47–49.

sermonized for decades, and they are still babes in Christ.[84] We Christians are not transformed simply by hearing sermons week after week. We are transformed by regular encounters with the Lord Jesus Christ.[85] Those who minister, therefore, are called to preach Christ and not information about Him. They are also called to make their ministry intensely practical. They are called not only to reveal Christ by the spoken word, but to show their hearers how to experience, know, follow, and serve Him. The contemporary sermon too often lacks these all-important elements.

If a preacher cannot bring his hearers into a living spiritual experience of that which he is ministering, the results of his message will be short-lived. Therefore, the church needs fewer pulpiteers and more spiritual facilitators. It is in dire need of those who can proclaim Christ and know how to deploy God's people to experience Him who has been preached.[86] And on top of that, Christians need instruction on how to share this living Christ with the rest of the church for their mutual edification.

Consequently, the Christian family needs a restoration of the biblical practice of mutual exhortation and mutual ministry.[87] For the New Testament hinges spiritual transformation upon these two things.[88] Granted, the gift of teaching is present in the church. But teaching is to come from all the believers (1 Corinthians 14:26, 31) as well as from those who are specially gifted to teach (Ephesians 4:11, James 3:1). We move far outside of biblical bounds when we allow teaching to take the form of a conventional sermon and relegate it to a class of professional orators.

---

[84] Alexander R. Hay, *The New Testament Order for Church and Missionary* (Audubon, NJ: New Testament Missionary Union, 1947), 292–293, 414.

[85] One may encounter Christ either in glory or in suffering (2 Corinthians 3:18; Hebrews 12:1ff.).

[86] Acts 3:20, 5:42, 8:5, 9:20; Galatians 1:6; Colossians 1:27-28. Whether one is preaching (*kerygma*) to unbelievers or teaching (*didache*) believers, the message to both believer and unbeliever alike is Jesus Christ. C. H. Dodd, *The Apostolic Preaching and Its Developments* (London: Hodder and Stoughton, 1963), 7ff. Speaking of the early church, Michael Green writes, "They preached a person. Their message was frankly Christocentric. Indeed, the gospel is referred to simply as Jesus or Christ: 'He preached Jesus to him . . . Jesus the man, Jesus crucified, Jesus risen, Jesus exalted to the place of power in the universe . . . Jesus who meantime was present among His people in the Spirit. . . . The risen Christ was unambiguously central in their message." Green, *Evangelism in the Early Church* (London: Hodder and Stoughton, 1970), 150.

[87] For more on this topic, see Viola, *Reimagining Church*.

[88] Hebrews 3:12-13, 10:24-26. Notice the emphasis on "one another" in these passages. It is *mutual* exhortation that the author has in view.

WRAPPING IT UP

Is preaching and teaching the Word of God scriptural? Yes, absolutely. But the contemporary pulpit sermon is not the equivalent of the preaching and teaching that is found in the Scriptures.[89] It cannot be found in the Judaism of the Old Testament, the ministry of Jesus, or the life of the primitive church.[90] What is more, Paul told his Greek converts that he refused to be influenced by the communication patterns of his pagan contemporaries (1 Corinthians 1:17, 22; 2:1-5).

But what about 1 Corinthians 9:22-23 (NLT), where Paul says, "I try to find common ground with everyone, doing everything I can to save some"? We would argue that this would *not* include making a weekly sermon the focus of all worship gatherings, which would have stifled the believers' transformation and mutual edification.

The sermon was conceived in the womb of Greek rhetoric. It was born into the Christian community when pagans-turned-Christians began to bring their oratorical styles of speaking into the church. By the third century, it became common for Christian leaders to deliver a sermon. By the fourth century it became the norm.[91]

Christianity has absorbed its surrounding culture.[92] When your pastor mounts his pulpit wearing his clerical robes to deliver his sacred sermon, he is unknowingly playing out the role of the ancient Greek orator.

Nevertheless, despite the fact that the contemporary sermon does not have a shred of biblical merit to support its existence, it continues to be uncritically admired in the eyes of most present-day Christians. It has become so entrenched in the Christian mind that most Bible-believing pastors and laymen fail to see that they are affirming and perpetuating an unscriptural practice out of sheer tradition. The sermon has become permanently embedded in a

---

[89] Craig A. Evans, "Preacher and Preaching: Some Lexical Observations," *Journal of the Evangelical Theological Society* 24, no. 4 (December 1981), 315–322.
[90] Norrington, *To Preach or Not*, 69.
[91] Ibid.
[92] George T. Purves, "The Influence of Paganism on Post-Apostolic Christianity," *The Presbyterian Review* 36 (October 1888): 529–554.

complex organizational structure that is far removed from New Testament church life.[93]

In view of all that we have discovered about the contemporary sermon, consider these questions:

How can a man preach a sermon on being faithful to the Word of God while he is preaching a sermon? And how can a Christian passively sit in a pew and affirm the priesthood of all believers when he is passively sitting in a pew? To put a finer point on it, how can you claim to uphold the Protestant doctrine of sola scriptura ("by the Scripture only") and still support the pulpit sermon?

As one author so eloquently put it, "The sermon is, in practice, beyond criticism. It has become an end in itself, sacred—the product of a distorted reverence for 'the tradition of the elders' . . . it seems strangely inconsistent that those who are most disposed to claim that the Bible is the Word of God, the 'supreme guide in all matters of faith and practice' are amongst the first to reject biblical methods in favor of the 'broken cisterns' of their fathers (Jeremiah 2:13)."[94]

In light of what you have read in this chapter, is there really any room in the church's corral for sacred cows like the sermon?

>delving DEEPER

1. You take issue with making the proclamation of the Word the center of the church meeting. However, Paul seems to emphasize preaching when instructing Timothy. In 2 Timothy 4:2, he tells him: "Preach the Word; be prepared in season and out of season; correct, rebuke and encourage—with great patience and careful instruction" (NIV).

Timothy was an apostolic worker. His role was to equip God's people to function and to know the Lord. It was also to win lost souls with a view to building the church. (In 2 Timothy 4:5, Paul tells Timothy to "do the work of an evangelist.")

Therefore, preaching the Word of God is part of the apostolic call. Timothy certainly did this, just as Paul did when he preached in the marketplace in Athens and

93 See also chapter 5.
94 Norrington, *To Preach or Not*, 102, 104.

in the hall of Tyrannus in Ephesus. Those were apostolic meetings designed for equipping the church and for building the community by converting people to Christ.

By contrast, the normative church meeting is when every member of the church comes together to share his or her portion of Christ (1 Corinthians 14:26, Colossians 3:16, Hebrews 10:24-25). All are free to teach, preach, prophesy, pray, and lead a song.

2. Greeks and Romans may have used rhetoric to titillate a crowd; however, why does that fact make including the principles of rhetoric and verse-by-verse commentary wrong? After all, God tells us to love Him with "all our mind," as well as with all our heart and soul.

The point of our argument is that the sermon originated from Greco-Roman paganism rather than from Jesus or the apostles. It is for the reader to decide whether or not the Greco-Roman sermon is wrong or right—an improved development to apostolic preaching or a departure from it.

3. When you describe the work of a church planter, you say he "submerged the churches in a revelation of Jesus Christ." What exactly does that mean, and how do you think this experience affects how a church body assembles together?

The first-century church planters had a deep and profound revelation (or insight) of Jesus Christ. They knew Him, and they knew Him well. He was their life, their breath, and their reason for living. They, in turn, imparted that same revelation to the churches they planted. John 1:1-3 is a good example of this dynamic.

Paul of Tarsus preached a message of Christ that was so profound that it caused immoral, blood-drinking pagans to become full-fledged Christians in love with Jesus Christ in just a few short months. (These new believers made up the churches of Pisidian Antioch, Iconium, Lystra, Derbe, Philippi, Thessalonica, and Berea [Acts 13–17].) Paul shared the depths of Christ with them in such a way that they knew that they were holy in His eyes and that they could know Him internally, for Christ indwelt them. This profound, personal understanding of the indwelling Christ affected how they gathered together and what they did in those gatherings.

Furthermore, Paul typically spent several months with these new converts and then left them on their own for long periods of time, sometimes years. And when he returned, they were still gathering together, still loving one another, and still following their Lord.

What kind of gospel did he preach to cause this kind of remarkable effect? He called it "the unsearchable riches of Christ" (Ephesians 3:8, NIV). To put it another way, he submerged them in a revelation of Jesus Christ.

4. It almost sounds like you are arguing against preaching and teaching. Is that what you are saying? If not, what are you arguing?

We strongly believe in preaching, teaching, prophesying, exhorting, and all forms of sharing the Word of God. We are simply saying that the modern sermon, which we define as the *same* person (usually a clergyman) giving an oration to the *same* group of people week after week, month after month, and year after year is not only unbiblical, it is counterproductive. We want readers to look at the biblical and historical evidence for this point and decide for themselves whether or not we are correct in our analysis. In fact, research conducted by The Barna Group has shown that sermons are generally ineffective at facilitating worship, at drawing people closer to God, and at conveying life-changing information to those in the audience.

chapter five

> THE PASTOR: OBSTACLE TO EVERY-MEMBER FUNCTIONING

"It is a universal tendency in the Christian religion, as in many other religions, to give a theological interpretation to institutions which have developed gradually through a period of time for the sake of practical usefulness, and then read that interpretation back into the earliest periods and infancy of these institutions, attaching them to an age when in fact nobody imagined that they had such a meaning."
—RICHARD HANSON, TWENTIETH-CENTURY PATRISTIC SCHOLAR

"I majored in Bible in college. I went to the seminary and I majored in the only thing they teach there: the professional ministry. When I graduated, I realized that I could speak Latin, Greek, and Hebrew, and the only thing on earth I was qualified for was to be pope. But someone else had the job."
—ANONYMOUS PASTOR

THE PASTOR. He is the fundamental figure of the Protestant faith. So prevailing is the pastor in the minds of most

Christians that he is often better known, more highly praised, and more heavily relied upon than Jesus Christ Himself!

Remove the pastor and most Protestant churches would be thrown into a panic. Remove the pastor, and Protestantism as we know it would die. The pastor is the dominating focal point, mainstay, and centerpiece of the contemporary church. He is the embodiment of Protestant Christianity.

But here is the profound irony. There is not a single verse in the entire New Testament that supports the existence of the modern-day pastor! He simply did not exist in the early church.

Note that we are using the term *pastor* throughout this chapter to depict the contemporary pastoral office and role, not the specific individual who fills this role. By and large, those who serve in the office of pastor are wonderful people. They are honorable, decent, and very often gifted Christians who love God and have a zeal to serve His people. But it is the role they fill that both Scripture and church history are opposed to.[1]

THE PASTOR IS IN THE BIBLE . . . RIGHT?

The word *pastors* does appear in the New Testament:

And He gave some as apostles, and some as prophets, and some as evangelists, and some as pastors *and teachers.*

(EPHESIANS 4:11, NASB, AUTHORS' EMPHASIS)

The following observations are to be made about this text.

> This is the only verse in the entire New Testament where the word *pastor* is used.[2] One solitary verse is a mighty scanty piece of evidence on which to hang the Protestant faith! In this regard, there seems to be more biblical authority for snake handling (see Mark 16:18 and Acts 28:3-6) than there is for

---

[1] Today those who feel called to the ministry of the local church generally believe their options are limited to serving as a pastor or worship leader. While being called to the Lord's work is definitely a real experience, these positions did not exist in the first century. Nevertheless, though their office is without scriptural basis, pastors often do help people. But they help people *despite* their office, not because of it.

[2] A derivative form of the word *poimen* is used in Acts 20:28 and 1 Peter 5:2-3.

the present-day pastor. Roman Catholics have made the same error with the word *priest*. You can find the word *priest* used in the New Testament three times. In every case, it refers to all Christians.[3]

> The word is used in the plural. It is *pastors*. This is significant. For whoever these "pastors" are, they are plural in the church, not singular. Consequently, there is no biblical support for the practice of sola pastora (single pastor).

> The Greek word translated *pastors* is *poimenas*. It means shepherds. (*Pastor* is the Latin word for shepherd.) *Pastor*, then, is a metaphor to describe a particular function in the church. It is not an office or a title.[4] A first-century shepherd had nothing to do with the specialized and professional sense it has come to have in contemporary Christianity. Therefore, Ephesians 4:11 does not envision a pastoral office, but merely one of many functions in the church. Shepherds are those who naturally provide nurture and care for God's sheep. It is a profound error, therefore, to confuse shepherds with an office or title as is commonly conceived today.[5]

> At best, Ephesians 4:11 is oblique. It offers absolutely no definition or description of who pastors are. It simply mentions them. Regrettably, we have filled this word with our own Western concept of what a pastor is. We have read our idea of the contemporary pastor back into the New Testament. Never would any first-century Christian have conceived of the contemporary pastoral office!

Richard Hanson observes, "For us the words bishops, presbyters, and deacons are stored with the associations of nearly two thousand

---

[3] Revelation 1:6, 5:10, 20:6. R. Paul Stevens, *The Other Six Days: Vocation, Work, and Ministry in Biblical Perspective* (Grand Rapids: Eerdmans, 1999), 173–181.

[4] Banks, *Paul's Idea of Community*, 131–135. The New Testament never uses the secular Greek words for civil and religious authorities to depict ministers in the church. Further, even though most New Testament authors were steeped in the Jewish priestly system of the Old Testament, they never use *hiereus* (priest) to refer to Christian ministry. Ordination to office presupposes a static and definable church leadership role that did not exist in the apostolic churches. Marjorie Warkentin, *Ordination: A Biblical-Historical View* (Grand Rapids: Eerdmans, 1982), 160–161, 166.

[5] The words of Job come to mind: "Let me not, I pray you, accept any man's person, neither let me give flattering titles unto man" (Job 32:21).

years. For the people who first used them, the titles of these offices can have meant little more than inspectors, older men and helpers. It was when unsuitable theological significance began to be attached to them that the distortion of the concept of Christian ministry began."[6]

First-century shepherds were the local elders (presbyters)[7] and overseers of the church.[8] Their function was at odds with the contemporary pastoral role.[9]

WHERE DID THE PASTOR COME FROM?

If contemporary pastors were absent from the early church, where did they come from? And how did they rise to such a prominent position in the Christian faith? The roots of this tale are tangled and complex, and they reach as far back as the fall of man.

With the Fall came an implicit desire in people to have a physical leader to bring them to God. For this reason, human societies throughout history have consistently created a special caste of revered religious leaders. The medicine man, the shaman, the rhapsodist, the miracle worker, the witch doctor, the soothsayer, the wise man, and the priest have all been with us since Adam's blunder.[10] And this person is always marked by special training, special garb, a special vocabulary, and a special way of life.[11]

We can see this instinct rear its ugly head in the history of ancient Israel. It made its first appearance during the time of Moses. Two servants of the Lord, Eldad and Medad, received God's Spirit and began to prophesy. In hasty response, a young zealot urged Moses to "restrain them" (Numbers 11:26-28, NASB). Moses reproved the

---

6 Hanson, *Christian Priesthood Examined*, 34–35.
7 This word is the spelling into English letters of the Greek word for "elder" (*presbuteros*).
8 The terms *overseers* and *servants* were ecclesiasticized into the words *bishops* and *deacons* (Smith, *From Christ to Constantine*, 32).
9 Christian Smith, *Going to the Root*, ch. 2–3; Jon Zens, *The Pastor* (St. Croix Falls, WI: Searching Together, 1981); Jon Zens, "The 'Clergy/Laity' Distinction: A Help or a Hindrance to the Body of Christ?" *Searching Together* 23, no. 4 (1995).
10 "Christianity . . . learnt from the example of pagan religions that most men find it difficult to understand or approach God without the aid of a man who in some sense stands for God, represents Him, and feels called to devote himself to this representative ministry" (Hanson, *Christian Priesthood Examined*, 100).
11 Walter Klassen, "New Presbyter Is Old Priest Writ Large," *Concern* 17 (1969): 5. See also W. Klassen, J. L. Burkholder, and John Yoder, *The Relation of Elders to the Priesthood of Believers* (Washington, DC: Sojourners Book Service, 1969).

young suppressor saying he wished all of God's people could prophesy. Moses had set himself against a clerical spirit that had tried to control God's people.

We see it again when Moses ascended Mount Horeb. The people wanted Moses to be a physical mediator between them and God because they feared a personal relationship with the Almighty (Exodus 20:19).

This fallen instinct made another appearance during the time of Samuel. God wanted His people to live under His direct headship. But Israel clamored for a human king instead (1 Samuel 8:19).

The seeds of the contemporary pastor can even be detected in the New Testament era. Diotrephes, who "love[d] to have the preeminence" in the church, illegitimately took control of its affairs (3 John 9-10). In addition, some scholars have suggested that the doctrine of the Nicolaitans that Jesus condemns in Revelation 2:6 is a reference to the rise of an early clergy.[12]

Alongside humanity's fallen quest for a human spiritual mediator is the obsession with the hierarchical form of leadership. All ancient cultures were hierarchical in their social structures to one degree or another. Regrettably, the postapostolic Christians adopted and adapted these structures into their church life as we shall see.

THE BIRTH OF ONE-BISHOP RULE

Up until the second century, the church had no official leadership. That it had leaders is without dispute. But leadership was unofficial in the sense that there were no religious "offices" or sociological slots to fill. New Testament scholarship makes this abundantly clear.[13]

In this regard, the first-century churches were an oddity indeed.

---

[12] F. W. Grant, *Nicolaitanism or the Rise and Growth of Clerisy* (Bedford, PA: MWTB, n.d.), 3–6. The Greek word *nicolaitane* means "conquering the people." *Nikos* means "to conquer over" and *laos* means "the people." Grant believes that Nicolaitans are those who make "laity" out of God's people by raising up "clergy" to lord it over them. See also Alexander Hay, *What Is Wrong in the Church?* (Audubon, NJ: New Testament Missionary Union, n.d.), 54.

[13] See Banks, *Paul's Idea of Community*, 131–135. The word *office* has no analog in the Greek New Testament when referring to Christian leaders. We read these conventions of human sociological organization back into our New Testament.

They were religious groups without priest, temple, or sacrifice.[14] The Christians themselves led the church under Christ's direct headship. Leaders were organic, untitled, and were recognized by their service and spiritual maturity rather than by a title or an office.

Among the flock were the elders (shepherds or overseers). These men all had equal standing. There was no hierarchy among them.[15] Also present were extra-local workers who planted churches. These were called "sent ones" or apostles. But they did not take up residency in the churches for which they cared. Nor did they control them.[16] The vocabulary of New Testament leadership allows no pyramidal structures. It is rather a language of horizontal relationships that includes exemplary action.[17]

Church leadership began to formalize at about the time of the death of the itinerant apostolic workers (church planters). In the late first and early second centuries, local presbyters began to emerge as the resident "successors" to the unique leadership role played by the apostolic workers. This gave rise to a single leading figure in each church.[18] Without the influence of the extra-local workers who had been mentored by the New Testament apostles, the church began to drift toward the organizational patterns of her surrounding culture.[19]

Ignatius of Antioch (35–107) was instrumental in this shift. He was the first figure in church history to take a step down the slippery slope toward a single leader in the church. We can trace the origin of the contemporary pastor and church hierarchy to him. Ignatius elevated one of the elders in each church above all the others.

---

14 James D. G. Dunn, *New Testament Theology in Dialogue* (Philadelphia: Westminster Press, 1987), 123, 127–129.

15 In the writings of the early church fathers, the words *shepherd, overseer,* and *elder* are always used interchangeably, as is the case in the New Testament. F. F. Bruce states, "That the language of the New Testament does not allow us to press a distinction between the Greek word translated 'bishop' (*episkopos*) and that translated 'elder' (*presbyteros*) need not be argued at length. Paul could address the assembled *elders* of the church of Ephesus as those whom the Holy Spirit had made *bishops*. Later, in the Pastoral Epistles (those to Timothy and Titus), the two terms still appear to be used interchangeably" (*The Spreading Flame* [Grand Rapids: Eerdmans, 1958] 65). In fact, bishops, elders, and shepherds (always in the plural) continue to be regarded as identical in the writings of 1 Clement, the *Didache,* and *The Shepherd of Hermas.* They were seen as identical up until the beginning of the second century. See also Mackinnon, *Calvin and the Reformation,* 80–81; Ferguson, *Early Christians Speak,* 169–173.

16 See Viola, *Reimagining Church* for details.

17 1 Corinthians 11:1; 2 Thessalonians 3:9; 1 Timothy 4:12; 1 Peter 5:3.

18 Ferguson, *Early Christians Speak,* 172.

19 In his book *To Preach or Not to Preach?* David Norrington gives an in-depth discussion of how hierarchical structures and ecclesiastical specialists began to emerge in the church (pp. 24–25).

The elevated elder was now called the bishop. All the responsibilities that belonged to the college of elders were exercised by the bishop.[20]

In AD 107, Ignatius wrote a series of letters when on his way to be martyred in Rome. Six out of seven of these letters strike the same chord. They exalt the authority and importance of the bishop's office.[21]

According to Ignatius, the bishop had ultimate power and should be obeyed absolutely. Consider the following excerpts from his letters: "Plainly therefore we ought to regard the bishop as the Lord Himself. . . . All of you follow the bishop as Jesus Christ follows the Father. . . . Wherever the bishop shall appear, there will the people be; even as where Jesus may be. . . . It is not lawful apart from the bishop either to baptize or to hold a love feast; but whatever he shall approve, this is well-pleasing also to God. . . . It is good to recognize God and the bishop. He that honors the bishop is honored of God. . . . Do nothing without the bishop. . . . Therefore as the Lord did nothing without the Father, being united with Him, either by Himself or by the Apostles, so neither do you anything without the bishop and the presbyters. . . . You should look on your bishop as a type of the Father."[22]

For Ignatius, the bishop stood in the place of God while the presbyters, or elders, stood in the place of the twelve apostles.[23] It fell to the bishop alone to celebrate the Lord's Supper, conduct baptisms, give counsel, discipline church members, approve marriages, and preach sermons.[24]

The elders sat with the bishop at the Lord's Supper. But it was the bishop who presided over it. He took charge of leading public prayers

---

[20] Ferguson, *Early Christians Speak*, 173.

[21] Bruce, *Spreading Flame*, 203–204.

[22] Epistle to the Ephesians, 6:1; Epistle to the Smyrnaeans, 8:1-2; Epistle to the Philadelphians, 7:1; Epistle to the Magnesians, 7:1; Epistle to the Trallians, 3:1. Ignatius's epistles are replete with this sort of language. See *Early Christian Writings: The Apostolic Fathers* (New York: Dorset Press, 1968), 75–130.

[23] Edwin Hatch, *The Organization of the Early Christian Churches* (London: Longmans, Green, and Co., 1895), 106, 185; *Early Christian Writings*, 88. Hatch's book shows that the gradual evolution of the organization of the church and various elements of that organization were borrowed from Greco-Roman society.

[24] Robert M. Grant, *The Apostolic Fathers: A New Translation and Commentary*, vol. 11 (New York: Thomas Nelson & Sons, 1964), 58, 171.

and ministry.[25] Only in the most extreme cases could a layman take the Lord's Supper without the bishop present.[26] For the bishop, said Ignatius, must "preside" over the elements and distribute them.

In Ignatius's mind, the bishop was the remedy for dispelling false doctrine and establishing church unity.[27] Ignatius believed that if the church would survive the onslaught of heresy, it had to develop a rigid power structure patterned after the centralized political structure of Rome.[28] Single-bishop rule would rescue the church from heresy and internal strife.[29]

Historically this is known as the "monoepiscopate" or "the monarchical episcopacy." It is the type of organization where the bishop is distinguished from the elders (the presbytery) and ranks above them.

At the time of Ignatius, the one-bishop rule had not caught on in other regions.[30] But by the mid-second century, this model was firmly established in most churches.[31] By the end of the third century, it prevailed everywhere.[32]

The bishop eventually became the main administrator and distributor of the church's wealth.[33] He was the man responsible for teaching the faith and knowing what Christianity was all about.[34] The congregation, once active, was now rendered passive. God's people merely watched the bishop perform.

In effect, the bishop became the solo pastor of the church[35]—the professional in common worship.[36] He was seen as the spokesperson

---

[25] R. Alastair Campbell, *The Elders: Seniority within Earliest Christianity* (Edinburgh: T. & T. Clark, 1994), 229.

[26] Hatch, *Organization of the Early Christian Churches*, 124.

[27] Ibid., 100.

[28] Kenneth Strand, "The Rise of the Monarchical Episcopate," in *Three Essays on Early Church History* (Ann Arbor, MI: Braun-Brumfield, 1967); Warkentin, *Ordination: A Biblical-Historical View*, 175.

[29] Hanson, *Christian Priesthood Examined*, 69; *Early Christian Writings*, 63–72.

[30] Bruce, *Spreading Flame*, 66–69; Niebuhr and Williams, *Ministry in Historical Perspectives*, 23–25. When Ignatius wrote his letters, the one-bishop rule was being practiced in such Asian cities as Ephesus, Philadelphia, Magnesia, and Smyrna. But it had not yet reached Greece or cities in the West, such as Rome. It appears that the one-bishop rule moved in a westward direction from Syria across the Empire.

[31] Hanson, *Christian Priesthood Examined*, 67; Bruce, *Spreading Flame*, 69. J. B. Lightfoot's "The Christian Ministry" in *Saint Paul's Epistle to the Philippians* (Wheaton, IL: Crossway, 1994) offers, in Frank's opinion, the most satisfactory explanation of the historical evidence of how the bishop gradually developed out of the presbytery.

[32] Niebuhr and Williams, *Ministry in Historical Perspectives*, 25.

[33] S. L. Greenslade, *Shepherding the Flock* (London: SCM Press, 1967), 8.

[34] Hanson, *Christian Priesthood Examined*, 68.

[35] Hatch, *Growth of Church Institutions*, 35.

[36] White, *Protestant Worship and Church Architecture*, 65–66.

and head of the congregation and the one who controlled all church activities. In short, he was the forerunner of the contemporary pastor.

FROM PRESBYTER TO PRIEST

Clement of Rome, who died in about 100, was the first Christian writer to make a distinction in status between Christian leaders and nonleaders. He was the first to use the word *laity* to distinguish them from the ministers.[37] Clement argued that the Old Testament order of priests should find fulfillment in the Christian church.[38]

Tertullian was the first writer to use the word *clergy* to refer to a separate class of Christians.[39] Both Tertullian and Clement popularized the word *clergy* in their writings.[40]

The New Testament, on the other hand, never uses the terms *clergy* and *laity* and does not support the concept that there are those who do ministry (clergy) and those to whom ministry is done (laity).[41] Thus what we have in Tertullian and Clement is a clear break from the New Testament Christian mind-set where all believers shared the same status. By the mid-third century, the authority of the bishop had hardened into a fixed office.[42]

Then Cyprian of Carthage appeared, furthering the impact. Cyprian was a former pagan orator and teacher of rhetoric.[43] When he became a Christian, he began to write prolifically. But Cyprian never abandoned some of his pagan ideas.

Due to Cyprian's influence, the door was open to resurrect the Old Testament economy of priests, temples, altars, and sacrifices.[44]

---

[37] 1 Clement 40:5. See also Ferguson, *Early Christians Speak*, 168; R. Paul Stevens, *The Abolition of the Laity* (Carlisle, UK: Paternoster Press, 1999), 5.

[38] Warkentin, *Ordination: A Biblical-Historical View*, 38.

[39] Tertullian, *On Monogamy*, 12.

[40] Stevens, *Abolition of the Laity*, 28.

[41] The term *laity* is derived from the Greek word *laos*, which means "the people" (see 1 Peter 2:9-10). The term *clergy* is derived from the Greek word *kleros*, which means "a lot, a share, or an inheritance." The New Testament never uses the word *kleros* for leaders. It rather uses it for the whole people of God. For it is God's people that are God's inheritance (see Ephesians 1:11; Galatians 3:29; Colossians 1:12; 1 Peter 5:3). In this connection, it is ironic that Peter in 1 Peter 5:3 exhorts the elders of the church to not lord over the *kleros* ("clergy")! Again, *kleros* and *laos* both refer to the whole of God's flock.

[42] J. G. Davies, *The Early Christian Church: A History of Its First Five Centuries* (Grand Rapids: Baker Books, 1965), 92. For a brief synopsis of how the clergy developed, see Stevens, *Other Six Days*, 39–48.

[43] "Come and See" Icons, Books, and Art, "St. Cyprian of Carthage," http://www.comeandseeicons.com/c/phm12.htm.

[44] Nichols, *Corporate Worship*, 25.

Bishops began to be called priests,[45] a custom that became common by the third century.[46] They were also called pastors on occasion.[47] In the third century, every church had its own bishop.[48] (At this time bishops were essentially heads over local churches. They were not diocesan superintendents as they are today in Roman Catholicism.) And bishops and presbyters together started to be called "the clergy."[49]

The origin of the unbiblical doctrine of "covering" can be laid at the feet of Cyprian also.[50] Cyprian taught that the bishop has no superior but God. He was accountable to God alone. Anyone who separated himself from the bishop separated himself from God.[51] Cyprian also taught that a portion of the Lord's flock was assigned to each individual shepherd (bishop).[52]

After the Council of Nicaea (325), bishops began to delegate the responsibility of the Lord's Supper to the presbyters.[53] Presbyters were little more than deputies of the bishop, exercising his authority in his churches.

Because the presbyters were the ones administering the Lord's Supper, they began to be called priests.[54] More startling, the bishop

---

[45] Ferguson, *Early Christians Speak*, 168. Cyprian normally called the bishop *sacerdos*, which is Latin for "priest." Sacerdotal language taken from the Old Testament to define church offices quickly caught on (Warkentin, *Ordination: A Biblical-Historical View*, 177; Smith, *From Christ to Constantine*, 136). J. B. Lightfoot wrote that the "sacerdotal view of the ministry is one of the most striking and important phenomena in the history of the church." "Christian Ministry," 144.

[46] Hanson, *Christian Priesthood Examined*, 35, 95. There is no evidence that anyone thought of Christian ministers as priests until the year AD 200. Tertullian is the first to apply the term *priest* to bishops and presbyters. Throughout his writings, he calls the bishop and the presbyters *sacerdos* (priests) and he calls the bishop *sacerdos summus* (high priest). He does so without any explanation, indicating that his readers were familiar with these titles (p. 38). See also Hans von Campenhausen, *Tradition and Life in the Church* (Philadelphia: Fortress Press, 1968), 220. Cyprian is also credited for saying that the bishop is the equivalent of the Old Testament high priest (Smith, *From Christ to Constantine*, 136). The historian Eusebius regularly calls clergy "priests" in his voluminous writings (Hanson, *Christian Priesthood Examined*, 61).

[47] "Thus it was the bishop, as chief pastor of the local church, who came to represent the fullness of the ministry. He was prophet, teacher, chief celebrant at the liturgical assembly, and chairman of the board of overseers of the Christian 'synagogue'" (Niebuhr and Williams, *Ministry in Historical Perspectives*, 28). Gregory the Great's work *The Book of Pastoral Rule* written in AD 591 is a discussion on the duties of the bishop's office. To Gregory, the bishop is a pastor, and preaching is one of his most important duties. Gregory's book is a Christian classic and is still used to train pastors in Protestant seminaries today. See also Philip Culbertson and Arthur Bradford Shippee, *The Pastor: Readings from the Patristic Period* (Minneapolis: Fortress Press, 1990).

[48] For a discussion of this development, see Ferguson, *Early Christians Speak*, 13–14.

[49] Niebuhr and Williams, *Ministry in Historical Perspectives*, 28.

[50] For a thorough discussion of this doctrine and its refutation, see Viola, *Reimagining Church*.

[51] Stevens, *Other Six Days*, 41–42.

[52] Cyprian said, "a portion of the flock has been assigned to each individual pastor, which he is to rule and govern, having to give account of his doing to the Lord" (*Letter to Cornelius of Rome*, LIV, 14). See also Hatch, *Organization of the Early Christian Churches*, 171.

[53] Niebuhr and Williams, *Ministry in Historical Perspectives*, 28–29.

[54] Campbell, *Elders*, 231; Niebuhr and Williams, *Ministry in Historical Perspectives*, 29.

came to be regarded as the high priest who could forgive sins![55] All of these trends obscured the New Testament reality that all believers are priests unto God.

By the fourth century, this graded hierarchy dominated the Christian faith.[56] The clergy caste was now cemented. At the head of the church stood the bishop. Under him was the college of presbyters. Under them stood the deacons.[57] And under all of them were the laymen. One-bishop rule became the accepted form of church government throughout the Roman Empire. (During this time, certain churches began to exercise authority over other churches—thus broadening the hierarchical structure.)[58]

By the end of the fourth century, the bishops walked with the great. As noted in chapter 2, Constantine was the first to give them tremendous privileges. They became involved in politics, which separated them further from the presbyters.[59] In his attempts to strengthen the bishop's office, Cyprian argued for an unbroken succession of bishops that traced back to Peter.[60] This idea is known as apostolic succession.[61]

Throughout his writings, Cyprian employed the official language of the Old Testament priesthood to justify this practice.[62] Like Tertullian (160–225) and Hippolytus (170–236) before him, Cyprian used the term *sacerdotes* to describe the presbyters and bishops.[63] But he went a step further.

---

[55] Davies, *Early Christian Church*, 131; *The Apostolic Tradition of Hippolytus*, trans. Burton S. Easton (Cambridge: Cambridge University Press, 1934). Hippolytus distinguishes sharply between the powers of the bishop and the presbyters. His writings give the bishop the power to forgive sins and to allot penance (Hanson, *Christian Priesthood Examined*, 39–40). Presbyters and deacons could only baptize with the bishop's authority (Campbell, *Elders*, 233).

[56] Davies, *Early Christian Church*, 187. In AD 318, Constantine recognized the jurisdiction of the bishop. In AD 333, the bishops were placed on an equal footing with Roman magistrates (p. 188).

[57] Hans Lietzmann, *A History of the Early Church*, vol. 2 (New York: The World Publishing Company, 1953), 247.

[58] According to the canons of the Council of Nicaea, Alexandria, Rome, and Antioch had special authority over the regions around them (Smith, *From Christ to Constantine*, 95).

[59] Hanson, *Christian Priesthood Examined*, 72. Hanson explains how the fall of the Roman Empire in the fifth century strengthened the bishop's office (pages 72–77).

[60] Ann Fremantle, ed., *A Treasury of Early Christianity* (New York: Viking Press, 1953), 301.

[61] Apostolic succession first appears in the writings of Clement of Rome and Irenaeus. It also appears in Hippolytus. But Cyprian turned it into a coherent doctrine. Grant, *Early Christianity and Society*, 38; Norman Sykes, *Old Priest and New Presbyter* (London: Cambridge University Press, 1956), 240.

[62] G. S. M. Walker, *The Churchmanship of St. Cyprian* (London: Lutterworth Press, 1968), 38. Many of the church fathers treated the Old Testament Scriptures as providing a normative ordering of the church. The use of Old Testament priest terminology for church officebearers became common as early as the second century (Warkentin, *Ordination: A Biblical-Historical View*, 50, 161; Hanson, *Christian Priesthood Examined*, 46, 51).

[63] Hanson, *Christian Priesthood Examined*, 59; Warkentin, *Ordination: A Biblical-Historical View*, 39.

The non–New Testament concept of sacerdotalism—the belief that there exists a divinely appointed person to mediate between God and the people—originated with Cyprian. He argued that because the Christian clergy were priests who offer the holy sacrifice (the Eucharist) they were sacrosanct (holy) themselves.[64]

We can also credit Cyprian with the notion that when the priest offered the Eucharist, he was actually offering up the death of Christ on behalf of the congregation.[65] To Cyprian's mind, the body and blood of Christ are once again sacrificed through the Eucharist.[66] Consequently, it is in Cyprian that we find the seeds of the medieval Catholic Mass.[67] This idea widened the wedge between clergy and laity. It also created an unhealthy dependence of the laity upon the clergy.

THE ROLE OF THE PRIEST

Until the Middle Ages, the presbyters (now commonly called "priests") played second fiddle to the bishop. But during the Middle Ages there was a shift. The presbyters began to represent the priesthood while the bishops were occupied with political duties.[68] The parish (local) priests became more central to the life of the church than the bishop.[69] The priest now stood in God's place and controlled the sacraments.

As Latin became the common language in the mid-fourth century, the priest would invoke the words *hoc est corpus meum*. These Latin words mean "This is my body."

With these words, the priest became the overseer of the mysterious happenings that were believed to have occurred during the Catholic Mass. Ambrose of Milan can be credited for the idea that the

---

[64] Hanson, *Christian Priesthood Examined*, 54.

[65] Ibid., 58. In both the *Didache* and 1 Clement, the Eucharist is referred to as a "sacrifice" and an "offering" performed by the bishops (von Campenhausen, *Tradition and Life in the Church*, 220).

[66] The word *sacrifice* as used in a liturgical sense first appears in the *Didache* (von Campenhausen, *Tradition and Life in the Church*, 220).

[67] The idea that the priest offers the sacrifice of Christ through the Eucharist is sacerdotalism. On this score, Richard Hanson poignantly remarks, "This sacerdotal concept of priesthood appears to obscure, if not actually abolish, the doctrine of the priesthood of all believers. It drains believers' priesthood all away into the priesthood of the clergy" (Hanson, *Christian Priesthood Examined*, 98).

[68] Ibid., 79.

[69] In the third century, each priest chose a bishop to oversee and coordinate his functioning. In the fourth century, things got more complex. Bishops needed supervision. Hence were born archbishops and metropolitans who governed the churches of a province (Durant, *Age of Faith*, 45, 756–760).

mere utterance of *hoc est corpus meum* supernaturally converted bread and wine into the Lord's physical body and blood.[70] (Some scholars say that the stage-magic phrase *hocus pocus* comes from *hoc est corpus meum*.) According to Ambrose, the priest was endowed with special powers to call God down out of heaven into bread.

Because of this sacramental function, the word *presbyteros* came to mean "sacerdos" (priest). Consequently, when the Latin word *presbyter* was taken into English, it had the meaning of "priest" rather than "elder."[71] Thus in the Roman Catholic church, *priest* was the widely used term to refer to the local presbyter.

THE INFLUENCE OF GRECO-ROMAN CULTURE

The Greco-Roman culture that surrounded the early Christians reinforced the graded hierarchy that was slowly infiltrating the church. Greco-Roman culture was hierarchical by nature. This influence seeped into the church when new converts brought their cultural baggage into the believing community.[72]

Human hierarchy and "official" ministry institutionalized the church of Jesus Christ. By the fourth century, these elements hardened the arteries of the once living, breathing ekklesia of God—within which ministry was functional, Spirit-led, organic, and shared by all believers.

By the fifth century, the concept of the priesthood of all believers had completely disappeared from Christian practice. Access to God was now controlled by the clergy caste. Clerical celibacy began to be enforced. Infrequent Communion became a regular habit of the so-called laity. The church building was now veiled with incense and smoke. Clergy prayers were said in secret. And the small but

---

[70] *Concerning the Mysteries*, 9:52, 54. In the Eastern churches a prayer is offered for the Spirit to do the magic. In the Western churches, the prayer was left out for the words themselves to do the trick (Dix, *Shape of the Liturgy*, 240–241, 275; Josef A. Jungmann, *The Mass of the Roman Rite*, vol. 1 [New York: Benziger, 1951], 52).

[71] Campbell, *Elders*, 234–235. The word *priest* is etymologically a contraction of "presbyter." By the close of the Old English period, the English term *priest* had become the current word for "presbyter" and "sacerdos" (Cross and Livingstone, *Oxford Dictionary of the Christian Church*, 1325).

[72] Hatch, *Organization of the Early Christian Churches*, 30–31.

profoundly significant screen that separated clergy from laity had been introduced.

The role of the bishop was also changing, elevating him from serving as the head of a local church to becoming the representative of everybody in a given area.[73] Bishops ruled over the churches just as Roman governors ruled over their provinces.[74] Eventually, the bishop of Rome was given the most authority of all, and his position finally evolved into the office of the pope.[75]

CONSTANTINE AND ROMAN HIERARCHY

The hierarchical leadership structure first emerged in ancient Egypt, Babylon, and Persia.[76] It was later carried over into the Greek and Roman culture where it was perfected.

Historian D. C. Trueman writes, "The Persians made two outstanding contributions to the ancient world: The organization of their empire and their religion. Both of these contributions have had considerable influence on our western world. The system of imperial administration was inherited by Alexander the Great, adopted by the Roman Empire, and eventually bequeathed to modern Europe."[77]

The social world into which Christianity spread was governed by a single ruler—the emperor. Soon after Constantine took the throne in the early fourth century, the church became a full-fledged, top-down, hierarchically organized society.[78]

---

[73] Hanson, *Christian Priesthood Examined*, 71.

[74] Robert F. Evans, *One and Holy: The Church in Latin and Patristic Thought* (London: S.P.C.K., 1972), 48.

[75] Before Constantine, the Roman bishop exercised no jurisdiction outside of Rome. While he was honored, he did not have that kind of ecclesiastical authority (Bruce Shelley, *Church History in Plain Language* [Waco, TX: Word, 1982], 151). The word *pope* comes from the title *papa*, a term used to express the fatherly care of any bishop. It was not until the sixth century that the term began to be used exclusively for the bishop of Rome. Here is a brief sketch of the origin of the Roman Catholic pope: At the end of the second century, Roman bishops were given great honor. Stephen I (d. 257) was the first to use the Petrine text (Matthew 16:18) to support the preeminence of the Roman bishop. But this was not universally held. The emergence of the modern pope can be traced to Leo the Great, who served from 440 to 461. Leo was the first to make a theological and biblical claim for the primacy of the Roman bishop. Under him, the primacy of Rome was finally established. With the coming of Gregory the Great (540–604), the "papal chair" was extended and enhanced. (Incidentally, Gregory became by far the largest landowner in Italy, setting a precedent for rich and powerful popes to follow.) By the mid-third century, the Roman church had 30,000 members, 150 clergymen, and 1,500 widows and poor people (Gonzalez, *Story of Christianity*, 1:242; Schaff, *History of the Christian Church*, vol:212, 218–219; Shelley, *Church History in Plain Language*, 150–151; Davies, *Early Christian Church*, 135–136, 250; Durant, *Age of Faith*, 521; Hanson, *Christian Priesthood Examined*, 76ff.). Gregory was also the first to use the term *servant of the servants of God* (Schaff, *History of the Christian Church*, 3:534; 4:329).

[76] Durant, *Caesar and Christ*, 670–671.

[77] D. C. Trueman, *The Pageant of the Past: The Origins of Civilization* (Toronto: Ryerson, 1965), 105.

[78] Grant, *Early Christianity and Society*, 11–12. "The organization of the church adapted itself to the political and geographical divisions of the Empire" (Schaff, *History of the Christian Church*, 3:7).

Edwin Hatch writes, "For the most part the Christian churches associated themselves together upon the lines of the Roman Empire." This not only applied to the graded hierarchy it adopted into its leadership structure, but also to the way the church divided itself up into gradations of dioceses, provinces, and municipalities all controlled by a top-down leadership system. "The development of the organization of the Christian churches was gradual," Hatch adds, "[and] the elements of which that organization were composed were already existing in human society."[79]

Will Durant makes a similar point, noting that Christianity "grew by the absorption of pagan faith and ritual; it became a triumphant church by inheriting the organizing patterns and genius of Rome. . . . As Judea had given Christianity ethics, and Greece had given it theology, so now Rome gave it organization; all these, with a dozen absorbed and rival faiths, entered into the Christian synthesis."[80]

By the fourth century, the church followed the example of the Roman Empire. Emperor Constantine organized the church into dioceses along the pattern of the Roman regional districts. (The word *diocese* was a secular term that referred to the larger administrative units of the Roman Empire.) Later, Pope Gregory shaped the ministry of the entire church after Roman law.[81]

Durant adds, "When Christianity conquered Rome the ecclesiastical structure of the pagan church, the title and vestments of the pontifex maximus . . . and the pageantry of immemorial ceremony, passed like maternal blood into the new religion, and captive Rome captured her conqueror."[82]

All of this was at gross odds with God's way for His church. Thus when Jesus entered the drama of human history, He obliterated both the religious professional icon as well as the hierarchical form of

---

[79] Hatch, *Organization of the Early Christian Churches*, 185, 213. As Bruce Shelley puts it, "As the church grew, it adopted, quite naturally, the structure of the Empire." *Church History in Plain Language*, 152.
[80] *Caesar and Christ*, 575, 618. Durant writes, "The Roman Church followed in the footsteps of the Roman State" (p. 618).
[81] Stevens, *Other Six Days*, 44; Trueman, *Pageant of the Past*, 311; Fox, *Pagans and Christians*, 573; Cross and Livingstone, *Oxford Dictionary of the Christian Church*, 482.
[82] Durant, *Caesar and Christ*, 671–672.

leadership.[83] As an extension of Christ's nature and mission, the early church was the first "lay-led" movement in history. But with the death of the apostles and the men they trained, things began to change.[84]

Since that time, the church of Jesus Christ has derived its pattern for church organization from the societies in which it has been placed—despite our Lord's warning that He was initiating a new society with a unique character (Matthew 23:8-11 and Mark 10:42ff.). In striking contrast to the Old Testament provisions made at Mt. Sinai, neither Jesus nor Paul imposed any fixed organizational patterns for the New Israel.

CONSTANTINE AND THE GLORIFICATION OF THE CLERGY

From AD 313 to 325, Christianity was no longer a struggling religion trying to survive the Roman government. It was basking in the sun of imperialism, loaded with money and status.[85] To be a Christian under Constantine's reign was no longer a handicap. It was an advantage. It was fashionable to become a part of the emperor's religion. And to be among the clergy was to receive the greatest of advantages.[86]

Clergymen received the same honors as the highest officials of the Roman Empire and even the emperor himself.[87] In fact, Constantine gave the bishops of Rome more power than he gave Roman governors.[88] He also ordered that the clergy receive fixed annual allowances (ministerial pay)!

In AD 313, he exempted the Christian clergy from paying taxes—something that pagan priests had traditionally enjoyed.[89] He also made them exempt from mandatory public office and other civic duties.[90] They were freed from being tried by secular courts and from

---

[83] Matthew 20:25-28, 23:8-12; Luke 22:25-27.
[84] Paul trained a number of men to take his place. Among them were Timothy, Titus, Gaius, Trophimus, Tychicus, etc. See Viola, *So You Want to Start a House Church?* for details.
[85] Hanson, *Christian Priesthood Examined*, 62.
[86] At this time, the term *clergy* broadened to include all officials in the church (Niebuhr and Williams, *Ministry in Historical Perspectives*, 29). See also Boggs, *Christian Saga*, 206–207.
[87] Jungmann, *Early Liturgy*, 130–131.
[88] Durant, *Caesar and Christ*, 618–619.
[89] Hanson, *Christian Priesthood Examined*, 62; Durant, *Caesar and Christ*, 656–657, 668.
[90] Duchesne, *Early History of the Christian Church*, 50; Johnson, *History of Christianity*, 77; Fox, *Pagans and Christians*, 667.

serving in the army.[91] (Bishops could be tried only by a bishop's court, not by ordinary law courts.)[92]

In all these things the clergy was given special class status. Constantine was the first to use the words *clerical* and *clerics* to depict a higher social class.[93] He also felt that the Christian clergy deserved the same privileges as governmental officials. So bishops sat in judgment like secular judges.[94]

The net result was alarming: The clergy had the prestige of church office bearers, the privileges of a favored class, and the power of a wealthy elite. They had become an isolated class with a separate civil status and way of life. (This included clergy celibacy.)[95]

They even dressed and groomed differently from the common people.[96] Bishops and priests shaved their heads. This practice, known as the tonsure, comes from the old Roman ceremony of adoption. All those who had shaved heads were known as clerks or clergy.[97] They also began wearing the clothes of Roman officials (see chapter 6).

It should come as no surprise that so many people in Constantine's day experienced a sudden "call to the ministry."[98] To their minds, being a church officer had become more of a career than a calling.[99]

A FALSE DICHOTOMY

Under Constantine, Christianity was both recognized and honored by the state. This blurred the line between the church and the world.

---

[91] Such exemptions had been granted to such professions as physicians and professors. David Andrews, *Christi-Anarchy* (Oxford: Lion Publications, 1999), 26.

[92] Collins and Price, *Story of Christianity*, 74.

[93] Johnson, *History of Christianity*, 77. A century later, Julian the Apostate was using these same terms (*clerical, clerics*) in a negative sense.

[94] Fox, *Pagans and Christians*, 667.

[95] Hatch, *Organization of the Early Christian Churches*, 153–155, 163. In the first three centuries of Christianity, priests were not required to be celibate. In the West, the Spanish Council of Elvira held in AD 306 was the first to require clergy to be celibate. This was reasserted by Pope Siricius in AD 386. Any priest who married or continued to live with his wife was defrocked. In the East, priests and deacons could marry before ordination, but not after. Bishops had to be celibate. Gregory the Great did a great deal to promote clerical celibacy, which many were not following. Clerical celibacy only widened the gulf between clergy and the so-called "ordinary" people of God (Cross and Livingstone, *Oxford Dictionary of the Christian Church*, 310; Schaff, *History of the Christian Church*, 1:441–446; Durant, *Age of Faith*, 45).

[96] The bishop's dress was the ancient robe of a Roman magistrate. Clergy were not to let their hair grow long like the pagan philosophers (Hatch, *Organization of the Early Christian Churches*, 164–165).

[97] Collins and Price, *Story of Christianity*, 74.

[98] Hanson, *Christian Priesthood Examined*, 62

[99] Niebuhr and Williams, *Ministry in Historical Perspectives*, 29.

The Christian faith was no longer a minority religion. Instead, it was protected by emperors. As a consequence, church membership grew rapidly—as large numbers of people with questionable conversions began to join. Such people brought into the church a wide variety of pagan ideas. In the words of Will Durant: "While Christianity converted the world; the world converted Christianity, and displayed the natural paganism of mankind."[100]

As we have seen in chapter 3, the practices of the mystery religions began to be employed in the church's worship. And the pagan notion of the dichotomy between the sacred and profane found its way into the Christian mind-set.[101] It can be rightfully said that the clergy/laity class distinction grew out of this very dichotomy. The Christian life was now being divided into two parts: secular and spiritual—profane and sacred.

By the third century, the clergy/laity gap widened to the point of no return.[102] Clergymen were the trained leaders of the church—the guardians of orthodoxy—the rulers and teachers of the people. They possessed gifts and graces not available to lesser mortals.

The laity were the second-class, untrained Christians. The great theologian Karl Barth rightly said, "The term 'laity' is one of the worst in the vocabulary of religion and ought to be banished from the Christian conversation."[103]

This false dichotomy led to the profoundly mistaken idea that there are sacred professions (a call to "the ministry") and ordinary professions (a call to a worldly vocation).[104] Historian Philip Schaff rightly describes these factors as creating "the secularization of the church" where the "pure stream of Christianity" had become polluted.[105] Take note that this mistaken dichotomy still lives in the minds of many believers today.

---

[100] Durant, *Caesar and Christ*, 657.
[101] Senn, *Christian Worship and Its Cultural Setting*, 40–41.
[102] Norrington, *To Preach or Not*, 25.
[103] Karl Barth, *Theologische Fragen und Antworten* (1957), 183–184, quoted in R. J. Erler and R. Marquard, eds., *A Karl Barth Reader*, trans. G. W. Bromiley (Grand Rapids: Eerdmans, 1986), 8–9.
[104] Everything ought to be done for God's glory, for He has sanctified the mundane (1 Corinthians 10:31). The false dichotomy between the sacred and profane has been forever abolished in Christ. Such thinking belongs to both paganism and ancient Judaism. For the Christian, "nothing is unclean in itself," and "what God has made clean, do not call common" (Romans 14:14, NASB; Acts 10:15, ESV). For an in-depth discussion on the fallacy of the sacred/profane disjunction, see Davies, *Secular Use of Church Buildings*, 222–237.
[105] Schaff, *History of the Christian Church*, 3:125–126.

But the concept is pagan, not Christian. It ruptures the New Testament reality that everyday life is sanctified by God.[106]

Along with these mind-set changes came a new vocabulary. Christians began to adopt the vocabulary of the pagan cults. The title *pontifex* (pontiff, a pagan title) became a common term for Christian clergy in the fourth century. So did "Master of Ceremonies," and "Grand Master of the Lodge."[107] All of this reinforced the mystique of the clergy as the custodians of the mysteries of God.[108]

In short, by the end of the fourth century on into the fifth, the clergy had become a sacerdotal caste—a spiritually elite group of "holy men."[109] This leads us to the thorny subject of ordination.

THE FALLACY OF ORDINATION

In the fourth century, theology and ministry were the exclusive domain of the priests. Work and war were the domain of the laity. What was the rite of passage into the sacred realm of the priest? Ordination.[110]

Before we examine the historical roots of ordination, let's look at how leadership was recognized in the early church. After beginning a church, the apostolic workers (church planters) of the first century would revisit that body after a period of time. In some of those churches, the workers would publicly acknowledge elders. In every case, the elders were already "in place" before they were publicly endorsed.[111]

Elders naturally emerged in a church through the process of time. They were not appointed to an external office.[112] Instead, they

---

[106] Dunn, *New Testament Theology in Dialogue*, 127.

[107] Hanson, *Christian Priesthood Examined*, 64. Terms like *coryphaeus* (Master of Ceremonies) and *hierophant* (Grand Master of the Lodge) were freely borrowed from pagan cults and used for the Christian clergy. Tertullian was the first to use the term *supreme pontiff* (bishop of bishops) to refer to the bishop of Rome in his work *On Chastity*, written at about AD 218. Tertullian, however, uses the term sarcastically (Bruce, *Spreading Flame*, 322).

[108] Hanson, *Christian Priesthood Examined*, 64.

[109] Ibid., 65–66; von Campenhausen, *Tradition and Life in the Church*, 222–223.

[110] Warkentin, *Ordination: A Biblical-Historical View*, 40, 167.

[111] See Acts 13–19; 1 Corinthians; 2 Corinthians. I (Frank) trace the chronology of when the apostles visited the churches they planted and when they acknowledged elders in Viola, *The Untold Story of the New Testament Church: An Extraordinary Guide to Understanding the New Testament* (Shippensburg, PA: Destiny Image, 2004).

[112] According to Bible commentator Alfred Plummer, the Greek words translated "ordain" in the New Testament do not have special ecclesiastical meanings. None of them implies the rite of ordination or a special ceremony. "The Pastoral Epistles," in W. Robertson Nicoll, ed., *The Expositor's Bible* (New York: Armstrong, 1903), 219–221.

were recognized by virtue of their seniority and spiritual service to the church. According to the New Testament, recognition of certain gifted members is something that is instinctive and organic.[113] Every believer has the discernment to recognize those within his or her church who are gifted to carry out various ministries.

Strikingly, only three passages in the New Testament tell us that elders were publicly recognized. Elders were acknowledged in the churches in Galatia (Acts 14:23). Paul had Timothy acknowledge elders in Ephesus (1 Timothy 3:1ff.). He also told Titus to recognize them in the churches in Crete (Titus 1:5ff.).

The word *ordain* (KJV) in these passages does not mean to place into office.[114] It rather carries the idea of endorsing, affirming, and showing forth what has already been happening.[115] It also conveys the thought of blessing.[116] Public recognition of elders and other ministries was typically accompanied by the laying on of hands by apostolic workers. (In the case of workers being sent out, this was done by the church or the elders.)[117]

In the first century, the laying on of hands merely meant the endorsement or affirmation of a function, not the installment into an office or the giving of special status. Regrettably, it came to mean the latter in the late second and early third centuries.[118]

During the third century, *ordination* took on an entirely different meaning. It was a formalized Christian rite.[119] By the fourth century, the ceremony of ordination was embellished by symbolic garments and solemn ritual.[120] Ordination produced an ecclesiastical caste that usurped the believing priesthood.

[113] Acts 16:2; 1 Corinthians 16:18; 2 Corinthians 8:22; Philippians 2:22; 1 Thessalonians 1:5, 5:12; 1 Timothy 3:10.
[114] Warkentin, *Ordination: A Biblical-Historical View*, 4. Translators of the KJV have used *ordain* for 21 different Hebrew and Greek words. Seventeenth-century ecclesiastical misunderstanding influenced this poor word choice.
[115] The Greek word *cheirotoneo* in Acts 14:23 literally means "to stretch forth the hand" as in voting. Hence, it is likely that the apostles laid hands on those whom the majority of the church deemed were already functioning as overseers among them.
[116] Campbell, *Elders*, 169–170.
[117] Acts 13:2; 1 Timothy 4:14. Paul, an older worker, also laid hands on Timothy, a younger worker (2 Timothy 1:6).
[118] Warkentin, *Ordination: A Biblical-Historical View*, 104, 111, 127, 130. Warkentin does a thorough study on the New Testament meaning of the "laying on of hands" in chapters 9–11 of her book. Her conclusion: "The laying on of hands has nothing to do with routine installation into office in the church, whether as elder, deacon, pastor, or missionary" (p. 156).
[119] The earliest record of the ordination rite is found in the *Apostolic Tradition of Hippolytus* (ca. 215). By the fourth century, references to it abound (Warkentin, *Ordination: A Biblical-Historical View*, 25, 41).
[120] Warkentin, *Ordination: A Biblical-Historical View*, 104.

From where did Christians get their pattern of ordination? They patterned their ordination ceremony after the Roman custom of appointing men to civil office. The entire process, down to the very words, came straight from the Roman civic world.[121]

By the fourth century, the terms used for appointment to Roman office and for Christian ordination became synonymous.[122] When Constantine made Christianity the religion of choice, church leadership structures were buttressed by political sanction. The forms of the Old Testament priesthood were combined with Greek hierarchy.[123] Sadly, the church was secure in this new form—just as it is today.

Soon ordination was viewed as a rite that resulted in an irrevocable position.[124] Augustine taught that ordination confers a "definite irremovable imprint" on the priest that empowers him to fulfill his priestly functions.[125]

Christian ordination, then, came to be understood as that which constitutes the essential difference between clergy and laity. By it, the clergy were empowered to administer the sacraments. It was believed that the priest, who performs the divine service, should be the most perfect and holy of all Christians.[126]

Gregory of Nazianzus (329–389) and Chrysostom had such a high view of those occupying the priesthood that danger loomed for the clergy if they failed to live up to the holiness of their service.[127] "The priest, [Chrysostom] observed, is ever judged by his parish as though he were an angel and not of the same frail stuff as the rest of men."[128]

How was the priest to live in such a state of pure holiness? How was he to be worthy to serve in "the choir of angels"? The answer was

---

[121] Hatch, *Organization of the Early Christian Churches*, 129–133. This same tendency was picked up by Judaism as early as the first century. Jewish scribes who were proficient in the interpretation of the Torah and the oral traditions ordained men for office in the Sanhedrin. These men were viewed as mediators of the will of God to all of Israel. The "ordained" of the Sanhedrin became so powerful that by the early second century the Romans put to death anyone who performed Jewish ordination! Warkentin, *Ordination: A Biblical-Historical View*, 16, 21–23, 25.

[122] Warkentin, *Ordination: A Biblical-Historical View*, 35. This is evident from the *Apostolic Constitutions* (AD 350–375).

[123] Ibid., 45.

[124] Niebuhr and Williams, *Ministry in Historical Perspectives*, 75.

[125] von Campenhausen, *Tradition and Life in the Church*, 224.

[126] Ibid., 227.

[127] Ibid., 228.

[128] Niebuhr and Williams, *Ministry in Historical Perspectives*, 71, 128.

ordination. By ordination, the stream of divine graces flowed into the priest, making him a fit vessel for God's use. This idea, also known as "sacerdotal endowment," first appears in the writings of Gregory of Nyssa (330–395).

Gregory argued that ordination makes the priest "invisibly but actually a different, better man," raising him high above the laity.[129] "The same power of the word," writes Gregory, "makes the priest venerable and honorable, separated. . . . While but yesterday he was one of the mass, one of the people, he is suddenly rendered a guide, a president, a teacher of righteousness, an instructor in hidden mysteries."[130]

Listen to the words of one fourth-century document: "The bishop, he is the minister of the Word, the keeper of knowledge, the mediator between God and you in several parts of your Divine worship. . . . He is your ruler and governor. . . . He is next after God your earthly god, who has a right to be honored by you."[131] Priests came to be identified as the "vicars of God on the earth."

To further show the priests' distinction from other people, both their lifestyle and dress were different from that of laymen.[132] Regrettably, this concept of ordination has never left the Christian faith. It is alive and well in contemporary Christianity. In fact, if you are wondering why and how the present-day pastor got to be so exalted as the "holy man of God," these are the roots.

Eduard Schweizer, in his classic work *Church Order in the New Testament*, argues that Paul knew nothing about an ordination that confers ministerial or clerical powers to a Christian.[133] First-century shepherds (elders, overseers) did not receive anything that resembles modern-day ordination. They were not set above the rest of the flock. They were those who served among them (see Acts 20:28, NASB, and 1 Peter 5:2-3, NASB).

---

[129] von Campenhausen, *Tradition and Life in the Church*, 229.
[130] *On the Baptism of Christ: A Sermon for the Day of Lights* by St. Gregory of Nyssa. See also Niehbur and Williams, *Ministry in Historical Perspectives*, 75. Ordination was believed to confer upon the recipient a *character indelibilis*. That is, something sacred had entered into him (Warkentin, *Ordination: A Biblical-Historical View*, 42; Schaff, *History of the Christian Church* 3:489).
[131] *Apostolic Constitutions* II.4.26.
[132] David D. Hall, *The Faithful Shepherd* (Chapel Hill: The University of North Carolina Press, 1972), 6.
[133] Schweizer, *Church Order in the New Testament*, 207.

First-century elders were merely endorsed publicly by traveling apostolic workers as being those who cared for the church. Such acknowledgment was simply the recognition of a function. It did not confer special powers. Nor was it a permanent possession.

The contemporary practice of ordination creates a special caste of Christian. Whether it be the priest in Catholicism or the pastor in Protestantism, the result is the same: The most important ministry is restricted to a few "special" believers.

Such an idea is as damaging as it is nonscriptural. The New Testament nowhere limits preaching, baptizing, or distributing the Lord's Supper to the "ordained." Eminent scholar James D. G. Dunn put it best when he said that the clergy-laity tradition has done more to undermine New Testament authority than most heresies.[134]

Since church office could only be held through the rite of ordination, the power to ordain became the crucial issue in holding religious authority. The biblical context was lost. And proof-texting methods were used to justify the clergy/laity hierarchy. Perhaps the best-known example is the early Catholics' use of Matthew 16 to justify the creation of a papal system and the doctrine of apostolic succession. The result: Ordinary believers, generally uneducated and ignorant, were at the mercy of a professional clergy.[135]

THE REFORMATION

The Reformers of the sixteenth century brought the Catholic priesthood sharply into question. They attacked the idea that the priest had special powers to convert wine into blood. They rejected apostolic succession. They encouraged the clergy to marry. They revised the liturgy to give the congregation more participation. They also abolished the office of the bishop and reduced the priest back to a presbyter.[136]

---

[134] Dunn, *New Testament Theology in Dialogue*, 138ff., 126–129.
[135] Warkentin, *Ordination: A Biblical-Historical View*, 45, 51; Hatch, *Organization of the Early Christian Churches*, 126–131. Ordination grew into an instrument to consolidate clerical power. Through it, the clergy could lord over God's people as well as secular authorities. The net effect is that modern ordination sets up artificial barriers between Christians and hinders mutual ministry.
[136] Hanson, *Christian Priesthood Examined*, 82.

Unfortunately, however, the Reformers carried the Roman Catholic clergy/laity distinction straight into the Protestant movement. They also kept the Catholic idea of ordination.[137] Although they abolished the office of the bishop, they resurrected the one-bishop rule, clothing it in new garb.

The rallying cry of the Reformation was the restoration of the priesthood of all believers. However, this restoration was only partial. Luther, Calvin, and Zwingli affirmed the believing priesthood with respect to one's individual relationship to God. They rightly taught that every Christian has direct access to God without the need of a human mediator. This was a wonderful restoration. But it was one-sided.

What the Reformers failed to do was to recover the corporate dimension of the believing priesthood. They restored the doctrine of the believing priesthood soteriologically—i.e., as it related to salvation. But they failed to restore it ecclesiologically—i.e., as it related to the church.[138]

In other words, the Reformers only recovered the priesthood of the believer (singular). They reminded us that every Christian has individual and immediate access to God. As wonderful as that is, they did not recover the priesthood of all believers (collective plural). This is the blessed truth that every Christian is part of a clan that shares God's Word one with another. (It was the Anabaptists who recovered this practice. Regrettably, this recovery was one of the reasons why Protestant and Catholic swords were red with Anabaptist blood.)[139]

While the Reformers opposed the pope and his religious hierarchy, they still held to the narrow view of ministry that they inherited. They believed that "ministry" was an institution that was closeted among the few who were "called" and "ordained."[140] Thus the Reform-

---

[137] While Luther rejected the idea that ordination changes the ordained person's character, he nevertheless held to its importance. To Luther's mind, ordination is a rite of the church. And a special ceremony was necessary for the carrying out of pastoral duties (Senn, *Christian Liturgy*, 297).

[138] "The priesthood of all believers refers not only to each person's relation to God and to one's priesthood to neighbors, as in Luther; it refers also to the equality of all people in the Christian community with respect to formal function." John Dillenberger and Claude Welch, *Protestant Christianity: Interpreted through Its Development* (New York: The Macmillan Company, 1988), 61.

[139] Hall, *Faithful Shepherd*, 8. For a compelling treatment of the Anabaptist story, see Peter Hoover's *The Secret of the Strength: What Would the Anabaptists Tell This Generation?* (Shippensburg, PA: Benchmark Press, 1998).

[140] J. L. Ainslie, *The Doctrines of Ministerial Order in the Reformed Churches of the 16th and 17th Centuries* (Edinburgh: T. & T. Clark, 1940), 2, 5.

ers still affirmed the clergy-laity split. Only in their rhetoric did they state that all believers were priests and ministers. In their practice they denied it. So after the smoke cleared from the Reformation, we ended up with the same thing that the Catholics gave us—a selective priesthood!

Luther held to the idea that those who preach needed to be specially trained. Like the Catholics, the Reformers believed that only the "ordained minister" could preach, baptize, and administer the Lord's Supper.[141] As a result, ordination gave the minister a special aura of divine favor that could not be questioned.

Tragically, Luther and the other Reformers violently denounced the Anabaptists for practicing every-member functioning in the church.[142] The Anabaptists believed it was every Christian's right to stand up and speak in a meeting. It was not solely the domain of the clergy. Luther was so opposed to this practice that he said it came from "the pit of hell" and those who were guilty of it should be put to death.[143]

In short, the Reformers retained the idea that ordination was the key to having power in the church. It was the ordained minister's duty to convey God's revelation to His people.[144] And he was paid for this role.

Like the Catholic priest, the Reformed minister was viewed by the church as the "man of God"—the paid mediator between God and His people.[145] He was not a mediator to forgive sins, but a mediator to communicate the divine will.[146] So in Protestantism an old problem took on a new form. The jargon changed, but the error remained.

---

[141] Warkentin, *Ordination: A Biblical-Historical View*, 57–58, 61–62.

[142] The Anabaptists both believed and practiced Paul's injunction in 1 Corinthians 14:26, 30-31 that every believer has the right to function at any time in a church meeting. In Luther's day, this practice was known as the *Sitzrecht*—"the sitter's right" (Hoover, *Secret of the Strength*, 58–59).

[143] Luther announced that "the *Sitzrecht* was from the pit of hell" and was a "perversion of public order . . . undermining respect for authority." Within 20 years, over 116 laws were passed in German lands throughout Europe making this "Anabaptist heresy" a capital offense (Hoover, *Secret of the Strength*, 59, 198). Further, Luther felt that if the whole church publicly administered the Lord's Supper it would be a "deplorable confusion." To Luther's mind, one person must take on this task—the pastor. Paul Althaus, *The Theology of Martin Luther* (Philadelphia: Fortress Press, 1966), 323.

[144] Warkentin, *Ordination: A Biblical-Historical View*, 105.

[145] Ibid. Protestants today speak of "the ministry" as a mediatorial body set within the larger body of Christ rather than a function shared by all.

[146] Just as the Roman Catholic clergy was seen as the gatekeeper of salvation, the Protestant clergy was viewed as the trustee of divine revelation. According to the *Augsburg Confession* of 1530, the highest office in the church was the preaching office. In ancient Judaism, the rabbi interpreted the Torah for the people. In the Protestant church, the minister is regarded as the custodian of God's mysteries (Warkentin, *Ordination: A Biblical-Historical View*, 168).

In the seventeenth century, Puritan writers John Owen (1616–1683) and Thomas Goodwin (1600–1680), like Luther and Calvin, viewed the pastorate as a permanent fixture in God's house. Owen and Goodwin led the Puritans to focus all authority into the pastoral role. To their minds, the pastor is given "the power of the keys." He alone is ordained to preach, administer the sacraments,[147] read Scripture publicly,[148] and be trained in the original biblical languages, as well as logic and philosophy.

Both the Reformers and the Puritans held the idea that God's ministers must be competent professionals. Therefore, pastors had to undergo extensive academic training to fulfill their office.[149]

FROM PRIEST TO PASTOR

John Calvin did not like using the word *priest* to refer to ministers.[150] He preferred the term *pastor*.[151] In Calvin's mind, *pastor* was the highest word one could use for ministry. He liked it because the Bible referred to Jesus Christ, "the great Shepherd of the sheep" (Hebrews 13:20).[152] Ironically, Calvin believed that he was restoring the New Testament bishop (*episkopos*) in the person of the pastor![153]

Luther also did not like using the word *priest* to define the new Protestant ministers. He wrote, "We neither can nor ought to give the name priest to those who are in charge of the Word and sacrament among the people. The reason they have been called priests is either because of the custom of the heathen people or as a vestige of the Jewish nation. The result is greatly injurious to the church."[154] So he too adopted the terms *preacher*, *minister*, and *pastor* to refer to this office.

Zwingli and Martin Bucer also favored the word *pastor*. They

[147] John Owen, *The True Nature of a Gospel Church and Its Government*, ed. John Huxtable (London: James Clarke, 1947), 41, 55, 68, 99; Ainslie, *Doctrines of Ministerial Order*, 37, 49, 56, 59, 61–69; Thomas Goodwin, *Works*, 11:309.

[148] Jon Zens, "Building Up the Body: One Man or One Another," *Baptist Reformation Review* 10, no. 2 (1981): 21–22.

[149] Hall, *Faithful Shepherd*, 28–29.

[150] John Calvin, *Institutes of the Christian Religion* (Philadelphia: Westminster Press, 1960), bk. 4, ch. 8, no. 14.

[151] *Pastor* is from the Latin, which was used to translate "shepherd." William Tyndale preferred the term *pastor* in his Bible translation. Tyndale debated Sir Thomas More over the issue of *pastor* vs. *priest*. Tyndale, a Protestant, took the position that "pastor" was exegetically correct (see *The Parker Society Series on the English Reformers* for this exchange).

[152] Hall, *Faithful Shepherd*, 16.

[153] Sykes, *Old Priest and New Presbyter*, 111.

[154] Luther, "Concerning the Ministry," *Luther's Works*, 35, 40.

wrote popular treatises on it.[155] As a result, the term began to permeate the churches of the Reformation.[156] However, given their obsession with preaching, the Reformers' favorite term for the minister was *preacher*. And this was what the common people generally called him.[157]

It was not until the eighteenth century that the term *pastor* came into common use, eclipsing *preacher* and *minister*.[158] This influence came from the Lutheran Pietists. Since then the term has become widespread in mainstream Christianity.[159]

Even so, the Reformers considered the pastor to be the functioning head of the church. According to Calvin, "The pastoral office is necessary to preserve the church on earth in a greater way than the sun, food, and drink are necessary to nourish and sustain the present life."[160]

The Reformers believed that the pastor possessed divine power and authority. He did not speak in his own name, but in the name of God. Calvin further reinforced the primacy of the pastor by treating acts of contempt or ridicule toward the minister as serious public offenses.[161]

This should come as no surprise when you realize what Calvin took as his model for ministry. He did not take the church of the

---

[155] One of the most influential books during the Reformation was Bucer's *Pastorale*. In the same spirit, Zwingli published a tract entitled *The Pastor*.

[156] Calvin's church order of pastors with governing elders in Geneva became the most influential model during the Reformation. It became the pattern of the Protestant churches in France, Holland, Hungary, and Scotland, as well as among the English Puritans and their descendants (Niebuhr and Williams, *Ministry in Historical Perspectives*, 115–117, 131). Calvin also gave rise to the idea that the pastor and teacher were the only two "ordinary" officers in Ephesians 4:11-12 that continue perpetually in the church (Hall, *Faithful Shepherd*, 28). During the seventeenth century, the Puritans used the term *pastor* in some of their published works. Seventeenth-century Anglican and Puritan works on pastoral care referred to parish (local) clergy as "parsons" or "pastors." (George Herbert, *The Country Parson and the Temple* (Mahwah, NJ: Paulist Press, 1981) and Richard Baxter, *The Reformed Pastor* (Lafayette, IN: Sovereign Grace Trust Fund, 2000), respectively.

[157] Niebuhr and Williams, *Ministry in Historical Perspectives*, 116. "The German Reformers also adhered to the medieval usage and called the preacher *Pfarrer*, i.e., parson (derived from *parochia*—parish and *parochus*—parson)." While Lutheran preachers are called pastors in the United States, they are still called *Pfarrer* (head of the parish) in Germany. Given the gradual transition from Catholic priest to Protestant pastor, it was not uncommon for people to still call their new Protestant preachers by the old Catholic titles like priest.

[158] The word *pastor* has always appeared in theological literature dating as far back as the Patristic Period. The word choice was dependent on the function you wished to highlight: A pastor guided in moral and spiritual ways. A priest officiated the sacraments. Even so, the term *pastor* was not on the lips of the common believer until after the Reformation.

[159] Niebuhr and Williams, *Ministry in Historical Perspectives*, 116. The word *priest* belongs to the Catholic/Anglican tradition, the word *minister* belongs to the Reformed tradition, and the word *pastor* belongs to the Lutheran and evangelical tradition (p. viii). The Reformers did speak of their minister as *pastor*, but they mostly called him *preacher*. The word *pastor* later evolved to become the predominant term in Christianity for this office. This was due to the mainstreaming of these groups which sought distance from "high church" vocabulary. The term *minister* was introduced gradually into the English-speaking world by the Nonconformists and Dissenters. They wished to distinguish the Protestant "ministry" from the Anglican clergy.

[160] Calvin, *Institutes of the Christian Religion*, IV: 3:2, p. 1055.

[161] Niebuhr and Williams, *Ministry in Historical Perspectives*, 138.

apostolic age. Instead, he took as his pattern the one-bishop rule of the second century.[162] This was true for the other Reformers as well.[163]

The irony here is that John Calvin bemoaned the Roman Catholic Church because it built its practices on "human inventions" rather than on the Bible.[164] But Calvin did the same thing. In this regard, Protestants are just as guilty as are Catholics. Both denominations base their practices on human tradition.

Calvin taught that the preaching of the Word of God and the proper administration of the sacraments are the marks of a true church.[165] To his mind, preaching, baptism, and the Eucharist were to be carried out by the pastor, not the congregation.[166] For all the Reformers, the primary function of a minister was preaching. The preeminent place of preaching is best reflected in Luther's German Mass, which included three services on Sunday. At 5 or 6 a.m., a sermon was given on the Epistle of the day. At the main service at 8 or 9 a.m., the minister preached on the Gospel of the day. The sermon at the Vesper service in the afternoon was based on the Old Testament.[167]

Like Calvin, Luther also made the pastor a separate and exalted office. While he argued that the keys of the Kingdom belonged to all believers, Luther confined their use to those who held offices in the church.[168] "We are all priests," said Luther, "insofar as we are Chris-

---

[162] "For his [Calvin's] model of the ministry goes back to the church of the early second century rather than to that of the strictly apostolic age. In the apostolic age the local Christian community was under the charge not of a single pastor, but of a number of functionaries known interchangeably, as he notes, as presbyters (elders) and bishops. It was only in the second century that the single bishop or pastor of the Christian community came into existence, as in the Epistles of Ignatius. . . . It was this stage of the development of the ministerial office in the early second-century church that Calvin took as his model" (Mackinnon, *Calvin and the Reformation*, 81–82).

[163] James H. Nichols writes, "The Reformers also generally accepted the second-century system of an institutionalized ministry of pastors or bishops to lead the laity in worship. . . . They did not attempt to return to the age of the apostles." (*Corporate Worship*, 21).

[164] Niebuhr and Williams, *Ministry in Historical Perspectives*, 111.

[165] Calvin, *Institutes of the Christian Religion*, IV: 1:9, p. 1023.

[166] John H. Yoder, "The Fullness of Christ," *Concern* 17 (1969): 71.

[167] Niebuhr and Williams, *Ministry in Historical Perspectives*, 131, 133, 135; "Powerful Preaching: A Sample of How Luther Could Bring Bible Characters to Life," *Christian History* 12, no. 3 (1993): 27. Luther was abrasive, powerful, and dramatic. He communicated his own person in his sermons without superimposing himself on the message. He was a voracious preacher, delivering an estimated 4,000 sermons. His messages were awe-inspiring, poetic, and creative. Zwingli preached directly and naturally, yet he was regarded as too intellectual. Calvin was consistent in his exhaustive expounding of passages, but he was always impersonal. Bucer was long-winded and had a penchant for rambling. Even so, early Protestant preaching was very doctrinaire, being obsessed with "correct and pure doctrine." For this reason, Reformation preachers were primarily Bible teachers.

[168] Hall, *Faithful Shepherd*, 8.

tians, but those whom we call priests are ministers selected from our midst to act in our name, and their priesthood is our ministry."[169]

This was sacerdotalism, pure and simple. Luther broke from the Catholic camp in that he rejected a sacrificing priesthood. But in its place, he believed that the sharing of God's Word belonged to a special order.[170]

The following are characteristic statements made by Luther in his exaltation of the pastor: "God speaks through the preacher. . . . A Christian preacher is a minister of God who is set apart, yea, he is an angel of God, a very bishop sent by God, a savior of many people, a king and prince in the Kingdom of Christ. . . . There is nothing more precious or nobler in the earth and in this life than a true, faithful parson or preacher."[171]

Said Luther, "We should not permit our pastor to speak Christ's words by himself as though he were speaking them for his own person; rather, he is the mouth of all of us and we all speak them with him in our hearts. . . . It is a wonderful thing that the mouth of every pastor is the mouth of Christ, therefore you ought to listen to the pastor not as a man, but as God."[172] You can hear the echoes of Ignatius ringing through these words.

Such ideas reveal a flawed view of the church. Luther felt the church was primarily a preaching station. "The Christian congregation," said Luther, "never should assemble unless God's Word is preached and prayer is made, no matter for how brief a time this may be."[173] Luther believed that the church is simply a gathering of people who listen to preaching. For this reason, he called the church building a Mundhaus, which means a mouth-house.[174] He also made this alarming statement: "The ears are the only organs of a Christian."[175] These are the roots of Protestantism.

---

[169] Niebuhr and Williams, *Ministry in Historical Perspectives*, 112. The Reformers substituted the word *minister* for *priest*. Jones, *Historical Approach to Evangelical Worship*, 141.

[170] B. A. Gerrish, "Priesthood and Ministry in the Theology of Luther," *Church History* 34 (1965), 404–422.

[171] Niebuhr and Williams, *Ministry in Historical Perspectives*, 114–115.

[172] Althaus, *Theology of Martin Luther*, 326.

[173] "Concerning the Ordering of Divine Worship in the Congregation," *Works of Martin Luther*, C. M. Jacobs, ed. (Philadelphia: Muhlenberg Press, 1932), VI, 60.

[174] Niebuhr and Williams, *Ministry in Historical Perspectives*, 114.

[175] *Luther's Works*, 29:224.

THE CURE OF SOULS

Calvin, Luther, and Bucer believed that the two key functions of the pastor were the proclamation of the Word (preaching) and the celebration of the Eucharist (Communion). But Calvin and Bucer added a third element. They emphasized that the pastor had a duty to provide care and healing to the congregation.[176] This is known as the "cure of souls." Bucer wrote the preeminent book on this subject, entitled *True Cure of the Souls*, in 1538.

The origin of "cure of souls" goes back to the fourth and fifth centuries.[177] We find it in the teaching of Gregory of Nazianzus. Gregory called the bishop a "pastor"—a physician of souls who diagnoses his patient's maladies and prescribes either medicine or the knife.[178]

Luther's early followers also practiced the care of souls.[179] But in Calvin's Geneva, it was raised to an art form. Each pastor and one elder were required to visit the homes of their congregants. Regular visits to the sick and those in prison were also observed.[180] For Calvin and Bucer, the pastor was not merely a preacher and a dispenser of the sacraments. He was the "cure of souls" or the "curate." His task was to bring healing, cure, and compassion to God's hurting people.[181]

This idea lives on in the Protestant world today. It is readily seen in the contemporary concepts of pastoral care, pastoral counseling, and Christian psychology. In the present-day church, the burden of such care typically falls on the shoulders of one man—the pastor. (In the first century, it fell on the shoulders of the entire church and upon a group of seasoned men called "elders.")[182]

---

[176] John T. McNeill, *A History of the Cure of Souls* (New York: Harper and Row, 1951).

[177] Gregory of Nazianzus, Chrysostom, Augustine, and Gregory the Great wrote a good deal on the "cure of souls" (McNeill, *History of the Cure of Souls*, 100). In AD 591, Gregory the Great wrote a treatise for pastors called *The Book of Pastoral Rule*. This work is still used in seminaries today, and it owes a great deal to Gregory of Nazianzus (p. 109). Gregory the Great was more of a pastor to the Western church than any of the other popes.

[178] McNeill, *History of the Cure of Souls*, 108. Gregory of Nazianzus articulated these things in his Second Oration, penned in AD 362.

[179] Ibid., 177.

[180] Niebuhr and Williams, *Ministry in Historical Perspectives*, 136. In 1550, an order was issued that ministers should visit each home at least once a year.

[181] This book came out in German and Latin versions (McNeill, *History of the Cure of Souls*, 177).

[182] See Viola, *Reimagining Church*. Human healing comes through connectedness in Christian community. See Larry Crabb's *Connecting: Healing Ourselves and Our Relationships* (Nashville: W Publishing, 2004).

THE PASTOR-DRIVEN CHURCH

In short, the Protestant Reformation struck a blow to Roman Catholic sacerdotalism. It was not a fatal blow, however, but merely a semantic change. The Reformers retained the one-bishop rule. The pastor now played the role of the bishop. The bishop-driven church evolved into the pastor-driven church. The pastor came to be regarded as the local head of a church—the leading elder.[183] As one writer put it, "In Protestantism, the preachers tend to be the spokesmen and representatives of the church and the church is often the preacher's church. This is a great danger and threat to the Christian religion, not unrelated to clericalism."[184]

In their rhetoric the Reformers decried the clergy-laity split. But in their practice they fully retained it. As Kevin Giles says, "Differences between Catholic and Protestant clergy were blurred in practice and theology. In both kinds of churches, the clergy were a class apart; in both, their special status was based on Divine initiatives (mediated in different ways); and in both, certain duties were reserved to them."[185]

The long-standing, postbiblical tradition of the one-bishop rule (now embodied in the pastor) prevails in the Protestant church today. Tremendous psychological factors make laypeople feel that ministry is the responsibility of the pastor. *It's his job. He's the expert* is often their thinking.

The New Testament word for minister is *diakonos*. It means "servant." But this word has been distorted because men have professionalized the ministry. We have taken the word *minister* and equated it with the pastor, with no scriptural justification whatsoever. In like

---

[183] Many Reformed churches distinguish between "teaching" elders and "ruling" elders. Teaching elders occupy the traditional position of bishop or minister, while ruling elders handle administration and discipline. This form of church polity was brought to New England from Europe (Hall, *Faithful Shepherd*, 95). Eventually, due to the unpopularity of the office, the ruling elders were dropped and the teaching elder remained. This was also true in the Baptist churches of the eighteenth and nineteenth centuries. Often these churches lacked the financial resources to support one "minister." In this way, by the end of the nineteenth century, the evangelical churches adopted the "single pastor" tradition. Mark Dever, *A Display of God's Glory* (Washington, DC: Center for Church Reform, 2001), 20; R. E. H. Uprichard, "The Eldership in Martin Bucer and John Calvin," *Irish Biblical Studies Journal* (June 18, 1996): 149, 154. So the single pastor in evangelical churches evolved from a plurality of elders in the Reformed tradition.

[184] Niebuhr and Williams, *Ministry in Historical Perspectives*, 114. The so-called "lay-preacher" emerged out of the evangelical revivals of the eighteenth century (p. 206).

[185] Kevin Giles, *Patterns of Ministry among the First Christians* (New York: HarperCollins, 1991), 195–196.

manner, we have mistakenly equated preaching and ministry with the pulpit sermon, again without biblical justification.

HOW THE PASTORAL ROLE DAMAGES BODY LIFE

Now that we have unearthed the little-known roots of the contemporary pastor, let's shift our attention to the practical effects that a pastor has on the people of God.

The unscriptural clergy/laity distinction has done untold harm to the body of Christ. It has divided the believing community into first- and second-class Christians. The clergy/laity dichotomy perpetuates an awful falsehood—namely, that some Christians are more privileged than others to serve the Lord.

The one-man ministry is entirely foreign to the New Testament, yet we embrace it while it suffocates our functioning. We are living stones, not dead ones. However, the pastoral office has transformed us into stones that do not breathe.

Permit us to get personal. We believe the pastoral office has stolen your right to function as a full member of Christ's body. It has distorted the reality of the body, making the pastor a giant mouth and transforming you into a tiny ear.[186] It has rendered you a mute spectator who is proficient at taking sermon notes and passing an offering plate.

But that is not all. The modern-day pastoral office has overthrown the main thrust of the letter to the Hebrews—the ending of the old priesthood. It has made ineffectual the teaching of 1 Corinthians 12–14, that every member has both the right and the privilege to minister in a church meeting. It has voided the message of 1 Peter 2 that every brother and sister is a functioning priest.

Being a functioning priest does not mean that you may only perform highly restrictive forms of ministry like singing songs in your pew, raising your hands during worship, setting up the PowerPoint

---

[186] To put this tragedy in the form of a biblical question, "And if they were all one member, where would the body be?" (1 Corinthians 12:19, NKJV).

presentation, or teaching a Sunday school class. That is not the New Testament idea of ministry! These are mere aids for the pastor's ministry. As one scholar put it, "Much Protestant worship, up to the present day, has also been infected by an overwhelming tendency to regard worship as the work of the pastor (and perhaps the choir) with the majority of the laity having very little to do but sing a few hymns and listen in a prayerful and attentive way."[187]

We expect doctors and lawyers to serve us, not to train us to serve others. And why? Because they are the experts. They are trained professionals. Unfortunately, we look upon the pastor in the same way. All of this does violence to the fact that every believer is a priest. Not only before God, but to one another.

But there is something more. The contemporary pastorate rivals the functional headship of Christ in His church. It illegitimately holds the unique place of centrality and headship among God's people, a place that is reserved for only one Person—the Lord Jesus. Jesus Christ is the only head over a church and the final word to it.[188] By his office, the pastor displaces and supplants Christ's headship by setting himself up as the church's human head.

For this reason, we believe the present-day pastoral role hinders the fulfillment of God's eternal purpose. Why? Because that purpose is centered on making Christ's headship visibly manifested in the church through the free, open, mutually participatory, every-member functioning of the body.[189] As long as the pastoral office is present in a particular church, that church will have a slim chance of witnessing such a glorious thing.

HOW THE PASTOR DAMAGES HIMSELF

The contemporary pastor not only does damage to God's people, he does damage to himself. The pastoral office has a way of chewing up

[187] Davies, *New Westminster Dictionary of Liturgy*, 292.
[188] In this regard (and contrary to popular opinion), the pastor is *not* "the cerebellum, the center for communicating messages, coordinating functions, and conducting responses between the Head and the Body." He is not called to give "authoritative communication of the truth from the Head to the Body." And he is not the "accurate communicator of the needs from the Body to the Head." The pastor is described with these inflated terms in David L. McKenna's "The Ministry's Gordian Knot," *Leadership* (Winter 1980) 50–51.
[189] See Ephesians 3:8-11. For a full discussion of this purpose, see Frank's book *God's Ultimate Passion*.

many who come within its parameters. Depression, burnout, stress, and emotional breakdown occur at abnormally high rates among pastors. At the time of this writing, there are reportedly more than 500,000 paid pastors serving churches in the United States.[190] Among this massive number of religious professionals, consider the following statistics that testify to the lethal danger of the pastoral office:

> ➤ 94 percent feel pressured to have an ideal family.
> ➤ 90 percent work more than forty-six hours a week.
> ➤ 81 percent say they have insufficient time with their spouses.
> ➤ 80 percent believe that pastoral ministry affects their family negatively.
> ➤ 70 percent do not have someone they consider a close friend.
> ➤ 70 percent have lower self-esteem than when they entered the ministry.
> ➤ 50 percent feel unable to meet the demands of the job.[191]
> ➤ 80 percent are discouraged or deal with depression.
> ➤ More than 40 percent report that they are suffering from burnout, frantic schedules, and unrealistic expectations.[192]
> ➤ 33 percent consider pastoral ministry an outright hazard to the family.[193]
> ➤ 33 percent have seriously considered leaving their position in the past year.[194]
> ➤ 40 percent of pastoral resignations are due to burnout.[195]

Most pastors are expected to juggle sixteen major tasks at once.[196] And many crumble under the pressure. For this reason,

[190] The Barna Group, "A Profile of Protestant Pastors," *The Barna Update* (September 25, 2001), (http://www.barna.org). Half of these churches have fewer than 100 active members (Larry Witham, "Flocks in Need of Shepherds," *The Washington Times* (July 2, 2001).
[191] H. B. London and Neil B. Wiseman, *Pastors at Risk* (Wheaton, IL: Victor Books, 1993); "Is the Pastor's Family Safe at Home?" *Leadership* (Fall 1992); *Physician Magazine* (September/October 1999), 22; The Barna Group, "Pastors Feel Confident in Ministry, but Many Struggle in Their Interaction with Others," *The Barna Update* (July 10, 2006). http://www.barna.org.
[192] Compilation of surveys from Focus on the Family Pastors Gatherings.
[193] Fuller Institute of Church Growth (Pasadena: Fuller Theological Seminary, 1991).
[194] Witham, "Flocks in Need of Shepherds."
[195] *Vantage Point*, Denver Seminary (June 1998), 2.
[196] The Barna Group, "A Profile of Protestant Pastors," *The Barna Update* (September 25, 2001). These tasks include casting vision, identifying and training leaders, preaching and teaching, raising money, serving the needy, providing strategy and planning, organizing church activities and programs, overseeing all administration, managing staff and volunteers, resolving conflicts, representing the congregation in the community, providing congregation care and counseling, evangelizing the unsaved, administering the sacraments, and discipling individuals.

1,400 ministers in all denominations across the United States are fired or forced to resign each month.[197] Over the past twenty years, the average length of a pastorate has declined from seven years to just over four years![198]

Unfortunately, few pastors have connected the dots to discover that it is their office that causes this underlying turbulence.[199] Simply put: Jesus Christ never intended any person to sport all the hats a present-day pastor is expected to wear. He never intended any one person to bear such a load.

The demands of the pastorate are crushing; they will drain any mortal dry. Imagine for a moment that you were working for a company that paid you on the basis of how good you made your people feel. What if your pay depended on how entertaining you were, how friendly you were, how popular your wife and children were, how well-dressed you were, and how perfect your behavior was?

Can you imagine the unmitigated stress this would cause you? Can you see how such pressure would force you into playing a pretentious role—all to keep your authority, your prestige, and your job security? (For this reason, many pastors are resistant to receiving any kind of help.)[200]

The pastoral profession dictates standards of conduct like any other profession, whether it be teacher, doctor, or lawyer. The profession dictates how pastors are to dress, speak, and act. This is one of the major reasons why many pastors live very artificial lives.

In this regard, the pastoral role fosters dishonesty. Congregants

---

[197] *The Christian Citizen* (November 2000) reported that 1,400 pastors leave the pastorate each month. In the same vein, *The Washington Times* ran a series of five articles by Larry Witham on the "clergy crisis" that is sweeping America. Witham reported: Very few of the clergy in this country are young. Only 8 percent are 35 or younger. Of the 70,000 students enrolled in the nation's 237 accredited theological seminaries, only a third want to lead a church as a pastor. The pastorate draws a greater number of older candidates. In like manner, a clergy shortage has hit most mainline Protestant churches in Canada. "While it may be personally enriching to minister to a flock, it's also daunting—for not a lot of money—to meet expectations as a theologian, counselor, public speaker, administrator and community organizer all in one" (Douglas Todd, "Canada's Congregations Facing Clergy Shortage," *Christian Century* [October 10, 2001], 13).

[198] Data drawn from PastorPoll surveys conducted by The Barna Group from 1984 through 2006.

[199] I (Frank) once read the following promotion for a pastors' resource book: "Man works from sun to sun, but a pastor's work is never done. That's because he must wear so many different hats: preacher, teacher, counselor, administrator, worship leader, and oftentimes fixer of the furniture too! For pastors who'd like a hand with some of these hats, we . . . have just the resource for you."

[200] For a firsthand account of the psychological pressures of the modern pastorate, see C. Welton Gaddy, *A Soul Under Siege: Surviving Clergy Depression* (Philadelphia: Westminster, 1991).

expect their pastor to always be cheerful, completely spiritual, and available at a moment's call. They also expect that he will have a perfectly disciplined family. Furthermore, he should never appear resentful or bitter.[201] Many pastors take to this role like actors in a Greek drama.[202]

Based on the scores of personal testimonies we have heard from erstwhile pastors, many—if not most—pastors cannot stay in their office without being corrupted on some level. The power-politics endemic to the office is a huge problem that isolates many of them and poisons their relationship with others.

In an insightful article to pastors entitled "Preventing Clergy Burnout," the author suggests something startling. His advice to pastors gives us a clear peek into the power-politics that goes with the pastorate.[203] He implores pastors to "fellowship with clergy of other denominations. These persons cannot harm you ecclesiastically, because they are not of your official circle. There is no political string they can pull to undo you."[204]

Professional loneliness is another virus that runs high among pastors. The lone-ranger plague drives some ministers into other careers. It drives others into crueler fates.[205]

All of these pathologies find their root in the history of the pastorate. It is "lonely at the top" because God never intended for anyone to be at the top—except His Son! In effect, the present-day pastor tries to shoulder the fifty-eight New Testament "one another" exhortations all by himself.[206] It is no wonder that many of them get crushed under the weight.[207]

---

[201] Larry Burkett, "First-Class Christians, Second-Class Citizens," *East Hillsborough Christian Voice* (February 2002), 3.

[202] Not all pastors play to this role. But the few who manage to resist this incredible pressure seem to be the exception to the rule.

[203] Alarmingly, 23 percent of Protestant clergy have been fired at least once, and 41 percent of congregations have fired at least two pastors. Survey done by *Leadership* printed in G. Lloyd Rediger's *Clergy Killers: Guidance for Pastors and Congregations Under Attack* (Philadelphia: Westminster/John Knox, 1997).

[204] J. Grant Swank, "Preventing Clergy Burnout," *Ministry* (November 1998), 20.

[205] Larry Yeagley, "The Lonely Pastor," *Ministry* (September 2001), 28; Michael L. Hill and Sharon P. Hill, *The Healing of a Warrior: A Protocol for the Prevention and Restoration of Ministers Engaging in Destructive Behavior* (Cyberbook, 2000).

[206] For example: Love one another (Romans 13:8); care for one another (1 Corinthians 12:25); serve one another (Galatians 5:13); edify one another (Romans 14:19); bear with one another (Ephesians 4:2, NKJV); exhort one another (Hebrews 3:13), etc.

[207] *Searching Together* 23, no.4 (Winter 1995) discusses this issue at length.

CONCLUSION

The contemporary pastor is the most unquestioned fixture in twenty-first-century Christianity. Yet not a strand of Scripture supports the existence of this office.

Rather, the present-day pastor was born out of the single-bishop rule first spawned by Ignatius and Cyprian. The bishop evolved into the local presbyter. In the Middle Ages, the presbyter grew into the Catholic priest. During the Reformation, he was transformed into the "preacher," "the minister," and finally "the pastor"—the person upon whom all of Protestantism hangs. To boil it down to one sentence: The Protestant pastor is nothing more than a slightly reformed Catholic priest. (Again, we are speaking of the office and not the individual.)

Catholic priests had seven duties at the time of the Reformation: preaching; the sacraments; prayers for the flock; a disciplined, godly life; church rites; supporting the poor; and visiting the sick.[208] The Protestant pastor takes upon himself all of these responsibilities—plus he sometimes blesses civic events.

The famed poet John Milton put it best when he said, "New presbyter is but old priest writ large!"[209] In other words, the contemporary pastor is but an old priest written in larger letters!

>delving DEEPER

1. *While you note that the early church received oversight from church planters who did not stay long-term in any one church, wasn't that largely because trained leaders were rare—a situation still true in many parts of the world even today—and had to be shared by a number of churches?*

No. Church planters deliberately left so that the church could function under the headship of Christ. If a church planter stays in a church, the members naturally look to him to lead. Every-member functioning is hindered. This is still true today.

---

[208] Johann Gerhard in *Church Ministry* by Eugene F. A. King (St. Louis: Concordia Publishing House, 1993), 181.
[209] From Milton's 1653 poem "On the New Forcers of Conscience under the Long Parliament."

The pattern throughout the entire New Testament is that church planters (apostolic workers) always left the church after they laid the foundation. For more details, see *The Normal Christian Church Life* by Watchman Nee (Anaheim: Living Stream Ministry, 1980).

2. James 3:1 says, "Not many of you should become teachers in the church, for we who teach will be judged more strictly" (NLT). First Corinthians 12:27-31 clearly states that the Holy Spirit has gifted every person differently—not everyone is gifted as an apostle, prophet, or teacher, and each believer has a different function. Don't these Scriptures support the idea that God calls only some to preach, teach, and minister to the church at large?

Yes, absolutely. We agree that there are teachers, preachers, prophets, apostles, evangelists, and even shepherds in the church of Jesus Christ. The contemporary pastoral office, however, is not what these texts envision. In fact, since pastors today are generally expected to take on so many roles, they often must operate outside their giftedness. That is unfair, both to them and to those within the body who possess these very gifts and are not permitted to use them.

3. While you characterize ordination as a formal Christian rite with pagan roots, this process ensures that church leaders have a proper grasp of the Scriptures and publicly commit themselves to building up the church. Doesn't ordination, therefore, serve as an important safeguard for those within a church?

This question is based on the assumption that the modern clergy system is the model for Christian ministry. As we have shown, the early Christians knew nothing of a clergy. And they certainly did not know anything about an ordained clergy.

Apostolic workers acknowledged local elders in some churches. (Acts 20:28, 1 Timothy 3, and Titus 1 describe the qualities of these elders.) And churches sent out apostolic workers to do the work of church planting. But these practices have few points of contact with modern ordination ceremonies, which elevate some Christians above others.

4. What do you mean when you say that "many—if not most—pastors cannot stay in their office without being corrupted on some level"? Some of the most godly, giving people I know are pastors who work incredibly hard for the Kingdom.

We know many hard-working, godly, and giving pastors also. But we also know countless pastors who have admitted, often late in their careers, that they were corrupted by the office on some level. Some have personally confessed to us, "It didn't affect me for a number of years, but after a while, it began to change me without my realizing it." They explained how they became people pleasers, trying to play to their "audience" and maintain a particular image. This observation has nothing to do with a pastor's motives. It has to do with the powerful influence of an unbiblical system.

All that aside, the real question is, should we support an office and a role that has no basis in the New Testament? If the modern pastoral office and role is a God-inspired development, then we should support it. But if it is not, we should not be surprised to learn it has harmful effects on those who fill the role.

5. What would you say to pastors who read this chapter and feel that you are attacking them personally?

It is not in our hearts to demean any pastor or minister. We believe that most of them are called of God, love God, and are servants to His people (see p. 106). Yet we understand that some pastors may feel attacked when reading this chapter. We suggest that, in some cases, that may be because their identity is so tied up with their position, which isn't surprising considering the leadership structure and system we have created and passed down through the years. Pastors who are secure in their office or role should not feel threatened as they read this book. We do not claim to be infallible in our conclusions. We simply ask that our readers be open to considering them.

chapter six

> SUNDAY MORNING COSTUMES: COVERING UP THE PROBLEM

"Beware of [those] who like to walk around in long robes."
   —JESUS CHRIST IN LUKE 20:46, NASB

"Beware lest any man spoil you through philosophy and vain deceit, after the tradition of men, after the rudiments of the world, and not after Christ."
   —PAUL OF TARSUS IN COLOSSIANS 2:8

EVERY SUNDAY MORNING, millions of Protestants throughout the world put on their best clothes to attend Sunday morning church.[1] But no one seems to question why. Hundreds of

---

[1]   Denominations like the Vineyard are the exception. Such neo-denominations espouse a casual form of worship that typically includes coffee and doughnuts before the service. Shorts and T-shirts are common apparel in a Vineyard church service. Most congregants in the 320,000 U.S. Protestant churches "dress up" for Sunday morning church. If we add the number of non-Protestant Christians who dress up for church, the number is astronomical.

thousands of pastors wear special garb that separates them from their congregants. And no one seems to care.

Admittedly the dress has become more casual in a number of churches over the past few decades. A person dressed in denim can walk into the sanctuaries of many churches today without getting dirty looks. Yet dressing up for church is still a common practice in many churches. In this chapter, we will explore the origin of "dressing up" for church. We will also trace the roots of the clergy's special attire.

DRESSING UP FOR CHURCH

The practice of dressing up for church is a relatively recent phenomenon.[2] It began in the late-eighteenth century with the Industrial Revolution, and it became widespread in the mid-nineteenth century. Before this time, "dressing up" for social events was known only among the very wealthy. The reason was simple. Only the well-to-do aristocrats of society could afford nice clothing! Common folks had only two sets of clothes: work clothes for laboring in the field and less tattered clothing for going into town.[3]

Dressing up for any occasion was only an option for the wealthiest nobility.[4] From medieval times until the eighteenth century, dress was a clear marker of one's social class. In places like England, poor people were actually forbidden to wear the clothing of the "better" people.[5]

This changed with the invention of mass textile manufacturing and the development of urban society.[6] Fine clothes became more affordable to the common people. The middle class was born, and those within it were able to emulate the envied aristocracy. For the first time, the middle class could distinguish themselves from the

---

[2] Dressing "decently" for church service goes back to around the third century. Clement of Alexandria (150–215) put it this way: "Woman and man are to go to church decently attired, with natural step, embracing silence . . . let the woman observe this further. Let her be entirely covered, unless she happens to be at home." ("Going to Church," *The Instructor*, bk. 3. ch. 11.)

[3] Max Barsis, *The Common Man through the Centuries* (New York: Unger, 1973).

[4] Leigh Eric Schmidt, "A Church Going People Is a Dress-Loving People," *Church History* (58), 38–39.

[5] Ibid.

[6] James Hargreaves invented the "spinning jenny" in 1764, creating finer, more colorful clothing that was affordable to the masses. Elizabeth Ewing, *Everyday Dress 1650–1900* (London: Batsford, 1984), 56–57.

peasants.[7] To demonstrate their newly improved status, they could now "dress up" for social events just like the well-to-do.[8]

Some Christian groups in the late eighteenth and early nineteenth centuries resisted this cultural trend. John Wesley wrote against wearing expensive or flashy clothing.[9] The early Methodists so resisted the idea of dressing up for church that they turned away anyone who wore expensive clothing to their meetings.[10] The early Baptists also condemned fine clothing, teaching that it separated the rich from the poor.[11]

Despite these protests, mainstream Christians began wearing fine clothes whenever they could. The growing middle class prospered, desiring bigger homes, larger church buildings, and fancier clothing.[12] As the Victorian enculturation of the middle class grew, fancier church buildings began to draw more influential people in society.[13]

This all came to a head when in 1843, Horace Bushnell, an influential Congregational minister in Connecticut, published an essay called "Taste and Fashion." In it, Bushnell argued that sophistication and refinement were attributes of God and that Christians should emulate them.[14] Thus was born the idea of dressing up for church to honor God. Church members now worshipped in elaborately decorated buildings sporting their formal clothes to honor God.[15]

---

7 Bushman, *Refinement of America*, 313.

8 Henry Warner Bowden and P. C. Kemeny, eds., *American Church History: A Reader* (Nashville: Abingdon Press, 1971), 87–89. Dress and hierarchy were closely connected in colonial America. A pamphlet published anonymously in Philadelphia in 1722 entitled *The Miraculous Power of Clothes, and Dignity of the Taylors: Being an Essay on the Words, Clothes Make Men* suggested the following: Social status, station, and power were displayed, expressed, and sustained through dress. The connection between dress and hierarchy in colonial society invested clothes with symbolic power. This mind-set eventually seeped into the Christian church.

9 Rupert Davies, *A History of the Methodist Church in Great Britain* (London: Epworth, 1965), 193; Nehemiah Curnock, ed., *Journals of Wesley* (London: Epworth Press, 1965), 193. Wesley's teaching on clothing has been called "a gospel of plainness." His main message was that Christians ought to dress plainly, neatly, and simply. Wesley spoke on this subject so often that he is credited for coining the phrase "Cleanliness is next to godliness." However, he borrowed it from a rabbi (Phinehas Ben-Yair, *Song of Songs*, Midrash Rabbah, I.1:9).

10 Davies, *History of the Methodist Church*, 197.

11 Schmidt, "A Church Going People Is a Dress-Loving People," 40.

12 Bushman, *Refinement of America*, 335, 352.

13 Ibid., 350. Denominations with a greater number of wealthy members (Episcopal, Unitarian, etc.) began selling pews to wealthy families to fund elaborate church building programs. "On top of pew costs, worshippers had to wear clothes in keeping with the splendor of the building, and the style of the congregation became an insurmountable barrier for many. A century earlier a common farmer could dress up for church by putting on a blue check shirt. In the genteel atmosphere of the new beautiful churches, more was required."

14 Ibid., 328, 331.

15 Ibid., 350.

In 1846, a Virginia Presbyterian named William Henry Foote wrote that "a church-going people are a dress loving people."[16] This statement simply expressed the formal dress ritual that mainstream Christians had adopted when going to church. The trend was so powerful that by the 1850s, even the "formal-dress-resistant" Methodists got absorbed by it. And they, too, began wearing their Sunday best to church.[17]

Accordingly, as with virtually every other accepted church practice, dressing up for church is the result of Christians being influenced by their surrounding culture. Today, many Christians "suit up" for Sunday morning church without ever asking why. But now you know the story behind this mindless custom.

It is purely the result of nineteenth-century middle-class efforts to become like their wealthy aristocrat contemporaries, showing off their improved status by their clothing. (This effort was also helped along by Victorian notions of respectability.) It has nothing to do with the Bible, Jesus Christ, or the Holy Spirit.

SO WHAT'S WRONG WITH IT?

What's the big deal about "dressing up" for church? It is hardly a burning issue. However, it is what dressing up for church represents that is the burning issue.

First, it reflects the false division between the secular and the sacred. To think that God cares one whit if you wear dressy threads on Sunday to "meet Him" is a violation of the New Covenant. We have access to God's presence at all times and in all circumstances. Does He really expect His people to dress up for a beauty pageant on Sunday morning?

Second, wearing attractive, flashy clothes on Sunday morning screams out an embarrassing message: that church is the place where

---

16 Schmidt, "A Church Going People Is a Dress-Loving People," 36.
17 Bushman, *Refinement of America*, 319. "The early Methodists knew fashionable dress was the enemy, and now the enemy was winning." Schmidt writes, "People were concerned on the Sabbath . . . to dress themselves in their best clothes; Sunday best was already proverbial. Even pietists and evangelicals who insisted on plain dress nonetheless made sure that their bodies were gravely and decently clothed" (Schmidt, "A Church Going People Is a Dress-Loving People," 45).

Christians hide their real selves and "dress them up" to look nice and pretty.[18] Think about it. Wearing your Sunday best for church is little more than image management. It gives the house of God all the elements of a stage show: costumes, makeup, props, lighting, ushers, special music, master of ceremonies, performance, and the featured program.[19]

Dressing up for church violates the reality that the church is made up of real people with messy problems—real people who may have gotten into a major-league bickering match with their spouses just before they drove into the parking lot and put on colossal smiles to cover it up!

Wearing our "Sunday best" conceals a basic underlying problem. It fosters the illusion that we are somehow "good" because we are dressing up for God. It is a study in pretense that is dehumanizing and constitutes a false witness to the world.

Let's face it. As fallen humans, we are seldom willing to appear to be what we really are. We almost always rely on our performance or dress to give people a certain impression of what we want them to believe we are. All of this differs markedly from the simplicity that marked the early church.

Third, dressing up for church smacks against the primitive simplicity that was the sustaining hallmark of the early church. The first-century Christians did not "dress up" to attend church meetings. They met in the simplicity of living rooms. They did not dress to exhibit their social class. In fact, the early Christians made concrete efforts to show their absolute disdain for social class distinctions.[20]

In the church, all social and racial distinctions are erased. The early Christians knew well that they were a new species on this

---

[18] God looks at the heart; He is not impressed with the garb we wear (1 Samuel 16:7; Luke 11:39; 1 Peter 3:3-5). Our worship is in the spirit, not in physical outward forms (John 4:20-24).

[19] Christian Smith, "Our Dressed Up Selves," *Voices in the Wilderness* (September/October, 1987), 2.

[20] In his book *Ante Pacem: Archaeological Evidence of Church Life Before Constantine*, Graydon Snyder states that there are about thirty extant letters written by Christians before Constantine. According to these letters, the Christians typically dropped their general family name, which indicated their social status. They also called one another "brother" and "sister." Graydon Snyder, e-mail messages to Frank Viola, October 12 and 14, 2001, and July 10, 2007.

planet.[21] For this reason, James levels a rebuke to those believers who were treating the rich saints better than the poor saints. He boldly reproves the rich for dressing differently from the poor.[22]

And yet, many Christians are under the false delusion that it is "irreverent" to dress in informal clothing when attending a Sunday morning church service. This is not dissimilar to how the Scribes and the Pharisees accused the Lord and His disciples of being irreverent for not following the tradition of the elders (Mark 7:1-13).

In short, to say that the Lord expects His people to dress in fine clothing when the church gathers is to add to the Scriptures and speak where God has not spoken.[23] Such a practice is human tradition at its best.

THE GARB OF THE CLERGY

Let's now shift gears and look at the development of the clergy attire. Christian clergy did not dress differently from the common people until the coming of Constantine.[24]

Contrary to popular opinion, clergy apparel (including the "ecclesiastical vestments" of the high church tradition) did not originate with the priestly dress of the Old Testament. It rather has its origin in the secular dress of the Greco-Roman world.[25]

Here is the story: Clement of Alexandria argued that the clergy should wear better garments than the laity. (By this time the church liturgy was regarded as a formal event.) Clement said that the minister's clothes should be "simple" and "white."[26]

---

[21] The early Christians saw themselves as a new creation, a new humanity, and a new species that transcends all natural distinctions and barriers (1 Corinthians 10:32; 2 Corinthians 5:17; Galatians 3:28; Ephesians 2:15; Colossians 3:11).

[22] James 2:1-5. This passage also suggests that a person wearing fashionable clothing to the church meeting was the exception, not the standard.

[23] Deuteronomy 4:2; Proverbs 30:6; Revelation 22:18.

[24] *The Catholic Encyclopedia 1913 On-Line Edition*, s.v. "Vestments," http://www.newadvent.org/cathen/15388a.htm; *Encyclopedia Britannica Online*, s.v. "Sacred Rights Ceremonies: The Concept and Forms of Ritual: Christianity" (1994–1998). Shortly before Constantine, clergymen wore a cloak of fine material when administering the Eucharist.

[25] *Catholic Encyclopedia*, s.v. "Vestments." Under "Origin" the entry reads: "The Christian vestments did not originate in the priestly dress of the Old Testament, they have, rather, developed from the secular dress of the Graeco-Roman world." See also Janet Mayo, *A History of Ecclesiastical Dress* (New York: Holmes & Meier Publishers, 1984), 11–12. Mayo writes, "A consideration of ecclesiastical vestments will reveal that they had their origins in secular Roman dress. The view that vestments were of Levitical origin and came from Jewish priestly garments is a later idea." For a rare history of the religious costume, see Amelia Mott Gummere, *The Quaker: A Study in Costume* (Philadelphia: Ferris and Leach, 1901). Note that the vestments of the priesthood in the Old Testament were types and shadows of the spiritual garments that Christians are clothed with in Christ Jesus (Hebrews 10:1; Colossians 2:16-17, 3:10-14; Ephesians 4:24; 1 Peter 5:5; Revelation 19:8).

[26] "On Clothes," *The Instructor*, bk. 3, ch. 11.

White was the color of the clergy for centuries. This custom appears to have been borrowed from the pagan philosopher Plato who wrote that "white was the color of the gods." In this regard, both Clement and Tertullian felt that dyed colors were displeasing to the Lord.[27]

With the coming of Constantine, distinctions between bishop, priest, and deacon began to take root.[28] When Constantine moved his court to Byzantium and renamed it Constantinople in AD 330, the official Roman dress was gradually adopted by the priests and deacons.[29] The clergy were now identified by their garb, which matched that of secular officials.[30]

After the Germanic conquests of the Roman Empire from the fourth century onward, fashions in secular dress changed. The flowing garments of the Romans gave way to the short tunics of the Goths. But the clergy, wishing to remain distinct from the laity, continued to wear the archaic Roman costumes![31]

The clergy wore these outdated garments during the church service following the model of the secular court ritual.[32] When laymen adopted the new style of dress, the clergy believed that such dress was "worldly" and "barbarian." They retained what they considered to be "civilized" dress. And this is what became the clerical attire.[33] This practice was supported by the theologians of the day. For example, Jerome (ca. 342–420) remarked that the clergy should never enter into the sanctuary wearing everyday garments.[34]

From the fifth century onward, bishops wore purple.[35] In the sixth

---

[27] Ibid., bk 2, ch. 11; Mayo, *A History of Ecclesiastical Dress*, 15.

[28] Mayo, *History of Ecclesiastical Dress*, 14–15.

[29] Ibid., Latourette, *A History of Christianity*, 211; Brauer, *The Westminster Dictionary of Church History* (Philadelphia: The Westminster Press, 1971), 284.

[30] "The bishop's dress was the ancient robe of a Roman magistrate." Hatch, *Organization of the Early Christian Churches*, 164. The bishop's dress indicated a specific caste structure. It included a white fringed saddlecloth or *mappula*, flat black slippers or *campagi*, and *udones* or white stockings. This was the dress of the Roman magistrates. Johnson, *History of Christianity*, 133.

[31] Senn, *Christian Worship and Its Cultural Setting*, 41; "Sacred Rights Ceremonies," *Encyclopedia Britannica Online*.

[32] Eugene TeSelle, professor of church history and theology, Vanderbilt University, in e-mail message to Frank Viola, January 18, 2000.

[33] Mayo, *History of Ecclesiastical Dress*, 15; Jones, *Historical Approach to Evangelical Worship*, 117.

[34] Jerome said that God is honored if the bishop wears a white tunic more handsome than usual. Frank Senn, liturgical scholar, in e-mail message to Frank Viola, July 18, 2000. See also Jerome, "Against Jovinianus" bk. 2.34 (*Nicene and Post-Nicene Fathers*, series 2, vol. 6) and "Lives of Illustrious Men," ch. 2 (*Nicene and Post-Nicene Fathers*, series 2, vol. 3).

[35] Collins and Price, *The Story of Christianity*, 25, 65.

and seventh centuries, clergy garb became more elaborate and costly.[36] By the Middle Ages, their clothing acquired mystical and symbolic meanings.[37] Special vestments were spawned around the sixth and seventh centuries. And there grew up the custom of keeping a special set of garments in the vestry to put over one's street clothes.[38]

During the seventh and eighth centuries, the vestments were accepted as sacred objects inherited from the robes of Levitical priests in the Old Testament.[39] (This was a rationalization to justify the practice.) By the twelfth century, the clergy also began wearing street clothes that distinguished them from everyone else.[40]

WHAT THE REFORMATION CHANGED

During the Reformation, the break with tradition and clerical vestments was slow and gradual.[41] In the place of the clergy vestments, the Reformers adopted the scholar's black gown.[42] It was also known as the philosopher's cloak, as it had been worn by philosophers in the fourth and fifth centuries.[43] So prevalent was the new clerical garb that the black gown of the secular scholar became the garment of the Protestant pastor.[44]

The Lutheran pastor wore his long black gown in the streets. He also wore a round "ruff" around his neck that grew larger with time. It grew so large that by the seventeenth century the ruff was

---

[36] Jones, *Historical Approach to Evangelical Worship*, 116–117. Mayo's *History of Ecclesiastical Dress* goes into great detail on the development of each piece of the clerical vestments through each stage of history in each tradition. No distinctive headdress was worn for the first thousand years, and the girdle was not known until the eighth century. Elias Benjamin Sanford, ed., *A Concise Cyclopedia of Religious Knowledge* (New York: Charles L. Webster & Company, 1890), 943.

[37] Mayo, *History of Ecclesiastical Dress*, 27; Isidore of Pelusium (d. around 440) was the first to ascribe symbolic interpretations to parts of the vestments. The entire priestly garb was given symbolic meanings around the eighth century in the West and the ninth century in the East (*Catholic Encyclopedia*, s.v. "Vestments."). The Medievals had a love affair with symbolism, so they could not resist giving all the vestments religious "spiritual" meanings. These meanings are still alive today in liturgical churches.

[38] Senn, *Christian Worship and Its Cultural Setting*, 41. The vestry, or sacristy, was a special room in the church building where the clerical vestments and sacred vessels were kept.

[39] Mayo, *History of Ecclesiastical Dress*, 27.

[40] Collins and Price, *Story of Christianity*, 25, 65.

[41] Mayo, *History of Ecclesiastical Dress*, 64. Zwingli and Luther quickly discarded the garments of the Catholic priest. Hall, *Faithful Shepherd*, 6.

[42] Zwingli was the first to introduce the scholar's gown, in Zurich in the autumn of 1523. Luther began to wear it in the afternoon of October 9, 1524 (Niebuhr and Williams, *Ministry in Historical Perspectives*, 147). See also George Marsden, *The Soul of the American University: From Protestant Establishment to Established Nonbelief* (New York: Oxford University Press, 1994), 37.

[43] H. I. Marrou, *A History of Education in Antiquity* (New York: Sheed and Ward, 1956), 206. "The philosopher could be recognized by his cloak, which was short and dark and made of coarse cloth." See also Smith, *From Christ to Constantine*, 105.

[44] Niebuhr and Williams, *Ministry in Historical Perspectives*, 147. The black gown was "clerical streetwear" in the sixteenth century (Senn, *Christian Worship and Its Cultural Setting*, 42).

called "the millstone ruff."[45] (The ruff is still worn in some Lutheran churches today.)

Interestingly, however, the Reformers still retained the clerical vestments. The Protestant pastor wore them when he administered the Lord's Supper.[46] This is still the case today in many Protestant denominations. Just like Catholic priests, many pastors will put on their clerical robes before lifting the bread and the cup.

The garb of the Reformed pastor (the black gown) symbolized his spiritual authority.[47] This trend continued throughout the seventeenth and eighteenth centuries. Pastors always wore dark clothing, preferably black. (This was the traditional color for "professionals" such as lawyers and doctors during the sixteenth century.)

Black soon became the color of every minister in every branch of the church.[48] The black scholar's gown eventually evolved into the "frock coat" of the 1940s. The frock coat was later replaced by the black or grey "lounge suit" of the twentieth century.[49]

At the beginning of the twentieth century, many clergymen wore white collars with a tie. In fact, it was considered highly improper for a clergyman to appear without a tie.[50] Low church clergy (Baptists, Pentecostals, etc.) wore the collar and necktie. High church clergy (Anglicans, Episcopalians, Lutherans, etc.) adopted the clerical collar—often dubbed the "dog collar."[51]

The origin of the clerical collar goes back to 1865. It was not a Catholic invention as is popularly believed. It was invented by the Anglicans.[52] Priests in the eighteenth and nineteenth centuries traditionally wore black cassocks (floor-length garments with collars that stood straight up) over white garments (sometimes called the alb).

---

45 Chadwick, *Reformation*, 422–423.
46 Mayo, *History of Ecclesiastical Dress*, 66.
47 Bowden and Kemeny, *American Church History*, 89.
48 Mayo, *History of Ecclesiastical Dress*, 77–78.
49 Ibid., 118.
50 Ibid., 94.
51 Ibid., 94, 118.
52 Niebuhr and Williams, *Ministry in Historical Perspectives*, 164. According to *The London Times* (March 14, 2002), the clerical collar was invented by the Rev. Dr. Donald McLeod of Glasgow. A popular belief is that the clerical collar was invented by the Catholic Counter-Reformation to prevent priests from wearing large ruffs like Protestant pastors wore (Chadwick, *Reformation*, 423). But it seems to have come into being well after this.

In other words, they wore a black collar with white in the middle. The clerical collar was simply a removable version of this collar. It was invented so that priests, both Anglican and Catholic, could slip it over their street clothes and be recognized as "men of God" in any place!

Today, it is the dark suit with a tie that is the standard attire of most Protestant pastors. Many pastors would not be caught dead without it! Some Protestant pastors wear the clergy collar as well. The collar is the unmistakable symbol that the person wearing it is a clergyman.

IS SPECIAL CLERGY ATTIRE HARMFUL?

A specially attired clergy is an affront to the spiritual principles that govern the house of God. It strikes at the heart of the church by separating God's people into two classes: "professional" and "nonprofessional."

Like "dressing up" for church, clerical clothing—whether it be the elaborate vestments of the "high church" minister or the dark suit of the evangelical pastor—is rooted in worldly culture. The distinctive garb of the clergy goes back to the fourth century, when clergymen adopted the dress of Roman secular officials.

The Lord Jesus and His disciples knew nothing of wearing special clothing to impress God or to distinguish themselves from God's people.[53] Wearing special garb for religious purposes was rather a characteristic of the Scribes and Pharisees.[54] And neither Scribe nor Pharisee could escape the Lord's penetrating gaze when He said, "Beware of the teachers of the law. They like to walk around in flowing robes and love to be greeted in the marketplaces and have the most important seats in the synagogues and the places of honor at banquets" (Luke 20:46, NIV).

---

[53] Luke 7:25; 2 Corinthians 8:9. It appears that the nicest clothes that Jesus owned while on earth were given to him in mockery—Luke 23:11. Recall that the Son of God entered this earth not in kingly garments, but wrapped in swaddling clothes (Luke 2:7). Note that John the Baptist is the most extreme case of those who did not seek to impress God by their clothing (Matthew 3:4).

[54] Matthew 23:5; Mark 12:38.

>delving DEEPER

1. You imply that people should never be encouraged to dress up for church; however, for me, doing so serves as a reminder that we should give God the respect He deserves. In this sense, isn't wearing good clothes to church a positive thing?

If you feel that dressing up for church gatherings is a positive thing and you can do it unto the Lord with pure motives, then by all means do so. But we should be careful not to judge or look down upon those who do not dress up for such gatherings.

2. Do you believe that dressing up for church is inherently wrong, or do you think it is a human-invented practice that can be redeemed?

The latter. Unlike some of the other traditional practices that we have traced in this book, we believe this one is an extrabiblical practice that can be redeemed (see answer above). There is nothing inherently wrong with wearing dressy clothes to a Christian gathering. As with all our religious traditions, we simply believe it is important to ask why we do it and get in touch with our motives behind it.

chapter seven

➤ MINISTERS OF MUSIC: CLERGY SET TO MUSIC

"The hallmark of an authentic evangelicalism is not the uncritical repetition of old traditions, but the willingness to submit every tradition, however ancient, to fresh biblical scrutiny and, if necessary, reform."

   —JOHN STOTT, TWENTIETH-CENTURY BRITISH MINISTER AND
   BIBLE SCHOLAR

"The real trouble is not in fact that the church is too rich but that it has become heavily institutionalized, with a crushing investment in maintenance. It has the characteristics of the dinosaur and battleship. It is saddled with a plant and a programme beyond its means, so that it is absorbed in problems of supply and preoccupied with survival. The inertia of the machine is such that the financial allocations, the legalities, the channels of organization, the attitudes of mind, are all set in the direction of continuing and enhancing the status quo. If one wants to pursue a course which cuts across these channels, then most of one's energies are exhausted before one ever reaches the enemy lines."

   —JOHN A. T. ROBINSON, TWENTIETH-CENTURY ENGLISH
   NEW TESTAMENT SCHOLAR

WALK INTO ANY CHRISTIAN CHURCH service and you'll find it will usually begin with the singing of hymns, choruses, or praise and worship songs. One person (or a team of people) will both lead and direct the singing. In more traditional churches, it will be the choir director or the music minister. (In some churches, this role is even played by the senior pastor.) Or it may be handled by the choir itself. In contemporary churches, it will be the worship leader or the praise and worship team.

Leading up to the sermon, those who "lead worship" select the songs that are to be sung. They begin those songs. They decide how those songs are to be sung. And they decide when those songs are over. Those sitting in the audience in no way, shape, or form lead the singing. They are led by someone else who is often part of the clerical staff—or who has similar stature.

This is in stark contrast to New Testament teaching and example. In the early church, worship and singing were in the hands of all of God's people.[1] The church herself led her own songs. Singing and leading songs was a corporate affair, not a professional event led by specialists.

THE ORIGINS OF THE CHOIR

This all began to change with the rise of the clergy and the advent of the Christian choir, which dates back to the fourth century. Shortly after the Edict of Milan (AD 313), the persecution of Christians ceased. During Constantine's reign, choirs were developed and trained to help celebrate the Eucharist. The practice was borrowed from Roman custom, which began its imperial ceremonies with processional music. Special schools were established, and choir singers were given the status of a second-string clergy.[2]

The roots of the choir are found in the pagan Greek temples

---

[1] Ephesians 5:19; Colossians 3:16. Note the words "speaking to yourselves" and "one another" in these passages.
[2] Liemohn, *The Organ and Choir in Protestant Worship*, 8.

and Greek dramas.[3] Will Durant states it beautifully: "In the Middle Ages, as in ancient Greece, the main fountainhead of drama was in religious liturgy. The Mass itself was a dramatic spectacle; the sanctuary a sacred stage; the celebrants wore symbolic costumes; priest and acolytes engaged in dialogue; and the antiphonal responses of priest and choir, and of choir to choir, suggested precisely that same evolution of drama from dialogue that had generated the sacred Dionysian play."[4]

With the advent of the choir in the Christian church, singing was no longer done by all of God's people but by clerical staff composed of trained singers.[5] This shift was partly due to the fact that heretical doctrines were spread through hymn singing. The clergy felt that if the singing of hymns was in their control, it would curb the spread of heresy.[6] But it was also rooted in the ever-growing power of the clergy as the main performers in the Christian drama.[7]

By AD 367, congregational singing was altogether banned. It was replaced by music from the trained choirs.[8] Thus was born the trained professional singer in the church. Singing in Christian worship was now the domain of the clergy and choir.

Ambrose is credited for creating the first postapostolic Christian hymns.[9] These hymns were modeled on the old Greek modes and

---

[3] The Greeks had trained choirs to accompany their pagan worship (H. W. Parke, *The Oracles of Apollo in Asia Minor* [London: Croom Helm, 1985], 102–103). Greek plays, both tragedy and comedy, were accompanied by orchestras (Marion Bauer and Ethel Peyser, *How Music Grew* [New York: G. P. Putnam's Sons, 1939], 36, 45; Elizabeth Rogers, *Music through the Ages* [New York: G. P. Putnam Sons, 1967], 87; Carl Shaulk, *Key Words in Church Music* [St. Louis: Concordia Publishing House, 1978], 64; Quasten, *Music and Worship in Pagan and Christian Antiquity*, 76; Alfred Sendrey, *Music in the Social and Religious Life of Antiquity* [Rutherford, NJ: Fairleigh Dickinson University Press, 1974], 327, 412). There were typically between fifteen and twenty-four people in the Greek choirs (Claude Calame, *Choruses of Young Women in Ancient Greece* [Lanham, MD: Rowman & Littlefield, 2001], 21). Some have tried to argue that the Christians borrowed choirs and chanting from the Jewish synagogue. But this is highly unlikely as the third- and fourth-century Christians borrowed little to nothing from the Jews. Instead, they drew heavily from their surrounding Greco-Roman culture. Interestingly, Greek music had its genesis in the Orient and Asia Minor (Rogers, *Music through the Ages*, 95).

[4] Durant, *Age of Faith*, 1027.

[5] Liemohn, *Organ and Choir in Protestant Worship*, 8–9. Up until the fourth century, congregational singing was a characteristic feature of Christian worship.

[6] Edward Dickinson, *The Study of the History of Music* (New York: Charles Scribner's Sons, 1905), 16, 24.

[7] Bauer and Peyser, *How Music Grew*, 71–72.

[8] Rogers, *Music through the Ages*, 108. The Council of Laodicea (AD ca. 367) forbade all others to sing in church besides the canonical singers. This act was to ensure that the quality of singing could be more homogeneous and controllable by those directing the worship (Davies, *The New Westminster Dictionary of Liturgy*, 131; Arthur Mees, *Choirs and Choral Music* [New York: Greenwood Press, 1969], 25–26).

[9] Ambrose's hymns were orthodox. The Arians used hymns plentifully to promote their heretical teachings about Jesus. (Arians believed that Jesus was a creature created by God.)

called by Greek names.[10] Ambrose also created a collection of liturgical chants that are still used today in some Catholic churches.[11] The liturgical chant is the direct descendant of the pagan Roman chant, which goes back to the ancient Sumerian cities.[12]

Papal choirs began in the fifth century.[13] When Gregory the Great became pope near the end of the sixth century, he reorganized the Schola Cantorum (school of singing) in Rome. (This school was founded by Pope Sylvester, who died in AD 335.)[14]

With this school, Gregory established professional singers who trained Christian choirs all throughout the Roman Empire. The singers trained for nine years. They had to memorize every song that they sang—including the famous Gregorian chant.[15] Gregory wiped out the last vestiges of congregational singing, believing music was a clerical function and the exclusive right of trained singers.

Trained choirs, trained singers, and the end of congregational singing all reflected the cultural mind-set of the Greeks. Much like oratory (professional speaking), the Greek culture was built around an audience-performer dynamic. Tragically, this trait was carried over from the temples of Diana and the Greek dramas straight into the Christian church. The congregation of God's people became spectators not only in spoken ministry, but in singing as well.[16] Regrettably, the spirit of Greek spectatorship still lives in the contemporary church.

Christian boys' choirs also go back to the days of Constantine. Some still exist. Most were created from orphanages.[17] The Vienna

10 Bauer and Peyser, *How Music Grew*, 71. "The Greek musical system was the precursor of that of the early Christian church, and the line of descent is unbroken from Greece, through Rome, to the Middle Ages and modern times" (Dickinson, *The Study of the History of Music*, 9). Actually, the earliest full text we have of a Christian hymn is dated around AD 200. Ambrose simply made hymn writing a common practice in the church. Christian music at this time drew from popular Greek idioms. Barry Leisch, *The New Worship: Straight Talk on Music and the Church* (Grand Rapids: Baker Book House, 1996). 35.

11 Rogers, *Music through the Ages*, 106.

12 Bauer and Peyser, *How Music Grew*, 70; Rogers, *Music through the Ages*, 61. "From words which have survived we know that each [Sumerian] temple practiced well-organized liturgies chanted in the techniques of solo and response (between priest and choir) and antiphony (choir to choir)." See also Dickinson, *The Study of the History of Music*, 25.

13 Dickinson, *Study of the History of Music*, 18.

14 Rogers, *Music through the Ages*, 109; Andrew Wilson-Dickson, *The Story of Christian Music* (Oxford: Lion Publications, 1992), 43; Appleby, *History of Church Music*, 28.

15 Bauer and Peyser, *How Music Grew*, 73–75; Rogers, *Music through the Ages*, 109. All singing at this time was without musical instruments.

16 Dickinson, *Study of the History of Music*, 14.

17 *The Catholic Encyclopedia*, s.v. "Choir," http://www.newadvent.org/cathen/03693b.htm; Shaulk, *Key Words in Church Music*, 64–65. Iris V. Cully and Kendig Brubaker Cully, eds., *Harper's Encyclopedia of Religious Education*, s.v. "Choir" (San Francisco: Harper & Row Publishers, 1971).

Boys Choir, for example, was founded in Vienna, Austria, in 1498. The choir sang exclusively for the court, at Mass, and at private concerts and state events.[18] The first boys' choirs were actually established by pagans who worshipped Greco-Roman gods.[19] These pagans believed that the voice of young boys possessed special powers.[20]

THE FUNERAL DIRGE AND PROCESSION

Another form of music with pagan roots is the funeral dirge. It was brought into the Christian church in the early third century. As one scholar put it, "The pagan cult of the dead was too much a part of the past lives of many Christians, formerly pagans, for them simply to be able to replace pagan dirges and funeral music with Psalmody."[21]

During the days of Constantine, Roman betrothal practices and funeral processions were adapted and transformed into Christian "funerals."[22] This was borrowed from pagan practice.[23] The so-called funeral dirge that is observed and accepted by Christians also came out of paganism.[24] It was brought into the Christian church in the early third century. Tertullian was opposed to Christian funeral procession simply because it had pagan origins.[25]

Not only did the funeral procession emerge out of paganism; so did the funeral oration. It was the common practice of pagans in the Roman Empire to hire one of the town's eloquent professors to speak at the funeral of a loved one. The speaker followed a little handbook for such occasions. He would work himself up to a passionate pitch and then say of the deceased, "He now lives among the gods, traversing the heavens and looking down on life below."[26] It was his job to

---

[18] http://www.bach-cantatas.com/Bio/Wiener-Sangerknaben.htm. For a discussion on the pagan origin of women's choirs, see Quasten, *Music and Worship in Pagan and Christian Antiquity*, 77–86.

[19] Parke, *Oracles of Apollo in Asia Minor*, 102–103; Quasten, *Music and Worship*, 87ff. "The pagans frequently used boys choirs in their worship, especially on festive occasions."

[20] Quasten, *Music and Worship*, 87.

[21] Ibid., 86, 160ff.

[22] Senn, *Christian Worship and Its Cultural Setting*, 41. Senn also explains how Roman betrothal practices were incorporated into Christian weddings.

[23] See chapter 3.

[24] Quasten, *Music and Worship*, 163.

[25] Ibid., 164–165.

[26] MacMullen, *Christianizing the Roman Empire*, 11–13.

comfort the loved ones of the deceased. This role is filled today by the contemporary pastor. Even the words of the oration are strikingly similar!

THE CONTRIBUTION OF THE REFORMATION

The major musical contribution of the Reformers was the restoration of congregational singing and the use of instruments. John Huss (1372–1415) of Bohemia and his followers (called Hussites) were among the first to bring both back into the church.[27]

Luther also encouraged congregational singing during certain parts of the service.[28] But congregational hymn singing did not reach its peak until the eighteenth century during the Wesleyan revival in England.[29]

In Reformation churches, the choir remained. It both supported and led congregational singing.[30] About 150 years after the Reformation, congregational singing became a generally accepted practice.[31] By the eighteenth century, the organ would take the place of the choir in leading Christian worship.[32]

Interestingly, there is no evidence of musical instruments in the Christian church service until the Middle Ages.[33] Before then, all singing during the service was unaccompanied by musical instruments.[34]

---

[27] Jones, *Historical Approach to Evangelical Worship*, 257. The Hussites created the first Protestant hymnbook in 1505 in Prague. See also Terry, *Evangelism: A Concise History*, 68.

[28] Jones, *Historical Approach to Evangelical Worship*, 257. During Luther's day, some sixty hymnbooks were published. More specifically, Luther augmented congregational singing as part of the liturgy. He left a Latin Mass, which was sung by the choir in towns and universities, and a German Mass, which was sung by the congregation in villages and rural places. These two models were merged in Lutheran practice in the sixteenth to eighteenth centuries. The Reformed were opposed to both choral music and congregational hymns. They approved only the singing of metrical (versified) Psalms and other biblical canticles. From their perspective, choirs and hymns were Roman. So Lutheran use of them demonstrated a half-baked reform (Frank Senn, e-mail message to Frank Viola, November 18, 2000).

[29] Jones, *Historical Approach to Evangelical Worship*, 257. The hymns of Isaac Watts, John Wesley, and Charles Wesley were widely used. Hymn writing and singing swept all Free Churches on two continents during this time.

[30] Liemohn, *Organ and Choir in Protestant Worship*, 15. John F. White remarks that "to this day there remains considerable confusion of exactly what the function of the choir is in Protestant worship, and there is no single good rationale for the existence of the choir in Protestantism" (*Protestant Worship and Church Architecture*, 186).

[31] Liemohn, *Organ and Choir in Protestant Worship*, 15–16.

[32] Ibid., 19. In the seventeenth century, the organ would play parts against the unison singing of the congregation, thus drowning out the people. Geneva churches tore out the organs from their church buildings because they did not want worship to be stolen from the people (Wilson-Dickson, *Story of Christian Music*, 62, 76–77). As with the steeple and other embellishments, evangelical churches eventually imported organs from the Anglicans during the 1800s to keep up with the competition. Bushman, *Refinement of America*, 336–337.

[33] Ferguson, *Early Christians Speak*, 157.

[34] Church fathers like Clement of Alexandria (of the third century), Ambrose, Augustine, and Jerome (of the fourth and fifth centuries) all opposed using musical instruments in their worship. Like Calvin later on, they associated musical instruments with pagan ceremonies and Roman theatrical productions. Liemohn, *Organ and Choir in Protestant Worship*, 2; Quasten, *Music and Worship*, 64.

The church fathers took a dim view of musical instruments, associating them with immorality and idolatry.[35] Calvin agreed, viewing musical instruments as pagan. Consequently, for two centuries, Reformed churches sang psalms without the use of instruments.[36]

The organ was the first instrument used by post-Constantinian Christians.[37] Organs were found in Christian churches as early as the sixth century. But they were not used during the Mass until the twelfth century. By the thirteenth century, the organ became an integral part of the Mass.[38]

The organ was first used to give the tone to the priests and the choir.[39] During the Reformation, the organ became the standard instrument used in Protestant worship—except among the Calvinists, who removed and demolished church organs.[40] The first organ to be purchased by an American church was in 1704.[41]

The first Protestant choirs began flourishing in the mid-eighteenth century.[42] Special seats were assigned to choir members to show their special status.

At first, the function of the choir was to set the pitch for congregational singing. But before long, the choir began to contribute special selections.[43] Thus was born special music by the choir as the congregation watched it perform.

By the end of the nineteenth century, the children's choir made its appearance in American churches.[44] By this time, it became customary for the choir in nonliturgical churches to play special music. (This practice was eventually carried over to liturgical churches as well.)[45]

---

[35] Ferguson, *Early Christians Speak*, 157.
[36] Jones, *Historical Approach to Evangelical Worship*, 255–256. The *Genevan Psalter*, published in 1522, was the standard hymnbook for Reformed churches in Europe and the United States for over 200 years.
[37] Ibid., 256.
[38] Liemohn, *Organ and Choir in Protestant Worship*, 4.
[39] Ibid., 3.
[40] Ibid., 3, 32–33. Wesleyans forbade organs in 1796, preferring the bass viol as the only legal instrument in worship. But organs were installed twelve years later in Wesleyan churches (pp. 91–92). The Lutheran organ became an indispensable feature of Lutheran worship. Ironically, the Lutheran organ music tradition was founded by a Dutch Calvinist named Jan Pieterszoon Sweelinck in the early seventeenth century (Senn, *Christian Liturgy*, 534).
[41] The church was Trinity Church in New York. For a discussion on the first organs used in America, see Liemohn, *Organ and Choir in Protestant Worship*, 110–111.
[42] Ibid., 113; White, *Protestant Worship and Church Architecture*, 110.
[43] Liemohn, *Organ and Choir in Protestant Worship*, 115.
[44] Ibid., 125. The First Presbyterian Church in Flemington, New Jersey, is credited with being the first to organize a children's choir.
[45] Ibid.

The location of the choir is worth noting. In the late sixteenth century, the choir moved from the chancel (clergy platform) to the rear gallery where a pipe organ was installed.[46] But during the Oxford Movement of the late nineteenth and early twentieth centuries, the choir returned to the chancel. It was at this time that choir members began wearing ecclesiastical robes.[47] By the 1920s and 1930s, it was customary for American choirs to wear these special vestments to match the newly acquired neo-Gothic church buildings.[48] The choir in their archaic clerical clothes were now standing with the clergy in front of the people![49]

THE ORIGIN OF THE WORSHIP TEAM

In many contemporary churches, whether charismatic or noncharismatic, the choir has been replaced by the worship team.[50] Such churches have sanctuaries that boast few religious symbols (except possibly banners or flags).

At the front of the stage is a simple podium, some plants, amplifiers, speakers, and lots of wires. The dress is usually casual. Folding chairs or theater seats typically are used in place of pews. The standard worship team includes an amplified guitar, drums, keyboard, possibly a bass guitar, and some special vocalists. Words are usually projected onto a screen or a bare wall by an overhead (or video) projector or by PowerPoint slides. The songs are typically selected before the worship service. There are rarely songbooks or hymnals.

In such churches, worship means following the band's prescribed songs. The praise and worship time typically lasts from twenty to forty minutes. The first songs are usually upbeat praise choruses.[51] The worship team will then lead a lively, hand-clapping, body-swaying,

---

46 Senn, *Christian Liturgy*, 490.
47 Liemohn, *Organ and Choir in Protestant Worship*, 127; Wilson-Dickson, *Story of Christian Music*, 137.
48 Senn, *Christian Worship and Its Cultural Setting*, 49.
49 A. Madeley Richardson, *Church Music* (London: Longmans, Green, & Co., 1910), 57.
50 Denominations like the Vineyard, Calvary Chapel, and Hope Chapel hold the market share for these sorts of churches. However, many denominational and nondenominational churches have adopted the same style of worship.
51 The recovery of singing choruses of Scripture was brought in by the Jesus movement of the 1970s. David Kopp, *Praying the Bible for Your Life* (Colorado Springs: Waterbrook Press, 1999), 6–7.

hand-raising, (sometimes dancing) congregation into a potpourri of individualistic, gentle, worshipful singing. (Typically, the focus of the songs is on individual spiritual experience. First person singular pronouns—*I, me, my*—dominate a good number of the songs.[52] In some contemporary churches, the trend is moving more toward corporate, first person plural lines—*we, us, our*. This is a wonderful shift.)

As the band leaves the stage, ushers pass the offering plates. This is usually followed by the sermon, and the pastor dominates the rest of the service. In many churches, the pastor will call the worship team to return to the stage to play a few more worshipful songs as he winds up his sermon. "Ministry time" may ensue as the band plays on.

The song liturgy just described works like clockwork in the typical charismatic and nondenominational church. But where did it come from?

In 1962, a group of dissatisfied British church musicians in Dunblane, Scotland, tried to revitalize traditional Christian songs. Led by Congregational minister Erik Routley, these artists were influenced by Bob Dylan and Sydney Carter. George Shorney Jr. of Hope Publishing Company brought their new style to the United States. These new Christian hymns were a reform, but not a revolution. The revolution came when rock and roll was adapted into Christian music with the coming of the Jesus movement. This reform set the stage for the revolutionary musical changes to take root in the Christian church through Calvary Chapel and the Vineyard.[53]

The origin of the worship team goes back to the founding of Calvary Chapel in 1965. Chuck Smith, the founder of the denomination, started a ministry for hippies and surfers. Smith welcomed the newly converted hippies to retune their guitars and play their now redeemed music in church. He gave the counterculture a stage for their music—allowing them to play Sunday night performances and

---

[52] This maps perfectly with the baby boomers' self-focus.

[53] Since the advent of contemporary Christian music, the "worship wars" have begun, constituting a divisive force that has balkanized Christian churches into "old-styled-traditional-music lovers" vs. "new-styled-contemporary-music lovers." Not a few churches have been splintered right down the middle over what form of music is to be used during the church service. Contemporary vs. traditional music has become the root, stem, and branch of the new sectarian, Christian tribalism that plagues the modern church.

concerts."[54] The new musical forms began to be called "praise and worship."[54] As the Jesus movement began to flourish, Smith founded the record company Maranatha Music in the early 1970s. Its goal was to distribute the songs of these young artists.[55]

The Vineyard, under the influence of musical genius John Wimber, followed suit with the worship team. Wimber, a former Calvary Chapel pastor, became head of the Vineyard movement in 1982. Since that time, the Vineyard has probably had more influence on establishing worship teams and worship music than Calvary Chapel. Vineyard music is regarded as more intimate and worshipful, while Calvary Chapel's music is known for its upbeat, praise-oriented songs.[56]

In due time, the guitar replaced the organ as the central instrument that led worship in the Protestant church. Although patterned after the rock concert of secular culture, the worship team has become as common as the pulpit.

SO WHAT'S THE GRIPE?

Perhaps you are wondering, *What's wrong with having a choir leader, a worship leader, or a worship team to lead the church's singing?* Nothing . . . if every member of the church is content with it. However, many Christians feel that it robs God's people of a vital function: to select and lead their own singing in the meetings—to have divine worship in their own hands—to allow Jesus Christ to direct the singing of His church rather than have it led by a human facilitator. Singing in the early church was marked by these very features.

Listen to Paul's description of a New Testament church meeting: "Every one of you hath a psalm" (1 Corinthians 14:26). "Speak to one another with psalms, hymns and spiritual songs" (Ephesians 5:19, NIV). Consider the words "every one of you." Song leaders, choirs, and worship teams make this impossible by limiting the headship of

---

[54] Michael S. Hamilton, "The Triumph of Praise Songs: How Guitars Beat Out the Organ in the Worship Wars," *Christianity Today* (July 12, 1999).

[55] Donald E. Miller, *Reinventing American Protestantism* (Berkeley: University of Berkeley Press, 1997), 65, 83.

[56] Ibid., 19, 46–52, 84.

Christ—specifically His ministry of leading His brethr‹
ing praise songs to His Father. Of this ministry (which is l
today), the writer of Hebrews says, "Both the one who n
holy and those who are made holy are of the same family. S‹
not ashamed to call them brothers. He says, 'I will declare you
to my brothers; in the presence of the congregation [ekklesia] I will
sing your praises'" (Hebrews 2:11-12, NIV).

When worship songs can only be announced, initiated, and led by
the talented, this element of the service becomes more like entertainment than corporate worship.[57] And only those who "make the cut"
are allowed to participate in the ministry of leading songs. We would
argue that according to New Testament principle, the ministry of
singing belongs in the hands of all of God's people. And there should
be an outlet for this ministry to be expressed.

I (Frank) am no theoretician. For almost twenty years I have
gathered with churches where every member has been trained to start
a song spontaneously.[58] Imagine: Every brother and sister free to lead
songs under the headship of Jesus Christ—even to write his or her
own songs and bring them to the meeting for all to learn. I have met
with numerous churches that have experienced this glorious dynamic.
Someone starts a song and everyone joins in. Then someone else
begins another song, and so worship continues without long pauses
and with no visible leader present.

This is exactly how the first-century Christians worshipped, by
the way. Yet it is a rare experience in the modern-day institutional
church. The good news is that it is possible and available for all who
wish to experience Christ's headship through song in a church meeting. The singing in such churches is intensely corporate rather than
individualistic and subjective.[59]

"By the rivers of Babylon, there we sat down, yea, we wept, when

---

[57] I have no problem at all with talented musicians performing for an audience to encourage, instruct, inspire, or even entertain them. However, that ought not to be confused with the ministry of praise and worship singing, which belongs to the whole church.

[58] I (Frank) explain practically how a group of Christians can lead their own songs and write their own songs in my book *Gathering in Homes* (Gainesville, FL: Present Testimony Ministry, 2006).

[59] Ephesians 5:19 and Colossians 3:16 capture the flavor of the corporate nature of first-century Christian singing.

.emembered Zion. We hanged our harps upon the willows in the midst thereof. For there they that carried us away captive required of us a song; and they that wasted us required of us mirth, saying, Sing us one of the songs of Zion. How shall we sing the LORD's song in a strange land?" . . . "When the LORD turned again the captivity of Zion, we were like them that dream. Then was our mouth filled with laughter, and our tongue with singing: then said they among the heathen, The LORD hath done great things for them" (Psalm 137:1-4; 126:1-2).

>delving DEEPER

1. You expose the "pagan roots" of the church choir; yet I don't see why that in and of itself makes it less valuable. I don't have the gift of singing but appreciate that those who love music and are gifted in that area take the time and effort to prepare to lead me into worship through song. Your thoughts?

We also appreciate those who are musically gifted and who can use their musical talents to bless others. However, to relegate the song selections in every church gathering to a select few (i.e., a choir or worship team) disallows the rest of the body from participating in this ministry. This contradicts Scripture. As Paul says, "every one of you hath a psalm" in the gathering (1 Corinthians 14:26; see also Ephesians 5:19 and Colossians 3:16).

2. Currently my pastor and the worship team leader choose music that corresponds with the morning's message. I may not "connect" with every song chosen but don't see how that would be any different if everyone present were invited to choose and lead a song.

If one has never seen a group of Christians choosing and leading their own songs spontaneously under Christ's headship, it is difficult to grasp what this would look like. Suffice it to say that there is a world of difference between having a select group of people pick the songs and having every believer participate in initiating songs. It is the difference between passively following one person (or a small group) and everyone actively participating together spontaneously.

3. In the Old Testament period (see 1 Chronicles 23:5, 30; 25:1-31, 2 Chronicles 7:6), God instituted "professional" worship leaders among the Levitical families who led public worship and wrote many of the Psalms (e.g., those by Asaph and the descendants of Korah). Do you think this provides a biblical basis for a valid music ministry? Why or why not?

We believe these passages actually support our point. The Old Testament priesthood was restricted to a select group of people—the Levites. In the New Covenant, that selective priesthood has been done away with, and every Christian has been made a priest unto God. We are not part of the Levitical priesthood; we are priests after the order of Melchizedek (Hebrews 5–7). Christ is our High Priest, and every believer is a priest under Him (1 Peter 2:5, 9; Revelation 1:6). Therefore, to our minds, these passages show that every Christian has the right to participate in "leading worship" under Christ's headship.

4. Do you feel it's wrong for a Christian to sing a solo in a church gathering or for a band to play a song and lead a group of believers into worshipful singing?

Not at all. We are simply arguing that if these things eclipse, make void, and completely replace the ministry given to every believer to lead and participate in singing praise and worship songs to the Lord, we should consider the possibility that we may have squelched a God-ordained ministry of the church.

chapter eight

> TITHING AND CLERGY SALARIES: SORE SPOTS ON THE WALLET

"Unlike so many, we do not peddle the Word of God for profit."
—PAUL OF TARSUS IN 2 CORINTHIANS 2:17, NIV

"The church, embracing the mass of the population of the Empire, from the Caesar to the meanest slave, and living amidst all its institutions, received into her bosom vast deposits of foreign material from the world and from heathenism. . . . Although ancient Greece and Rome have fallen forever, the spirit of Graeco-Roman paganism is not extinct. It still lives in the natural heart of man, which at this day as much as ever needs regeneration by the Spirit of God. It lives also in many idolatrous and superstitious usages of the Greek and Roman churches, against which the pure spirit of Christianity has instinctively protested from the beginning, and will protest, till all remains of gross and refined idolatry shall be outwardly as well as inwardly overcome, and baptized and sanctified not only with water, but also with the spirit and fire of the gospel."
—PHILIP SCHAFF, NINETEENTH-CENTURY CHURCH HISTORIAN

"**WILL A MAN ROB GOD?** Yet you rob me. But you ask, "How do we rob you?" In tithes and offerings. You are under a curse—the whole nation of you—because you are robbing me. Bring the whole tithe into the storehouse, that there may be food in my house. Test me in this,' says the LORD Almighty, 'and see if I will not throw open the floodgates of heaven and pour out so much blessing that you will not have room enough for it'" (Malachi 3:8-10, NIV).

This passage seems to be many Christian leaders' favorite Bible text, especially when giving is at low tide. If you have spent any time in the contemporary church, you have heard this passage read from the pulpit on numerous occasions. Consider some of the rhetoric that goes with it:

"God has commanded you to faithfully give your tithes. If you do not tithe, you are robbing God Almighty, and you put yourself under a curse."

"Your tithes and offerings are necessary if God's work will go on!" ("God's work," of course, includes paying the pastoral staff and footing the monthly electric bill to keep the building afloat.)

What is the result of this sort of pressure? God's people are persuaded to give one-tenth of their incomes every week. When they do, they feel they have made God happy. And they can expect Him to bless them financially. When they fail, they feel they are being disobedient, and they worry that a financial curse looms over them.

But let's take a few steps backward and ask the penetrating question: "Does the Bible teach us to tithe? And . . . are we spiritually obligated to fund the pastor and his staff?"

The answer to these two questions may shock you.

IS TITHING BIBLICAL?

Tithing does appear in the Bible. So, yes, tithing is biblical. But it is not Christian. The tithe belongs to ancient Israel. It was essentially their income tax. Never do you find first-century Christians tithing in the New Testament.

Numerous Christians do not have the foggiest idea about what the Bible teaches regarding the tithe. So let's look at it. The word *tithe* simply means the tenth part.[1] The Lord instituted three kinds of tithes for Israel as part of their taxation system. They are:

> A tithe of the produce of the land to support the Levites who had no inheritance in Canaan.[2]

> A tithe of the produce of the land to sponsor religious festivals in Jerusalem. If the produce was too burdensome for a family to carry to Jerusalem, they could convert it into money.[3]

> A tithe of the produce of the land collected every third year for the local Levites, orphans, strangers, and widows.[4]

This was the biblical tithe. God commanded Israel to give 23.3 percent of their income every year, not 10 percent.[5] These tithes consisted of the produce of the land—which included the seed of the land, the fruit of the land, and the herd or the flock. It was the product of the land, not money.

A clear parallel can be seen between Israel's tithing system and the modern taxation system present in America. Israel was obligated to support their national workers (priests), their holidays (festivals), and their poor (strangers, widows, and orphans) with their annual tithes. Most modern tax systems serve a similar purpose.

With the death of Jesus, all ceremonial codes that belonged to the Jews were nailed to Christ's cross and buried, never to be used again to condemn us. For this reason, we never see Christians tithing in the New Testament, just as we don't see them sacrificing goats and bulls to cover their sins.

Paul writes, "When you were dead in your transgressions and the uncircumcision of your flesh, He made you alive together with Him, having forgiven us all our transgressions, having canceled out the certificate

---

[1] In the Old Testament, the Hebrew word for "tithe" is *maaser*, which means a tenth part. In the New Testament, the Greek word is *dekate*, which again means a tenth. The word is not taken from the religious world, but from the world of mathematics and finance.
[2] Leviticus 27:30-33; Numbers 18:21-31.
[3] Deuteronomy 14:22-27. This is sometimes called "the festival tithe."
[4] Deuteronomy 14:28-29, 26:12-13. Jewish historian Josephus and other scholars believe this is a third tithe used in a different way from the second. Stuart Murray, *Beyond Tithing* (Carlisle, UK: Paternoster Press, 2000), 76, 90; "What Is a Tithe?" Questions about Tithing, Generous Giving, http://www.generousgiving.org/page.asp?sec=43&page=589.
[5] Twenty percent yearly and 10 percent every three years equals 23.3 percent per year. God commanded all three tithes (Nehemiah 12:44; Malachi 3:8-12; Hebrews 7:5).

of debt consisting of decrees against us, which was hostile to us; and He has taken it out of the way, having nailed it to the cross. . . . Therefore no one is to act as your judge in regard to food or drink or in respect to a festival or a new moon or a Sabbath day—things which are a mere shadow of what is to come; but the substance belongs to Christ."[6]

Tithing belonged exclusively to Israel under the Law. When it comes to financial stewardship, we see the first-century Christians giving cheerfully according to their ability—not dutifully out of a command.[7] Giving in the early church was voluntary.[8] And those who benefited from it were the poor, orphans, widows, sick, prisoners, and strangers.[9]

We can hear someone making the following objection right now: "But what about Abraham? He lived before the Law. And we see him tithing to the high priest Melchizedek (Genesis 14:17-20). Does this not overturn your argument that the tithe is part of the Mosaic Law?"

No, it does not. First, Abraham's tithe was completely voluntary. It was not compulsory. God did not command it as He did with the tithe for Israel.

Second, Abraham tithed out of the spoils that he acquired after a particular battle he fought. He did not tithe out of his own regular income or property. Abraham's act of tithing would be akin to you winning the lottery or a mega jackpot, or receiving a work bonus, then tithing it.

Third, and most important, this is the only recorded time that Abraham tithed out of his 175 years of life on this earth. We have no evidence that he ever did such a thing again. Consequently, if you wish to use Abraham as a "proof text" to argue that Christians must tithe, then you are only obligated to tithe one time![10]

---

6   Colossians 2:13-14, 16-17, NASB; see also Hebrews 6–10.
7   This is very clear from 2 Corinthians 8:3-12, 9:5-13. Paul's word on giving is this: Give as God has prospered you—according to your ability and means.
8   Gough, Early Christians, 86.
9   "How We Christians Worship," Christian History 12, no. 1 (1993): 15.
10 The same is true for Jacob. According to Genesis 28:20-22, Jacob vowed to tithe to the Lord. But like Abraham's tithe, Jacob's tithe was completely voluntary. And as far as we know, it was not a lifetime practice. If Jacob began tithing regularly (and this cannot be proven), he waited for twenty years to pass before he started! To quote Stuart Murray, "Tithing appears to be almost incidental to the stories (of Abraham and Jacob) and no theological significance is accorded to this practice by the author."

This brings us back to that oft-quoted text in Malachi 3. What was God saying there? First, this passage was directed to ancient Israel when they were under the Mosaic Law. God's people were holding back their tithes and offerings. Consider what would happen if a large portion of a country's citizens refused to pay their taxes. This would be viewed as a form of stealing by many, and in some countries, those unwilling to pay would face consequences.[11]

In the same way, when Israel held back her taxes (tithes), she was stealing from God—the One who instituted the tithing system. The Lord then commanded His people to bring their tithes into the storehouse. The storehouse was located in the chambers of the Temple. The chambers were set apart to hold the tithes (which were produce, not money) for the support of the Levites, the poor, the strangers, and the widows.[12]

Notice the context of Malachi 3:8-10. In verse 5, the Lord says that He will judge those who oppress the widow, the fatherless, and the stranger. He says, "So I will come near to you for judgment. I will be quick to testify against sorcerers, adulterers and perjurers, against those who defraud laborers of their wages, who oppress the widows and the fatherless, and deprive aliens of justice, but do not fear me" (NIV).

The widows, fatherless, and strangers were the rightful recipients of the tithe. Because Israel was withholding her tithes, she was guilty of ignoring the needs of these three groups. Herein is the heart of God in Malachi 3:8-10: He opposes oppression of the poor.

How many times have you heard pastors point this out when they preached on Malachi 3? In scores of sermons I have heard on tithing, I was never told what the passage was actually talking about. That is, tithes were given to support the widows, the fatherless, the strangers, and the Levites (who owned nothing).

---

11 Note that some believe paying taxes is not a legal obligation in certain countries. We are simply using this as an illustration and nothing more.
12 Nehemiah 12:44, 13:12-13; Deuteronomy 14:28-29, 26:12.

THE ORIGIN OF THE TITHE AND THE CLERGY SALARY

The New Testament urges believers to give according to their ability. Christians in the early church gave to help other believers as well as to support apostolic workers, enabling them to travel and plant churches.[13] One of the most outstanding testimonies of the early church has to do with how generous the Christians were to the poor and needy.[14] This is what provoked outsiders, including the philosopher Galen, to watch the awesome, winsome power of the early church and say: "Behold how they love one another."[15]

In the third century, Cyprian of Carthage was the first Christian writer to mention the practice of financially supporting the clergy. He argued that just as the Levites were supported by the tithe, so the Christian clergy should be supported by the tithe.[16] But this is misguided thinking. Today, the Levitical system has been abolished. We are all priests now. So if a priest demands a tithe, then all Christians should tithe to one another!

Cyprian's plea was exceedingly rare for his time. It was neither picked up nor echoed by the Christian populace until much later.[17] Other than Cyprian, no Christian writer before Constantine ever used Old Testament references to advocate tithing.[18] It was not until the fourth century, three hundred years after Christ, that some Christian leaders began to advocate tithing as a Christian practice to support the clergy.[19] But it did not become widespread among Christians until the eighth century.[20] According to one

[13] Helping other believers: Acts 6:1-7, 11:27-30, 24:17; Romans 15:25-28; 1 Corinthians 16:1-4; 2 Corinthians 8:1-15, 9:1-12; 1 Timothy 5:3-16. Supporting church planters: Acts 15:3; Romans 15:23-24; 1 Corinthians 9:1-14, 16:5-11; 2 Corinthians 1:16; Philippians 4:14-18; Titus 3:13-14; 3 John 1:5-8. There is a close connection between the wallet and the heart. One out of every six verses in Matthew, Mark, and Luke have to do with money. Of the thirty-eight parables in the New Testament, twelve have to do with money.

[14] A telling and moving historical account of third- and fourth-century Christian generosity is found in Kreider, *Worship and Evangelism in Pre-Christendom*, 20. See also Tertullian's testimony of Christian charity in Johnson, *History of Christianity*, 75, and Tan, *Lost Heritage*, 51–56.

[15] Tertullian, *Apology* 39:7; Robert Wilken, *The Christians as the Romans Saw Them* (New Haven, CT: University Press, 1984), 79–82.

[16] Cyprian, Epistle 65.1; Murray, *Beyond Tithing*, 104.

[17] Murray, *Beyond Tithing*, 104–105; Ferguson, *Early Christians Speak*, 86.

[18] Murray, *Beyond Tithing*, 112. Chrysostom advocated tithing to the poor in some of his writings (pp. 112–117).

[19] Ibid., 107. *The Apostolic Constitutions* (c. 380) support tithing to fund the clergy by arguing from the Old Testament Levitical system (pp. 113–116). Augustine argued for tithing, but he did not present it as the norm. In fact, Augustine knew that he did not represent the historic position of the church in his support of tithing. Tithing was practiced by some pious Christians in the fifth century, but it was by no means a widespread practice (pp. 117–121).

[20] Hatch, *Growth of Church Institutions*, 102–112.

scholar, "For the first seven hundred years they [tithes] are hardly ever mentioned."[21]

Charting the history of Christian tithing is a fascinating exercise.[22] Tithing spread from the state to the church. Here's the story. In the seventh and eighth centuries, leasing land was a familiar characteristic of the European economy. The use of the tithe, or the tenth, was commonly used to calculate payments to landlords. As the church increased its ownership of land across Europe, the 10 percent rent-charge shifted from secular landlords to the church. Ecclesiastical leaders became the landlords. And the tithe became the ecclesiastical tax. This gave the 10 percent rent charge new meaning. It was creatively applied to the Old Testament law and came to be identified with the Levitical tithe![23] Consequently, the Christian tithe as an institution was based on a fusion of Old Testament practice and a common system of land-leasing in medieval Europe.[24]

By the eighth century, the tithe became required by law in many areas of Western Europe.[25] But by the end of the tenth century, the tithe as a rent charge for leasing land had all but faded. The tithe, however, remained and it came to be viewed as a moral requirement supported by the Old Testament. The tithe had evolved into a legally mandatory religious practice throughout Christian Europe.[26]

To put it another way, before the eighth century the tithe was practiced as a voluntary offering.[27] But by the end of the tenth century, it had devolved into a legal requirement to fund the state church—demanded by the clergy and enforced by the secular authorities![28]

---

[21] Ibid., 102.

[22] Murray traces its entire history in *Beyond Tithing*, ch. 4–6.

[23] Hatch, *Growth of Church Institutions*, 103. The pseudo-Isodorian Decretals prove that tithes evolved from rent payments for the use of church lands. The Council of Valence in 855 states that this "decree deals with the payment of tithes as rent, about which some of the lessees of church lands appear to have been slack, and then urges their general payment by all Christians" (pp. 104–105). See also Murray, *Beyond Tithing*, 138.

[24] *Beyond Tithing*, 137. Murray writes, "Many aspects of Christendom emerged from just such a fusion of biblical and secular elements, Old Testament motifs and practices with Roman and pagan institutions and ideas."

[25] Ibid., 134. Charlemagne codified tithing and made it obligatory throughout his enlarged kingdom in 779 and 794 (p. 139); Durant, *Age of Faith*, 764.

[26] Murray, *Beyond Tithing*, 111, 140.

[27] The exception to this was in Gaul during the sixth century. The Synod of Tours in 567 made tithing mandatory in the region. The Synod of Macon in 585 threatened those who refused to tithe with excommunication. For a short but detailed discussion on Christian giving in the patristic church, see Kreider, *Worship and Evangelism in Pre-Christendom*, 34–35.

[28] Murray, *Beyond Tithing*, 2, 140. Theologians and legislators worked out the details of the tithing system.

Today, the tithe is no longer a legal requirement in any nation.[29] Yet the obligatory practice of tithing is as much alive today as it was when it was legally binding. Sure, you may not be physically punished if you fail to tithe. But in many ministries you will either be told or be made to feel that you are sinning.

In fact, in some churches, if you are not a tither, you will be barred from holding a ministry position. A friend of mine was considered for eldership in one well-known congregation. However, because he believed in giving anonymously (he didn't use checks), he was barred from being an elder. The reason? He was told that the church had to know who was obeying God by tithing and who wasn't. This was the across-the-board policy of that particular denomination. Only tithers could be elders.

As far as clergy salaries go, ministers were unsalaried for the first three centuries. But when Constantine appeared, he instituted the practice of paying a fixed salary to the clergy from church funds and municipal and imperial treasuries.[30] Thus was born the clergy salary, a harmful practice that has no root in the New Testament.[31]

There is no doubt that it is imperative for believers to support the Lord's work financially and to give generously to the poor. Scripture enjoins both, and the Kingdom of God desperately needs both. The issue under scrutiny in this chapter is the appropriateness of the tithe as a Christian "law" and how it is normally used: to fund clergy salaries, operational costs, and church building overhead.

A BURDEN ON THE POOR

If a believer wishes to tithe out of a personal decision or conviction, that is fine. Tithing becomes a problem when it is represented as God's command, binding upon every believer.

---

[29] Strikingly, the Church of England did away with the tithe as a legal requirement as recently as the 1930s (Murray, *Beyond Tithing*, 3–6).

[30] C. B. Hassell, *History of the Church of God, from Creation to AD 1885* (Middletown, NY: Gilbert Beebe's Sons Publishers, 1886), 374–392, 472; Smith, *From Christ to Constantine*, 123. The Montanists of the second century were the first to pay their leaders, but this practice did not become widespread until Constantine came along (Smith, *From Christ to Constantine*, 193).

[31] For a response to those biblical passages that some have used to defend clergy (pastor) salaries, see Viola, *Reimagining Church*.

Under the Old Testament system, tithing was good news to the poor. However, in our day, mandatory tithing equals oppression to the poor.[32] Not a few poor Christians have been thrown into deeper poverty because they have felt obligated to give beyond their means. They have been told that if they do not tithe, they are robbing God and breaking His command.[33] In such cases, the gospel is no longer "good news to the poor."[34] Rather, it becomes a heavy burden. Instead of liberty, it becomes oppression. We are so apt to forget that the original tithe that God established for Israel was to benefit the poor, not hurt them!

Conversely, contemporary tithing is good news to the rich. To a high earner, 10 percent is but a paltry sum. Tithing, therefore, appeases the consciences of the prosperous without impacting their lifestyles. Not a few wealthy Christians are deluded into thinking they are "obeying God" because they throw 10 percent of their income into the offering plate.

But God has a very different view of giving. Recall the parable of the widow's mite: "Jesus saw the rich putting their gifts into the temple treasury. He also saw a poor widow put in two very small copper coins. 'I tell you the truth,' he said, 'this poor widow has put in more than all the others. All these people gave their gifts out of their wealth; but she out of her poverty put in all she had to live on'" (Luke 21:1-4, NIV).

Sadly, tithing is often viewed as a litmus test for discipleship. If you are a good Christian, you will tithe (so it is thought). But this is a bogus application. Tithing is no sign of Christian devotion. If it were, the first-century Christians in the churches that Paul raised up would be condemned as being undevoted because all available evidence shows that they did not tithe![35]

---

[32] Not to mention the overlooked complexities of tithing. Consider the following: Does one tithe on net or gross? How do tax exemptions apply? Murray details the ignored complexities of trying to import the biblical system of tithing as practiced by ancient Israel to our culture today. In a system of jubilee years, Sabbaths, gleanings, and firstfruits, tithing made sense and helped to distribute the nation's wealth. Today, it often leads to gross injustices (see *Beyond Tithing*, ch. 2).

[33] Murray powerfully demonstrates that tithing ends up hurting the poor (*Beyond Tithing*, 8–10, 35–38).

[34] Matthew 11:5; Luke 4:18, 7:22; 1 Corinthians 1:26-29; James 2:5-6 (all NIV).

[35] Paul planted approximately fourteen churches. They were all heavily Gentile. Paul never put the Law on them (see Galatians). To say that the Gentile churches that Paul planted tithed is an argument from silence, and it runs against the entire grain of his law-free gospel. To Paul's mind, if someone tithed, that made him a debtor to do the whole law, which includes circumcision (Galatians 5:3).

One of the lingering roots behind the sustained push for tithing in the church today is the clergy salary. Not a few pastors feel that they must preach tithing to remind their congregation of its obligation to support them, their operational costs, and their programs. Regrettably, the promise of financial blessing or the fear of a financial curse has been employed too often as an incentive to ensure that the tithes keep rolling in.

In this way, tithing today is sometimes presented as the equivalent of a Christian stock investment. Pay the tithe, and God will give you more money in return. Refuse to tithe, and God will punish you. Such thoughts rip at the heart of the good news of the gospel.

The same can be said about the clergy salary. It, too, has no New Testament merit. In fact, the clergy salary runs against the grain of the entire New Covenant.[36] Elders (shepherds) in the first century were not salaried.[37] They were men with an earthly vocation.[38] They gave to the flock rather than taking from it. It was to a group of elders that Paul uttered these sobering words: "I have not coveted anyone's silver or gold or clothing. You yourselves know that these hands of mine have supplied my own needs and the needs of my companions. In everything I did, I showed you that by this kind of hard work we must help the weak, remembering the words the Lord Jesus himself said: 'It is more blessed to give than to receive'" (Acts 20:33-35, NIV).

Giving a salary to pastors elevates them above the rest of God's people. It creates a clerical caste that turns the living body of Christ into a business. Since the pastor and his staff are compensated for ministry, they are the paid professionals. The rest of the church lapses into a state of passive dependence.

If all Christians got in touch with the call that lies upon them to

---

[36] See Acts 20:17-38. Note that these are Paul's last words to the Ephesian elders, thinking he would never see them again—so they are significant (1 Thessalonians 2:9; 1 Peter 5:1-2).

[37] See Simon J. Kistemacher, *New Testament Commentary: Acts* (Grand Rapids: Baker Book House, 1990), 737, 740; Rolland Allen, *Missionary Methods: St. Paul's or Ours?* (Grand Rapids: Eerdmans, 1962), 50; Watchman Nee, *The Normal Christian Church Life* (Anaheim, CA: Living Stream Ministry, 1980), 62–63, 139–143; R. C. H. Lenski, *Commentary on St. Paul's Epistles to Timothy* (Minneapolis: Augsburg Publishing House, 1937), 683; and R. C. H. Lenski, *Commentary on St. Paul's Epistle to the Galatians* (Minneapolis: Augsburg Publishing House, 1961), 303–304; F. F. Bruce, *The Book of Acts* (Grand Rapids: Eerdmans, 1988), 389, 395.

[38] The New Testament references to elders makes this plain. In addition, 1 Timothy 3:7 says that an overseer must be well thought of in the community. The natural implication of this is that he is regularly employed in secular work.

be functioning priests in the Lord's house (and they were permitted to exercise that call), the question would immediately arise: "What on earth are we paying our pastor for!?"

But in the presence of a passive priesthood, such questions are never asked.[39] On the contrary, when the church functions as she should, a professional clergy becomes unnecessary. Suddenly, the thought *That is the job of the pastor* looks heretical. Put simply, a professional clergy fosters the pacifying illusion that the Word of God is classified (and dangerous) material that only card-carrying experts can handle.[40]

But that is not all. Paying a pastor encourages him to be a man pleaser. It makes him the slave of men. His meal ticket is attached to how much his congregation likes him. Thus he is not able to speak freely without the fear that he may lose some heavy tithers. (Many a pastor has confessed this very thing to us.)

A further peril of the paid pastorate is that it produces clergy who feel "stuck" in the pastorate because they believe they lack employable skills.[41] I (Frank) personally know a good number of pastors who felt convicted to leave the ministry. All of their schooling and training had been dedicated to studying and preaching the Bible. While these skills are noteworthy, they are of limited appeal in the secular job market. The major hurdle they now face is forging a new career to support their families. A friend of mine, an ex-pastor himself, is writing a booklet on how pastors can find employment and enter new careers after leaving the clergy system. His ideas are not based on theory. He and others like him have fleshed them out.

Even so, it is exceedingly difficult for many contemporary pastors to acknowledge the lack of scriptural support for their office simply because they are financially dependent upon it. As Upton

---

[39] According to Elton Trueblood, "Our opportunity for a big step lies in opening the ministry of the ordinary Christian in much the same manner that our ancestors opened Bible reading to the ordinary Christian. To do this means, in one sense, the inauguration of a new Reformation while in another it means the logical completion of the earlier Reformation in which the implications of the position taken were neither fully understood nor loyally followed" (*Your Other Vocation* [New York: Harper & Brothers, 1952], 32).

[40] The words of Jesus come to mind: "Woe to you experts in the law, because you have taken away the key to knowledge . . ." (Luke 11:52, NIV).

[41] The Greeks spoke publicly for a fee. Jewish rabbis learned a skill and could not accept money for religious services. In this way, the modern preacher has adopted the Greek custom rather than the Jewish custom that Paul of Tarsus followed even as a Christian.

Sinclair once said, "It is difficult to get a man to understand something when his salary depends upon his not understanding it." No wonder it takes a person of tremendous courage and faith to step out of the pastorate.

A number of my (Frank's) ex-pastor friends have admitted that they were part of a religious system that subtly but profoundly injured them and their families.[42] Unfortunately, most of us are deeply naive about the overwhelming power of the religious system. It is a faceless system that does not tire of chewing up and spitting out its own.[43]

USHERS AND THE COLLECTION PLATE

Despite these problems, collecting tithes and offerings is now a part of almost every church service. How did the practice of ushers passing collection plates take shape? This is another postapostolic invention. It began in 1662, although alms dishes and alms chests were present before then.[44]

The usher originated from Queen Elizabeth I's (1533–1603) reorganization of the liturgy of the Church of England. Ushers were responsible for walking people to their seats (in part to ensure that reserved spots weren't taken by the wrong people), collecting the offering, and keeping records of who took Communion. The predecessor of the usher was the church "porter," a minor order (lesser clergy) that can be traced back to the third century.[45] Porters had the

---

[42] I've detailed a number of these effects in chapter 5, under "How the Pastor Damages Himself."

[43] Many pastors are completely unaware of what they are getting into when they enter professional ministry. I have a young friend who recently resigned from being a Methodist pastor. He told me, "I had no idea what I was getting into until I got into it. It deeply hurt my wife. It was nothing like I had ever imagined." This was not the first time I heard these words. According to Eugene Peterson, "American pastors are abandoning their posts, left and right, and at an alarming rate. They are not leaving their churches and getting other jobs. Congregations still pay their salaries. . . . But [these pastors] are abandoning their calling." *Working the Angles: The Shape of Pastoral Integrity* (Grand Rapids: Eerdmans, 1987), 1.

[44] James Gilchrist, *Anglican Church Plate* (London: The Connoisseur, 1967), 98–101. Early offering plates were called "alms dishes." The silver alms dish did not appear as a normal part of church furnishing until after the Reformation (Michael Clayton, *The Collector's Dictionary of the Silver and Gold of Great Britain and North America* [New York: The Word Publishing Company, 1971], 11). According to Charles Cox and Alfred Harvey, the use of alms boxes, collecting boxes, and alms dishes is almost entirely a post-Reformation practice. In medieval times, church buildings had alms chests with a slot in the lid. In the fourteenth century, the alms dish appeared. In the seventeenth century, alms basins began to be passed around by deacons or churchwardens. J. G. Davies, ed., *A New Dictionary of Liturgy and Worship* (London: SCM Press, 1986), 5–6; Charles Oman, *English Church Plate 597-1830* (London: Oxford University Press, 1957); J. Charles Cox and Alfred Harvey, *English Church Furniture* (EP Publishing Limited, 1973), 240–245; David C. Norrington, *"Fund-Raising: The Methods Used in the Early Church Compared with Those Used in English Churches Today," EQ 70*, no. 2 (1998): 130. Norrington's entire article is a worthwhile read. He shows that present day "soliciting" methods in church have no analog in the New Testament (pages 115–134).

[45] *The Catholic Encyclopedia*, s.v. "porter, doorkeeper," http://www.newadvent.org/cathen/12284b.htm.

duty of locking and opening the church doors, keeping order in the building, and providing general direction to the deacons.[46] Porters were replaced by "churchwardens" in England before and during the Reformation period.[47] After the churchwarden came the usher.

CONCLUSION

As we've seen, tithing, while biblical, is not Christian. Jesus Christ did not teach it to His disciples.[48] The first-century Christians did not observe it. And for three hundred years, followers of Christ did not do it. Tithing did not become a widely accepted practice among Christians until the eighth century, though they gave generously—often well above 10 percent of their resources—from the beginning.

Tithing is mentioned only four times in the New Testament. But none of these instances apply to Christians.[49] Tithing belonged to the Old Testament era where a taxation system was needed to support the poor and a special priesthood that had been set apart to minister to the Lord. With the coming of Jesus Christ, there has been a "change of the law"—the old has been "set aside" and rendered obsolete by the new (Hebrews 7:12-18; 8:13, NIV).

We are all priests now—free to function in God's house. The Law, the old priesthood, and the tithe have all been crucified. There is now no Temple curtain, no Temple tax, and no special priesthood that stands between God and man. You have been set free from the bondage of tithing and from the obligation to support the unbiblical clergy system. May you, like the first-century Macedonian Christians, give freely, out of a cheerful heart, without guilt, religious obligation, or manipulation . . . generously helping those in need (2 Corinthians 8:1-4; 9:6-7).

---

[46] Professor John McGuckin, e-mail message to Frank Viola, September 23, 2002. The word *usher* comes from Anglo-Saxon and refers to a person who guides people into court or church. Professor Eugene A. Teselle, e-mail message to Frank Viola, September 22, 2002.

[47] Cox and Harvey, *English Church Furniture*, 245.

[48] In Matthew 23:23, Jesus was challenging the inconsistency of the Pharisees and teachers of the Law. He was not prescribing guidelines for His disciples.

[49] Murray handles all four instances in detail, proving that they are not proof texts for Christians tithing. He also shows that according to Jesus, tithing is linked to legalism and self-righteousness rather than a model to imitate (see *Beyond Tithing*, ch. 3).

➤delving DEEPER

1. You seem to assume that many pastors encourage tithing among their members simply because they want to be sure they will get paid—and have money to fund their programs. Isn't it just as likely that pastors encourage giving because Jesus and the apostle Paul encouraged it? Can you elaborate on what attitude churches should have toward giving?

Actually, both are true. Many pastors have confessed that their salary is a strong influence. We also know that other pastors have different motives. As for your other question, Christians who wish to tithe are free to do so. And if they do not wish to tithe, they are free not to do so. Paul outlines the proper attitude of giving when he writes, "Each man should give what he has decided in his heart to give, not reluctantly or under compulsion, for God loves a cheerful giver" (2 Corinthians 9:7, NIV).

2. First Timothy 5:17 says that "elders who do their work well should be respected and paid well" (NLT). Doesn't this support the idea of paying pastors? If not, what do you think this passage means?

To begin with, this passage deals with elders, not with the modern pastoral office. The actual Greek says that the elders who care for God's people well are worthy of double honor. The New American Standard, the King James Version, and the New International Version translate the text with the words *double honor*.

In verse 18, Paul quotes the Old Testament to buttress his argument. Just as the working ox deserves corn, and just as the laborer deserves payment, the elder who cares for God's people well deserves "double honor," that is, greater respect.

So the critical question becomes, what does "double honor" mean? Does it mean a clergy salary, an honorarium, or simply greater respect?

First, the specific Greek words that the New Testament uses for *pay* or *wages* are not used in this text. Rather, the Greek word for *honor* in this passage means to respect or value someone or something. The same word is used four times in 1 Timothy. In every case, it means respect.

Second, all Christians are called to honor one another (Romans 12:10). It would be absurd to take this to mean that all believers are to receive payment from one another. Again, those elders who serve well are to receive more honor—or greater respect.

Third, the fact that respect is what Paul had in mind is borne out by verse 19. Paul goes on to say that the elders are not to be accused (dishonored) unless there are two or three witnesses to confirm an accusation.

Granted, double honor may have included free-will offerings as a token of blessing from time to time (Galatians 6:6). But this was not the dominating thought. Scripture tells us elders deserve honor (respect), not a salary.

Consequently, 1 Timothy 5 is perfectly consistent with Paul's words to the elders recorded in Acts 20:33-35. There he told the elders in Ephesus that he did not take money from God's people but instead supplied his own needs. Paul then told the elders to follow his example in this. That passage alone argues against the idea of a hired clergy or a paid pastoral staff.

Strikingly, 1 Timothy 5:17-18 and Acts 20:33-35 were addressed to the same group of people—the elders in Ephesus. Thus there is no contradiction. Because the elders were local men, they were not biblically sanctioned to receive full financial support like itinerant apostles who traveled from region to region to plant churches (1 Corinthians 9:1-18).

Paul was an itinerant apostolic worker. Therefore, he had a legitimate right to receive full financial support from the Lord's people (see 1 Corinthians 9). But he intentionally waived that right whenever he worked with a group of Christians (1 Corinthians 9:14-18; 2 Corinthians 11:7-9; 12:13-18; 1 Thessalonians 2:6-9; 2 Thessalonians 3:8-9). We wonder what would happen if more ministers today would follow in the steps of Paul.

Paul's argument in 1 Timothy 5:17-18 is simply this: Just as the working ox deserves food and the working employee deserves payment, the elders who serve well should receive double respect. (In 1 Corinthians 9, Paul uses this same analogy. In that text, however, Paul is speaking of apostolic workers rather than local elders, and he makes it clear that finances rather than honor are in view.)

chapter nine

> BAPTISM AND THE LORD'S SUPPER: DILUTING THE SACRAMENTS

"Many institutions and elements of institutions which have sometimes been thought to belong to primitive Christianity belong, in fact, to the Middle Ages."

—EDWIN HATCH, NINETEENTH-CENTURY ENGLISH THEOLOGIAN

"The Protestant clergy have rescued the Bible from the darkness of papal libraries and have scattered it abroad over the whole earth. They have exalted it in the highest terms of human praise. They have studied, commented, and explained, nay even tortured every word, phrase, and expression in the original and translations, for every possible interpretation. The result is that Christianity is smothered in theology and criticism: the truths of revelation are wire-drawn and spun and twisted into the most fantastical shapes human fancy or human logic can devise. A system of technical Divinity has been constructed which rivals the complexity of all the machinery of the Romish church."

—STEPHEN COLWELL, NINETEENTH-CENTURY AUTHOR OF
NEW THEMES FOR THE PROTESTANT CLERGY

COUNTLESS BOOKS have been written on the two Protestant sacraments: baptism and the Lord's Supper. However, little to nothing exists in print to trace the origin of how we practice them today. In this chapter, we will see how far afield we have gotten in our practice of water baptism and the Lord's Supper.

DILUTING THE WATERS OF BAPTISM

Most evangelical Christians believe in and practice believer's baptism as opposed to infant baptism.[1] Likewise, most Protestants believe and practice baptism by immersion or pouring rather than by sprinkling. The New Testament as well as early church history stand with both of these positions.[2]

However, it is typical in most contemporary churches for baptism to be separated from conversion by great lengths of time. Many Christians were saved at one age and baptized at a much later age. In the first century, this was unheard of.

In the early church, converts were baptized immediately upon believing.[3] One scholar says of baptism and conversion, "They belong together. Those who repented and believed the Word were baptized. That was the invariable pattern, so far as we know."[4] Another writes, "At the birth of the church, converts were baptized with little or no delay."[5]

In the first century, water baptism was the outward confession of a person's faith.[6] But more than that, it was the way someone came to the Lord. For this reason, the confession of baptism is vitally linked to the exercise of saving faith. So much so that the New Testament writers often use *baptism* in place of the word *faith* and link it to being

---

[1] Though we can't offer a detailed examination of what Scripture teaches about baptism in this chapter, consider that from a theological standpoint, infant baptism divorces two things that the Scriptures consistently join together: (1) faith and repentance and (2) water baptism.

[2] *Baptism* in the Greek (*baptizo*) can have a number of meanings depending on the context in which it is used. Immersion was the common practice of the Christian church until the late Middle Ages in the West (Ferguson, *Early Christians Speak*, 43–51).

[3] Acts 2:37-41; 8:12ff., 27-38; 9:18; 10:44-48; 16:14-15, 31-33; 18:8; 19:1-5; 22:16.

[4] Green, *Evangelism in the Early Church*, 153.

[5] David F. Wright, *The Lion Handbook of the History of Christianity* (Oxford: Lion Publications, 1990), "Beginnings," see the section on "Instruction for Baptism."

[6] Augustine called baptism a "visible word" (*Tractates on the Gospel According to Saint John*, LXXX, 3).

"saved."[7] This is because baptism was the early Christian's initial confession of faith in Christ.

In our day, the "sinner's prayer" has replaced the role of water baptism as the initial confession of faith. Unbelievers are told, "Say this prayer after me, accept Jesus as your personal Savior, and you will be saved." But nowhere in all the New Testament do we find any person being led to the Lord by a sinner's prayer. And there is not the faintest whisper in the Bible about a "personal" Savior.

Instead, unbelievers in the first century were led to Jesus Christ by being taken to the waters of baptism. Put another way, water baptism was the sinner's prayer in century one! Baptism accompanied the acceptance of the gospel. For example, when Lydia heard Paul preach the gospel, she believed and was immediately baptized with her household (Acts 16:14-15). In the same way, when Paul led the Philippian jailor and his household to the Lord, they were immediately baptized (Acts 16:30-33). This was the New Testament pattern (see also Acts 2:41; 8:12, 35-37). Baptism marked a complete break with the past and a full entrance into Christ and His church. Baptism was simultaneously an act of faith as well as an expression of faith.[8]

So when did baptism get separated from receiving Christ? It began in the early second century. Certain influential Christians taught that baptism must be preceded by a period of instruction, prayer, and fasting.[9] This trend grew worse in the third century when young converts had to wait three years before they could be baptized!

If you were a baptismal candidate in this era, your life was meticulously scrutinized.[10] You had to show yourself worthy of baptism by your conduct.[11] Baptism became a rigid and embellished ritual that borrowed much from Jewish and Greek culture—elaborate with

---

[7] Mark 16:16; Acts 2:38; Acts 22:16; and 1 Peter 3:21 are some examples.

[8] The importance of water baptism in the Christian faith is depicted in early Christian art (Andre Grabar, *Christian Iconography* [Princeton: Princeton University Press, 1968]).

[9] Ferguson, *Early Christians Speak*, 33.

[10] Wright, *Lion Handbook of the History of Christianity*, "Beginnings," section on "Instruction for Baptism." Wright points out that by the fourth century, the clergy took over the instructions for converts and the bishop became personally responsible for the teaching and discipline that preceded baptism. This is the precursor for the prebaptismal class overseen by the pastor in many modern Protestant churches. From the second century onward, baptisms normally took place at Easter. Herein is the origin of Lent (Smith, *From Christ to Constantine*, 151).

[11] Ferguson, *Early Christians Speak*, 35.

BAPTISM AND THE LORD'S SUPPER: DILUTING THE SACRAMENTS

189

blessing the water, full disrobing, the uttering of a creed, anointing oil with exorcism, and giving milk and honey to the newly baptized person.[12] It had devolved into an act associated with works rather than with faith.

The legalism that accompanied baptism led to an even more startling concept: Only baptism forgives sins. If a person committed sin after baptism, he could not be forgiven. For this reason, the delay of baptism became quite common by the fourth century. Since it was believed that baptism brought the forgiveness of sins, many felt it was best to delay baptism until the maximum benefits could be obtained.[13] Therefore, some people, like Constantine, waited until they were on their deathbeds to be baptized.[14]

THE SINNER'S PRAYER AND A PERSONAL SAVIOR

As stated earlier, the sinner's prayer eventually replaced the biblical role of water baptism. Though it is touted as gospel today, this prayer developed only recently. D. L. Moody was the first to employ it.

Moody used this "model" of prayer when training his evangelistic coworkers.[15] But it did not reach popular usage until the 1950s with Billy Graham's *Peace with God* tract and later with Campus Crusade for Christ's *Four Spiritual Laws*.[16] There is nothing particularly wrong with it. Certainly, God will respond to the heartfelt prayers of any indi-

[12] Ibid., 35–36; W. R. Halliday, *The Pagan Background of Early Christianity* (New York: Cooper Square Publishers, 1970), 313. The giving of milk and honey was borrowed from paganism. The new convert ("catechumens" as they came to be called, from which *catechism* is derived) was typically baptized on a Sunday Passover or Pentecost. The Thursday beforehand the candidate had to be bathed. He spent Friday and Saturday in fasting, and then he was exorcised by the bishop to drive out any demons. By the end of the second century, this was a fairly uniform baptismal ceremony in the West. Gregory Dix points out that the introduction of the creed in Christianity begins in the first half of the second century with the baptismal creed. The creed was made up of a series of three questions dealing respectively with the three Persons of the Trinity. The Council of Nicaea of AD 325 carried the creed a step further. The creed evolved into a test of fellowship for those within the church rather than a test of faith for those outside of it (Dix, *The Shape of the Liturgy*, 485; Norrington, *To Preach or Not*, 59).

[13] Ferguson, *Early Christians Speak*, 60.

[14] Green, *Evangelism in the Early Church*, 156.

[15] C. L. Thompson, *Times of Refreshing, Being a History of American Revivals with Their Philosophy and Methods* (Rockford: Golden Censer Co. Publishers, 1878); Paul H. Chitwood, "The Sinner's Prayer: An Historical and Theological Analysis" (Dissertation, Southern Baptist Theological Seminary, Louisville, KY, 2001).

[16] Here is the classic "Sinner's Prayer" that appears in the *Four Spiritual Laws* tract: "Lord Jesus, I need You. Thank You for dying on the cross for my sins. I open the door of my life and receive You as my Savior and Lord. Thank You for forgiving my sins and giving me eternal life. Take control of the throne of my life. Make me the kind of person You want me to be." In the first century, water baptism was the visible testimony that publicly demonstrated the heart of this prayer.

vidual who reaches out to Him in faith. However, it should not replace water baptism as the outward instrument for conversion-initiation.

The phrase *personal Savior* is yet another recent innovation that grew out of the ethos of nineteenth-century American revivalism.[17] It originated in the mid-1800s to be exact.[18] But it grew to popular parlance by Charles Fuller (1887–1968). Fuller literally used the phrase thousands of times in his incredibly popular *Old Fashioned Revival Hour* radio program that aired from 1937 to 1968. His program reached from North America to every spot on the globe. At the time of his death, it was heard on more than 650 radio stations around the world.[19]

Today, the phrase *personal Savior* is used so pervasively that it seems biblical. But consider the ludicrousness of using it. Have you ever introduced one of your friends by such a designation? "This is my 'personal friend,' Billy Smith."

In Jesus Christ, you and I have received something far greater than a personal Savior. We have received Jesus Christ's very own relationship with His Father! According to New Testament teaching, what the Father was to Jesus Christ, Jesus Christ is to you and me. Because we are now "in Christ," the Father loves us and treats us just as He does His own Son. In other words, we share and participate in Christ's perfect relationship with His Father.[20]

This relationship is corporate just as much as it is individual. All Christians share that relationship together. In this regard, the phrase *personal Savior* reinforces a highly individualistic Christianity. But the New Testament knows nothing of a "Just-me-and-Jesus" Christian faith. Instead, Christianity is intensely corporate. Christianity is a life lived out among a body of believers who know Christ together as Lord and Savior.

---

[17] See chapter 3 for a discussion of contributions from Finney, Moody, and others.

[18] The phrase is absent from the "Making of America" database from 1800–1857. It begins appearing in 1858 in the "Ladies Repository," a periodical put out by the Methodist Episcopal Church during the mid-1800s. Interestingly, 1858 is the year that Charles Finney concluded his prayer revivals, which are now so famous.

[19] See http://www.answers.com/topic/charles-e-fuller.

[20] John 17:23, 20:21; Romans 8:15; Galatians 4:6; Ephesians 1:4-6. For a fuller discussion on this topic, see Bill Freeman's *The Church Is Christ* (Scottsdale, AZ: Ministry Publications, 1993), ch. 3.

THE LORD'S SUPPER

Rivers of blood have been shed at the hands of Protestant and Catholic Christians alike over the doctrinal intricacies related to Holy Communion.[21] The Lord's Supper, once precious and living, became the center of theological debate for centuries. Tragically, it moved from a dramatic and concrete picture of Christ's body and blood to a study in abstract and metaphysical thought.

We cannot concern ourselves with the theological minutiae that surround the Lord's Supper in this book. But clearly Protestants (as well as Catholics) do not practice the Supper the way it was observed in the first century. For the early Christians, the Lord's Supper was a festive communal meal.[22] The mood was one of celebration and joy. When believers first gathered for the meal, they broke the bread and passed it around. Then they ate their meal, which then concluded after the cup was passed around. The Lord's Supper was essentially a Christian banquet. And there was no clergyman to officiate.[23]

Today, tradition has forced us to take the Supper as a tongue-tickling thimble of grape juice and a tiny, tasteless bite-size cracker. The Supper is often taken in an atmosphere of solemnity. We are told to remember the horrors of our Lord's death and to reflect on our sins.

In addition, tradition has taught us that taking the Lord's Supper can be a dangerous thing. Thus many contemporary Christians would never take Communion without an ordained clergyman present. Often, they point to 1 Corinthians 11:27-33. In verse 27, the apostle Paul does warn believers not to participate in the Lord's Supper "unworthily." In this instance, however, he appears to have been speaking to church members who were dishonoring the Supper by

---

[21] One of the better-known figures killed for his views on the Lord's Supper was Thomas Cranmer. Cranmer was named archbishop of Canterbury by Henry VIII, but his greatest influence was felt during the brief reign of Henry's son, Edward VI. Later, during the reign of Queen Mary, Cranmer was charged with sedition for defending Protestant sacramental theology. He was burned at the stake in March 1556 (Douglas, *Who's Who in Christian History*, 179–180).

[22] See Eric Svendsen, *The Table of the Lord* (Atlanta: NTRF, 1996); F. F. Bruce, *First and Second Corinthians*, NCB (London: Oliphant, 1971), 110; White, *The Worldliness of Worship*, 85; William Barclay, *The Lord's Supper* (Philadelphia: Westminister Press, 1967), 100–107; I. Howard Marshall, *Last Supper and Lord's Supper* (Grand Rapids: Eerdmans, 1980); Vernard Eller, *In Place of Sacraments* (Grand Rapids: Eerdmans, 1972), 9–15.

[23] Barclay, *Lord's Supper*, 102–103. The Lord's Supper was once a "lay" function, but it eventually devolved into the special duty of a priestly class.

not waiting for their poor brethren to eat with them, as well as those who were getting drunk on the wine.

TRUNCATING THE MEAL

So why was the full meal replaced with a ceremony including only the bread and the cup? Here is the story. In the first and early second centuries, the early Christians called the Lord's Supper the "love feast."[24] At that time, they took the bread and cup in the context of a festive meal. But around the time of Tertullian, the bread and the cup began to be separated from the meal. By the late second century, this separation was complete.[25]

Some scholars have argued that the Christians dropped the meal because they wanted to keep the Eucharist from becoming profaned by the participation of unbelievers.[26] This may be partly true. But it is more likely that the growing influence of pagan religious ritual removed the Supper from the joyful, down-to-earth, nonreligious atmosphere of a meal in someone's living room.[27] By the fourth century, the love feast was prohibited among Christians![28]

With the abandonment of the meal, the terms *breaking of bread* and *Lord's Supper* disappeared.[29] The common term for the now truncated ritual (just the bread and the cup) was the *Eucharist*.[30] Irenaeus (130–200) was one of the first to call the bread and cup an offering.[31] After him, it began to be called the "offering" or "sacrifice."

The altar table where the bread and cup were placed came to be

24 It was called the *Agape*. Jude 1:12.
25 Dix, *Shape of the Liturgy*, 23; Ferguson, *Early Christians Speak*, 82–84, 96–97, 127–130. In the first and early second centuries, the Lord's Supper seems to have been taken in the evening as a meal. Second-century sources show it was taken only on Sundays. In the *Didache*, the Eucharist is still shown to be taken with the *Agape* meal (love feast). See also Davies, *Secular Use of Church Buildings*, 22.
26 Svendsen, *Table of the Lord*, 57–63.
27 For the pagan influences on the evolving Christian Mass, see Edmund Bishop's essay "The Genius of the Roman Rite"; Duchesne, *Christian Worship*, 86–227; Jungmann, *Early Liturgy*, 123, 130–144, 291–292; Smith, *From Christ to Constantine*, 173; Durant, *Caesar and Christ*, 599–600, 618–619, 671–672.
28 It was prohibited by the Council of Carthage in AD 397. Barclay, *Lord's Supper*, 60; Charles Hodge, *First Corinthians* (Wheaton, IL: Crossway Books, 1995), 219; R. C. H. Lenski, *The Interpretation of 1 and 2 Corinthians* (Minneapolis: Augsburg Publishing House, 1963), 488.
29 Gough, *The Early Christians*, 100.
30 Ibid., 93. *Eucharist* means "thanksgiving."
31 Tad W. Guzie, *Jesus and the Eucharist* (New York: Paulist Press, 1974), 120.

seen as an altar where the victim was offered.[32] The Supper was no longer a community event. It was rather a priestly ritual that was to be watched at a distance. Throughout the fourth and fifth centuries, there was an increasing sense of awe and dread associated with the table where the sacred Eucharist was celebrated.[33] It became a somber ritual. The joy that had once been a part of it had vanished.[34]

The mystique associated with the Eucharist was due to the influence of the pagan mystery religions, which were clouded with superstition.[35] With this influence, the Christians began to ascribe sacred overtones to the bread and the cup. They were viewed as holy objects in and of themselves.[36]

Because the Lord's Supper became a sacred ritual, it required a sacred person to administer it.[37] Enter now the priest offering the sacrifice of the Mass.[38] He was believed to have the power to call God down from heaven and confine Him to a piece of bread.[39]

Around the tenth century, the meaning of the word *body* changed in Christian literature. Previously, Christian writers used the word *body* to refer to one of three things: (1) the physical body of Jesus, (2) the church, or (3) the bread of the Eucharist.

The early church fathers saw the church as a faith community that identified itself by the breaking of bread. But by the tenth century, there was a shift in thinking and language. The word *body* was

---

[32] Ibid.

[33] Writers as early as Clement of Alexandria, Tertullian, and Hippolytus (early third century) began to use language speaking of a presence of Christ generally in the bread and wine. But no attempt was made at that early stage to argue for a physical realism that "changed" the bread and wine into flesh and blood. Later, some Eastern writers (Cyril of Jerusalem; Serapion, bishop of Thmuis; and Athanasius) introduced a prayer to the Holy Spirit to transform the bread and wine into the body and blood. But it was Ambrose of Milan (late fourth century) who began to locate the consecratory power in the reciting of the words of institution. The words "This is my body" (in Latin *hoc est corpus meum*) were believed to contain in them the power to transform the bread and the wine (Jungmann, *The Mass of the Roman Rite*, 52, 203–204; Dix, *The Shape of the Liturgy*, 239, 240–245). Incidentally, Latin started in North Africa in the late 100s and spread slowly toward Rome until it was common by the end of the 300s. Bard Thompson, *Liturgies of the Western Church* (Cleveland: Meridian Books, 1961), 27.

[34] This shift is also reflected in Christian art. There are no gloomy visages of Jesus before the fourth century (Graydon Snyder, e-mail message to Frank Viola, October 12, 2001; see also his book *Ante Pacem*).

[35] Guzie, *Jesus and the Eucharist*, 121.

[36] This occurred in the ninth century. Before this, it was the *act* of taking the Eucharist that was regarded as sacred. But in AD 830, a man named Radbert wrote the first treatise that approached the Eucharist by focusing directly on the bread and wine. All the Christian writers before Radbert described what Christians were doing when they took the bread and wine. They described the *action* of taking the elements. Radbert was the first to focus exclusively on the elements themselves—the bread and the wine that sat on the altar table (Guzie, *Jesus and the Eucharist*, 60–61, 121–123).

[37] Dunn, *New Testament Theology in Dialogue*, 125–135.

[38] This started around the fourth century.

[39] Hanson, *Christian Priesthood Examined*, 80.

no longer used to refer to the church. It was only used to refer to the Lord's physical body or the bread of the Eucharist.[40]

Consequently, the Lord's Supper became far removed from the idea of the church coming together to celebrate the breaking of bread.[41] The vocabulary change reflected this practice. The Eucharist had ceased to be part of a joyful communal meal but came to be viewed as sacred on its own—even as it sat on the table. It became shrouded in a religious mist. Viewed with awe, it was taken with glumness by the priest and completely removed from the communal nature of the ekklesia.

All of these factors gave rise to the doctrine of transubstantiation. In the fourth century, the belief that the bread and wine changed into the Lord's actual body and blood was explicit. Transubstantiation, however, was the doctrine that gave a theological explanation of how that change occurred.[42] (This doctrine was worked out from the eleventh through the thirteenth centuries.)

With the doctrine of transubstantiation, God's people approached the elements with a feeling of fear. They were reluctant even to approach them.[43] When the words of the Eucharist were uttered, it was believed that the bread literally became God. All of this turned the Lord's Supper into a sacred ritual performed by sacred people and taken out of the hands of God's people. So deeply entrenched was the medieval idea that the bread and cup were an "offering" that even some of the Reformers held to it.[44]

While contemporary Protestant Christians have discarded the Catholic *notion* that the Lord's Supper is a sacrifice, they have continued to embrace the Catholic *practice* of the Supper. Observe a Lord's

---

[40] Guzie, *Jesus and the Eucharist*, 125–127.
[41] For many slaves and poor folks, the Lord's Supper was their one real meal. Interestingly, it was not until the Synod of Hippo in AD 393 that the concept of fasting the Lord's Supper began to emerge (Barclay, *Lord's Supper*, 100).
[42] Gough, *Early Christians*, 111–112. The full-blown doctrine of transubstantiation is credited to Thomas Aquinas. In this regard, Martin Luther believed that the "opinion of Thomas" should have remained an opinion and not become church dogma (Senn, *Christian Liturgy*, 307).
[43] Hatch, *Growth of Church Institutions*, 216. Transubstantiation was defined as a doctrine in the Lateran Council in AD 1215 as the result of 350 years of controversy over the doctrine in the West (Dix, *Shape of the Liturgy*, 630; Hanson, *Christian Priesthood Examined*, 79; Philip Schaff, *History of the Christian Church*, 7 [Grand Rapids: Eerdmans, 1994], 614).
[44] Jones, *Historical Approach to Evangelical Worship*, 143.

Supper service (often called "Holy Communion") in most Protestant churches and you will observe the following:

> The Lord's Supper is a bite-size cracker (or a small piece of bread) and a shot glass of grape juice (or wine). As in the Catholic church, it is removed from the meal.

> The mood is somber and glum, just as it is in the Catholic church.

> Congregants are told by the pastor that they must examine themselves with regard to sin before they partake of the elements, a practice that came from John Calvin.[45]

> Like the Catholic priest, many pastors will sport clerical robes for the occasion. But always, the pastor administers the Supper and recites the words of institution, "This is my body," before dispensing the elements to the congregation.[46]

With only a few minor tweaks, all of this is medieval Catholicism through and through.

SUMMARY

Through our tradition, we have evacuated the true meaning and power behind water baptism. Properly conceived and practiced, water baptism is the believer's initial confession of faith before men, demons, angels, and God. Baptism is a visible sign that depicts our separation from the world,[47] our death with Christ, the burial of our old man,[48] the death of the old creation,[49] and the washing of the Word of God.[50]

Water baptism is the New Testament form of conversion-initiation. It is God's idea. To replace it with the human-invented sinner's prayer is to deplete baptism of its God-given testimony.

45 White, *Protestant Worship*, 66. First Corinthians 11:27-33 is not an exhortation to examine oneself with respect to personal sin. It is rather an exhortation to examine oneself in the area of taking the Supper in a "worthy manner." The Corinthians were dishonoring the Supper, for they were not waiting for their poor brethren to eat with them, and they were getting drunk on the wine.
46 Matthew 26:25-27; Mark 14:21-23; Luke 22:18-20.
47 Acts 2:38-40; 1 Corinthians 10:1-2.
48 Romans 6:3-5; Colossians 2:11-12.
49 1 Peter 3:20-21.
50 Acts 22:16; Ephesians 5:26.

In the same vein, the Lord's Supper, when separated from its proper context of a full meal, turns into a strange, pagan-like rite.[51] The Supper has become an empty ritual officiated by a clergyman, rather than a shared-life experience enjoyed by the church. It has become a morbid religious exercise, rather than a joyous festival—a stale individualistic ceremony, rather than a meaningful corporate event.

As one scholar put it, "It is not in doubt that the Lord's Supper began as a family meal or a meal of friends in a private house . . . the Lord's Supper moved from being a real meal into being a symbolic meal . . . the Lord's Supper moved from bare simplicity to elaborate splendor . . . the celebration of the Lord's Supper moved from being a lay function to a priestly function. In the New Testament itself, there is no indication that it was the special privilege or duty of anyone to lead the worshipping fellowship in the Lord's Supper."[52]

When Israel had departed from God's original thought, the prophet cried: "Thus says the LORD, 'Stand by the ways and see and ask for the ancient paths, where the good way is, and walk in it; and you will find rest for your souls'" (Jeremiah 6:16, NASB). In the same way, can we shun the vain traditions of men and return to the ancient paths . . . those holy traditions that were given to us by Jesus Christ and His apostles?[53]

>delving DEEPER

1. While the sinner's prayer may not be found in the Bible, saying it with a fellow believer when I committed my life to Christ helped me understand what I was doing: acknowledging my utter brokenness before God and recognizing my need for forgiveness. Are you saying it is wrong to pray the sinner's prayer or merely that it should not take the place of baptism as a public acknowledgment of conversion?

[51] Eduard Schweizer, *The Church As the Body of Christ* (Richmond, VA: John Knox Press, 1964), 26, 36–37.
[52] Barclay, *Lord's Supper*, 99–102.
[53] The New Testament repeatedly exhorts us to hold fast to the apostolic tradition given to the church by Jesus Christ and the apostles (1 Corinthians 11:2, 16; 2 Thessalonians 2:15, 3:6). See Viola, *Reimagining Church* for details.

The latter. We are merely saying that it should not replace water baptism as the biblical mode of conversion-initiation.

2. While you express your concern that the term *personal Savior* undermines the truth that our relationship is just as much corporate as individual, doesn't this phrase also remind us of the necessity of making our own confessions of faith and not assuming that merely being part of a church gives us a ticket to heaven?

We certainly should make our own confessions of faith. The early Christians confessed Jesus as Lord and Savior. Many Christians today feel this is sufficient. Therefore, they do not feel compelled to insert the word *personal* before it.

3. The apostle Paul's words in 1 Corinthians 11:23-26, in which he reminds believers of Jesus' words when instituting the Lord's Supper, seem to emphasize communion as a time to remember Christ's sacrificial death. Naturally, then, many believers use it as a time to confess their sin and remember God's mercy. It is hardly an "empty ritual" as you describe it. Your thoughts?

We agree that the Lord's Supper is not an empty ritual for all Christians. At the same time, we regret that so many churches have lost the focus the first Christians had when they celebrated communion. The early Christians took the supper in an atmosphere of joy and celebration. By it, they proclaimed Christ's victorious death and His future coming. They also took it as a full meal in fellowship with the body of Christ, the church. This is the way it was handed down to us by Jesus and the apostles. Therefore we ought to ask ourselves: Is stripping the Lord's Supper from the meal and making it a somber occasion a development or a departure? Have we improved upon what Jesus and the apostles passed down to us, or have we strayed from it?

chapter ten

> CHRISTIAN EDUCATION: SWELLING THE CRANIUM

"What has Athens to do with Jerusalem?"
> —TERTULLIAN, THIRD-CENTURY THEOLOGIAN

"'The Primitive Church had no New Testament, no thought-out theology, no stereotyped traditions. The men who took Christianity to the Gentile world had no special training, only a great experience—in which 'all maxims and philosophies were reduced to the simple task of walking in the light since the light had come.'"
> —B. H. STREETER, TWENTIETH-CENTURY ENGLISH THEOLOGIAN AND BIBLICAL SCHOLAR

IN THE MINDS of most Christians, formal Christian education qualifies a person to do the Lord's work. Unless a Christian has graduated from Bible college or seminary, he or she is viewed as being a "para"-minister. A pseudo Christian worker. Such a person cannot preach, teach, baptize, or administer the Lord's Supper since he or she has not been formally trained to do such things . . . right?

The idea that a Christian worker must attend Bible college or seminary to be legitimate is deeply ingrained—so much so that when people feel a "call" of God on their lives, they are conditioned to begin hunting for a Bible college or seminary to attend.

Such thinking fits poorly with the early Christian mind-set. Bible colleges, seminaries, and even Sunday schools were utterly absent from the early church. All are human innovations that came hundreds of years after the apostles' death.

How, then, were Christian workers trained in the first century if they did not go to a religious school? Unlike today's ministerial training, first-century training was hands-on, rather than academic. It was a matter of apprenticeship, rather than of intellectual learning. It was aimed primarily at the spirit, rather than at the frontal lobe.

In the first century, those called to the Lord's work were trained in two ways: (1) They learned the essential lessons of Christian ministry by living a shared life with a group of Christians. In other words, they were trained by experiencing body life as nonleaders. (2) They learned the Lord's work under the tutelage of an older, seasoned worker.

Remarking about the first-century church, Puritan John Owen writes, "Every church was then a seminary, in which provision and preparation was made."[1] Echoing these words, R. Paul Stevens states, "The best structure for equipping every Christian is already in place. It predates the seminary and the weekend seminar and will outlast both. In the New Testament no other nurturing and equipping is offered than the local church. In the New Testament church, as in the ministry of Jesus, people learned in the furnace of life, in a relational, living, working and ministering context."[2]

In stark contrast, contemporary ministerial training can be

---

[1] John Owen, *Hebrews,* Alister McGrath and J. I. Packer, eds. (Wheaton, IL: Crossway Books, 1998), 131.
[2] R. Paul Stevens, *Liberating the Laity* (Downers Grove, IL: InterVarsity Press, 1985), 46. Note that these words cannot be said of the modern institutional church. They rather apply to all first-century-styled churches.

described by the religious talk of Job's miserable comforters: rational, objective, and abstract. Very little is practical, experiential, or spiritual.

A complete examination of the methods by which Christian workers were trained in the first century is beyond the scope of this book. However, a small chorus of books have been dedicated to the subject.[3] In this chapter, we will trace the origin of the seminary, the Bible college, and the Sunday school. We will also trace the history of the youth pastor. And we will discuss how each of these is at odds with the way of Christ—for each is based upon the educational system of the world.[4]

FOUR STAGES OF THEOLOGICAL EDUCATION

Throughout church history there have been four stages of theological education. They are: episcopal, monastic, scholastic, and seminarian (pastoral).[5] Let's briefly examine each one:

Episcopal. Theology in the patristic age (third to fifth centuries) was called episcopal because the leading theologians of the day were bishops.[6] This system was marked by the training of bishops and priests on how to perform the various rituals and liturgies of the church.[7]

---

[3] Among them are Viola, *So You Want to Start a House Church?*; Robert E. Coleman, *The Master Plan of Evangelism* (Grand Rapids: Fleming H. Revell, 1993); A. B. Bruce, *The Training of the Twelve* (New Canaan, CT: Keats, 1979); and Gene Edwards, *Overlooked Christianity* (Sargent, GA: Seedsowers, 1997). The following books by Watchman Nee are also worth noting. They contain messages given to his younger coworkers during Nee's worker trainings: *The Character of God's Workman, The Ministry of God's Word,* and *The Release of the Spirit.* Second Timothy 2:2 refers to the concept of training Christian workers that is exemplified in the Gospels and Acts.

[4] For an insightful discussion on the educational aspect of the world system, see Watchman Nee's *Love Not the World* (Carol Stream, IL: Tyndale House Publishers, 1978).

[5] Robinson, *New Reformation*, 60–65. Robinson argues that patristic theology was written by bishops, medieval theology was written by university professors, Reformed theology was written by pastors, and the theology of the "new Reformation" will be written by and for the whole people of God. A "theology for the whole people of God" focuses on the concerns and experiences of all Christians, not just the concerns and experiences of a specialized group doing a specialized job (clergy). Contemporary scholars like R. Paul Stevens in *Abolition of the Laity* and *Other Six Days* and Robert Banks in *Reenvisioning Theological Education* (Grand Rapids: Eerdmans, 1999) have written much on this brand of theology. Also, Harold H. Rowdon's article "Theological Education in Historical Perspective," *Vox Evangelica* 7 (Carlisle, UK: Paternoster Press, 1971), 75–87, gives an overview of theological education throughout history.

[6] Augustine was one such person. A group of clergy gathered around him in the fifth century for training (Rowdon, "Theological Education in Historical Perspective," 75).

[7] Episcopal schools did not take on an academic character to train clergy until the sixth century. Before then, prospective priests would learn under the direction of their bishops how to perform rituals and conduct liturgies. Edward J. Power, *A Legacy of Learning: A History of Western Education* (Albany: State University of New York Press, 1991), 98, 108.

Monastic. The monastic stage of theological education was tied to the ascetic and mystical life. It was taught by monks living in monastic communities (and later cathedral schools).[8] Monastic schools were founded in the third century. These schools sent missionaries to uncharted territories after the fourth century.[9]

During this stage, the Eastern church fathers became steeped in Platonic thought. They held to the misguided view that Plato and Aristotle were schoolmasters whose techniques could be used to bring men to Christ. Though they did not intend to lead people astray, their heavy reliance on these pagan philosophers severely diluted the Christian faith.[10]

Since many of the church fathers were pagan philosophers and orators prior to their conversions, the Christian faith soon began to take on a philosophical bent. Justin Martyr (100–165), one of the most influential Christian teachers of the second century, "dressed in the garb of a philosopher."[11] Justin believed that philosophy was God's revelation to the Greeks. He claimed that Socrates, Plato, and others had the same standing for the Gentiles as Moses had for the Jews.[12]

After AD 200, Alexandria became the intellectual capital of the Christian world as it had been for the Greeks. A special school was formed there in AD 180. This school was the equivalent of a theological college.[13]

In Alexandria, the institutional study of Christian doctrine began.[14] Origen (185–254), one of the school's early and most influential teachers, was deeply influenced by pagan philosophy. He was a colleague of Plotinus, the father of Neoplatonism, and drew much from his teaching. According to Neoplatonic thought, an individual must ascend through different stages of purification in order to attain

---

8 Before the twelfth century, the only education in the West was provided by monastic and cathedral schools.

9 Marrou, *History of Education in Antiquity*, 329.

10 In his book, *Ascension and Ecclesia* (Grand Rapids: Eerdmans, 1999), Douglas Farrow exposes how Greek thinking took hold of theology through Origen and then Augustine and how it inevitably affected many areas of church life.

11 Eusebius, *The History of the Church*, IV, 11, 8.

12 Boggs, *Christian Saga*, 151; Hatch, *Influence of Greek Ideas and Usages*, 126–127.

13 Some say it was founded by Pantaenus, the teacher of Clement of Alexandria. Others say it was founded by Demetrius. B. H. Streeter, *The Primitive Church* (New York: The Macmillan Company, 1929), 57; James Bowen, *A History of Western Education* 1 (New York: St. Martin's Press, 1972), 240; Rowdon, "Theological Education in Historical Perspective," 76.

14 Bowen, *History of Western Education* 1:240; Collins and Price, *Story of Christianity*, 25.

to oneness with God.[15] Origen was the first to organize key theological concepts into a systematic theology.[16]

Of this period Will Durant has observed: "The gap between philosophy and religion was closing, and reason for a thousand years consented to be the handmaiden of theology."[17] Edwin Hatch echoes these thoughts, saying, "Within a century and a half after Christianity and philosophy first came into closest contact, the ideas and methods of philosophy had flowed in such mass into Christianity, and filled so large a place in it, as to have made it no less a philosophy than a religion."[18]

After Origen's death, Christian schools disappeared. Theological education reverted back to the episcopal form. Bishops were trained by personal contact with other bishops.[19] The sum and substance of clerical learning at this time was the study of Gregory the Great's pastoral theology.[20] Gregory taught bishops how to be good pastors.[21] By the mid-eighth century, bishops' schools were founded. In the tenth century, cathedrals began sponsoring their own schools.[22]

Scholastic. The third stage of theological education owes much to the culture of the university.[23] By 1200, a number of cathedral schools had evolved into universities. The University of Bologna in Italy was the first university to appear. The University of Paris came in a close second, followed by Oxford.[24]

The University of Paris became the philosophical and theological

---

[15] Durant, *Caesar and Christ*, 610. Neoplatonism flourished between 245 and 529, and it influenced Christian thought directly through Origen, Clement of Alexandria, Augustine, and Pseudo-Dionysius. Such an idea is still very prevalent in Catholic thought. See Philip S. Watson, *Neoplatonism and Christianity: 928 Ordinary General Meeting of the Victoria Institute*, vol. 87 (Surrey, UK: The Victoria Institute), 1955.

[16] *Pastor's Notes* 5, no. 2: 7.

[17] Durant, *Caesar and Christ*, 611.

[18] Hatch, *Influence of Greek Ideas and Usages*, 125.

[19] Marrou, *History of Education in Antiquity*, 329.

[20] Schaff, *History of the Christian Church*, 4:400.

[21] Gregory's work, *Book of Pastoral Rule*, was written in AD 591. It is a discussion on the duties of the bishop's office.

[22] Douglas, *New Twentieth Century Encyclopedia of Religious Knowledge*, 289. Notre Dame was one of the earliest cathedral schools. The University of Paris grew out of a cathedral school. Bowen, *History of Western Education* 2:111. After 1100, the cathedral schools expanded, being broken up into "grammar schools" for boys and a higher school for advanced learning.

[23] The word *university* comes from, the medieval Latin *universitas*, which was the term used for the medieval craft guilds (Bowen, *History of Western Education* 2:109).

[24] William Boyd, *The History of Western Education* (New York: Barnes & Noble, 1967), 128. For a discussion on the origin of the university system, see Helen Wieruszowski, *The Medieval University* (Princeton: Van Nostrand, 1966).

center of the world at that time.[25] (It would later become the seed of the Protestant seminary.)[26] Higher education was the domain of the clergy.[27] And the scholar was viewed as the guardian of ancient wisdom.

The present-day university grew from the bishops' responsibility to provide clerical training.[28] Theology was regarded as the "Queen of Sciences" in the university.[29] From the mid-twelfth century to the end of the fourteenth century, seventy-one universities were established in Europe.[30]

Contemporary theology cut its teeth on the abstractions of Greek philosophy.[31] University academics adopted an Aristotelian model of thinking that centered on rational knowledge and logic. The dominating drive in scholastic theology was the assimilation and communication of knowledge. (For this reason, the Western mind has always been fond of creedal formulations, doctrinal statements, and other bloodless abstractions.)

One of the most influential professors in the shaping of contemporary theology was Peter Abelard (1079–1142). Abelard is partly responsible for giving us "modern" theology. His teaching set the table and prepared the menu for scholastic philosophers like Thomas Aquinas (1225–1274).[32]

Distinguished by Abelard, the school of Paris emerged as the model for all universities to follow.[33] Abelard applied Aristotelian logic to revealed truth, though even he understood the tension between the

[25] Bowen, *History of Western Education* 1:110.
[26] The word *seminary* comes from the Latin *seminarium*, meaning "seedbed" (Reid, *Concise Dictionary of Christianity in America*, 1071).
[27] Collins and Price, *Story of Christianity*, 112.
[28] Rowdon, "Theological Education in Historical Perspective," 79. The Lateran Council of 1215 exhorted every metropolitan bishop to ensure theology was taught in every cathedral church.
[29] Ibid.
[30] Power, *Legacy of Learning*, 149. The history of university degrees is quite interesting. People who passed academic standards were called *masters*. Lawyers were the first to be called *doctors*. *Doctor* means "one who teaches." It comes from *doctrina* which means "learning." A *doctor*, then, is a *master* who teaches. Eager students who wanted recognition were called *bachelors* (p. 153). The cathedral *chancellor* had ultimate control of the university. *Masters* gave lectures to the *bachelors* who at first lived in privately hired rooms, then later in halls lent to them by the *masters* (Rowdon, "Theological Education in Historical Perspective," 79). The word *faculty* which means "strength, power, and ability," appeared around 1270. It represented the various subject divisions of the medieval guild. The word *faculty* eventually replaced *guild* and came to refer to the group of scholars in each subject. Bowen, *A History of Western Education* 2:111; Charles Homer Haskins, *The Rise of Universities* (New York: H. Holt, 1923), 17.
[31] Stevens, *Other Six Days*, 12–13; and Stevens, *Abolition of the Laity*, 10–22.
[32] D. W. Robertson, *Abelard and Heloise* (New York: The Dial Press, 1972), xiv.
[33] Bowen, *History of Western Education* 2:109.

two: "I do not wish to be a philosopher, if that means I contradict St. Paul; I do not wish to be a disciple of Aristotle, if that means I separate myself from Christ." He also gave the word *theology* the meaning it has today. (Before him, this word was only used to describe pagan beliefs.)[34]

Taking his cue from Aristotle, Abelard mastered the pagan philosophical art of dialectic—the logical disputation of truth. He applied this art to the Scriptures.[35] Christian theological education never recovered from Abelard's influence. Athens is still in its bloodstream. Aristotle, Abelard, and Aquinas all believed that reason was the gateway to divine truth. So from its beginnings, Western university education involved the fusion of pagan and Christian elements.[36]

Martin Luther had it right when he said, "What else are the universities than places for training youth in Greek glory."[37] Although Luther was a university man himself, his critique was aimed at the practice of teaching Aristotelian logic at the university level.[38]

Seminarian. Seminary theology grew out of the scholastic theology that was taught in the universities. As we have seen, this theology was based on Aristotle's philosophical system.[39] Seminary theology was dedicated to the training of professional ministers. Its goal was to produce seminary-trained religious specialists. It taught the theology—not of the early bishop, monk, or professor—but of the professionally "qualified" minister. This is the theology that prevails in the contemporary seminary.

One of the greatest theologians of this century, Karl Barth, reacted against the idea that theological education should be relegated to an elite class of professional orators. He wrote, "Theology is not a private reserve of theologians. It is not a private affair of

---

[34] To the disgust of many in his day, Abelard called one of his books *Christian Theology* (Robertson, *Abelard and Heloise*, xii–xiii).
[35] This shouldn't be confused with the approach of the apostle Paul, who may have used Greek logic to reason with the Greeks and rhetoric to communicate with them but did not use dialectic (Greek logic) to understand or interpret Scripture.
[36] Marsden, *Soul of the American University*, 34.
[37] Ibid., 35.
[38] Ibid., 36. For Luther's ideas on education, see Boyd, *History of Western Education*, 188ff. Ironically, Luther's coworker Melanchthon combined humanism (which has pagan roots) and Protestantism in the education of Northern Europe.
[39] Rowdon, "Theological Education in Historical Perspective," 79.

professors. . . . Nor is it a private affair of pastors. . . . Theology is a matter for the church. . . . The term 'laity' is one of the worst in the vocabulary of religion and ought to be banished from Christian conversation."[40]

Concerning the seminary, we might say that Peter Abelard laid the egg and Thomas Aquinas hatched it. Aquinas had the greatest influence on contemporary theological training. In 1879, his work was endorsed by a papal bull as an authentic expression of doctrine to be studied by all students of theology. Aquinas's main thesis was that God is known through human reason. He "preferred the intellect to the heart as the organ for arriving at truth."[41] Thus the more highly trained people's reason and intellect, the better they will know God. Aquinas borrowed this idea from Aristotle. And that is the underlying assumption of many—if not most—contemporary seminaries.

The teaching of the New Testament is that God is Spirit, and as such, He is known by revelation (spiritual insight) to one's human spirit.[42] Reason and intellect can cause us to know about God. And they help us to communicate what we know. But they fall short in giving us spiritual revelation. The intellect is not the gateway for knowing the Lord deeply. Neither are the emotions. In the words of A. W. Tozer: "Divine truth is of the nature of spirit and for that reason can be received only by spiritual revelation. . . . God's thoughts belong to the world of spirit, man's to the world of intellect, and while spirit can embrace intellect, the human intellect can never comprehend spirit. . . . Man by reason cannot know God; he can only know about God. . . . Man's reason is a fine instrument and useful within its field. It was not given as an organ by which to know God."[43]

In short, extensive Bible knowledge, a high-powered intellect, and razor-sharp reasoning skills do not automatically produce spiritual men and women who know Jesus Christ profoundly and who can

40 Barth, *Theologische Fragen und Antworten*, 175, 183–184, quoted in Erler and Marquard, *Karl Barth Reader*, 8–9.
41 Durant, *Age of Faith*, 964.
42 John 4:23-24; 1 Corinthians 2:9-16.
43 *Gems from Tozer* (Camp Hill, PA: Christian Publications, 1969), 36–37.

impart a life-giving revelation of Him to others.[44] (This, by the way, is the basis of spiritual ministry.) As Blaise Pascal (1623–1662) once put it, "It is the heart which perceives God, and not the reason."[45]

Today, Protestants and Catholics alike draw upon Aquinas's work, using his outline for their theological studies.[46] Aquinas's crowning work, *Summa Theologica* (*The Sum of All Theology*), is the model used in virtually all theological classes today—whether Protestant or Catholic. Consider the order in which Aquinas's theology is laid out:

God
Trinity
Creation
Angels
Man
The Divine Government (Salvation, etc.)
The Last End[47]

Now compare this outline to a typical systematic theology textbook used in Protestant seminaries:

God
Unity and Trinity
Creation
Angelology
The Origin and Character of Man

---

[44] This topic is far beyond the scope of this book. Four great resources that open up the Scriptures on the subject are T. Austin-Sparks, *What Is Man?* (Pensacola, FL: Testimony Publications, n.d.); Watchman Nee, *The Spiritual Man* (New York: Christian Fellowship Publishers, 1977); Mary McDonough, *God's Plan of Redemption* (Anaheim: Living Stream Ministry, 1999); and Ruth Paxson, *Life on the Highest Plane* (Grand Rapids: Kregel, 1996).

[45] *Pensées* #424. For an outstanding discussion on how God can be encountered beyond the bounds of human reason and intellect, see Dr. Bruce Demarest's *Satisfy Your Soul: Restoring the Heart of Christian Spirituality* (Colorado Springs: NavPress, 1999).

[46] "Thomas Aquinas Concludes Work on *Summa Theologiae*," *Christian History* 9, no. 4 (1990): 23. Later in his life, Thomas had a spiritual experience with the Lord. It went beyond his intellect to his spirit. The experience was so profound that Thomas declared: "All that I have hitherto written seems to me nothing but straw . . . compared to what has been revealed to me." After this experience of Christ, Thomas gave up all of his voluminous writing. His mammoth *Summa Theologica* was never completed. He laid down his pen on December 6, 1273, saying, "And I now await the end of my life" (*Summa Theologica*, Great Books of the Western World, vol. 19, Thomas Aquinas I, vi; Collins and Price, *Story of Christianity*, 113).

[47] *Summa Theologica*, vii.

Soteriology (Salvation, etc.)

Eschatology: The Final State[48]

Without a doubt, Aquinas is the father of contemporary theology.[49] His influence spread to the Protestant seminaries through the Protestant scholastics.[50] The tragedy is that Aquinas relied so completely on Aristotle's method of logic chopping when he expounded on holy writ.[51] In the words of Will Durant, "The power of the Church was still adequate to secure, through Thomas Aquinas and others, the transmogrification [transformation] of Aristotle into a medieval theologian." In another book Durant says that "he began a long series of works presenting Aristotle's philosophy in Christian dress."[52] Aquinas also quotes from another pagan philosopher profusely throughout his *Summa Theologica*.[53] Regardless of how much we wish to deny it, contemporary theology is a blending of Christian thought and pagan philosophy.

So we have four stages of theological education: episcopal, the theology of the bishops; monastic, the theology of the monks; scholastic, the theology of the professor; and seminarian, the theology of the professional minister.[54]

Each stage of Christian education is and always has been highly

---

[48] Henry C. Thiessen, *Lectures in Systematic Theology* (Grand Rapids: Eerdmans, 1979), v. Any standard Protestant systematic theology text follows this same template. All of it was derived from Aquinas.

[49] Aquinas's theological system continues to get reinforced. For instance, most Protestant seminaries in America and Europe follow what is known as the Berlin Model of theological education. This model started in Berlin in 1800. It was an outgrowth of enlightened rationalism that reinforced theology as a cerebral exercise. Most modern seminaries use this model today (*Vantage Point: The Newsletter of Denver Seminary*, June 1998, 4). According to Dr. Bruce Demarest, "As a legacy of the eighteenth-century Enlightenment, evangelicals often extol 'reason' as the key that unlocks the knowledge of God. Theology then becomes an intellectual undertaking—an activity of the mind and for the mind. Morton Kelsey observes that 'In Protestantism, God became a theological idea known by inference rather than a reality known by experience.' Through a 'left-brain' approach to the faith, God easily becomes an abstraction removed from lived experience. A. W. Tozer noted that even as many scientists lose God in His world (for example, Carl Sagan), so many theologians lose God in His Word" (*Satisfy Your Soul*, 95–96).

[50] Francis Turretin (Reformed) and Martin Chemnitz (Lutheran) were the two leading Protestant scholastics.

[51] The term *logic chopping* denotes going to great lengths to force the logic of an argument to fit a particular idea. If you doubt that Aquinas did this, simply read his *Summa Theologica*. Aquinas relied heavily upon Aristotelian logic and philosophy to support his theological views. Aquinas also wrote commentaries on Aristotle's work. According to Durant, Aquinas knew Aristotle's works more thoroughly than any other medieval thinker except for Averroes. For a full discussion on how Aquinas adopted Aristotle's philosophical system, see Douglas, *Who's Who in Christian History*, 30–34, and Durant, *Age of Faith*, 961–978.

[52] Durant, *Story of Philosophy* (New York: Washington Square Press, 1952), 104; Durant, *Age of Faith*, 962. The French chair of philosophy at Paris upbraided Thomas for tarnishing Christian theology with the philosophy of a pagan.

[53] Aquinas quotes Pseudo-Dionysius, a Neoplatonist, over 100 times in his *Summa Theologica*. Aquinas no doubt thought that the Dionysius he quoted was the man that Paul converted to Christ when in Athens (Acts 17:34). It was not, however. Pseudo-Dionysius was a Neoplatonist who lived much later than Dionysius the Areopagite.

[54] A fifth brand of theology called "lay theology" or a "theology for the whole people of God" is being championed by some contemporary scholars. See footnote 5 in this chapter.

intellectual and study driven.[55] As one scholar put it, "Whether a school was monastic, episcopal, or presbyterial, it never separated teaching from religious education, from instruction in church dogma and morals. Christianity was an intellectual religion."[56] As products of the Reformation, we are taught to be rationalistic (and very theoretical) in our approach to the Christian faith.[57]

THE FIRST SEMINARIES

For much of the medieval age, clerical education was minimal.[58] At the time of the Reformation, many Protestant pastors who converted from Roman Catholicism had no experience in preaching. They lacked both training and education.

As the Reformation progressed, however, provisions were made for uneducated pastors to attend schools and universities. Protestant ministers were not trained in oratory. They were instead trained in exegesis and biblical theology. It was assumed that if they knew theology, they could preach. (This assumption accounted for the long sermons in the sixteenth century, which often lasted two or three hours!)[59]

This type of theological training produced a "new profession"— the theologically trained pastor. Educated pastors now wielded tremendous influence, holding doctor's degrees in theology or other academic titles that gave them prestige.[60] By the mid-sixteenth century, most Protestant ministers were university trained in some way.[61]

So from its inception, Protestantism promoted a well-educated clergy, which became the backbone of the movement.[62] Throughout

---

[55] The exception is perhaps the "monastic" form. Some monastic schools studied the writings of the Christian mystics along with Aristotle and Plato.

[56] Marrou, *History of Education in Antiquity*, 343; Marsden, *Soul of the American University*, 38.

[57] Consider the following quote: "Christ did not appoint professors, but followers. If Christianity . . . is not reduplicated in the life of the person expounding it, then he does not expound Christianity, for Christianity is a message about living and can only be expounded by being realized in men's lives" (Søren Kierkegaard).

[58] Marsden, *Soul of the American University*, 38.

[59] Niebuhr and Williams, *Ministry in Historical Perspectives*, 133.

[60] Ibid., 144.

[61] Ibid., 142.

[62] Marsden, *Soul of the American University*, 37.

Protestant lands, the clergy were the best educated citizens. And they used their education to wield their authority.[63]

While Protestant ministers were sharpening their theological savvy, about one-fourth of the Catholic clergy had no university training. The Catholic church reacted to this at the Council of Trent (1545–1563). In order for the church to fight the new Protestant Reformation, it had to better educate its clergy. The solution? The founding of the very first seminaries.[64]

The Catholics wanted the learning and devotion of their priests to match that of the Protestant pastors.[65] Therefore, the Council of Trent required that all cathedral and greater churches "maintain, to educate religiously, and to train in ecclesiastical discipline, a certain number of youths of their city and diocese." So we may credit the founding of the seminary to the Catholics in the late sixteenth century.

The origin of the first Protestant seminary is clouded in obscurity. But the best evidence indicates that the Protestants copied the Catholic model and established their first seminary in America. It was established in Andover, Massachusetts, in 1808.[66]

Christian education in the United States was just as Aristotelian and highly systematized as it was in Europe.[67] By 1860, there were sixty Protestant seminaries on American soil.[68] This fast-paced growth was largely the result of the influx of converts produced during the Second Great Awakening (1800–1835) and the perceived need to train ministers to care for them.[69]

---

[63] Ibid., 37.
[64] Reid, *Concise Dictionary of Christianity in America*, 309; Durant, *Reformation*, 932. Trent made provision for a seminary in each diocese. A. G. Dickens, *Reformation and Society in Sixteenth-Century Europe* (London: Hartcourt, Brace, & World, Inc., 1966), 189; Collins and Price, *Story of Christianity*, 149.
[65] Rowdon, "Theological Education in Historical Perspective," 81.
[66] Reid, *Concise Dictionary of Christianity in America*, 113. John Calvin established the Geneva Academy in 1559, but this was not technically a seminary. While the Academy was used to train theologians, it was not conceived originally as a theological school. It gave a total education to nonclergy as well. Interestingly, Theodore Beza (Calvin's right-hand man) traced the scholastic pedigree of the Geneva Academy to the Greeks who in turn received their "true philosophy" from the Egyptians. It was argued that this was good, since Moses was educated in all the wisdom of the Egyptians (Robert W. Henderson, *The Teaching Office in the Reformed Tradition* [Philadelphia: Westminster Press, 1962], 51–61).
[67] John Morgan, *Godly Learning* (New York: Cambridge University Press, 1986), 107. American seminary education was also dominated by the Scottish "common sense" philosophy of Thomas Reid. Later, liberal seminaries came to prefer G. W. F. Hegel, while conservative seminaries stuck with Reid.
[68] Reid, *Concise Dictionary of Christianity in America*, 113.
[69] Ibid., 113.

Before Andover Seminary was founded, the Protestants had Yale (1701) and Harvard (1636) to train their clergy. Ordination was granted upon completing a formal examination by graduation.[70] But in time, these universities rejected orthodox Christian beliefs. (Harvard, for example, adopted Unitarianism.)[71] The Protestants no longer trusted an undergraduate education at Yale and Harvard, so they established their own seminaries to do the job themselves.[72]

BIBLE COLLEGE

The Bible college is essentially a nineteenth-century North American evangelical invention. A Bible college is a cross between a Bible institute (training center) and a Christian liberal arts school. Its students concentrate in religious studies and are trained for Christian service. The founders of the first Bible colleges were influenced by London pastors H. G. Guinness (1835–1910) and Charles Spurgeon (1834–1892).

In response to the revivalism of D. L. Moody, the Bible college movement blossomed in the late nineteenth and early twentieth centuries. The first two Bible colleges were the Missionary Training Institute (Nyack College, New York) in 1882 and Moody Bible Institute (Chicago) in 1886.[73] Their focus was to train ordinary laypeople to become "full-time" Christian workers.[74]

What led to the founding of the Bible college? From the mid-nineteenth century, little attention had been given to traditional Christian values as an integral part of higher education. Liberal theology had begun to dominate state universities across America. In the face of these elements, the demand for missionaries, parachurch leaders, and ministers provoked the creation of the Bible college to equip "the

---

70 Warkentin, *Ordination: A Biblical-Historical View*, 75.
71 Unitarianism denies the Trinity, the divinity of Jesus, and other orthodox Christian beliefs.
72 The first Catholic seminary to hit American soil was established in Baltimore in 1791. Reid, *Concise Dictionary of Christianity in America*, 1071.
73 The Moody Bible Institute was formally constituted in 1889 (Virginia Brereton, "The Popular Educator," *Christian History* 9, no. 1 [1990]: 28).
74 Reid, *Concise Dictionary of Christianity in America*, 42–43; *Harper's Encyclopedia of Religious Education*, 61.

called" with a Bible education.[75] Today, there are over four hundred Bible schools and colleges in the United States and Canada.[76]

SUNDAY SCHOOL

The Sunday school is also a relatively recent invention, born some 1,700 years after Christ. A newspaper publisher named Robert Raikes (1736-1811) from Britain is credited with being its founder.[77] In 1780, Raikes established a school in "Scout Alley," Gloucester, for poor children. Raikes did not begin the Sunday school for the purpose of religious instruction. Instead, he founded it to teach poor children the basics of education.

Raikes was concerned with the low level of literacy and morality among common children. Many of the children who attended his school were the victims of social and employer abuse. Because the children could not read, it was easy for others to take advantage of them. Although Raikes was an Anglican layman, the Sunday school took off like wildfire, spreading to Baptist, Congregational, and Methodist churches throughout England.[78]

The Sunday school movement came to a peak when it hit the United States. The first American Sunday school began in Virginia in 1785.[79] Then in 1790, a group of Philadelphians formed the Sunday School Society. Its purpose was to provide education to indigent children to keep them off the streets on Sunday.[80] In the eighteenth and nineteenth centuries, many Sunday schools operated separately from churches. The reason: Pastors felt that laymen could not teach the Bible.[81] In the mid-1800s, Sunday schools spread far and wide

---

[75] *Harper's Encyclopedia of Religious Education*, 61.

[76] "Bible College Movement," *The Evangelical Dictionary of Christian Education* (Grand Rapids: Baker Book House, 2001).

[77] *Harper's Encyclopedia of Religious Education*, 625. Most historical books credit Raikes with being the father of the Sunday school. But others are said to have been founders along with Raikes, Hannah More and Sarah Trimmer being among them (Thomas W. Laqueur, *Religion and Respectability: Sunday Schools and Working Class Culture, 1780-1850* [New Haven, CT: Yale University Press, 1976], 21). It has also been said that Rev. Thomas Stock of Gloucester gave Raikes the idea of Sunday education (p. 22).

[78] *Harper's Encyclopedia of Religious Education*, 625. The Sunday school grew as part of the evangelical revival of the 1780s and 1790s (Laqueur, *Religion and Respectability*, 61). When Raikes died in 1811, there were 400,000 children attending Sunday schools in Great Britain. C. B. Eavey, *History of Christian Education* (Chicago: Moody Press, 1964), 225–227.

[79] Terry, *Evangelism: A Concise History*, 180.

[80] *Harper's Encyclopedia of Religious Education*, 625.

[81] Terry, *Evangelism: A Concise History*, 181.

throughout America. In 1810, the Sunday school began to shift from being a philanthropic effort to help poor children to an evangelical mechanism.

D. L. Moody is credited with popularizing the Sunday school in America.[82] Under Moody's influence, the Sunday school became the primary recruiting ground for the contemporary church.[83] Today, the Sunday school is used both to recruit new converts and to train young children in the doctrines of the faith.[84] Public education has taken over the role for which Sunday school was designed.[85]

It should be noted that the nineteenth century was an era of institution building in America. Corporations, hospitals, asylums, prisons, as well as children's establishments like orphanages, reform schools, and free public schools were formed during this time.[86] The Sunday school was just another such institution.[87] Today, it is a permanent fixture in the traditional church.

As a whole, we don't view the contemporary Sunday school as an effective institution. According to some studies, Sunday school attendance has been on the decline over the last two decades.[88]

Describing the way of the early church, one scholar says, "There is no evidence to suggest that teachers divided groups on the basis of age and sex. The responsibility of the child's early education and, in particular, religious education lay with the parents. . . . No special arrangements seem to have been made for children by the early church. The Christian school was a long way off (around AD 372)— the Sunday School even more so."[89]

---

[82] Brereton, "Popular Educator," 28; Collins and Price, *Story of Christianity*, 187. Moody's Sunday school ministry cared for over 1,500 children.

[83] Anne M. Boylan, *Sunday School: The Formation of an American Institution 1790–1880* (New Haven, CT: Yale University Press, 1988), 167. This was the case by 1880. Arthur Flake developed the Sunday school program within the Southern Baptist Convention. He also popularized Sunday school growth principles that were adopted by other denominations. (Terry, *Evangelism: A Concise History*, 181). See also Elmer Towns, "Sunday School Movement," *New Twentieth Century Encyclopedia of Religious Knowledge*, 796–798.

[84] Ibid., 170; Reid, *Concise Dictionary of Christianity in America*, 331.

[85] *Pastor's Notes* 4, no. 1 (Worcester: Christian History Institute, 1991), 6.

[86] Boylan, *Sunday School*, 1.

[87] In 1824, there were 48,681 children in Sunday schools affiliated with the American Sunday School Union in the United States. In 1832, that figure grew to 301,358 (Boylan, *Sunday School*, 11). The American Sunday School Union was founded in 1824, comprising 724 schools, including 68 in Philadelphia. In 1970, the Union was renamed the American Missionary Society (Reid, *Concise Dictionary of Christianity in America*, 18).

[88] Bobby H. Welch, *Evangelism through the Sunday School: A Journey of Faith* (Nashville: Lifeway Press, 1997). Other studies show that attendance has been stable over the last decade.

[89] Norrington, *To Preach or Not*, 59.

THE YOUTH PASTOR

The youth pastor began appearing in churches long after Sunday schools, largely because society did not recognize or cater to the needs of this age group until the twentieth century.[90] In 1905, G. Stanley Hall popularized the concept of the "adolescent" as distinct from the young adult and the older child.[91]

Then in the 1940s, the term *teenager* was born. And for the first time a distinct youth subculture was created. People ages thirteen to nineteen were no longer simply "youths." They were now "teenagers."[92]

After World War II, Americans developed great concern for the young people of our nation. This concern spilled over into the Christian church. Youth rallies in the 1930s laboring under the banner "Youth for Christ" spawned a parachurch organization by the same name around 1945.[93]

With new understanding and concern for the "teenagers," the idea that someone needed to be employed to work with them emerged. Thus was born the professional youth minister. The youth pastor began working in large urban churches in the 1930s and 1940s.[94] Calvary Baptist Church in Manhattan had one of the very first youth pastors. *Moody Monthly* magazine wrote about him in the late 1930s.[95]

The majority of youth ministers in this era, however, worked for the emerging parachurch organizations that filled the Christian landscape.[96] By the early 1950s, thousands of professional youth min-

---

[90] Warren Benson and Mark H. Senter III, *The Complete Book of Youth Ministry* (Chicago: Moody Press, 1987), 66.

[91] Mark Senter III, *The Coming Revolution in Youth Ministry* (Chicago: Victor Books, 1992), 93.

[92] Michael V. Uschan, *The 1940s: Cultural History of the US through the Decades* (San Diego: Lucent Books, 1999), 88; Mary Helen Dohan, *Our Own Words* (New York: Alfred Knopf, 1974), 289.

[93] Mark Senter III, *The Youth for Christ Movement As an Educational Agency and Its Impact upon Protestant Churches: 1931–1979* (Ann Arbor: University of Michigan, 1990), 7–8. On pages 26ff., Senter discusses the social and historical factors that created a raft of youth organizations. Billy Graham became Youth for Christ's (YFC) traveling evangelist. In the 1950s, YFC established Bible clubs across the country (Reid, *Concise Dictionary of Christianity in America*, 377). In Manhattan, the charismatic Lloyd Bryant appears to be the first to organize regular youth rallies. Christopher Schlect, *Critique of Modern Youth Ministry* (Moscow, ID: Canon Press, 1995), 8.

[94] Calvary Baptist Church in Manhattan (1932), Vista Community Church in North San Diego County (1948), and Moody Memorial Church in Chicago (1949) all hired "youth directors." As Young Life and YFC clubs flourished in the country in the 1930s and 40s, smaller churches began employing youth ministers (Senter, *Coming Revolution in Youth Ministry*, 142).

[95] Mark Senter, e-mail message to Frank Viola, September 22, 1999.

[96] Young Life (1941), Youth for Christ (1945), Fellowship of Christian Athletes (1954), Youth with a Mission (1960). Senter, *Coming Revolution in Youth Ministry*, 27–28, 141; Mark Senter, "A Historical Framework for Doing Youth Ministry," *Reaching a Generation for Christ* (Chicago: Moody Press), 1997.

isters were meeting the spiritual needs of young people, who now had their own music, dress, literature, language, and etiquette.[97] During this time, the Christian church began to segregate teenagers from everyone else.

From the mid-1950s to the end of the 1960s, the youth pastor became an established part of evangelical churches. (The position took off a bit more slowly in the mainline denominations.)[98] By the end of the 1980s, youth ministry's shift from the parachurch organizations to institutional churches was pretty well complete.

Today, youth pastors are part of the professional clergy. Their position is built on the contemporary church's misguided choice to honor a division that was born in secular culture less than a century ago—namely, the division between teenager and everyone else.

Put another way, the youth pastor did not exist until a separate demographic group called teenagers emerged. In so doing, we created a problem that never before existed—what to do for (and with) the young people. It is not at all unlike the problem we created when a new class of Christian—the "laymen"—was invented. The question "How do we equip the laity?" was never asked before the institutional church made them a separate class of Christian.

EXPOSING THE HEART OF THE PROBLEM

The Greek philosophers Plato and Socrates taught that knowledge is virtue. Good depends on the extent of one's knowledge. Hence, the teaching of knowledge is the teaching of virtue.[99]

Herein lies the root and stem of contemporary Christian education. It is built on the Platonic idea that knowledge is the equivalent of moral character. Therein lies the great flaw.

Plato and Aristotle (both disciples of Socrates) are the fathers of contemporary Christian education.[100] To use a biblical metaphor,

---

[97] Schlect, *Critique of Modern Youth Ministry*, 6.
[98] Senter, *Coming Revolution in Youth Ministry*, 142.
[99] William Boyd and Edmund King, *The History of Western Education* (Lanham, MD: Barnes & Noble Books, 1995), 28.
[100] Power, *Legacy of Learning*, 29–116.

present-day Christian education, whether it be seminarian or Bible college, is serving food from the wrong tree: the tree of the knowledge of good and evil rather than the tree of life.[101]

Contemporary theological learning is essentially cerebral. It can be called "liquid pedagogy."[102] We pry open people's heads, pour in a cup or two of information, and close them up again. They have the information, so we mistakenly conclude the job is complete.

Contemporary theological teaching is data-transfer education. It moves from notebook to notebook. In the process, our theology rarely gets below the neck. If a student accurately parrots the ideas of his professor, he is awarded a degree. And that means a lot in a day when many Christians obsess over (and sometimes deify) theological degrees in their analysis of who is qualified to minister.[103]

Theological knowledge, however, does not prepare a person for ministry.[104] This does not mean that the knowledge of the world, church history, theology, philosophy, and the Scriptures is without value. Such knowledge can be very useful.[105] But it is not central. Theological competence and a high-voltage intellect alone do not qualify a person to serve in God's house.

The fallacy is that men and women who have matriculated from seminary or Bible college are instantly viewed as "qualified." Those who have not are viewed as "unqualified." By this standard, many of the Lord's choicest vessels would have failed the test.[106]

In addition, formal theological training does not equip students for many of the challenges of ministry. According to the Faith Communities Today (FACT) study released by Hartford Seminary in

---

101 Time and space will not permit us to explain the meaning of the two trees. For a fuller discussion, see Watchman Nee, *The Normal Christian Life*, ch. 7.

102 Pedagogy is the art and science of teaching.

103 One of the key problems in Christianity is that it inherited the intellectual standards of the ancient world (Marsden, *Soul of the American University*, 34).

104 Keep in mind that Joseph Stalin attended Tiflis Theological Seminary from ages 14 to 19 (Adam B. Ulam, *Stalin the Man and His Era* [New York: Viking Press, 1973], 18–22; Alan Bullock, *Hitler and Stalin: Parallel Lives* [New York: Knopf, 1992], 6, 13).

105 Paul of Tarsus was highly educated, and he was vital to the spread of early Christianity. Peter, on the other hand, was uneducated.

106 Jesus and the twelve apostles were all unlearned men: "The Jews were amazed and asked, 'How did this man [Jesus] get such learning without having studied?'" (John 7:15, NIV); "Now when they saw the boldness of Peter and John, and perceived that they were unlearned and ignorant men, they marveled; and they took knowledge of them, that they had been with Jesus" (Acts 4:13). Some noted Christians used of God who never received formal theological training include A. W. Tozer, G. Campbell Morgan, John Bunyan, C. H. Spurgeon, D. L. Moody, and A. W. Pink. In addition, some of the greatest Bible expositors in church history, such as Watchman Nee, Stephen Kaung, and T. Austin-Sparks, were not seminary trained.

Connecticut, seminary graduates and clergymen who had advanced degrees scored lower in both their ability to deal with conflict and in demonstrating a "clear sense of purpose" than did the nonseminary graduates.[107]

The survey showed that clergy with no ministerial education or formal certificate program scored the highest on tests that revealed how well one deals with conflict and stress. Bible college graduates scored slightly lower. Seminary graduates scored the lowest!

The major finding of the study was that "congregations with leaders who have a seminary education are, as a group, far more likely to report that in their congregations they perceive less clarity of purpose, more and different kinds of conflict, less person-to-person communication, less confidence in the future and more threat from changes in worship."[108]

All of this indicates that a person who matriculates from the theory-laden seminary or Bible college has been given little to no hands-on experience in the crucible of body life. By body life, we are not referring to the common experience of being in an institutional church setting. We are referring to the rough-and-tumble, messy, raw, highly taxing experience of the body of Christ where Christians live as a close-knit community and struggle to make corporate decisions together under Christ's headship without a stated leader over them. In this regard, the seminary is spiritually stultifying on some pretty basic levels.

The approach taken by seminaries is also self-referential. It sets its own criteria for who should minister and on what terms. It then often judges those who do not think the criteria are particularly useful or important.

But perhaps the most damaging problem of the seminary and Bible college is that they perpetuate the humanly devised system in which the clergy live, breathe, and have their being. That system—

---

[107] This study was based on more than 14,000 congregations from forty-one different denominations and "faith groups." It used twenty-six different surveys. The *FACT* study is considered to be the most comprehensive look at U.S. religion. The findings are published at http://www.fact.hartsem.edu.

[108] *FACT* study, 67.

along with every other outmoded human tradition addressed in this book—is protected, kept alive, and spread through our ministerial schools.[109]

Instead of offering the cure to the ills of the church, our theological schools worsen them by assuming (and even defending) all of the unscriptural practices that produce them.

The words of one pastor sum up the problem nicely: "I came through the whole system with the best education that evangelicalism had to offer—yet I really didn't receive the training that I needed . . . seven years of higher education in top-rated evangelical schools didn't prepare me to (1) do ministry and (2) be a leader. I began to analyze why I could preach a great sermon and people afterwards would shake my hand and say, 'Great sermon, Pastor.' But these were the very people who were struggling with self-esteem, beating their spouses, struggling as workaholics, succumbing to their addictions. Their lives weren't changing. I had to ask myself why this great knowledge I was presenting didn't move from their heads to their hearts and their lives. And I began to realize that the breakdown in the church was actually based on what we learned in seminary. We were taught that if you just give people information, that's enough!"[110]

>delving DEEPER

1. If you do not believe seminaries provide the right environment for the education of Christian leaders, can you give specifics on how you believe Christian workers should be prepared for Christian service?

This is a very big topic. But in short, the way that Jesus Christ trained Christian workers was to live with them for a period of years. It was "on the job" training. He mentored His disciples at close range. They also lived in community together. Jesus did the work, they watched, and then they went on a trial mission which He

---

[109] Ironically, Protestants are noted for their critical reflection on doctrine. But they have not applied that critical reflection to their church practices.

[110] Dr. Clyde McDowell, quoted in *Vantage Point: The Newsletter of Denver Seminary*, June 1998.

critiqued. Eventually, He sent them out, and they carried on the work themselves. Paul of Tarsus followed the same pattern, training Christian workers in the city of Ephesus. They were part of the community in Ephesus, they watched Paul, and eventually, they were sent out to do the work.

2. Can you elaborate on your statement that "the intellect is not the gateway for knowing the Lord deeply. Neither are the emotions"? How does Tozer's observation that we can only obtain divine truth through spiritual revelation affect how we should go about providing Christian training?

Those who train others in Christian work should be familiar with those spiritual realities that transcend intellect and emotion. Consequently, spiritual formation, spiritual understanding, and spiritual insight are vital ingredients in training for spiritual service. This includes spending time with the Lord, learning to bear His cross, living in authentic community, sharpening one's spiritual instincts, and discerning how to hear God's voice and be guided by Him inwardly.

3. What are your recommendations on how the church should instruct our children and youth?

The New Testament is absolutely silent on this question, though it seems to suggest that the responsibility for the moral teaching of children falls on the shoulders of the parents (see Ephesians 6:4 and 2 Timothy 1:5, 3:15).

That said, our suggestion is to let the creative juices of each local assembly discover new and effective ways to minister to the young ones.

chapter eleven

> REAPPROACHING THE NEW TESTAMENT: THE BIBLE IS NOT A JIGSAW PUZZLE

"In handling the subject of ministry in the New Testament it is essential to remember the order in which the books of the New Testament were written. If we assume, as the order in which the books of the New Testament are now presented would lead us to assume, that the Gospels were written first, and then Acts and then the letters of Paul, beginning with Romans and ending with the Pastoral Epistles to Timothy to Titus and the Letter to Philemon, we shall never be able to understand the development of the institutions and the thought of the early church."
—RICHARD HANSON, TWENTIETH-CENTURY PATRISTIC SCHOLAR

"In the last 50 or 100 years New Testament research has unremittingly and successfully addressed itself to the task of elucidating for us what was known as the 'Ecclesia' in primitive Christianity—so very different from what is to-day called the church both in Roman and

Protestant camps. . . . This insight—which an unprejudiced study of the New Testament and the crying need of the church have helped us to reach—may be expressed as follows: the New Testament 'Ecclesia,' the fellowship of Jesus Christ, is a pure communion of persons and has nothing to do with the character of an institution about it; it is therefore misleading to identify any single one of the historically developed churches, which are all marked by an institutional character, with the true Christian communion."

—EMIL BRUNNER, TWENTIETH-CENTURY SWISS THEOLOGIAN

WHY IS IT THAT WE CHRISTIANS can follow the same rituals every Sunday without ever noticing that they are at odds with the New Testament?[1] The incredible power of tradition has something to do with it. As we have seen, the church has often been influenced by the surrounding culture, seemingly unaware of its negative effects. At other times, it has, quite properly, recognized overt threats—such as heretical teachings about the person and divinity of Jesus Christ. But in an effort to combat those threats, it has moved away from the organic structure that God wrote into the church's DNA.

But there is something else—something more fundamental that most Christians are completely unaware of. It concerns our New Testament. The problem is not in what the New Testament says. The problem is in how we approach it.

The approach most commonly used among contemporary Christians when studying the Bible is called "proof texting." The origin of proof texting goes back to the late 1590s. A group of men called Protestant scholastics took the teachings of the Reformers and systematized them according to the rules of Aristotelian logic.[2]

The Protestant scholastics held that not only is the Scripture the Word of God, but every part of it is the Word of God in and of

---

[1] This chapter is based on a message Frank Viola delivered at a house church conference at Oglethorpe University in Atlanta, Georgia, on July 29, 2000.

[2] For a discussion on Protestant scholasticism, see Walter Elwell's *Evangelical Dictionary of Theology* (Grand Rapids: Baker Book House, 1984), 984–985. Francis Turretin (Reformed) and Martin Chemnitz (Lutheran) were the two main shakers among the Protestant scholastics (Elwell, *Evangelical Dictionary of Theology*, 1116 and 209 respectively).

itself—irrespective of context. This set the stage for the idea that if we lift a verse out of the Bible, it is true in its own right and can be used to prove a doctrine or a practice.

When John Nelson Darby emerged in the mid-1800s, he built a theology based on this approach. Darby raised proof texting to an art form. In fact, it was Darby who gave fundamentalist and evangelical Christians a good deal of their presently accepted teachings.[3] All of them are built on the proof-texting method. Proof texting, then, became the common way that we contemporary Christians approach the Bible.

As a result, we Christians rarely, if ever, get to see the New Testament as a whole. Rather, we are served up a dish of fragmented thoughts that are drawn together by means of fallen human logic. The fruit of this approach is that we have strayed far afield from the principles of the New Testament church. Yet we still believe we are being biblical. Allow us to illustrate the problem with a fictitious story.

MEET MARVIN SNURDLY

Marvin Snurdly is a world-renowned marital counselor. In his twenty-year career as a marriage therapist, Marvin has counseled thousands of troubled couples. He has an Internet presence. Each day hundreds of couples write letters to Marvin about their marital sob stories. The letters come from all over the globe. And Marvin answers them all.

A hundred years pass, and Marvin Snurdly is resting peacefully in his grave. He has a great-great-grandson named Fielding Melish. Fielding decides to recover the lost letters of his great great grandfather. But Fielding can find only thirteen of Marvin's letters. Out of the thousands of letters that Marvin wrote in his lifetime, just thirteen have survived! Nine were written to couples in marital crisis. Four were written to individual spouses.

---

[3] Dispensationalism and the pretribulational rapture are just two of them. The very successful *Left Behind* series is built upon these teachings (see *Time*, July 1, 2002, 41–48). For the fascinating origin of Darby's pretribulational doctrine, see MacPherson, *Incredible Cover-Up*.

These letters were all written within a twenty-year time frame: from 1980 to 2000. Fielding Melish plans to compile these letters into a volume. But there is something interesting about the way Marvin wrote his letters that makes Fielding's task somewhat difficult.

First, Marvin had an annoying habit of never dating his letters. No days, months, or years appear on any of the thirteen letters. Second, the letters only portray half the conversation. The initial letters written to Marvin that provoked his responses no longer exist. Consequently, the only way to understand the backdrop of each of Marvin's letters is by reconstructing the marital situation from Marvin's response.

Each letter was written at a different time, to people in a different culture, about a different problem. For example, in 1985, Marvin wrote a letter to Paul and Sally from Virginia, who were experiencing sexual problems early in their marriage. In 1990, Marvin wrote a letter to Jethro and Matilda from Australia, who were having problems with their children. In 1995, Marvin wrote a letter to a wife from Mexico who was experiencing a midlife crisis. Unfortunately, Fielding has no way of knowing when the letters were written.

Take note: twenty years—thirteen letters—all written to different people at different times in different cultures—all experiencing different problems.

It is Fielding Melish's desire to put these thirteen letters in chronological order. But without the dates, he cannot do this. So Fielding puts them in the order of descending length. That is, he takes the longest letter that Marvin wrote and puts it first. He puts Marvin's second longest letter after that. He takes the third longest and puts it third. The compilation ends with the shortest letter that Marvin penned. The thirteen letters are arranged, not chronologically, but by their length.

The volume hits the presses and becomes an overnight best seller.

One hundred years pass, and *The Collected Works of Marvin Snurdly* compiled by Fielding Melish stands the test of time. The work is still very popular. Another one hundred years pass, and this volume is being used copiously throughout the Western world.

The book is translated into dozens of languages. Marriage counselors quote it left and right. Universities employ it in their sociology classes. It is so widely used that someone gets a bright idea on how to make the volume easier to quote and handle.

What is that idea? It is to divide Marvin's letters into chapters and numbered sentences (or verses). So chapters and verses are added to *The Collected Works of Marvin Snurdly*.

But by adding chapter and verse to these once living letters, something changes that goes unnoticed. The letters lose their personal touch. Instead, they take on the texture of a manual.

Different sociologists begin writing books about marriage and the family. Their main source? *The Collected Works of Marvin Snurdly*. Pick up any book in the twenty-fourth century on the subject of marriage, and you will find the author quoting chapters and verses from Marvin's letters.

It usually looks like this: In making a particular point, an author will quote a verse from Marvin's letter written to Paul and Sally. The author will then lift another verse from the letter written to Jethro and Matilda. He will extract another verse from another letter. Then he will sew these three verses together and upon them he will build his particular marital philosophy.

Virtually every sociologist and marital therapist that authors a book on marriage does the same thing. Yet the irony is this: Each of these authors frequently contradicts the others, even though they are all using the same source!

But that is not all. Not only have Marvin's letters been turned into cold prose when they were originally living, breathing epistles to real people in real places, they have become a weapon in the hands of agenda-driven men. Not a few authors on marriage begin employing isolated proof texts from Marvin's work to hammer away at those who disagree with their marital philosophy.

How is this possible? How are all of these sociologists contradicting each other when they are using the exact same source? It is because the letters have been lifted out of their historical context. Each letter has been plucked from its chronological sequence and removed from its real-life setting.

Put another way, the letters of Marvin Snurdly have been transformed into a series of isolated, disjointed, fragmented sentences—so anyone can lift one sentence from one letter, another sentence from another letter, and then paste them together to create the marital philosophy of his or her choice.

An amazing story, is it not? Well, here is the punch line. Whether you realize it or not, this is a description of your New Testament!

THE ORDER OF PAUL'S LETTERS

The New Testament is made up mostly of the apostle Paul's letters; in fact, he wrote two-thirds of it. He penned thirteen letters in about a twenty-year time span. Nine letters were written to churches in different cultures, at different times, experiencing different problems. Four letters were written to individual Christians. The people who received those letters were also dealing with different issues at different times.

Take note: twenty years—thirteen letters—all written to different people at different times in different cultures—all experiencing different problems.[4]

In the early second century, someone began to take the letters of Paul and compile them into a volume. The technical term for this volume is "canon."[5] Scholars refer to this compiled volume as "the Pauline canon." The New Testament is essentially this compilation with a few letters added after it, the four Gospels and Acts placed before it, and Revelation tacked on the very end.

At the time, no one knew when Paul's letters were written.

---

[4] See Donald Guthrie's *New Testament Introduction*, revised edition (Downers Grove, IL: InterVarsity Press, 1990). For a good discussion on how we got our Bible, see *Christian History* 13, no. 3, and Ronald Youngblood, "The Process: How We Got Our Bible," *Christianity Today* (February 5, 1988), 23–38.

[5] Bruce, *Paul: Apostle of the Heart Set Free*, 465. Scholars refer to Paul's canon as the "Pauline corpus." To learn about the history of the New Testament canon, see F. F. Bruce, *The Canon of Scripture* (Downers Grove, IL: InterVarsity Press, 1988), ch. 8–23.

Even if they had, it would not have mattered. There was ..
dent for alphabetical or chronological ordering. The first-cei..
Greco-Roman world ordered its literature according to decreasing
length.[6]

Look at how your New Testament is arranged. What do you find? Paul's longest letter appears first.[7] It is Romans. First Corinthians is the second longest letter, so it follows Romans. Second Corinthians is the third longest letter. Your New Testament follows this pattern until you come to that tiny little book called Philemon.[8]

In 1864, Thomas D. Bernard delivered a series of talks as part of the Bampton Lectures. These lectures were published in 1872 in a book entitled *The Progress of Doctrine in the New Testament*. In the book, Bernard argued that the present order of Paul's letters in the New Testament was divinely inspired and commended. This book became very popular among Bible teachers of the nineteenth and twentieth centuries. As a result, virtually every theological text, exegetical text, or biblical commentary written in the nineteenth and twentieth centuries follows the present chaotic order, which blinds us from seeing the entire panoramic view of the New Testament. Canonical criticism is big among seminarians. This is the study of the canon as a unit in order to acquire an overall biblical theology. What is needed today is a theology built, not on the present canon and its misarrangement, but on the chronological narrative of the New Testament church.

Here is the present order as it appears in your New Testament. The books are arranged according to descending length:

Romans
1 Corinthians
2 Corinthians
Galatians

---

[6] Jerome Murphy-O'Connor, *Paul the Letter-Writer* (Collegeville, MN: The Liturgical Press, 1995), 121, 120. This practice is known as stichometry.

[7] For a thorough discussion on the order of the Pauline canon, see Murphy-O'Connor, *Paul the Letter-Writer*, ch. 3.

[8] Hebrews does not appear to be Pauline, so it was not part of the Pauline corpus.

Titus
Philemon

What, then, is the proper chronological order of these letters? According to the best available scholarship, here is the order in which they were written:[10]

Galatians
1 Thessalonians
2 Thessalonians
1 Corinthians
2 Corinthians
Romans
Colossians
Philemon
Ephesians
Philippians
1 Timothy
Titus
2 Timothy

THE ADDITION OF CHAPTERS AND VERSES

In the year 1227, a professor at the University of Paris named Stephen Langton added chapters to all the books of the Bible. Then

---

[9] Ephesians is actually a hair longer than Galatians, but the books were misarranged due to a scribal gloss. This is not surprising since the difference in length is so slight (Murphy-O'Connor, *Paul the Letter-Writer*, 124).

[10] See Guthrie's *New Testament Introduction*, revised edition; F. F. Bruce's *The Letters of Paul: An Expanded Paraphrase* (Grand Rapids: Eerdmans, 1965); F. F. Bruce's *Paul: Apostle of the Heart Set Free*.

in 1551, a printer named Robert Stephanus (sometimes called Robert Estienne) numbered the sentences in all the books of the New Testament.[11]

According to Stephanus's son, the verse divisions that his father created do not do service to the sense of the text. Stephanus did not use any consistent method. While riding on horseback from Paris to Lyons, he versified the entire New Testament within Langton's chapter divisions.[12]

So verses were born in the pages of holy writ in the year 1551.[13] And since that time God's people have approached the New Testament with scissors and glue, cutting and pasting isolated, disjointed sentences from different letters, lifting them out of their real-life setting, lashing them together to build floatable doctrines, and then calling it "the Word of God."

Seminarians and Bible college students alike are rarely if ever given a panoramic view of the free-flowing story of the early church with the New Testament books arranged in chronological order.[14] As a result, most Christians are completely out of touch with the social and historical events that lay behind each of the New Testament letters. Instead, they have turned the New Testament into a manual that can be wielded to prove any point. Chopping the Bible up into fragments makes this relatively easy to pull off.

HOW WE APPROACH THE NEW TESTAMENT

We Christians have been taught to approach the Bible in one of eight ways:

---

[11] Norman Geisler and William Nix, *A General Introduction of the Bible: Revised and Expanded* (Chicago: Moody Press, 1986), 340–341, 451; Bruce Metzger and Michael Coogan, *The Oxford Companion to the Bible* (New York: Oxford University Press, 1993), 79.

[12] H. von Soden, *Die Schriften des Newen Testamentes* (Gottingen, Germany: Vandenhoek, 1912), 1, 484; Connolly, *The Indestructible Book*, 154. One Bible historian made this remark about Stephanus's versification of the New Testament: "I think it had been better done on his knees in a closet."

[13] The versification of the Hebrew Bible occurred in 1571. Theodore Beza put Stephanus's verses in his version of the Textus Receptus (1565), which gave them the preeminent place that they have today. Kurt Galling, ed., *Die Religion in der Geschichte und der Gegenwart*, 3rd ed (Tubingen, Germany: J. C. B. Mohr, 1957), 3:114.

[14] In many seminaries and Bible colleges, the story of the early church is taught in a "church history" class while the books of the New Testament are taught in an "NT studies" class. And rarely do the twain meet. If you do not believe me, try this: The next time you meet a seminary student (or graduate), ask him or her to rehearse for you the entire chronological series of events from Paul's writing of Galatians to his writing of Romans.

> You look for verses that inspire you. Upon finding such verses, you either highlight, memorize, meditate upon, or put them on your refrigerator door.

> You look for verses that tell you what God has promised so that you can confess it in faith and thereby obligate the Lord to do what you want.

> You look for verses that tell you what God commands you to do.

> You look for verses that you can quote to scare the devil out of his wits or resist him in the hour of temptation.

> You look for verses that will prove your particular doctrine so that you can slice-and-dice your theological sparring partner into biblical ribbons. (Because of the proof-texting method, a vast wasteland of Christianity behaves as if the mere citation of some random, decontextualized verse of Scripture ends all discussion on virtually any subject.)

> You look for verses in the Bible to control and/or correct others.

> You look for verses that "preach" well and make good sermon material. (This is an ongoing addiction for many who preach and teach.)

> You sometimes close your eyes, flip open the Bible randomly, stick your finger on a page, read what the text says, and then take what you have read as a personal "word" from the Lord.

Now look at this list again. Which of these approaches have you used? Look again: Notice how each is highly individualistic. All of them put you, the individual Christian, at the center. Each approach ignores the fact that most of the New Testament was written to corporate bodies of people (churches), not to individuals.

But that is not all. Each of these approaches is built on isolated proof texting. Each treats the New Testament like a manual and blinds us to its real message. It is no wonder that we can approvingly nod our heads at paid pastors, the Sunday morning order of worship, sermons, church buildings, religious dress, choirs, worship teams, seminaries, and a passive priesthood—all without wincing.

We have been taught to approach the Bible like a jigsaw puzzle. Most of us have never been told the entire story that lies behind the letters that Paul, Peter, James, John, and Jude wrote. We have been taught chapters and verses, not the historical context.[15]

For instance, have you ever been given the story behind Paul's letter to the Galatians? Before nodding, see if you can answer these questions off the top of your head: Who were the Galatians? What were their issues? When and why did Paul write to them? What happened just before Paul penned his Galatian treatise? Where was he when he wrote it? What provoked him to write the letter? And where in Acts do you find the historical context for this letter? All of these background matters are indispensable for understanding what our New Testament is about. Without them, we simply cannot understand the Bible clearly or properly.[16]

One scholar put it this way, "The arrangement of the letters of Paul in the New Testament is in general that of their length. When we rearrange them into their chronological order, fitting them as far as possible into their life-setting within the record of the Acts of the Apostles, they begin to yield up more of their treasure; they become self-explanatory, to a greater extent than when this background is ignored."[17]

Another writes, "If future editions [of the New Testament] want to aid rather than hinder a reader's understanding of the New Testament, it should be realized that the time is ripe to cause both the verse and chapter divisions to disappear from the text and to be put on the margin in as inconspicuous a place as possible. Every effort must be made to print the text in a way which makes it possible

---

[15] Some of us have been taught a little about the historical background of the Bible. But it is just enough to inoculate us from searching further and getting the whole story.

[16] F. F. Bruce, ed., *The New International Bible Commentary* (Grand Rapids: Zondervan, 1979), 1095.

[17] G. C. D. Howley in "The Letters of Paul," *New International Bible Commentary*, 1095.

for the units which the author himself had in mind to become apparent."[18]

You could call our method of studying the New Testament the "clipboard approach." If you are familiar with computers, you are aware of the clipboard component. If you happen to be in a word processor, you may cut and paste a piece of text via the clipboard. The clipboard allows you to cut a sentence from one document and paste it into another.

Pastors, seminarians, and laymen alike have been conditioned by the clipboard approach when studying the Bible. This is how we justify our man-made, encased traditions and pass them off as biblical. It is why we routinely miss what the early church was like whenever we open up our New Testaments. We see verses. We do not see the whole picture.

This approach is still alive and well today, not only in institutional churches but in house churches as well. Let me use another illustration to show how easily anyone can fall into it—and the harmful effects it can have.

MEET JOE HOUSECHURCH

Joe Housechurch grew up in the institutional church. For the last ten years, he has been dissatisfied with it. Yet he has a heart for God and sincerely wants to be used by Him.

When Joe picks up a book on house churches, he has a crisis of conscience. He ends up learning some amazing things. Namely, that there is no contemporary pastor in the New Testament. There are no church buildings. There is no paid clergy, and church meetings are open for all to share.

All of these discoveries rock Joe's world, so much so that he leaves the institutional church (after facing the fury of the pastor, by the way). You see, Joe makes the mistake of sharing these "great revela-

---

[18] von Soden, *Die Schriften des Newen Testamentes*, 482.

tions" with other people in his church. When the pastor gets wind of it, Joe finds himself in the pastor's crosshairs and is called a heretic.

After licking his wounds, Joe picks up his New Testament, never realizing that the cut-and-paste approach still lives in his brain. The "clipboard mentality" was never extracted from his thinking. And he is blissfully unaware of it—as are most Christians.

Joe begins looking for the ingredients to start a New Testament church. So he begins to do what most Christians are conditioned to do when seeking God's will. He cherry-picks verses out of the New Testament, ignoring the social and historical background of those verses.

Joe comes across Matthew 18:20: "Where two or three are gathered together in my name, there am I in the midst of them." Joe keeps reading and discovers in Acts 2:46 that the early Christians regularly "met in homes" (NLT). Joe gets a revelation. "All I have to do is open up my house, have two or three people gather here, and voila! I have planted a New Testament church!"

So the next Sunday, Joe opens his home and starts a "house church" based on the New Testament (so he thinks). Soon he has another revelation: "I am a church planter like Paul. I started a house church just like he did." Joe does not realize that he has just lifted two sentences from two documents—completely out of historical context—and sewn them together to do something that has no root in Scripture.

Matthew 18:20 is not a recipe for founding a church. That passage is dealing with an excommunication meeting! Acts 2:46 is simply a report of what the early Christians did. Yes, the early Christians met in homes. And it is highly recommended that we meet in homes today.[19] But opening up one's home and inviting people to meet there does not make a church. Nor does it make the owner of the home a church planter.

The churches that were planted in the first century were planted

---

[19] See Viola, *Reimagining Church*.

out of blood and sweat. The people who planted them did not leave the synagogue on Saturday and decide they were going to plant house churches on Sunday. Every man in the New Testament who was involved in planting churches was first an ordinary brother in an already existing church. And in time that man—after a lot of tribulation and exposure in a church that knew him very well—was recognized and sent with the approval of that church. This is a consistent pattern throughout the New Testament.[20]

You can prove anything with verses. Birthing a church that maps to New Testament principles takes a whole lot more work than opening up your house and having people sit on comfy couches to drink java, eat cookies, and talk about the Bible.

What do we mean by a New Testament–styled church? It is a group of people who know how to experience Jesus Christ and express Him in a meeting without any human officiation. Such a group of people can function organically together as a body when they are left on their own after the church planter leaves them. (This does not mean that church planters never return. There are many times when they are needed to help the church. But after planting a church, church planters should be absent more than they are present.)

The one who plants a New Testament–styled church leaves that church without a pastor, elders, a music leader, a Bible facilitator, or a Bible teacher. If that church is planted well, those believers will know how to sense and follow the living, breathing headship of Jesus Christ in a meeting. They will know how to let Him invisibly lead their gatherings. They will bring their own songs, they will write their own songs, they will minister out of what Christ has shown them—with no human leader present! What is described here is not armchair philosophy. I (Frank) have worked with churches that fit this bill.

To equip people to do that takes a lot more than opening up your house and saying, "Come, let's have Bible study."

---

[20] See Viola, *So You Want to Start a House Church?*

Let's go back to our story. Joe Housechurch now has what he considers a New Testament church. As in all small groups like Joe's, the issue of leadership is raised. What does Joe do? He gets his cherry picker out and begins looking for verses on leadership. He stops at Acts 14 and is arrested by verse 23. It says, "Paul and Barnabas also appointed elders in every church" (NLT). Joe gets another revelation! *The word of God declares that every New Testament church has elders,* he muses. *Therefore, our house church needs elders!* (Joe makes this discovery only two weeks after opening up his home.)

After lifting that verse out of context, Joe appoints elders. (Joe happens to be one of those elders, by the way.)

What is the historical context of Acts 14? Two church planters, Paul and Barnabas, are sent out from their home church in Antioch. Before this sending, both men had already experienced church life as brothers, not leaders (Barnabas in Jerusalem and Paul in Antioch).

Acts 14:23 is part of a description of what took place after these two church planters were sent out. They are in south Galatia. The two men have just planted four churches. Now they are returning to visit those churches six months to one year after those churches were planted. Paul and Barnabas return to each of the Galatian churches and "publicly endorse old men" in each church.[21]

Joe has made another, more subtle mistake while interpreting this passage. The verse says that Paul and Barnabas appointed elders in every church. Joe takes this to mean that every genuine church has elders. Yet this text says no such thing. The verse is referring to an event in south Galatia during the first century. "Every church" means every church in south Galatia in AD 49![22] Luke is talking about the four churches that Paul and Barnabas just planted. Do you see the problem that we run into when we blithely lift verses from their historical setting?

The truth is, Joe Housechurch is totally outside biblical bounds. First, he is not an itinerant church planter. (These are the men who

---

[21] See Viola, *Reimagining Church.*
[22] Antioch of Syria and Corinth had no elders as far as we can tell.

acknowledged elders in the first century.) Second, his church is far too young to have elders. In Jerusalem, it took at least fourteen years for elders to emerge. But Joe Housechurch has his verse, so he is "standing on Scripture" (in his imagination).

Later, the issue of giving money comes up. So Joe parks at 1 Corinthians 16:2, "On the first day of each week, you should each put aside a portion of the money you have earned" (NLT). Based on this verse, Joe institutes a rule that everyone in his house church should give money to the church fund on Sunday morning.

Again, Joe has taken a passage out of context and built a practice upon it. First Corinthians 16:2 is dealing with a onetime request. It was written about AD 55 to the church in Corinth. At the time, Paul was collecting money from all the Gentile churches that he had planted. Paul had one goal for this: He wanted to bring that collection to the brothers and sisters in Jerusalem who were going through severe poverty. Paul was saying to the Corinthians, "By the way, when I come and visit, I want that money up front to bring to Jerusalem. So every Sunday when you come together, would you please gradually lay aside a portion of your earnings to create a relief fund?" First Corinthians 16:2, therefore, has nothing to do with a perfunctory ritual of taking up an offering every Sunday morning.[23]

Next Joe's house church begins to discuss the question of the church's mission. Naturally, Joe takes out his cherry picker and seeks verses that will yield an answer. He stops at Matthew 28:19, "Go ye therefore, and teach all nations." He cross-references this to Mark 16:15, which says: "Go ye into all the world, and preach the gospel." He continues on to Acts 5:42: "They ceased not to teach and preach Jesus Christ."

Joe muses to himself, *Our mission is to preach the gospel. That is why we exist. Why shucks, if God did not want us to preach the gospel He would have killed us after we got saved! So the only reason we breathe oxygen—the only reason why we have house churches—is to preach the gospel. This is what*

---

[23] We fully support regularly giving to the needs of the church (*not* pastor salaries or church buildings, mind you). But you cannot use this verse to make a law out of a Sunday morning offering.

the New Testament says. I just read it. And if we don't preach the gospel regularly, then we are sinning against God!

Once again, Mr. Joe Housechurch has lifted three verses totally out of context. In Matthew 28:19 and Mark 16:15, Jesus is sending His apostles. And in Acts 5:42, these same apostles are preaching the gospel. In the original Greek, the "Great Commission" reads: "Having gone on your way . . . " Therefore, it is a prophecy ("having gone"), not a command ("Go").[24] The Lord did not command the apostles to "go." He told them that they would be going. There is a valuable point here.

Unlike Christians today, the early Christians did not share Christ out of guilt, command, or duty. They shared Him because He was pouring out of them, and they could not help it! It was a spontaneous, organic thing—born out of life, not guilt.

Joe's thought processes about the church's mission have been shaped by two things: nineteenth-century revivalism (see chapter 3), and the clipboard approach to the Bible.

THE NET EFFECT OF THE CLIPBOARD APPROACH

Let's step back and analyze Joe's story. Joe has grossly mishandled the New Testament. Is his motive pure? Yes. Does he have a heart for God? Yes. Did this keep him from misapplying Scripture? No.

Joe has come to the New Testament as many of us were taught to do—with scissors and glue, ready to cut, paste, and create a basis for our favorite doctrines and practices.

The net effect of the clipboard approach is tragic. It has produced a raft of present-day churches that have no scriptural basis upon which to exist. (We speak of the institutional church as we know it today.) But more, it has generated scores of mechanical pro forma "house churches" that are lifeless, colorless, and sterile.

Recall the vision that Ezekiel had of the valley of dry bones (see Ezekiel 37). The Lord took Ezekiel to a valley of bones, and

---

[24] Kenneth S. Wuest, *The New Testament: An Expanded Translation* (Grand Rapids: Eerdmans, 1961).

the living, breathing Word of God came forth to resurrect those bones. The Scripture says that bone was put upon bone. The bones were clothed with sinew and flesh. And when the breath of God came into them like a rushing wind, those dead bones became a mighty army.

Many contemporary house church "planters" can be described as men who have come to the valley of dry bones with glue, needle, thread, and New Testament verses in hand. They have taken the bones and glued them together. They have put thread through the sinew and stitched flesh upon it. Then they have stood back and said, "Look, a New Testament church built on the New Testament. We have elders, we meet in a house, we do not have a hired clergy, we take up a collection every Sunday, and we preach the gospel."

But there is no rushing mighty wind!

The church of Jesus Christ cannot be started. It cannot be welded together. There is no blueprint or model that we can tease out of the New Testament by extracting verses and trying to imitate them mechanically. The church of Jesus Christ is a biological, living entity! It is organic; therefore, it must be born.

We do well to pay attention to the way that churches were raised up in the first century. I believe that Scripture holds for us enduring principles on this score. If you count all the churches mentioned in the New Testament, you'll find about thirty-five. Every one of them was either planted or aided by a traveling church planter who preached only Christ. There are no exceptions. The church was raised up as a result of the apostolic presentation of Jesus Christ.

There are more verses to back this principle up than there are for meeting in homes. There are more verses to back that up than there are for open, participatory meetings. There are more verses to back that up than there are for taking a collection on Sunday morning. The book of Acts is a record of churches being planted by extra-local workers in Judaea, South Galatia, Macedonia, Achaia, Asia Minor, and Rome. The epistles are letters written by apostolic workers to churches in crises, to individuals, and to those they were training for spiritual ministry. The principle of the extra-local church planter dominates the New Testament.[25]

And as we have seen, there is much more Scripture to support this practice than there is for all the unscriptural things we do in the contemporary church—including hiring a pastor. The pattern of extra-local workers planting and helping a church pervades the entire New Testament. And it is one that is deeply rooted in divine principle.[26]

A PRACTICAL REMEDY

What, then, is the antidote to the clipboard approach to the New Testament? What is the remedy that will bring you into a living expression of the body of Christ for our time? The antidote begins with understanding our New Testament.

We have been conditioned to come to the New Testament with a microscope and extract verses to find out what the early Christians did. We need to abandon that whole mentality, step back, and take a fresh look at the Scriptures. We must become familiar with the whole sweeping drama from beginning to end. We need to learn to view the New Testament panoramically, not microscopically.

F. F. Bruce, one of the greatest scholars of our time, once made a riveting statement. He said reading the letters of Paul is like listening to one end of a phone conversation.[27] Thanks to recent biblical scholarship, we can now reconstruct the entire saga of the early church. In other words, we can hear the other side of the conversation! Frank's book *The Untold Story of the New Testament Church* reconstructs both sides of the conversation, creating one fluid narrative of the early church.

To learn the story of the early church is to be forever cured of the cut-and-paste, clipboard approach to the New Testament. Learning

---

[25] To see this principle emerge in Scripture chronologically, see Viola, *The Untold Story of the New Testament Church.*
[26] See Viola, *So You Want to Start a House Church?* which is a detailed discussion on the four ways that churches were planted in the first century and the spiritual principles that governed them.
[27] F. F. Bruce, *Answers to Questions* (Grand Rapids: Zondervan, 1972), 93.

the story will lay bare the spiritual principles that are in God Himself and that are consistent throughout all of the New Testament. We consistently miss these principles because of the way we approach the Bible and because Paul's letters are not arranged chronologically.

When we learn the story, our verses must bow and bend to it. No longer are we able to take a verse out of context and say, "Look, we are supposed to do this." Many of the verses that we Christians routinely pull out of the Bible will simply not yield. More significantly, approaching the Bible in this way enables us to see the passion and unity with which the first Christians lived as they sought to faithfully follow and represent their Lord Jesus. And what was that passion? That is the question we turn to in the final chapter.

>delving DEEPER

1. Are you saying it is always dangerous to handle Scripture topically, either in individual study or while preparing to teach on some specific issue? Or do you think, if Christians took the time to gain a panoramic understanding of Scripture, they could avoid the dangers of proof texting?

Topical studies can easily lead one astray if the particular texts that are part of the "topic" are not understood in their historical contexts. For that reason, it is best to begin with the narrative of Scripture, seeing the whole fluid story in its historical context. Once that foundation is laid, topical studies can prove quite meaningful.

2. Is "organic church" a synonym for "house church"? If not, what is the distinction?

No, it is not a synonym. Some house churches are organic, while others are not. A number of present-day house churches are glorified Bible studies. Many others are supper-fests (the meetings revolve around a shared meal and that is about it). Some house churches are just as institutionalized as traditional churches—with a living room pulpit and chairs arranged in rows so attendees can listen to a forty-five-minute sermon.

Organic church life is a grassroots experience that is marked by face-to-face community, every-member functioning, open-participatory meetings, nonhierarchical leadership, and the centrality and supremacy of Jesus Christ as the functional leader and head of the group. Put another way, organic church life is the "experience" of the Body of Christ. In its purest form, it is the fellowship of the triune God brought to earth and experienced by human beings.

3. What are the signs of a healthy organic church? What are the signs of an unhealthy organic church?

Some of the signs of a healthy organic church are:

- the building together of sisters and brothers into a close-knit, Christ-centered community
- the transformation of character in the lives of the members
- meetings that express and reveal Jesus Christ and in which every member functions and shares
- community life that is vibrant, thriving, authentic, and where the members grow to love one another more and more
- a community of believers who are magnificently obsessed with their Lord, and who are neither legalistic nor libertine in their lifestyle

The signs of an unhealthy organic church are similar to the problems the apostle Paul pointed out to the church in Corinth:

- a perversion of the grace of God to be a license to sin
- a sectarian and elitist attitude
- self-centeredness among members

Since organic churches are face-to-face communities, they experience the whole gamut of problems that Christians face in close-knit relationships. Those problems are dealt with in Paul's letters. Healthy churches survive those problems and become stronger after passing through them. Unhealthy ones typically do not survive them.

chapter twelve

► A SECOND GLANCE AT THE SAVIOR: JESUS, THE REVOLUTIONARY

"A true radical must be a man of roots. In words that I have used else-where, 'The revolutionary can be an "outsider" to the structure he would see collapse: indeed, he must set himself outside of it. But the radical goes to the roots of his own tradition. He must love it: he must weep over Jerusalem, even if he has to pronounce its doom.'"
   —JOHN A. T. ROBINSON, TWENTIETH-CENTURY ENGLISH
   NEW TESTAMENT SCHOLAR

"If Christianity is to receive a rejuvenation it must be by other means than any now being used. If the church in the second half of [the twentieth] century is to recover from the injuries she suffered in the first half, there must appear a new type of preacher. The proper, ruler-of-the-synagogue type will never do. Neither will the priestly type of man who carries out his duties, takes his pay and asks no questions, nor the smooth-talking pastoral type who knows how to make the Christian religion acceptable to everyone. All these have been tried and found wanting. **Another kind of religious leader must arise among us. He must be of the old prophet type, a man who has seen visions of God and has heard a voice from the Throne. When he comes (and I pray God there will not be one but many) he will stand in flat contradiction to everything our smirking, smooth civilization holds dear. He will contradict, denounce and protest in the name of God and will earn the hatred and opposition of a large segment of Christendom."**

—A. W. TOZER, TWENTIETH-CENTURY AMERICAN MINISTER AND AUTHOR

JESUS CHRIST IS NOT ONLY the Savior, the Messiah, the Prophet, the Priest, and the King. He is also the Revolutionary. Yet few Christians know Him as such. Doubtlessly, some readers have struggled with this thought while reading this book: *Why do you have to be so negative about the contemporary church? Jesus is not a critical person. It is so unlike our Lord to talk about what is wrong with the church. Let's focus on the positive and ignore the negative!*

Such sentiments reveal complete unfamiliarity with Christ as revolutionary teacher—radical prophet—provocative preacher—controversialist—iconoclast—and the implacable opponent of the religious establishment.

Granted, our Lord is not critical or harsh with His own. He is full of mercy and kindness, and He loves His people passionately. However, this is precisely why He is jealous over His bride. And it is why He will not compromise with the entrenched traditions to which His people have been held captive. Nor will He ignore our fanatical devotion to them.

Consider our Lord's conduct while on earth.

Jesus was never a rabble-rouser nor a ranting rebel (Matthew 12:19-20). Yet He constantly defied the traditions of the scribes and Pharisees. And He did not do so by accident, but with great deliberation. The Pharisees were those who, for the sake of the "truth" as they saw it, tried to extinguish the truth they could not see. This explains why there was always a blizzard of controversy between the "tradition of the elders" and the acts of Jesus.

Someone once said that "a rebel attempts to change the past; a revolutionary attempts to change the future." Jesus Christ brought drastic change to the world. Change to man's view of God. Change to God's view of man. Change to men's view of women. Our Lord came to bring radical change to the old order of things, replacing it with a new order.[1] He came to bring forth a new covenant—a new Kingdom—a new birth—a new race—a new species—a new culture—and a new civilization.[2]

As you read through the Gospels, behold your Lord, the Revolutionary. Watch Him throw the Pharisees into a panic by intentionally flaunting their conventions. Numerous times Jesus healed on the Sabbath day, flatly breaking their cherished tradition. If the Lord wanted to placate His enemies, He could have waited until Sunday or Monday to heal some of these people. Instead, He deliberately healed on the Sabbath, knowing full well it would make His opponents livid.

This pattern runs pretty deep. In one instance, Jesus healed a blind man by mixing clay with spittle and putting it in the man's eyes. Such an act was in direct defiance of the Jewish ordinance that prohibited healing on the Sabbath by mixing mud with spittle![3] Yet your Lord intentionally shattered this tradition publicly and with absolute resolve. Watch Him eat food with unwashed hands under the judgmental gaze of the Pharisees, again intentionally defying their fossilized tradition.[4]

In Jesus, we have a man who refused to bow to the pressures of religious conformity. A man who preached a revolution. A man who would not tolerate hypocrisy. A man who was not afraid to provoke

---

[1] The following passages throw light on Christ's revolutionary nature: Matthew 3:10-12, 10:34-38; Mark 2:21-22; Luke 12:49; John 2:14-17, 4:21-24.

[2] The church of Jesus Christ is not a blending of Jew and Gentile. It is a new humanity—a new creation—that transcends both Jew and Gentile (Eph. 2:15). The ekklesia is a biologically new entity on this planet . . . it is a people who possess divine life (1 Corinthians 10:32; 2 Corinthians 5:17; Galatians 3:28; Colossians 3:11). Even the Christians of the second century spoke of themselves as "the new race" and "the third race." See Clement of Alexandria, *Stromata*, or *Miscellanies*, book 6, ch. 5. "We who worship God in a new way, as the third race, are Christians"; *Epistle to Diognetus*, ch. 1, "this new race."

[3] In the Mishnah it is stated: "To heal a blind man on the Sabbath it is prohibited to inject wine in his eyes. It is also prohibited to make mud with spittle and smear it on his eyes" (Shabbat 108:20).

[4] According to the Mishnah, "One should be willing to walk four miles to water in order to wash your hands rather than to eat with unwashed hands" (Sotah, 4b); "He who neglects hand washing is as he who is a murderer" (Challah, J, 58:3).

those who suppressed the liberating gospel He brought to set men free. A man who did not mind evoking anger in His enemies, causing them to gird their thighs for battle.

What is the point? It is this: Jesus Christ came not only as Messiah, the Anointed One of God, to deliver His people from the bondage of the Fall.

He came not only as Savior, paying a debt He did not owe to wash away the sins of mankind.

He came not only as Prophet, comforting the afflicted and afflicting the comfortable.

He came not only as Priest, representing people before God and representing God before people.

He came not only as King, triumphant over all authority, principality, and power.

He also came as Revolutionary, tearing apart the old wineskin with a view to bringing in the new.

Behold your Lord, the Revolutionary!

For most Christians, this is a side of Jesus Christ they have never known before. Yet we believe it explains why exposing what is wrong with the contemporary church so that Christ's body can fulfill God's ultimate intention is so critical. It is simply an expression of our Lord's revolutionary nature. The dominating aim of that nature is to put you and me at the center of the beating heart of God. To put you and me in the core of His eternal purpose—a purpose for which everything was created.[5]

The early church understood that purpose. They not only understood God's passion for His church, they lived it out. And what did such body life look like? Consider the brief glimpse below:[6]

> The early Christians were intensely Christ-centered. Jesus Christ was their pulse beat. He was their life, their breath, and their central point of reference. He was the object of their

---

5 See Viola, *God's Ultimate Passion* for a discussion on the eternal purpose.
6 The subject of the organic church is so broad that it cannot be covered in this book. However, Frank's book *Reimagining Church* (Colorado Springs: David C. Cook, 2008) provides a thorough, Scripture-based look at the organic practices of the New Testament church.

worship, the subject of their songs, and the content of their discussion and vocabulary. The New Testament church made the Lord Jesus Christ central and supreme in all things.

> The New Testament church had no fixed order of worship. The early Christians gathered in open-participatory meetings where all believers shared their experience of Christ, exercised their gifts, and sought to edify one another. No one was a spectator. All were given the privilege and the responsibility to participate. The purpose of these church meetings was twofold. It was for the *mutual* edification of the body. It was also to make visible the Lord Jesus Christ through the every-member functioning of His body. The early church meetings were not religious "services." They were informal gatherings that were permeated with an atmosphere of freedom, spontaneity, and joy. The meetings belonged to Jesus Christ and to the church; they did not serve as a platform for any particular ministry or gifted person.

> The New Testament church lived as a face-to-face community. While the early Christians gathered for corporate worship and mutual edification, the church did not exist to merely meet once or twice a week. The New Testament believers lived a shared life. They cared for one another outside of scheduled meetings. They were, in the very real sense of the word, family.

> Christianity was the first and only religion the world has ever known that was void of ritual, clergy, and sacred buildings. For the first 300 years of the church's existence, Christians gathered in homes. On special occasions, Christian workers would sometimes make use of larger facilities (like Solomon's Porch [John 10:23, Acts 3:11] and the Hall of Tyrannus [Acts 19:9]). But they had no concept of a sacred edifice nor of spending large amounts of money on buildings. Nor would they ever call a building a "church" or the "house of God." The only sacred

building the early Christians knew was the one not made with human hands.

> The New Testament church did not have a clergy. The Catholic priest and the Protestant pastor were completely unknown. The church had traveling apostolic workers who planted and nurtured churches. But these workers were not viewed as being part of a special clergy caste. They were part of the body of Christ, and they *served* the churches (not the other way around). Every Christian possessed different gifts and different functions, but only Jesus Christ had the exclusive right to exercise authority over His people. No man had that right. Eldering and shepherding were just two of those gifts. Elders and shepherds were ordinary Christians with certain gifts. They were not special offices. And they did not monopolize the ministry of the church meetings. They were simply seasoned Christians who naturally cared for the members of the church during times of crisis and provided oversight for the whole assembly.

> Decision making in the New Testament church fell upon the shoulders of the whole assembly. Traveling church planters would sometimes give input and direction. But ultimately, the whole church made local decisions under the lordship of Jesus Christ. It was the church's responsibility to find the Lord's mind together and act accordingly.

> The New Testament church was organic, not organizational. It was not welded together by putting people into offices, creating programs, constructing rituals, and developing a top-down hierarchy or chain-of-command structure. The church was a living, breathing organism. It was born, it would grow, and it naturally produced all of what was in its DNA. That would include all the gifts, ministries, and functions of the body of Christ. In the eyes of God, the church is a beautiful

woman. The bride of Christ. She was a colony from heaven, not a man-made organization from earth.

> Tithing was not a practice of the New Testament church. The early Christians used their funds to support the poor among them, as well as the poor in the world. They also supported traveling itinerant church planters so that the gospel could be spread and churches could be raised up in other lands. They gave according to their ability, not out of guilt, duty, or compulsion. Pastor/clergy salaries were unheard of. Every Christian in the church was a priest, a minister, and a functioning member of the body.

> Baptism was the outward expression of Christian conversion. When the early Christians led people to the Lord, they *immediately* baptized them in water as a testimony to their new position. The Lord's Supper was an ongoing expression whereby the early Christians reaffirmed their faith in Jesus Christ and their oneness with His body. The Supper was a full meal which the church enjoyed together in the spirit and atmosphere of joy and celebration. It was the fellowship of the body of Christ, not a token ritual or a religious rite. And it was never officiated by a clergy or a special priesthood.

> The early Christians did not build Bible schools or seminaries to train young workers. Christian workers were educated and trained by older workers in the context of church life. They learned "on the job." Jesus provided the initial model for this "on-the-job" training when He mentored the Twelve. Paul duplicated it when he trained young Gentile workers in Ephesus.

> The early Christians did not divide themselves into various denominations. They understood their oneness in Christ and expressed it visibly in every city. To their minds, there was only one church per city (even though it may have met in many

different homes throughout the locale). If you were a Christian in the first century, you belonged to that one church. The unity of the Spirit was well guarded. Denominating themselves ("I am of Paul," "I am of Peter," "I am of Apollos") was regarded as sectarian and divisive (see 1 Corinthians 1:12).

We believe these are some aspects of God's vision for every church. In fact, we have written this book for one reason: to make room for the absolute centrality, supremacy, and headship of Christ in His church. Fortunately, more and more Revolutionaries today are catching that vision. They recognize that what is needed is a revolution within the Christian faith—a complete upheaval of those Christian practices that are contrary to biblical principle. We must begin all over again, on the right foundation. Anything less will prove defective.

And so our hope as you finish this book is threefold. First, we hope that you will begin asking questions about church as you presently know it. How much of it is truly biblical? How much of it expresses the absolute headship of Jesus Christ? How much of it allows the members of His body the freedom to function? Second, we hope you will share this book with every Christian you know so that they too can be challenged by its message. And third, we hope you will pray seriously about what your response should be to that message.

If you are a disciple of the Revolutionary from Nazareth . . . the radical Messiah[7] who lays His axe to the root . . . you must eventually ask a specific question. It is the same question that was asked of our Lord's disciples while He walked this earth. That question is: "Why do your disciples break the tradition of the elders?" (Matthew 15:2).

---

[7] The word *radical* is derived from the Latin *radix*, which means "root." A radical, therefore, is someone that goes to the root or origin of something. Jesus Christ was both a radical and a revolutionary. See John A. T. Robinson's definition for both terms in the epigraph that begins this chapter.

>delving DEEPER

1. Why are you so critical of the church? God loves the church. It angers me that you're so judgmental about it.

This question is a good example of the problem we are trying to expose in this book. Namely, many Christians are confused about what the Bible means when it uses the word *church*. The word *church* refers to God's people. More specifically, it refers to the gathered community of those who follow Jesus. It does not refer to a system, a denomination, a building, an institution, or a service.

We have written this book because we love the church very much. And we want to see her function in a way that brings glory to God. The institutional church system and structure are not biblical. And as we have argued, they hamper God's people from functioning the way God intended.

When Martin Luther challenged the institutional church of his day, it made many people angry. As a matter of fact, if Luther had not had the support of Frederick the Wise and his armies, he would have been killed for his beliefs (like many other Reformers were).

Today, Protestants look back on Luther and hail him as a hero. Luther loved God and the church, but he strongly disagreed with the church system that surrounded him, arguing that it was not biblical. And he had the courage to prophetically declare that disagreement in public. (By the way, Luther was far stronger in his rhetoric than we have been. If you think this book has been difficult to absorb, try reading some of Luther's diatribes against the church system of his day.)

In short, it is because of our love for the church and our desire to see God's people set free that we have written this book. And it is our hope that God will use it to help change the course of church history.

2. You say that in a healthy organic church, each week "every member has contributed something of Christ in the gathering." Does that mean that every week every believer in the gathering is expected to share some way in which Christ has been revealed to him or her? How do you ensure that an unbeliever or someone with a poor grasp of Scripture doesn't get up and speak falsehood? Also, don't some attendees just feel pressured into contributing, even if they really have nothing to offer that particular morning?

If the church is properly equipped, these problems rarely occur. Paul's instruction to "let the others pass judgment" (1 Corinthians 14:29, NASB) when someone ministers in the meeting goes a long way toward providing a safety net for healthy participatory meetings.

Note that it takes time for a church to be equipped to conduct an open meeting. And herein lies the role of church planters. Their job is to equip the members to function in a coordinated way. That includes encouraging those who rarely participate to function more and those who tend to dominate the meeting to function less. It also involves showing God's people how to fellowship with the Lord in such a way that they will have something to contribute in every meeting.

In addition, the fear that someone will say something "false" in a meeting should never compel us to replace open participatory meetings with services directed by someone from the clergy. Like Paul, we should trust God's people enough that if someone does share something amiss in a meeting, the church will take this as an opportunity to highlight and magnify the truth. The amazing thing is that when God's people are properly equipped, they do just that.

3. If Christ were to send a message to the institutional church today (much as he did to the early churches in Revelation 2–3), what do you think he would say? Would he offer any words of commendation?

It would be highly presumptuous to answer such a question with any certainty. And since the institutional church is not a monolith, what Christ would say would no doubt vary from church to church.

Yet we suspect He would probably say some of the same things He said to the churches in Revelation 2 and 3, as they apply to all Christians in every age. He would also probably have a great deal to commend about certain churches. Perhaps He would commend some for caring for the lost and faithfully preaching the gospel to them. He might commend others for standing with the widows, orphans, and the oppressed. Maybe He would commend others for their faithfulness to follow His teachings without compromise.

At the same time, He would probably address specific shortcomings in each church, just as He did in Revelation. In addition, He would probably give a rebuke to those churches where God's people have been suppressed, manipulated, abused, and silenced into doing certain things. And there's a good chance He would give a word of correction to the Lord's people for allowing themselves to be treated in this way. As He said in days past, "The prophets prophesy lies, the priests rule by their own authority, and my people love it this way. But what will you do in the end?" (Jeremiah 5:31, NIV).

>THE NEXT STEP

"Now when they heard this, they were pierced to the heart, and said to Peter and the rest of the apostles, 'Brethren, what shall we do?'"
—ACTS 2:37, NASB

"And you will know the truth, and the truth will set you free."
—JESUS CHRIST IN JOHN 8:32, NLT

READING THIS BOOK TAKES COURAGE.

Such courage is required not because of what the book says, but because of what you, as a follower of Christ, should do in response to what you have read.

Is it *possible* for a believer to know the truth and ignore it? Yes, as evidenced by the little steps away from God's plan for the church that Christians have consistently taken over the past two millennia.

Is it *appropriate* for us to move away from God's plan for His church? Absolutely not. Is it acceptable to simply acknowledge that we have taken many wrong turns in the past without realigning with God's plan in the present? Of course not. One of the distinguishing marks of Christians is their integrity. We demonstrate that integrity by following our Lord, regardless of what others do, just because He is Lord.

Having read this book, you must make a decision: Will you *act* upon what you have read, or will you simply be *informed* by it?

Many people find themselves in a real dilemma today. They want to be the church, as God intended, but they are not exactly sure how. Especially in a day when unbiblical expressions of the church are the norm.

To put it in a question: Now that you have discovered that the institutional church is not scriptural, what is the next step? What should you do now?

Here are some areas to ponder and pray over:

A NEW APPROACH TO WORSHIP

If you are like many Christians, you view worship as something you do on Sunday morning (and possibly Wednesday night) when the worship team or the worship minister leads the congregation into songs of "praise and worship." Or . . . it's when you are at home singing to a worship CD or tape.

The New Testament, however, paints a very different picture of worship. First, worship is extremely important to God. Thus, it should be a lifestyle, not an event (see Romans 12:1). Second, from the beginning of the Old Testament when God gave the law to Israel and throughout the New Testament era, worship was very much a *corporate* exercise. It was not the exclusive domain of the individual. Third, God has given us specific instructions on *how* to worship Him.

Recall when King David wanted to bring the Ark of the Covenant to Jerusalem. Israel responded to his desire and brought the holy Ark to the chosen city on a wooden cart. As the cart headed toward the Holy City, Israel danced, sang, celebrated with music. That is, they worshipped! And they worshipped with great fervor and passion. It was a wonderful celebration. But tragedy struck, and God ended the celebration (see 2 Samuel 6:1-15).

Why did this happen? It is because the people had violated the Lord's prescribed will on *how* the Ark was to be carried. God had a specific way in which He was to be worshipped, and He didn't compromise that expectation.

Even though the hearts of God's people were right and even though David's intentions were pure, the error was that they didn't "inquire of him about how to [worship] in the prescribed way" (1 Chronicles 15:13, NIV). God made clear through Moses that the Ark of the Lord's presence was to be carried upon the sanctified shoulders of Levitical priests. It was never to be placed on a wooden cart.

David got it right the second time around and placed the Ark on the shoulders of the Levites, just as God prescribed. God was pleased. Consider David's sobering words about Israel's mistake the first time around:

"It was because you, the Levites, did not bring it up the first time that the LORD our God broke out in anger against us. We did not inquire of him about how to do it in the prescribed way" (1 Chronicles 15:13, NIV).

Israel's error was that they didn't seek God according to "the prescribed way." That is, they didn't worship God according to His way. They worshipped Him in their own way. It's important to note that Israel borrowed the idea to place the holy Ark on a wooden cart from the heathen Philistines! (See 1 Samuel 6:1-12.)

In the same way, God has not been silent about how He wishes to be worshipped. He wishes to be worshipped in spirit and in truth (John 4:23). "In truth" simply means in reality and according to His way. Regrettably, however, the holy vessels of the Lord are still being carried on wooden carts. You have already read the story in this book.

A NEW APPROACH TO SPIRITUAL GROWTH

The early church produced followers of Christ who turned their world upside down. Even today, these first-century Christians have much to teach us about how we are to live as we grow in Christ. True discipleship is about bearing fruit for the Kingdom of God based on the development and activation of Christlike character. True discipleship is knowing Jesus Christ and allowing Him to live His life in us.

It's unfortunate that we have made Christian discipleship an academic exercise as well as an individual pursuit. Across the country we have defined "success" in spiritual formation in terms of the quantity of knowledge received and retained. We often measure this in terms of programs or courses of study that have been completed. We have lost sight of the authentic aim of discipleship in favor of impractical, passive outcomes that do not reshape who we are and how we live.

Yet Jesus never told us that "He who dies with the most religious knowledge, wins." Nor did He ever make discipleship an individual task accomplished solely through personal sweat and toil.

Jesus spent His life equipping others to live a life for God and showing them firsthand what that looked like. He began with a *community* of twelve men and a handful of women who lived a shared life together. And that community expanded into communities all over the Roman world. Those communities were the early churches.

Jesus' approach to affecting lives was interactive and hands-on. His lectures were few and far between and always led to implementing the point of the lesson in the trenches of life. His perspective was drawn from the big picture of God's Kingdom—that is, based upon a worldview that was shaped by a comprehensive understanding of God's ways and His desired outcomes.

How does this translate into practical, personal action?

Very simple. The school of Christ is none other than the community of the believers—the ekklesia of God. We learn Christ from one another and with one another in a close-knit, shared-life community, where every member is free to share the Lord with their brothers and sisters, just as the first-century Christians did.

According to Paul, Jesus Christ is someone to be *learned* in the believing community (Ephesians 4:20). It is in that community that we "learn Christ" to be better disciples. It's in that community that we learn Christ to be parents, children, husbands, and wives. It's in that community where every member learns Him together, hears Him together, and follows Him together.

There is no substitute for that. The Christian life was never meant to be lived outside of Christian community. And that is precisely what the church is in the biblical sense . . . a shared-life community under Christ's leadership.

A NEW APPROACH TO MANAGING RESOURCES

With our lives so packed with activity and commitments, we naturally appreciate responsibilities that are easy to remember and quick to fulfill. Tithing may well fit into that category (even though it has no New Testament support—see chapter 8).

As we have seen, handling God's resources is not something to be taken lightly. Nor is it an obligation that can be satisfied by simply writing a check that satisfies a legalistic limit and then forgetting about it.

Being part of a family includes protecting the family's resources. It is no different with the family of God. The tangible resources of God's Kingdom have been placed at our disposal. We have the privilege of investing those resources—not just our money, but our time, possessions, ideas, relationships, skills, spiritual gifts, and so forth—to produce positive results for the Kingdom. The progress of God's work depends to some extent upon how we utilize the ample resources that He has entrusted to us. You are, in effect, a portfolio manager for the Kingdom of God.

Is investing your money, effort, expertise, relational capital, and creativity in constructing more religious buildings the best investment for His Kingdom? Is investing 3 percent of your total household income—that's the average devoted by Americans to religious activity of any type—sufficient to advance His work?[1] Can you justify giving money to an organization to take care of the needs of the poor as your only involvement in the lives of the impoverished? Like every investor, you will be seduced by opportunities that are likely to produce good outcomes as well as by other opportunities that will squander

---

[1] Every year, The Barna Group tracks people's giving to churches and other nonprofit organizations. A recent review of donations is described in the report "Americans Donate Billions to Charity, But Giving to Churches Has Declined." That report can be accessed at http://www.barna.org.

resources. Every choice you make has eternal consequences. How you choose to allocate the Kingdom's resources will affect the lives of many people.

Although the notion of giving God one-tenth of what you have is perceived as a stretch by most believers, keep in mind that you have been freed from such a target. Instead, God has given you the checkbook and told you to invest it in whatever ways will bring about the best outcomes for His glory and purposes. And, of course, you will be evaluated for how wisely you invested those resources.

It has often been said that you can tell a person's priorities by examining his or her checkbook. If someone were to examine your checkbook—as well as your schedule and personal goals—what message would he or she receive?

A NEW LOOK AT YOUR IDENTITY

Our studies have shown that most Americans are struggling to clarify their identity. They tend to see themselves as unique individuals, Americans, members of their family, occupational professionals, consumers, and then as followers of Christ—in that order of priority. In the minds and hearts of most Americans—even those whose beliefs classify them as "born-again Christians"—their identity as a follower of Christ pales in importance in comparison to the other roles they embrace. Oddly, most of the born-again Christians consider themselves to be servants of God and to have been transformed by their faith in Christ. Clearly, there are some missing connections in this self-evaluation.[2]

Perhaps the confusion is due to the enormous number of interactions and responsibilities that people take on each day. Maybe it has to do with the disjointed, topical teaching that most of us receive from our churches. It may even be attributable to the lure of competing perspectives and images bombarding us from the ever-present media.

------

2 This research is described in greater detail in *Think Like Jesus* by George Barna (Nashville: Integrity Publishers, 2003).

But the bottom line is really quite simple. You are a priest of God, a minister of the Lord Jesus Christ, and a member of His glorious body. Through your declaration of allegiance to Jesus and your stated desire to live with Him forever, you have a responsibility to be a *functioning* priest, minister, and member of the body.

The organized church has moved down a crooked path over the past two thousand years. The only way to get it back on track is for each of us to begin prayerfully exploring the original plan that God had for His people and then to be willing to respond faithfully to that plan. In this way, the Revolution that has begun to take root in our day will spread far and wide. And God will get what He has always been after.

› FINAL THOUGHTS

1. I belong to an institutional church. If I attended an organic church meeting this week, how would the experience be different from that of my church service?

In organic church life, the meetings look different every week. While the brothers and sisters in an organic church may prayerfully plan the focus of their own meetings (for instance, they might set aside a month for the body to concentrate on Ephesians 1), they do not plan a specific order of worship. Instead, everyone is free to function, share, participate, and minister spiritually during gatherings, so the creativity expressed in them is endless.

Participants do not know who will stand up and share next nor what they will share. There might be skits; there might be poems read; there might be new songs introduced and sung; there might be exhortations, testimonies, short teachings, revelations, and prophetic words. Because everyone is involved and people contribute spontaneously, boredom is not a problem. The most meaningful meetings are generally those in which everyone participates and functions.

Jesus Christ is the center of the meeting. He is glorified through the songs, the lyrics, the prayers, the ministry, and the sharing. The meeting is completely open for the Holy Spirit to reveal Christ through each member as He sees fit. In the words of 1 Corinthians 14:26, "every one of you" contributes something of Christ to the gathering. In organic church life, the corporate church meeting is an explosive outflow of what the Lord revealed of Himself to each member during the week. These features are virtually absent in the typical institutional church service.

2. Some have suggested that much of the structure and hierarchy within present-day churches grew out of the need to protect against potential cults and heresies in the early church. What are the safeguards against these dangers in organic churches?

Actually, we believe that, as a result of our fallen nature, people always move to adopt hierarchy and top-down relationships because they give human beings a sense of control and security.

Yet history teaches us that hierarchical organizations do not curb heresy. In fact, the testimony of church history is that they can foster and increase it. When the leaders of a denomination or movement embrace a heresy, it becomes perpetuated throughout all the churches connected to that denomination or movement.

On the contrary, when the autonomous nature of every church is preserved, the spreading of error is more likely to be localized. When a church is autonomous, it is difficult for an ambitious false teacher to seize control of unrelated churches.

By the way, virtually all the major cults are hierarchical organizations. (Notice we said "major" cults. We recognize that some cults are headed by a single leader who dominates all decisions and squelches any dissension. Sometimes these figures even claim to be leading a "house church." Yet any church headed by a person who is (1) dictatorial and (2) advances his own wisdom over that of Scripture is most certainly not headed by Christ and must be avoided at all costs.)

For the reasons outlined above, we believe hierarchical structures neither curb heresy nor prevent cultism. The only safeguard against heresy in a church is believers' mutual subjection to one another under the headship of Christ. And this requires face-to-face community and relationships that are centered on Christ.

The body of Christ has been in existence for two thousand years. That said, mutual subjection not only includes subjection to one another in a local fellowship, but subjection to the truth that the general body of Christ has agreed upon throughout the ages. In this way, the historic creeds can be helpful guideposts to keep a church on track when it comes to the essential teachings of our faith.

3. Why are you convinced that the first-century model of church is the one we must follow? Our twenty-first century world is so different from that of the first Christians.

We believe the Bible, not human tradition, is the divine guide for Christian faith and practice—including church practice.

The Bible is not silent on how the church of Jesus Christ functions. The New Testament gives a clear theology of the church. It also gives concrete examples of how that theology fleshes itself out.

Because the church is a spiritual organism, not an institutional organization, it is organic. (Evangelicals are in agreement that the church is an organism. Throughout the New Testament, the church is always depicted by living images—for example, one new man, a body, a bride, a family, a living temple made up of living stones.)

And because the church is organic, it has a natural expression—as all organisms do. For that reason, when a group of Christians follow their spiritual DNA, they will gather in a way that matches the DNA of the triune God—for they possess the same life that God Himself possesses. While we Christians are by no means divine, we have been privileged to be "partakers of the divine nature" (2 Peter 1:4).

Consequently, the DNA of the church is marked by the very traits that we find in the triune God; namely, mutual love, mutual dependence, mutual dwelling, mutual fellowship, and authentic community. As theologian Stanley Grenz once said, "The ultimate basis for our understanding of the church lies in its relationship to the nature of the triune God himself."

That said, the idea that the church should adapt to the present culture raises more questions than it answers. For example, which church practices should be discarded or adapted to the present culture and which are normative and should never be changed?

The DNA of the church produces certain identifiable features. Some of them are: the experience of authentic community, a familial love and devotion of its members one to another, the centrality of Jesus Christ, the native instinct to gather together without ritual, every-member functioning, the innate desire to form deep-seated relationships that are centered on Christ, and the internal drive for open-participatory gatherings. We believe that any church practice that obstructs these innate characteristics is unsound, and therefore, unbiblical.

While the seed of the gospel will *naturally* produce these particular features, how they are expressed will look slightly different from culture to culture. For instance, I (Frank) once planted an organic church in the country of Chile. The songs these believers wrote, the way they interacted with each other, the way they sat, what they did with their children, all looked different from organic churches born in Europe and the United States. However, the same basic features that reside in the DNA of the church were all present. And institutional church forms never appeared.

Healthy organic churches never produce a clergy system, a single pastor, a hierarchical leadership structure, or an order of worship that renders the majority passive. To our minds, such things rupture the church's genetic code and violate her native expression. They also run contrary to New Testament principles.

By Constantine's day, when the church became more concerned about its status in culture than its DNA, the form of the church began changing dramatically from what it was in the first century. New Testament scholar F. F. Bruce wisely writes, "When the church thinks more of her status than of her service, she has taken a wrong path and must immediately retrace her steps."[1] In this connection, we feel the church must retrace her steps and return to her biblical roots.

Put another way: Should we follow a model of church that is rooted in New Testament principle and example, or should we follow one that finds its origins in pagan traditions? That is the ultimate question that this book should lead us to address.

4. You said the Trinity is noted for its mutuality. Yet don't John 14:28 and 1 Corinthians 11:3 teach that there is a hierarchy in the Godhead?

No. These passages have in view the Son's temporal relationship as a human being who voluntarily submitted Himself to His Father's will. In the Godhead, the Son and Father experience communality and mutual submission.

It is for this reason that biblical orthodoxy rejects the eternal subordination of the Son of God. It instead accepts the temporal subordination of the Son in His incarnation.

As theologian Kevin Giles says, "Historic orthodoxy has never accepted hierarchical ordering in the Trinity."[2] To paraphrase the Athanasian Creed, the Son is only inferior to the Father in relation to His manhood; He is equal with the Father in relation to the Godhead.

5. Throughout church history, various people and movements have called for a return to the New Testament model of church governance and practice. Do you see yourselves as part of one of these movements or something completely new?

God has always had a people who have stood outside the institutional church. Historians have called them "the radical reformation." Some historians have called them "the trail of blood" because they were persecuted savagely for their stance.[3]

---

[1] F. F. Bruce, *A Mind for What Matters* (Eerdmans, Grand Rapids, 1990), 247.
[2] See Kevin Giles, *Jesus and the Father* (Grand Rapids: Zondervan, 2006); *The Trinity & Subordinationism* (Downers Grove, IL: InterVarsity Press, 2002); Gilbert Bilezikian, *Community 101* (Grand Rapids: Zondervan, 1997), Appendix.
[3] See John W. Kennedy, *The Torch of the Testimony* (Bombay: Gospel Literature Service, 1965); E.H. Broadbent, *The Pilgrim Church* (Grand Rapids: Gospel Folio Press, 1999); and Leonard Verduin, *The Reformers and Their Stepchildren* (Grand Rapids: Eerdmans, 1964).

These Christians, in every age, refused to conform to the institutional church of their day. They believed that the institutional church was a departure from, not a development of, the church that Jesus established. These nonconformists fiercely stood for the centrality of Jesus Christ, the every-member functioning of His body, the priesthood of all believers, and the oneness of the body of Christ. They held that torch high, and they were abused by their fellow Christians as a result. We (the authors) stand in that lineage.

6. You talk about how Christians are "conditioned to read the Bible with the lens handed to them by the Christian tradition to which we belong." How can I be sure you are not also interpreting the Bible to fit your own thoughts and experiences?

Every Christian who has ever lived interprets the Bible through the lens of his or her own experience and thoughts. We are no exception.

However, there is a strong consensus among evangelical scholars that the early church did not have a clergy, did not meet in sacred buildings, did not take the Lord's Supper outside of a full meal, did not have a fixed liturgy, and did not dress up for church meetings. In addition, the fact that the modern institutional church derived many of its practices from Greco-Roman paganism cannot be disputed. (This book provides the historical documentation.)

In short, we Christians have made acceptable and normative church practices that the New Testament neither teaches nor exemplifies. And we have abandoned those church practices that were acceptable and normative in the New Testament.

So the question really boils down to this: Are the practices of the institutional church (the clergy/laity system, salaried pastors, sacred buildings, the order of worship, etc.) God-approved developments to the church that the New Testament envisions? Or are they an unhealthy departure from it?

That is the question that we would like every reader to prayerfully consider.

7. While you attribute church practices like the building of sanctuaries and the rise of the clergy to pagan influences, don't humans naturally begin to organize and adapt to the surrounding culture?

If we obey our fallen nature, yes, we humans will organize and adapt to the world. One of the genius strokes of our God, however, is that He built into the DNA of the body of Christ people whose ministries were given to prevent this from happening. (See 1 Corinthians 3:5-15; 12:28-31; Ephesians 4:11-16; Acts 13-21.) These were itinerant apostolic workers who planted churches, left them on their own, then visited them periodically to equip, recenter, and encourage them. One of their tasks was to keep the churches from experiencing entropy. They also kept foreign elements out so that churches could grow healthy and remain true to their organic nature. Paul of Tarsus was such an itinerant worker, and his letters illustrate beautifully the role of such people.

Unfortunately, during the persecutions of the first and second century, the itinerant ministry died out. Nonetheless, it has been restored since then within organic churches. This particular ministry is an important check to keep them from gravitating toward the surrounding culture and adopting its values.

8. While you fault traditional churches for making members passive spectators, I not only attend Sunday morning service, but I belong to a church small group that sounds a lot like the organic church experience. We worship, study God's Word together, and turn to one another for support when we face challenges and crises. In my view, I have the best of both worlds.

If you feel that what you have described is the best of both worlds, then by all means, stay where you are. However, many of us have concerns about both. We have observed that most small groups attached to an institutional church have a leader present who is the head of the meetings. Thus to our minds, such meetings are directed by a human head who either controls or facilitates it.

I (Frank) have been in countless small group meetings of this nature across denominational lines. Never did I see a meeting that was completely under the headship of Jesus Christ in which all members came to that meeting to share their Lord with their sisters and brothers freely and without human control or interference.

All the gatherings operated more like a Bible study or traditional prayer meeting rather than a free-flowing, open-participatory gathering that is envisioned in the New Testament where Jesus Christ is made visible by the every-member functioning of His body.

I have met with some of the founders of the small group movement in the institutional church, and they tried to defend the idea that someone must lead such gatherings. I disagree. If God's people are properly equipped, they can have meetings that have no leader but Jesus Christ.

All that to say there is a huge difference between the typical small group that is attached to an institutional church and the organic church that is envisioned in the New Testament. Nevertheless, if a person feels comfortable with the former model of church, we believe he or she should remain in it until the Lord shows another path.

9. Some Christians are naturally drawn to traditional forms like liturgy and choral music, which help them connect with both God and the body of Christ through the ages. Do you believe the Holy Spirit will not work through those forms—or if He does, that it is not His preferred means of drawing others to Himself? How would you back up that claim through Scripture?

We believe that the question "Can you prove from the Bible that the Holy Spirit will not work through a certain traditional practice?" is really the wrong one to ask since it cannot be answered honestly. It is an unprovable tenet because Scripture never addresses it. The question we should be asking is: "What does the Word of God teach about church practice?"

We can be certain that God does not endorse any church practice that violates New Testament principles. For instance, we believe the clergy/laity distinction violates the New Testament principle of the priesthood of all believers (see chapter 5).

To our minds, if we are willing to abandon all traditions that conflict with God's Word, the question that will dominate our thinking is: "What does the Word of God teach regarding His church—its purpose, its function, and its expression?"

This question provides a useful grid by which to discern whether or not a church structure is enhancing or stifling New Testament principles. Again, if a church structure violates a New Testament directive, then it should be challenged.

And this is what we want our readers to be asking and exploring.

Having said this, we do not doubt that God can, and undoubtedly does, work through practices invented by humans, that have no scriptural basis. That God still works through people in the institutional church is beyond dispute. Both authors owe our salvation and baptism to people laboring in the institutional church.

But just because God may use His people in a particular system does not mean that He approves of that system. Remember, God used and even blessed Israel at a time when she rejected His will to be their only king. They instead wanted to follow the other nations and have an earthly king. God granted their request. And He still loved and used His people despite their rejection of His revealed will.

10. Isn't much of our problem with church the fact that so often we go with the attitude of "What will I get out of it?" rather than "How can I honor and glorify God through my worship?" Wouldn't regaining the proper perspective of worship make all the difference?

No, not really. This question assumes two things: first, that the only reason for a church gathering is for individual Christian worship, and second, that church is a place to "go." (Go back and read the question carefully.) Both assumptions are without scriptural merit, yet they are imbedded in the Christian mind-set as a result of years of religious tradition. The New Testament knows nothing of a "worship service." And people cannot "go" to church. They are the church.

The early church met for the purpose of displaying Jesus Christ through the every-member functioning of Christ's body. The goal was to make Christ visible and to edify the whole church in the process. Mutual edification through mutual sharing, mutual ministry, and mutual exhortation was the aim.

To our thinking, what would make all the difference is if God's people were equipped and then encouraged to have meetings where every member shared the Christ they had encountered that week, freely and openly, as 1 Corinthians 14:26, 31 and Hebrews 10:25 exhort. The result: God would be seen and thus glorified.

Consider your physical body. When every member of your body functions, your personality is expressed. It is the same way with Christ. When each member of His body shares his or her portion of Christ, then Christ is assembled (see 1 Corinthians 12–14).

This dynamic is similar to putting together a jigsaw puzzle. When all the pieces are fitted together, we see the whole picture. But if only a few pieces are visible, we cannot understand the whole picture. It is not without significance, then, that the Greek word translated "church" (*ekklesia*) in the New Testament actually means "assembly." The church meeting is for the purpose of reassembling Jesus Christ on the earth.

I (Frank) have been in so many New Testament–styled meetings that I have lost count. But I can tell you that there is nothing quite like them. I will rehearse one quick story to give you the flavor of the response such a meeting can produce.

One of the brothers in an organic church I was a part of brought an unbelieving friend to one of our meetings. We met in a large living room. In the meeting, every member shared his or her experience with the Lord that week. Jesus Christ was revealed, exalted, shared, declared, made known, and testified to by each member of the body. The meeting was so full of life that there were no pauses and no silence. We heard from our Lord from every member of the body in that room. The flow of the Spirit was undeniable. A common theme emerged in the gathering, though no agenda had been established for it.

As the meeting was winding down, the unbeliever fell to his knees in the middle of the living room and cried out, "I want to be saved! I have seen God here!" This man was not prompted or asked to do this. There was no "altar call" or "salvation invitation." It just happened.

This is one of the things that occurs organically when Jesus Christ is made visible through His Body (see 1 Corinthians 14:24-25). I have watched this phenomenon take place numerous times in such gatherings—not to mention the transformation I have seen such meetings produce in believers.

11. Your book really disturbs me because I think some people may leave their churches after finishing it. I'm particularly concerned about the reader who decides to drop out of his or her church and then fails to connect with another body of believers.

We hope that this book will give God's people permission to follow the guidance of the Holy Spirit, wherever that may lead them. No one should feel pressured to remain in a particular type of church if he or she feels the Lord is leading him or her out of it. And no one should feel pressured to leave, either.

With that in mind, the advice we would offer to those who feel called to leave the institutional church is threefold. 1) Leave quietly and do not take anyone else with you. In other words, do not cause division. 2) Resist becoming bitter against the institutional church. If you have been hurt by people in it, take your pain to the cross. Harboring bitterness is like taking poison and waiting for the other person to get sick. Few things are as lethal. 3) Actively seek Christians to fellowship with around Jesus Christ. The Web site http://www.housechurchresource.org provides resources for those interested in organic church life and puts people in contact with churches that are exploring fresh ways to be faithful to the New Testament vision of church. Take the time to visit such churches (they all differ) and get connected. And if you feel so led, relocate to be part of one.

For answers to more of the most commonly asked questions about the book, visit www.paganchristianity.org.

➤SUMMARY OF ORIGINS

"What history teaches us is that men have never learned anything from it."
— G. W. F. HEGEL, NINETEENTH-CENTURY GERMAN PHILOSOPHER

The following summary is neither complete nor detailed. Note that all of the practices covered are postbiblical, postapostolic, and mostly influenced by pagan culture.

CHAPTER 2: THE CHURCH BUILDING

The Church Building—First constructed under Constantine around AD 327. The earliest church buildings were patterned after the Roman basilicas, which were modeled after Greek temples.

The Sacred Space—Christians borrowed this idea from the pagans in the second and third centuries. The burial places of the martyrs were regarded as "sacred." In the fourth century, church buildings were erected on these burial places, thus creating "sacred" buildings.

The Pastor's Chair—Derived from the cathedra, which was the bishop's chair or throne. This chair replaced the seat of the judge in the Roman basilica.

Tax-Exempt Status for Churches and Christian Clergy—Emperor Constantine gave churches tax-exempt status in AD 323. He made clergy exempt from paying taxes in AD 313, a privilege that pagan priests enjoyed.

Stained-Glass Windows—First introduced by Gregory of Tours and brought to perfection by Suger (1081–1151), abbot of St. Denis.

Gothic Cathedrals—Twelfth century. These edifices were built according to the pagan philosophy of Plato.

271

The Steeple—Rooted in ancient Babylonian and Egyptian architecture and philosophy, the steeple was a medieval invention that was popularized and modernized by Sir Christopher Wren in London around 1666.

The Pulpit—Used in the Christian church as early as AD 250. It came from the Greek *ambo*, which was a pulpit used by both Greeks and Jews for delivering monologues.

The Pew—Evolved from the thirteenth through the eighteenth centuries in England.

CHAPTER 3: THE ORDER OF WORSHIP

The Sunday Morning Order of Worship—Evolved from Gregory's Mass in the sixth century and the revisions made by Luther, Calvin, the Puritans, the Free Church tradition, the Methodists, the Frontier-Revivalists, and the Pentecostals.

The Centrality of the Pulpit in the Order of Worship—Martin Luther in 1523.

Two Candles Placed on Top of the "Communion Table" and Incense Burning—Candles were used in the ceremonial court of Roman emperors in the fourth century. The Communion table was introduced by Ulrich Zwingli in the sixteenth century.

Taking the Lord's Supper Quarterly—Ulrich Zwingli in the sixteenth century.

The Congregation Standing and Singing When the Clergy Enters—Borrowed from the ceremonial court of Roman emperors in the fourth century. Brought into the Protestant liturgy by John Calvin.

Coming to Church with a Somber/Reverent Attitude—Based on the medieval view of piety. Brought into the Protestant service by John Calvin and Martin Bucer.

Condemnation and Guilt over Missing a Sunday Service—Seventeenth-century New England Puritans.

The Long "Pastoral Prayer" Preceding the Sermon—Seventeenth-century Puritans.

The Pastoral Prayer Uttered in Elizabethan English—Eighteenth-century Methodists.

The Goal of All Preaching to Win Individual Souls—Eighteenth-century Frontier-Revivalists.

The Altar Call—Instituted by seventeenth-century Methodists and popularized by Charles Finney.

The Church Bulletin (written liturgy)—Originated in 1884 with Albert Blake Dick's stencil duplicating machine.

The "Solo" Salvation Hymn, Door-to-Door Witnessing, and Evangelistic Advertising/Campaigning—D. L. Moody.

The Decision Card—Invented by Absalom B. Earle (1812–1895) and popularized by D. L. Moody.

Bowing Heads with Eyes Closed and Raising the Hand in Response to a Salvation Message—Billy Graham in the twentieth century.

"The Evangelization of the World in One Generation" Slogan—John Mott around 1888.

Solo or Choral Music Played during the Offering—Twentieth-century Pentecostals.

CHAPTER 4: THE SERMON

The Contemporary Sermon—Borrowed from the Greek sophists, who were masters at oratory and rhetoric. John Chrysostom and Augustine popularized the Greco-Roman homily (sermon) and made it a central part of the Christian faith.

The One-Hour Sermon, Sermon Crib Notes, and the Four-Part Sermon Outline—Seventeenth-century Puritans.

CHAPTER 5: THE PASTOR

The Single Bishop (predecessor of the contemporary pastor)—Ignatius of Antioch in early second century. Ignatius's model of one-bishop rule did not prevail in the churches until the third century.

The "Covering" Doctrine—Cyprian of Carthage, a former pagan orator. Revived under Juan Carlos Ortiz from Argentina and the "Fort Lauderdale Five" from the United States, creating the so-called "Shepherding-Discipleship Movement" in the 1970s.

Hierarchical Leadership—Brought into the church by Constantine in the fourth century. This was the leadership style of the Babylonians, Persians, Greeks, and Romans.

Clergy and Laity—The word *laity* first appears in the writings of Clement of Rome (d. 100). *Clergy* first appears in Tertullian. By the third century, Christian leaders were universally called clergy.

Contemporary Ordination—Evolved from the second century to the fourth. It was taken from the Roman custom of appointing men to civil office. The idea of the ordained minister as the "holy man of God" can be traced to Augustine, Gregory of Nazianzus, and Chrysostom.

The Title "Pastor"—Catholic priests who became Protestant ministers were not universally called pastors until the eighteenth century under the influence of Lutheran Pietists.

CHAPTER 6: SUNDAY MORNING COSTUMES

Christians Wearing Their "Sunday Best" for Church—Began in the late-eighteenth century with the Industrial Revolution and became widespread in the mid-nineteenth century. The practice is rooted in the emerging middle-class effort to become like their wealthy aristocrat contemporaries.

Clergy Attire—Began in AD 330 when Christian clergy started wearing the garb of Roman officials. By the twelfth century, the clergy began wearing everyday street clothes that distinguished them from the people.

The Evangelical Pastor's Suit—A descendant of the black scholar's gown worn by Reformation ministers, the black lounge suit of the twentieth century became the typical costume of the contemporary pastor.

The Clerical (Backwards) Collar—Invented by Rev. Dr. Donald McLeod of Glasgow in 1865.

CHAPTER 7: MINISTERS OF MUSIC

The Choir—Provoked by Constantine's desire to mimic the professional music used in Roman imperial ceremonies. In the fourth century, the Christians borrowed the choir idea from the choirs used in Greek dramas and Greek temples.

The Boys Choir—Began in the fourth century, borrowed from the boys choirs used by the pagans.

Funeral Processions and Orations—Borrowed from Greco-Roman paganism in the third century.

The Worship Team—Calvary Chapel in 1965, patterned after the secular rock concert.

CHAPTER 8: TITHING AND CLERGY SALARIES

Tithing—Did not become a widespread Christian practice until the eighth century. The tithe was taken from the 10 percent rent charge used in the Roman Empire and later justified using the Old Testament.

Clergy Salaries—Instituted by Constantine in the fourth century.

The Collection Plate—The alms dish appeared in the fourteenth century. Passing a collection plate began in 1662.

The Usher—Began with Queen Elizabeth I (1533–1603). The predecessor of the usher is the church porter, a position that can be traced back to the third century.

CHAPTER 9: BAPTISM AND THE LORD'S SUPPER

Infant Baptism—Rooted in the superstitious beliefs that pervaded the Greco-Roman culture, it was brought into the Christian faith in the late second century. By the fifth century, it replaced adult baptism.

Sprinkling Replacing Immersion—Began in the late Middle Ages in the Western churches.

Baptism Separated from Conversion—Began in the early second century as a result of the legalistic view that baptism was the only medium for the forgiveness of sins.

The "Sinner's Prayer"—Originated with D. L. Moody and made popular in the 1950s through Billy Graham's *Peace with God* tract and later with Campus Crusade for Christ's *Four Spiritual Laws*.

Use of the Term "Personal Savior"—Spawned in the mid-1800s by the Frontier-Revivalist influence and popularized by Charles Fuller (1887–1968).

The Lord's Supper Condensed from a Full "Agape" Meal to Only the Cup and the Bread—The late second century as a result of pagan ritual influences.

CHAPTER 10: CHRISTIAN EDUCATION

The Catholic Seminary—The first seminary began as a result of the Council of Trent (1545–1563). The curriculum was based on the teachings of Thomas Aquinas, which was a blending of Aristotle's philosophy, Neoplatonic philosophy, and Christian doctrine.

The Protestant Seminary—Began in Andover, Massachusetts, in 1808. Its curriculum, too, was built on the teachings of Thomas Aquinas.

The Bible College—Influenced by the revivalism of D. L. Moody, the first two Bible colleges were the Missionary Training Institute (Nyack College, New York) in 1882 and Moody Bible Institute (Chicago) in 1886.

The Sunday School—Created by Robert Raikes from Britain in 1780. Raikes did not found the Sunday school for the purpose of religious instruction. He founded it to teach poor children the basics of education.

The Youth Pastor—Developed in urban churches in the late 1930s and 1940s as a result of seeking to meet the needs of a new sociological class called "teenagers."

CHAPTER 11: REAPPROACHING THE NEW TESTAMENT

Paul's Letters Combined into a Canon and Arranged according to Descending Length—Early second century.

Chapter Numbers Placed in the New Testament—University of Paris professor Stephen Langton in 1227.

Verses Added to New Testament Chapters—Printer Robert Stephanus in 1551.

►KEY FIGURES IN CHURCH HISTORY

Abelard, Peter, French scholastic philosopher and shaper of modern theology (1079–1142)

Ambrose, bishop of Milan who created the first postapostolic hymns and chants (339–397)

Aquinas, Thomas, Italian theologian and philosopher who wrote *Summa Theologica*; he was the first to articulate the doctrine of transubstantiation (1225–1274)

Aristotle, Greek philosopher (384–322 BC)

Arnobius of Sicca, early Christian apologist in Africa (d. 330)

Athanasius, theologian and bishop of Alexandria (296–373)

Augustine of Hippo, bishop of Hippo and influential theologian and writer (354–430)

Barth, Karl, Swiss Reformed theologian (1886–1968)

Beza, Theodore, John Calvin's "right-hand man" (1519–1605)

Bruce, F. F., British Bible scholar (1910–1990)

Brunner, Emil, Swiss theologian (1889–1966)

Bucer, Martin, German Reformer (1491–1551)

Bushnell, Horace, Congregationalist minister (1802–1876)

Calvin, John, French Reformer (1509–1564)

Carlstadt, Andreas, German Reformer (1480–1541)

Charlemagne, Emperor of the Holy Roman Empire (ca. 742–814)

Chemnitz, Martin, Lutheran theologian who was part of the "Protestant Scholastics" (1522–1586)

Chrysostom, John, Christian orator from Constantinople (347–407)

Clement of Alexandria, Christian teacher who united Greek philosopohy with Christian doctrine and the first to use the phrase "going to church" (150–215)

Clement of Rome, bishop of Rome who first used the term *laity* in contrast with *clergy* (died about 100)

Constantine I, emperor who promoted Christianity throughout the Roman Empire (ca. 285–337)

Cyprian of Carthage, bishop of Carthage, theologian, and writer (ca. 200–258)

Cyril of Jerusalem, bishop of Jerusalem who introduced a prayer for the Holy Spirit to transform the elements of the Eucharist (315–386)

Darby, John Nelson, one of the founders of the Plymouth Brethren movement who built his theology on "proof-texting" (1800–1882)

Dick, Albert Blake, inventor of stencil duplicating (1856–1934)

Dow, Lorenzo, Methodist evangelist who invited people forward to receive prayer (1777–1834)

Durant, Will, American historian, writer, and philosopher (1885–1981)

Earle, Absolom B., inventor of the "decision" card (1812–1895)

Edwards, Jonathan, Congregational minister and theologian (1703–1758)

Elizabeth I, queen of England who reorganized the liturgy of the Church of England (1533–1603)

Eusebius, bishop of Caesarea and early church historian (ca. 260–ca. 340)

Finney, Charles, American evangelist who popularized the "altar call" (1792–1875)

Foote, William Henry, Presbyterian minister (1794–1869)

Fuller, Charles, American clergyman and radio evangelist who popularized the phrase "personal savior" (1887–1968)

Goodwin, Thomas, Puritan preacher, writer, and chaplain to Oliver Cromwell (1600–1680)

Gregory of Nazianzus, Cappadocian church father who developed the idea of the priest as a "holy man" (329–389)

Gregory of Nyssa, Cappadocian church father who developed the idea of "sacerdotal endowment" (330–395)

Gregory of Tours, bishop of Tours who introduced colored glass into church buildings (538–593)

Gregory the Great, pope who shaped the Mass (540–604)

Guinness, H. G., London pastor (1835–1910)

Gutenberg, Johann, printer of the Bible (1396–1468)

Hastings, Thomas, composer who worked with Charles Finney (1784–1872)

Hatch, Edwin, English theologian and historian (1835–1889)

Hippolytus, Roman priest who wrote that the bishop has power to forgive sins (170–236)

Huss, John, Bohemian Reformer (1372–1415)

Ignatius of Antioch, bishop of Antioch who elevated the "bishop" above other elders (35–107)

Innocent I, pope who made infant baptism mandatory (d. 417)

Irenaeus, bishop of Lyons and theologian who wrote about apostolic succession (130–200)

Isidore of Pelusium, monk and writer who ascribed symbolic interpretations to priestly vestments (d. ca. 450)

Jerome, Latin church father and creator of the Latin *Vulgate*; he advocated special robes for the clergy (342–420)

Justin Martyr, influential Christian teacher and apologist (100–165)

Kierkegaard, Søren, Danish philosopher and theologian (1813–1855)

Knox, John, Scottish Reformer (1513–1572)

Lactantius, Latin Christian apologist and teacher of rhetoric (ca. 240–ca. 320)

Langton, Stephen, professor of the University of Paris and later Archbishop of Canterbury; he added chapters to the Bible (ca. 1150–1228)

Leo I (Leo the Great), pope who established the primacy of Rome (d. 440)

Luther, Martin, German Reformer (1483–1546)

Moody, D. L., influential American evangelist (1837–1899)

More, Hannah, cofounder of Sunday school (1745–1833)

More, Sir Thomas, English lawyer, author, and statesman (1478–1535)

Mott, John, American Methodist and founder of the Student Volunteer Movement for Foreign Missions (1865–1955)

Newton, John, Anglican clergyman and author of the hymn "Amazing Grace" (1725–1807)

Origen, Christian scholar and theologian who organized doctrinal concepts into systematic theology (185–254)

Owen, John, English theologian and Puritan writer (1616–1683)

Pascal, Blaise, religious philosopher and mathematician (1623–1662)

Plato, Greek philosopher (427–347 BC)

Plotinus, founder of the influential pagan philosophy of Neoplatonism (205–270)

Radbertus, Paschasius (Radbert), French theologian (790–865)

Raikes, Robert, English philanthropist and Anglican layman who founded and promoted the Sunday school (1736–1811)

Robinson, John A. T., Anglican bishop and writer (1919–1983)

Routley, Erik, English Congregationalist minister, composer, and hymn writer (1917–1982)

Schaff, Philip, Swiss theologian and historian (1819–1893)

Serapion, bishop of Thmuis who introduced a prayer for the Holy Spirit to transform the elements of the Eucharist (d. after 360)

Simons, Menno, Anabaptist leader (1496–1561)

Siricius, pope who required that clergy be celibate (334–399)

Smith, Chuck, founder of Calvary Chapel and the "worship team" concept (1927–)

Socrates, Greek philosopher (470–399 BC)

Spurgeon, Charles, British Reformed Baptist preacher (1834–1892)

Stephanus, Robert (Estienne), Parisian scholar and printer who added verses to the New Testament (1503–1559)

Stephen I, pope who argued for the preeminence of the Roman bishop (d. 257)

Stock, Thomas, Gloucester minister who may have given Robert Raikes the idea of Sunday school (1750–1803)

Suger, abbot of St. Denis who introduced glass with sacred paintings (1081–1151)

Sunday, Billy, American evangelist (1862–1935)

Tertullian, theologian and apologist from Carthage who first used the term *clergy* to set apart church leaders (160–225)

Trimmer, Sarah, cofounder of Sunday school (1741–1810)

Turretin, Francis, Swiss Reformed pastor and theologian who was part of the "Protestant Scholastics" (1623–1687)

Tyndale, William, English Reformer and scholar who translated the Bible into English (ca. 1494–1536)

Watts, Isaac, prolific English hymn writer (1674–1748)

Wesley, Charles, English Methodist who is remembered for his hymns (1707–1788)

Wesley, John, English Methodist evangelist and theologian (1703–1791)

Whitefield, George, English evangelist during the First Great Awakening (1714–1770)

Wimber, John, leader of the Vineyard Movement (1934–1997)

Wren, Sir Christopher, architect of London cathedrals who popularized the steeple (1632–1723)

Zwingli, Ulrich, Swiss Reformer (1484–1531)

"The greatest advances in human civilization have come when we recovered what we had lost: when we learned the lessons of history."
—WINSTON CHURCHILL

Adams, Doug. *Meeting House to Camp Meeting.* Austin, TX: The Sharing Company, 1981.

Ainslie, J. L. *The Doctrines of Ministerial Order in the Reformed Churches of the 16th and 17th Centuries.* Edinburgh: T. & T. Clark, 1940.

Allen, Roland. *Missionary Methods: St. Paul's or Ours?* Grand Rapids: Eerdmans, 1962.

Althaus, Paul. *The Theology of Martin Luther.* Philadelphia: Fortress Press, 1966.

Andrews, David. *Christi-Anarchy.* Oxford: Lion Publications, 1999.

Anson, Peter F. *Churches: Their Plan and Furnishing.* Milwaukee: Bruce Publishing Co., 1948.

Appleby, David P. *History of Church Music.* Chicago: Moody Press, 1965.

Aquinas, Thomas. *Summa Theologica.* Allen, TX: Thomas More Publishing, 1981.

Atkerson, Steve. *Toward a House Church Theology.* Atlanta: New Testament Restoration Foundation, 1998.

Bainton, Roland. *Here I Stand: A Life of Martin Luther.* Nashville: Abingdon Press, 1950.

Banks, Robert. *Paul's Idea of Community.* Peabody, MA: Hendrickson, 1994.

———. *Reenvisioning Theological Education: Exploring a Missional Alternative to Current Models.* Grand Rapids: Eerdmans, 1999.

——— **and Julia Banks.** *The Church Comes Home.* Peabody, MA: Hendrickson, 1998.

Barclay, William. *Communicating the Gospel.* Sterling: The Drummond Press, 1968.

———. *The Lord's Supper.* Philadelphia: Westminster Press, 1967.

Barna, George. *Revolution.* Carol Stream, IL: Tyndale House, 2005.

Barsis, Max. *The Common Man through the Centuries.* New York: Unger, 1973.

Barth, Karl. "Theologische Fragen und Antworten." *In Dogmatics in Outline.* Translated by G. T. Thomson. London: SCM Press, 1949.

Bauer, Marion, and Ethel Peyser. *How Music Grew.* New York: G. P. Putnam's Sons, 1939.

Baxter, Richard. *The Reformed Pastor.* Lafayette, IN: Sovereign Grace Trust Fund, 2000.

Bede, *A History of the English Church and People.* Translated by Leo Sherley-Price. New York: Dorset Press, 1985.

Benson, Warren, and Mark H. *Senter III. The Complete Book of Youth Ministry.* Chicago: Moody Press, 1987.

Bercot, David W. *A Dictionary of Early Christian Beliefs.* Peabody, MA: Hendrickson, 1998.

Bernard, Thomas Dehaney. *The Progress of Doctrine in the New Testament.* New York: American Tract Society, 1907.

Bishop, Edmund. "The Genius of the Roman Rite." *In Studies in Ceremonial: Essays Illustrative of English Ceremonial.* Edited by Vernon Staley. Oxford: A. R. Mowbray, 1901.

Boettner, Loraine. *Roman Catholicism.* Phillipsburg, NJ: The Presbyterian and Reformed Publishing Company, 1962.

Boggs, Norman Tower. *The Christian Saga.* New York: The Macmillan Company, 1931.

Bowden, Henry Warner, and P. C. Kemeny, eds. *American Church History: A Reader.* Nashville: Abingdon Press, 1971.

Bowen, James. *A History of Western Education.* Vol. 1. New York: St. Martin's Press, 1972.

Boyd, William. *The History of Western Education.* New York: Barnes & Noble Books, 1967.

Boylan, Anne M. *Sunday School: The Formation of an American Institution 1790–1880.* New Haven, CT: Yale University Press, 1988.

Bradshaw, Paul F. *The Search for the Origins of Christian Worship.* New York: Oxford University Press, 1992.

Brauer, Jerald C., ed. *The Westminster Dictionary of Church History.* Philadelphia: Westminster Press, 1971.

Bray, Gerald. *Documents of the English Reformation.* Cambridge: James Clarke, 1994.

Brilioth, Yngve. *A Brief History of Preaching.* Philadelphia: Fortress Press, 1965.

Broadbent, E. H. *The Pilgrim Church.* Grand Rapids: Gospel Folio Press, 1999.

Bruce, A. B. *The Training of the Twelve.* New Canaan, CT: Keats Publishing Inc., 1979.

Bruce, F. F. *The Canon of Scripture.* Downers Grove, IL: InterVarsity Press, 1988.

———. *First and Second Corinthians* (New Century Bible Commentary). London: Oliphant, 1971.

———. *The Letters of Paul: An Expanded Paraphrase.* Grand Rapids: Eerdmans, 1965.

———, ed. *The New International Bible Commentary.* Grand Rapids: Zondervan, 1979.

———. *The New International Commentary on the New Testament.* Grand Rapids: Eerdmans, 1986.

———. *Paul: Apostle of the Heart Set Free.* Grand Rapids: Eerdmans, 1977.

———. *The Spreading Flame.* Grand Rapids: Eerdmans, 1958.

Brunner, Emil. *The Misunderstanding of the Church.* London: Lutterworth Press, 1952.

Bullock, Alan. *Hitler and Stalin: Parallel Lives.* New York: Alfred A. Knopf, 1992.

Burgess, Stanley M., and Gary B. McGee, eds. *Dictionary of Pentecostal and Charismatic Movements.* Grand Rapids: Zondervan, 1988.

Bushman, Richard. *The Refinement of America.* New York: Knopf, 1992.

Calame, Claude. *Choruses of Young Women in Ancient Greece.* Lanham, MD: Rowman & Littlefield, 2001.

Calvin, John. *Institutes of the Christian Religion.* Philadelphia: Westminster Press, 1960.

Campbell, R. Alastair. *The Elders: Seniority within Earliest Christianity.* Edinburgh: T. & T. Clark, 1994.

Case, Shirley J. *The Social Origins of Christianity.* New York: Cooper Square Publishers, 1975.

Casson, Lionel. *Everyday Life in Ancient Rome.* Baltimore: Johns Hopkins University Press, 1998.

Castle, Tony. *Lives of Famous Christians.* Ann Arbor, MI: Servant Books, 1988.

Chadwick, Owen. *The Reformation.* London: Penguin Books, 1964.

Chitwood, Paul H. "The Sinner's Prayer: An Historical and Theological Analysis." unpublished dissertation, Southern Baptist Theological Seminary, 2001.

Clowney, Paul and Teresa Clowney. *Exploring Churches.* Grand Rapids: Eerdmans, 1982.

Cobb, Gerald. *London City Churches.* London: Batsford, 1977.

Coleman, Robert E. *The Master Plan of Evangelism.* Grand Rapids: Fleming H. Revell Co., 1993.

Collins, Michael, and Matthew A. Price. *The Story of Christianity.* New York: DK Publishing, 1999.

Connolly, Ken. *The Indestructible Book.* Grand Rapids: Baker Books, 1996.

Craig, Kevin. "Is the Sermon Concept Biblical?" *Searching Together* 15, no. 1-2 (1986).

Cross, F. L., and E. A. Livingstone, eds. *The Oxford Dictionary of the Christian Church.* 3rd ed., New York: Oxford University Press, 1997.

Cullmann, Oscar. *Early Christian Worship.* London: SCM Press, 1969.

Cully, Iris V., and Kendig Brubaker Cully, eds. *Harper's Encyclopedia of Religious Education.* San Francisco: Harper & Row Publishers, 1971.

Cunningham, Colin. *Stones of Witness.* Gloucestershire, UK: Sutton Publishing, 1999.

Curnock, Nehemiah, ed. *Journals of Wesley.* London: Epworth Press, 1965.

Davies, Horton. *Christian Worship: Its History and Meaning.* New York: Abingdon Press, 1957.

———. *Worship and Theology in England: 1690–1850.* Princeton: Princeton University Press, 1961.

Davies, J. G. *The Early Christian Church: A History of Its First Five Centuries.* Grand Rapids: Baker Book House, 1965.

———. *A New Dictionary of Liturgy and Worship.* London: SCM Press, 1986.

———. *The New Westminster Dictionary of Liturgy and Worship.* Philadelphia: Westminster Press, 1986.

———. *The Secular Use of Church Buildings.* New York: The Seabury Press, 1968.

———. *The Westminster Dictionary of Worship.* Philadelphia: Westminster Press, 1972.

Davies, Rupert. *A History of the Methodist Church in Great Britain.* London: Epworth Press, 1965.

Dawn, Marva J. *Reaching Out without Dumbing Down: A Theology of Worship for the Turn-of-the-Century Culture.* Grand Rapids: Eerdmans, 1995.

Dever, Mark. *A Display of God's Glory.* Washington, DC: Center for Church Reform, 2001.

Dickens, A. G. *Reformation and Society in Sixteenth-Century Europe.* London: Hartcourt, Brace, & World, Inc., 1966.

Dickinson, Edward. *The Study of the History of Music.* New York: Charles Scribner's Sons, 1905.

Dillenberger, John, and Claude Welch. *Protestant Christianity: Interpreted through Its Development.* New York: The Macmillan Company, 1988.

Dix, Gregory. *The Shape of the Liturgy.* London: Continuum International Publishing Group, 2000.

Dodd, C. H. *The Apostolic Preaching and Its Developments.* London: Hodder and Stoughton, 1963.

Dohan, Mary Helen. *Our Own Words.* New York: Alfred A. Knopf, 1974.

Douglas, J. D. *New Twentieth Century Encyclopedia of Religious Knowledge.* Grand Rapids: Baker Book House, 1991.

————. *Who's Who in Christian History.* Carol Stream, IL: Tyndale House Publishers, 1992.

Duchesne, Louis. *Christian Worship: Its Origin and Evolution.* New York: Society for Promoting Christian Knowledge, 1912.

————. *Early History of the Christian Church: From Its Foundation to the End of the Fifth Century.* London: John Murray, 1912.

Dunn, James D. G. *New Testament Theology in Dialogue.* Philadelphia: Westminster Press, 1987.

Dunn, Richard R., and Mark H. Senter III, eds. *Reaching a Generation for Christ.* Chicago: Moody Press, 1997.

Durant, Will. *The Age of Faith.* New York: Simon & Schuster, 1950.

————. *Caesar and Christ.* New York: Simon & Schuster, 1950.

————. *The Reformation.* New York: Simon & Schuster, 1957.

Eavey, C. B. *History of Christian Education.* Chicago: Moody Press, 1964.

Edersheim, Alfred. *The Life and Times of Jesus the Messiah.* McLean, VA: MacDonald Publishing Company, 1883.

Ehrhard, Jim. *The Dangers of the Invitation System.* Parkville, MO: Christian Communicators Worldwide, 1999.

Eller, Vernard. *In Place of Sacraments.* Grand Rapids: Eerdmans, 1972.

Elwell, Walter. *Evangelical Dictionary of Theology.* Grand Rapids: Baker Book House, 1984.

Evans, Craig A. "Preacher and Preaching: Some Lexical Observations." *Journal of the Evangelical Theological Society* 24, no. 4 (December 1981).

Evans, Robert F. *One and Holy: The Church in Latin and Patristic Thought.* London: S.P.C.K., 1972.

Ewing, Elizabeth. *Everyday Dress: 1650–1900.* London: Batsford, 1984.

Ferguson, Everett. *Early Christians Speak: Faith and Life in the First Three Centuries,* 3rd ed. Abilene, TX: A.C.U. Press, 1999.

————, ed. *Encyclopedia of Early Christianity.* New York: Garland Publishing, 1990.

Finney, Charles. *Lectures on Revival.* Minneapolis: Bethany House Publishers, 1989.

Fox, Robin Lane. *Pagans and Christians.* New York: Alfred A. Knopf, 1987.

Foxe, John. *Foxe's Book of Martyrs.* Old Tappan, NJ: Spire Books, 1968.

Fremantle, Ann, ed. *A Treasury of Early Christianity.* New York: Viking Press, 1953.

Fromke, DeVern. *The Ultimate Intention.* Indianapolis: Sure Foundation, 1998.

Furst, Viktor. *The Architecture of Sir Christopher Wren.* London: Lund Humphries, 1956.

Galling, Kurt, ed. *Die Religion in der Geschichte und der Gegenwart,* 3rd ed. Tubingen, Germany: J. C. B. Mohr, 1957.

Geisler, Norman, and William Nix. *A General Introduction of the Bible: Revised and Expanded.* Chicago: Moody Press, 1986.

Gilchrist, James. *Anglican Church Plate.* London: The Connoisseur, 1967.

Giles, Kevin. *Patterns of Ministry among the First Christians.* New York: HarperCollins, 1991.

Gilley, Gary. *This Little Church Went to Market: The Church in the Age of Entertainment.* Webster, NY: Evangelical Press, 2005.

Gonzalez, Justo L. *The Story of Christianity.* Peabody, MA: Prince Press, 1999.

Gough, J. E. *Church, Delinquent and Society.* Melbourne: Federal Literature Committee of Churches of Christ in Australia, 1959.

Gough, Michael. *The Early Christians.* London: Thames and Hudson, 1961.

Grabar, Andre. *Christian Iconography.* Princeton: Princeton University Press, 1968.

Grant, F. W. *Nicolaitanism or the Rise and Growth of Clerisy.* Bedford, PA: MWTB, n.d.

Grant, Michael. *The Founders of the Western World: A History of Greece and Rome.* New York: Charles Scribner's Sons, 1991.

Grant, Robert M. *The Apostolic Fathers: A New Tranlsation and Commentary,* 6 vols. New York: Thomas Nelson & Sons, 1964.

———. *Early Christianity and Society.* San Francisco: Harper & Row Publishers, 1977.

Green, Joel B., ed. *Dictionary of Jesus and the Gospels.* Downers Grove, IL: InterVarsity Press, 1992.

Green, Michael. *Evangelism in the Early Church.* London: Hodder and Stoughton, 1970.

Greenslade, S. L. *Shepherding the Flock: Problems of Pastoral Discipline in the Early Church and in the Younger Churches Today.* London: SCM Press, 1967.

Gummere, Amelia Mott. *The Quaker: A Study in Costume.* Philadelphia: Ferris and Leach, 1901.

Guthrie, Donald. *New Testament Introduction.* rev. ed. Downers Grove, IL: InterVarsity Press, 1990.

Guzie, Tad W. *Jesus and the Eucharist.* New York: Paulist Press, 1974.

Hall, David D. *The Faithful Shepherd.* Chapel Hill: The University of North Carolina Press, 1972.

Hall, Gordon L. *The Sawdust Trail: The Story of American Evangelism.* Philadelphia: Macrae Smith Company, 1964.

Halliday, W. R. *The Pagan Background of Early Christianity.* New York: Cooper Square Publishers, 1970.

Hamilton, Michael S. "The Triumph of Praise Songs: How Guitars Beat Out the Organ in the Worship Wars." *Christianity Today* (July 12, 1999).

Hanson, Richard. *The Christian Priesthood Examined.* Guildford, UK: Lutterworth Press, 1979.

Hardman, Oscar. *A History of Christian Worship.* Nashville: Parthenon Press, 1937.

Haskins, Charles Homer. *The Rise of Universities.* New York: H. Holt, 1923.

Hassell, C. B. *History of the Church of God, from Creation to AD 1885.* Middletown, NY: Gilbert Beebe's Sons Publishers, 1886.

Hatch, Edwin. *The Growth of Church Institutions.* London: Hodder and Stoughton, 1895.

———. *The Influence of Greek Ideas and Usages upon the Christian Church.* Peabody, MA: Hendrickson, 1895.

———. *The Organization of the Early Christian Churches.* London: Longmans, Green, and Co., 1895.

Havass, Zahi. *The Pyramids of Ancient Egypt.* Pittsburgh: Carnegie Museum of Natural History, 1990.

Hay, Alexander R. *The New Testament Order for Church and Missionary.* Audubon, NJ: New Testament Missionary Union, 1947.

———. *What Is Wrong in the Church?* Audubon, NJ: New Testament Missionary Union, n.d.

Henderson, Robert W. *The Teaching Office in the Reformed Tradition.* Philadelphia: Westminster Press, 1962.

Herbert, George. *The Country Parson and the Temple.* Mahwah, NJ: Paulist Press, 1981.

Hislop, Alexander. *Two Babylons.* 2nd ed. Neptune, NJ: Loizeaux Brothers, 1990.

Hodge, Charles. *First Corinthians.* Wheaton, IL: Crossway Books, 1995.

Hoover, Peter. *The Secret of the Strength: What Would the Anabaptists Tell This Generation?* Shippensburg, PA: Benchmark Press, 1998.

Howe, Reuel L. *Partners in Preaching: Clergy and Laity in Dialogue.* New York: Seabury Press, 1967.

Jacobs, C. M., trans. *Works of Martin Luther.* Philadelphia: Muhlenberg Press, 1932.

Johnson, Paul. *A History of Christianity.* New York: Simon & Schuster, 1976.

Jones, Ilion T. *A Historical Approach to Evangelical Worship.* New York: Abingdon Press, 1954.

Jungmann, Josef A. *The Early Liturgy: To the Time of Gregory the Great.* Notre Dame: Notre Dame Press, 1959.

———. *The Mass of the Roman Rite, vol. 1.* New York: Benziger, 1951.

Kennedy, John W. *The Torch of the Testimony.* Bombay: Gospel Literature Service, 1965.

Kierkegaard, Søren. "Attack on Christendom." In *A Kierkegaard Anthology,* edited by Robert Bretall. Princeton: Princeton University Press, 1946.

King, Eugene F. A. *Church Ministry.* St. Louis: Concordia Publishing House, 1993.

Kistemaker, Simon J. *New Testament Commentary: Acts.* Grand Rapids: Baker Book House, 1990.

Klassen, W., J. L. Burkholder, and John Yoder. *The Relation of Elders to the Priesthood of Believers.* Washington, DC: Sojourners Book Service, 1969.

Klassen, Walter. "New Presbyter Is Old Priest Writ Large." *Concern* 17 (1969).

Kopp, David. *Praying the Bible for Your Life.* Colorado Springs: Waterbrook, 1999.

Krautheimer, Richard. *Early Christian and Byzantine Architecture.* London: Penguin Books, 1986.

Kreider, Alan. *Worship and Evangelism in Pre-Christendom.* Oxford: Alain/GROW Liturgical Study, 1995.

Larimore, Walter, and Rev. Bill Peel. "Critical Care: Pastor Appreciation." *Physician Magazine,* September/October 1999.

Latourette, Kenneth Scott. *A History of Christianity.* New York: Harper and Brothers, 1953.

Leisch, Barry. *The New Worship: Straight Talk on Music and the Church.* Grand Rapids: Baker Book House, 1996.

Lenski, R. C. H. *Commentary on St. Paul's Epistle to the Galatians.* Minneapolis: Augsburg Publishing House, 1961.

———. *Commentary on St. Paul's Epistles to Timothy.* Minneapolis: Augsburg Publishing House, 1937.

———. *The Interpretation of 1 and 2 Corinthians.* Minneapolis: Augsburg Publishing House, 1963.

Liemohn, Edwin. *The Organ and Choir in Protestant Worship.* Philadelphia: Fortress Press, 1968.

Lietzmann, Hans. *A History of the Early Church*, vol. 2. New York: The World Publishing Company, 1953.

Lightfoot, J. B. "The Christian Ministry." In *Saint Paul's Epistle to the Philippians*. Wheaton, IL: Crossway Books, 1994.

Lockyer, Herbert Sr., ed. *Nelson's Illustrated Bible Dictionary*. Nashville: Thomas Nelson Publishers, 1986.

Mackinnon, James. *Calvin and the Reformation*. New York: Russell and Russell, 1962.

MacMullen, Ramsay. *Christianizing the Roman Empire: AD 100–400*. London: Yale University Press, 1984.

MacPherson, Dave. *The Incredible Cover-Up*. Medford, OR: Omega Publications, 1975.

Marrou, H. I. *A History of Education in Antiquity*. New York: Sheed and Ward, 1956.

Marsden, George. *The Soul of the American University: From Protestant Establishment to Established Nonbelief*, New York: Oxford University Press, 1994.

Marshall, I. Howard. *Last Supper and Lord's Supper*. Grand Rapids: Eerdmans, 1980.

———. *New Bible Dictionary*. 2nd ed. Downers Grove, IL: InterVarsity Fellowship, 1982.

Maxwell, William D. *An Outline of Christian Worship: Its Developments and Forms*. New York: Oxford University Press, 1936.

Mayo, Janet. *A History of Ecclesiastical Dress*. New York: Holmes & Meier Publishers, 1984.

McKenna, David L. "The Ministry's Gordian Knot." *Leadership* (Winter 1980).

McNeill, John T. *A History of the Cure of Souls*. New York: Harper & Row Publishers, 1951.

Mees, Arthur. *Choirs and Choral Music*. New York: Greenwood Press, 1969.

Metzger, Bruce, and Michael Coogan. *The Oxford Companion to the Bible*. New York: Oxford University Press, 1993.

Middleton, Arthur Pierce. *New Wine in Old Wineskins*. Wilton, CT: Morehouse-Barlow Publishing, 1988.

Miller, Donald E. *Reinventing American Protestantism*. Berkeley: University of Berkeley Press, 1997.

Morgan, John. *Godly Learning*. New York: Cambridge University Press, 1986.

Muller, Karl, ed. *Dictionary of Mission: Theology, History, Perspectives*. Maryknoll, NY: Orbis Books, 1997.

Murphy-O'Connor, Jerome. *Paul the Letter-Writer*. Collegeville, MN: The Liturgical Press, 1995.

Murray, Iain H. *The Invitation System*. Edinburgh: Banner of Truth Trust, 1967.

———. *Revival and Revivalism: The Making and Marring of American Evangelicalism*. Carlisle, PA: Banner of Truth Trust, 1994.

Murray, Stuart. *Beyond Tithing*. Carlisle, UK: Paternoster Press, 2000.

Narramore, Matthew. *Tithing: Low-Realm, Obsolete and Defunct*. Graham, NC: Tekoa Publishing, 2004.

Nee, Watchman. *The Normal Christian Life*. Carol Stream, IL: Tyndale House Publishers, 1977.

Nevin, J. W. *The Anxious Bench*. Chambersburg, PA: German Reformed Church, 1843.

Nichols, James Hastings. *Corporate Worship in the Reformed Tradition.* Philadelphia: Westminster Press, 1968.

Nicoll, W. Robertson, ed. *The Expositor's Bible.* New York: Armstrong, 1903.

Niebuhr, H. Richard, and Daniel D. Williams. *The Ministry in Historical Perspectives.* San Francisco: Harper & Row Publishers, 1956.

Norman, Edward. *The House of God: Church Architecture, Style, and History.* London: Thames and Hudson, 1990.

Norrington, David C. *To Preach or Not to Preach? The Church's Urgent Question.* Carlisle, UK: Paternoster Press, 1996.

Oates, Wayne. *Protestant Pastoral Counseling.* Philadelphia: Westminster Press, 1962.

Old, Hughes Oliphant. *The Patristic Roots of Reformed Worship.* Zurich: Theologischer Veriag, 1970.

Oman, Charles. *English Church Plate 597–183.* London: Oxford University Press, 1957.

Osborne, Kenan B. *Priesthood: A History of the Ordained Ministry in the Roman Catholic Church.* New York: Paulist Press, 1988.

Owen, John. *Hebrews.* Edited by Alister McGrath and J. I. Packer. Wheaton, IL: Crossway Books, 1998.

———. *True Nature of a Gospel Church and Its Government.* London: James Clarke, 1947.

Park, Ken. *The World Almanac and Book of Facts 2003.* Mahwah, NJ: World Almanac Books, 2003.

Parke, H. W. *The Oracles of Apollo in Asia Minor.* London: Croom Helm, 1985.

Pearse, Meic, and Chris Matthews. *We Must Stop Meeting Like This.* E. Sussex, UK: Kingsway Publications, 1999.

Power, Edward J. *A Legacy of Learning: A History of Western Education.* Albany: State University of New York Press, 1991.

Purves, George T. "The Influence of Paganism on Post-Apostolic Christianity." *The Presbyterian Review.* No. 36 (October 1888).

Quasten, Johannes. *Music and Worship in Pagan and Christian Antiquity.* Washington DC: National Association of Pastoral Musicians, 1983.

Reid, Clyde H. *The Empty Pulpit.* New York: Harper & Row Publishers, 1967.

Reid, Daniel G. et al., *Concise Dictionary of Christianity in America.* Downers Grove, IL: InterVarsity Press, 1995.

———. *Dictionary of Christianity in America.* Downers Grove, IL: InterVarsity Press, 1990.

Richardson, A. Madeley. *Church Music.* London: Longmans, Green, & Co., 1910.

Robertson, A. T. *A Grammar of the Greek New Testament in the Light of Historical Research.* Nashville: Broadman & Holman Publishers, 1934.

Robertson, D. W. *Abelard and Heloise.* New York: The Dial Press, 1972.

Robinson, John A. T. *The New Reformation.* Philadelphia: Westminster Press, 1965.

Rogers, Elizabeth. *Music through the Ages.* New York: G. P. Putnam's Sons, 1967.

Rowdon, Harold H. "Theological Education in Historical Perspective." In *Vox Evangelica: Biblical and Other Essays from London Bible College.* Vol. 7. Carlisle, UK: Paternoster Press, 1971.

Sanford, Elias Benjamin, ed. *A Concise Cyclopedia of Religious Knowledge.* New York: Charles L. Webster & Company, 1890.

Saucy, Robert L. *The Church in God's Program.* Chicago: Moody Publishers, 1972.

Schaff, Philip. *History of the Christian Church.* Grand Rapids: Eerdmans, 1994.

Schlect, Christopher. *Critique of Modern Youth Ministry.* Moscow, ID: Canon Press, 1995.

Schweizer, Eduard. *The Church As the Body of Christ.* Richmond, VA: John Knox Press, 1964.

———. *Church Order in the New Testament.* Chatham, UK: W. & J. Mackay, 1961.

Sendrey, Alfred. *Music in the Social and Religious Life of Antiquity.* Rutherford, NJ: Fairleigh Dickinson University Press, 1974.

Senn, Frank C. *Christian Liturgy: Catholic and Evangelical.* Minneapolis: Fortress Press, 1997.

———. *Christian Worship and Its Cultural Setting.* Philadelphia: Fortress Press, 1983.

Senter, Mark H. III. *The Coming Revolution in Youth Ministry.* Chicago: Victor Books, 1992.

———. *The Youth for Christ Movement As an Educational Agency and Its Impact upon Protestant Churches: 1931–1979.* Ann Arbor, MI: University of Michigan, 1990.

Shaulk, Carl. *Key Words in Church Music.* St. Louis: Concordia Publishing House, 1978.

Shelley, Bruce. *Church History in Plain Language.* Waco, TX: Word Books, 1982.

Short, Ernest H. *History of Religious Architecture.* London: Philip Allan & Co., 1936.

Sizer, Sandra. *Gospel Hymns and Social Religion.* Philadelphia: Temple University Press, 1978.

Smith, Christian. *Going to the Root.* Scottdale, PA: Herald Press, 1992.

———. "Our Dressed Up Selves." *Voices in the Wilderness,* September/October 1987.

Smith, M. A. *From Christ to Constantine.* Downers Grove, IL: InterVarsity Press, 1973.

Snyder, Graydon F. *Ante Pacem: Archaeological Evidence for Church Life before Constantine.* Macon, GA: Mercer University Press, 1985.

———. *First Corinthians: A Faith Community Commentary.* Macon, GA: Mercer University Press, 1991.

Snyder, Howard. *Radical Renewal: The Problem of Wineskins Today.* Houston: Touch Publications, 1996.

Soccio, Douglas. *Archetypes of Wisdom: An Introduction to Philosophy.* Belmont, CA: Wadsworth ITP Publishing Company, 1998.

Sommer, Robert. "Sociofugal Space." *American Journal of Sociology* 72, no. 6, 1967.

Stevens, R. Paul. *The Abolition of the Laity.* Carlisle, UK: Paternoster Press, 1999.

———. *Liberating the Laity.* Downers Grove, IL: InterVarsity Press, 1985.

———. *The Other Six Days: Vocation, Work, and Ministry in Biblical Perspective.* Grand Rapids: Eerdmans, 1999.

Streeter, B. H. *The Primitive Church.* New York: The Macmillan Company, 1929.

Streett, R. Alan. *The Effective Invitation.* Old Tappan, NJ: Fleming H. Revell Co., 1984.

Stumpf, Samuel Enoch. *Socrates to Sartre.* New York: McGraw-Hill, 1993.

Swank, George W. *Dialogical Style in Preaching.* Valley Forge, PA: Judson Press, 1981.

Swank, J. Grant. "Preventing Clergy Burnout." *Ministry* (November 1998).

Sweet, Leonard. "Church Architecture for the 21st Century." *Your Church* (March/April 1999).

Sykes, Norman. *Old Priest and New Presbyter.* London: Cambridge University Press, 1956.

Tan, Kim. *Lost Heritage: The Heroic Story of Radical Christianity.* Godalming, UK: Highland Books, 1996.

Taylor, Joan E. *Christians and the Holy Places: The Myth of Jewish-Christian Origins.* Oxford: Clarendon Press, 1993.

Terry, John Mark. *Evangelism: A Concise History.* Nashville: Broadman & Holman Publishers, 1994.

Thiessen, Henry C. *Lectures in Systematic Theology.* Grand Rapids: Eerdmans, 1979.

Thompson, Bard. *Liturgies of the Western Church.* Cleveland: Meridian Books, 1961.

Thompson, C. L. *Times of Refreshing, Being a History of American Revivals with Their Philosophy and Methods.* Rockford: Golden Censer Co. Publishers, 1878.

Thomson, Jeremy. *Preaching As Dialogue: Is the Sermon a Sacred Cow?* Cambridge: Grove Books, 1996.

Tidball, D. J. *Dictionary of Paul and His Letters.* Downers Grove, IL: InterVarsity Press, 1993.

Trueman, D. C. *The Pageant of the Past: The Origins of Civilization.* Toronto: Ryerson, 1965.

Turner, Harold W. *From Temple to Meeting House: The Phenomenology and Theology of Places of Worship.* The Hague: Mouton Publishers, 1979.

Ulam, Adam B. *Stalin: The Man and His Era.* New York: Viking Press, 1973.

Uprichard, R. E. H. "The Eldership in Martin Bucer and John Calvin." *Irish Biblical Studies Journal* (June 18, 1996).

Uschan, Michael V. *The 1940's: Cultural History of the US through the Decades.* San Diego: Lucent Books, 1999.

Van Biema, David. "The End: How It Got That Way." *Time* (July 1, 2002).

Verduin, Leonard. *The Reformers and Their Stepchildren.* Grand Rapids: Eerdmans, 1964.

Verkuyl, Gerrit. *Berkeley Version of the New Testament.* Grand Rapids: Zondervan, 1969.

Viola, Frank. *God's Ultimate Passion.* Gainesville, FL: Present Testimony Ministry, 2006.

———. *Reimagining Church.* Colorado Springs: David C. Cook. 2008

———. *The Untold Story of the New Testament Church: An Extraordinary Guide to Understanding the New Testament.* Shippensburg, PA: Destiny Image, 2004.

von Campenhausen, Hans. *Tradition and Life in the Church.* Philadelphia: Fortress Press, 1968.

von Harnack, Adolf. *The Mission and Expansion of Christianity in the First Three Centuries.* New York: G. P. Putnam's Sons, 1908.

von Simson, Otto. *The Gothic Cathedral: Origins of Gothic Architecture and the Medieval Concept of Order.* Princeton: Princeton University Press, 1988.

von Soden, H. *Die Schriften des Newen Testamentes.* Gottingen, Germany: Vandenhoeck, 1912.

Walker, G. S. M. *The Churchmanship of St. Cyprian.* London: Lutterworth Press, 1968.

Wallis, Arthur. *The Radical Christian.* Columbia, MO: Cityhill Publishing, 1987.

Warkentin, Marjorie. *Ordination: A Biblical-Historical View.* Grand Rapids: Eerdmans, 1982.

Warns, J. *Baptism: Its History and Significance*. Exeter, UK: Paternoster Press, 1958.

Watson, Philip. *Neoplatonism and Christianity: 928 Ordinary General Meeting of the Victoria Institute*. Surrey, UK: The Victoria Institute, 1955.

Welch, Bobby H. *Evangelism through the Sunday School: A Journey of Faith*. Nashville: Lifeway Press, 1997.

Wesley, John. *Sermons on Several Occasions*. London: Epworth Press, 1956.

White, James F. *Protestant Worship: Traditions in Transition*. Louisville: Westminster/John Knox Press, 1989.

————. *The Worldliness of Worship*. New York: Oxford University Press, 1967.

White, L. Michael. *Building God's House in the Roman World*. Baltimore: Johns Hopkins University Press, 1990.

White, John F. *Protestant Worship and Church Architecture*. New York: Oxford University Press, 1964.

Whitham, Larry. "Flocks in Need of Shepherds." *Washington Times*, July 2, 2001.

Wickes, Charles. *Illustrations of Spires and Towers of the Medieval Churches of England*. New York: Hessling & Spielmeyer, 1900.

Wieruszowski, Helen. *The Medieval University*. Princeton: Van Nostrand, 1966.

Wilken, Robert. *The Christians as the Romans Saw Them*. New Haven, CT: University Press, 1984.

Williams, George. *The Radical Reformation*. Philadelphia: Westminster Press, 1962.

Williams, Peter. *Houses of God*. Chicago: University of Illinois Press, 1997.

Wilson-Dickson, Andrew. *The Story of Christian Music*. Oxford: Lion Publications, 1992.

Wright, David F. *The Lion Handbook of the History of Christianity*. Oxford: Lion Publications, 1990.

Wuest, Kenneth S. *The New Testament: An Expanded Translation*. Grand Rapids: Eerdmans, 1961.

Youngblood, Ronald. "The Process: How We Got Our Bible." *Christianity Today* (February 5, 1988), 23–38.

Zens, Jon. *The Pastor*. St. Croix Falls, WI: Searching Together, 1981.

FRANK VIOLA is an influential voice in the contemporary house church movement. For the last twenty years, he has been gathering with organic house churches in the United States. Frank has written eight revolutionary books on radical church restoration, including *God's Ultimate Passion* and *The Untold Story of the New Testament Church.* He is a nationally recognized expert on new trends for the church, holds conferences on the deeper Christian life, and is actively engaged in planting New Testament–styled churches. His Web site, www.frankviola.com, contains many free resources designed to enrich the spiritual lives of God's people. Frank and his family live in Gainesville, Florida.

GEORGE BARNA is the chairman of Good News Holdings, a multimedia firm in Los Angeles that produces movies, television programming, and other media content. He is also the founder and Directing Leader of The Barna Group, a research and resource firm in Ventura, California, whose clients have ranged from ministries such as the Billy Graham Evangelistic Association and Focus on the Family to corporations such as Ford and Walt Disney, as well as the U.S. Navy and U.S. Army. To date, Barna has written thirty-nine books, including best sellers such as *Revolution, Revolutionary Parenting, Transforming Children into Spiritual Champions, The Frog in the Kettle,* and *The Power of Vision.* He has been hailed as "the most quoted person in the Christian church today" and is counted among its most influential leaders. Barna lives with his wife, Nancy, and their three daughters (Samantha, Corban, and Christine) in Southern California.

FRANK VIOLA

- ➤ *Reimagining Church*
- ➤ *The Untold Story of the New Testament Church*
- ➤ *Rethinking the Will of God*
- ➤ *God's Ultimate Passion*
- ➤ *Gathering in Homes*
- ➤ *Straight Talk to Pastors*
- ➤ *Bethany*

GEORGE BARNA

- ➤ *Revolution*
- ➤ *Revolutionary Parenting*
- ➤ *Transforming Children into Spiritual Champions*
- ➤ *Think Like Jesus*
- ➤ *A Fish Out of Water*
- ➤ *Growing True Disciples*
- ➤ *The Power of Vision*
- ➤ *The Power of Team Leadership*

➤Available from Barna Books

Committed, born-again Christians are exiting the established church in massive numbers. Why are they leaving? Where are they going? And what does this mean for the future of the church? In this groundbreaking book, George Barna examines the state of the church today—and compares it to the biblical picture of the church as God intended it to be.

How can parents make a lasting impact on the spiritual lives of their children? To find the answer, George Barna researched the lives of thriving adult Christians and discovered the essential steps their parents took to shape their spiritual lives in childhood. *Revolutionary Parenting* shows parents how to instill in their children a vibrant commitment to Christ.

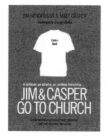

What happens when a Christian hires an atheist to accompany him to church? Find out by following Jim Henderson's journey across the country with skeptic Matt Casper as they visit twelve of America's churches and document their experiences at and reactions to each one. Their eye-opening, entertaining dialogue opens the way for authentic, attentive friendship between Christians and nonbelievers.

Many Christians take it for granted that their church's practices are rooted in Scripture. Yet how do our practices compare to those of first-century believers? *Pagan Christianity?* leads us on a fascinating tour through history that examines and challenges every aspect of the present-day church experience.

BARNA

REIMAGINING CHURCH
Pursuing the Dream of Organic Christianity

From
Frank Viola
and
David C. Cook, publisher

Now available from retailers and online outlets

CP0204